Toronto
Public
Library
Northern District
Resource Collection

3 9100 02526 947 6

AF575202

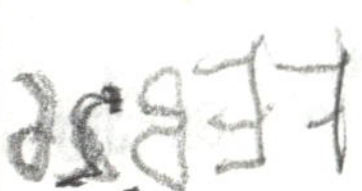

Toronto
Public
Library

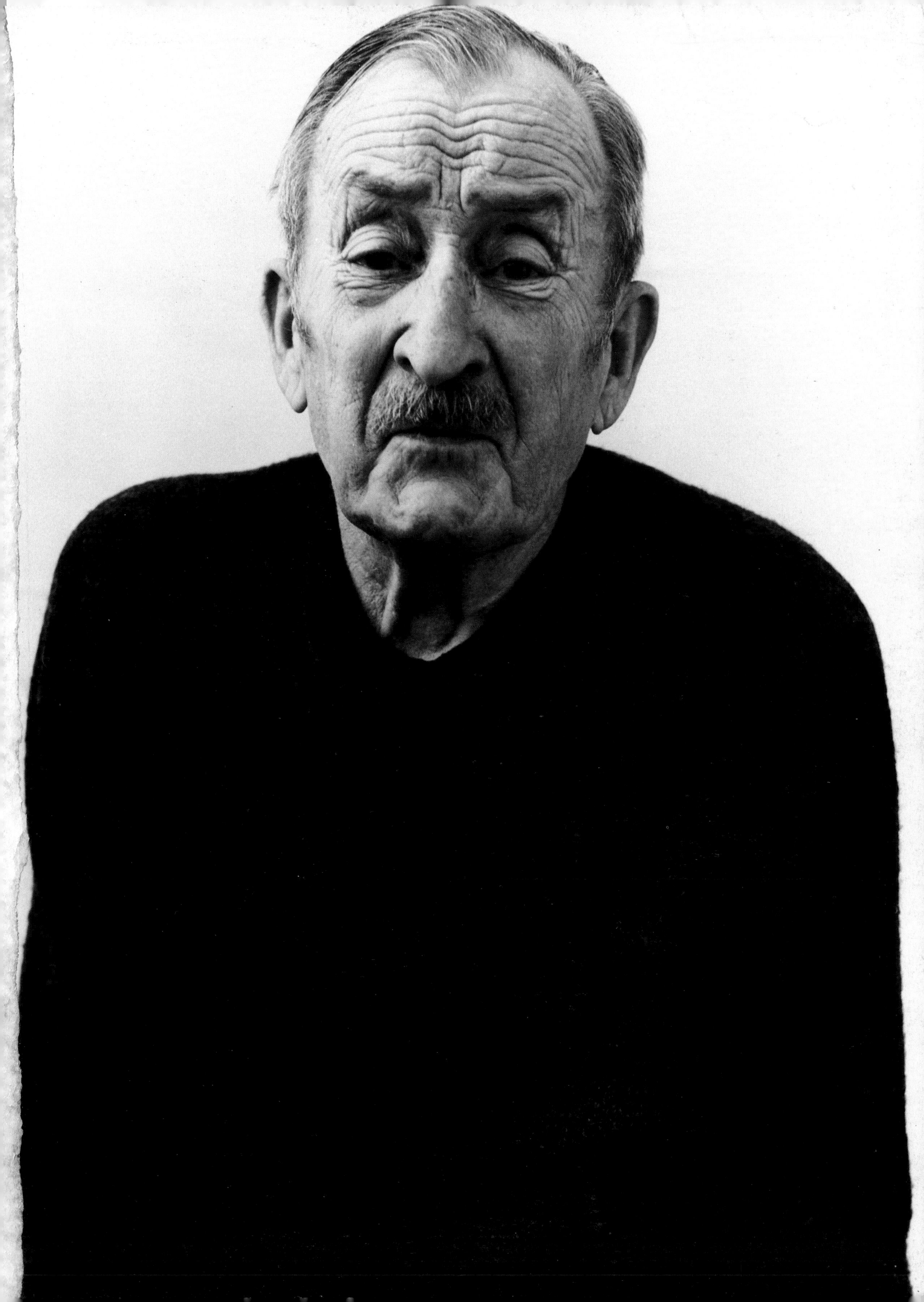

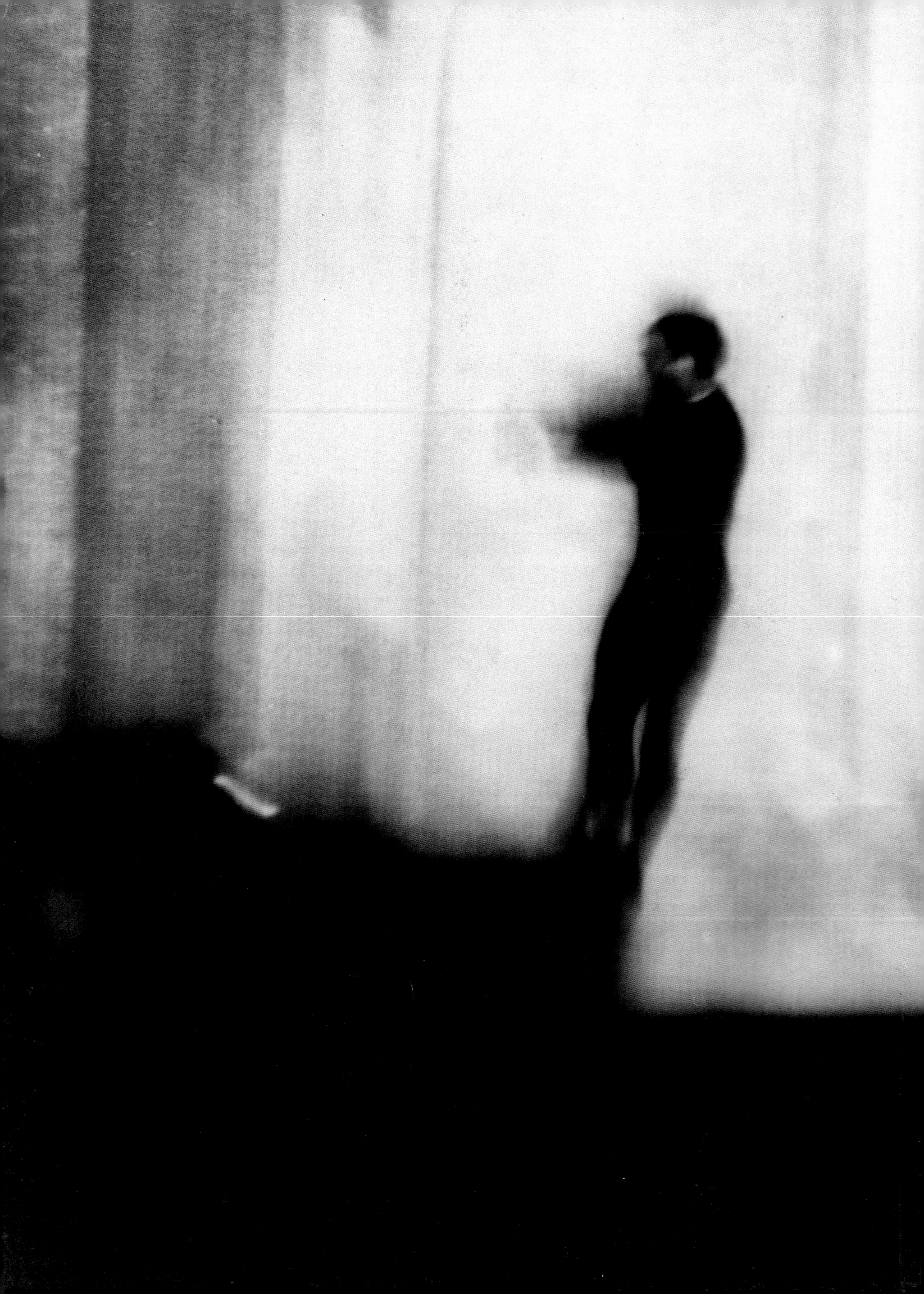

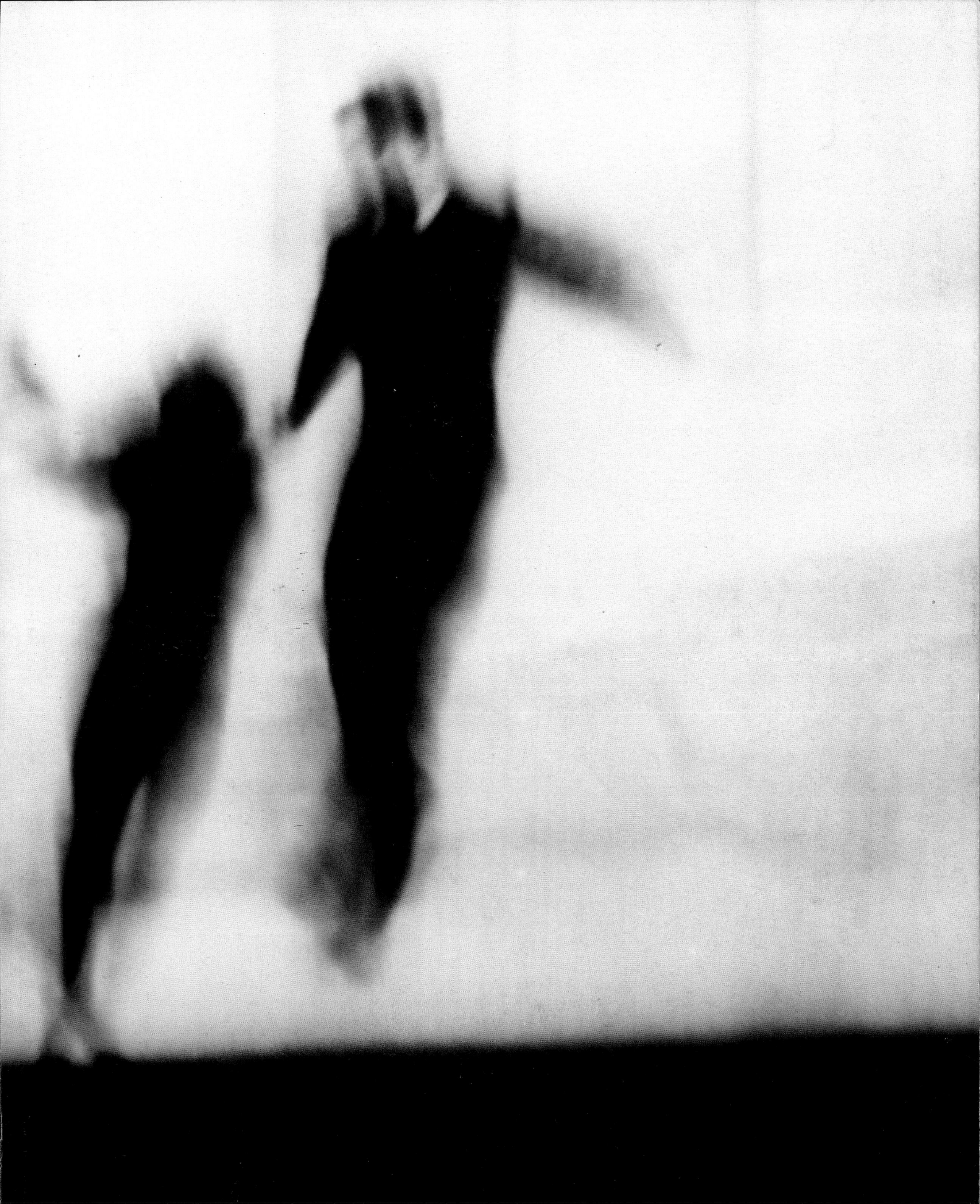

Page 1:

RICHARD AVEDON.

ALEXEY BRODOVITCH.

LE THOR, FRANCE, 10/2/69

Pages 2 and 3:

ALEXEY BRODOVITCH.

PHOTOGRAPH FROM *BALLET*

MASTERS OF
AMERICAN DESIGN

BRODOVITCH

ANDY GRUNDBERG

DOCUMENTS OF AMERICAN DESIGN
HARRY N. ABRAMS PUBLISHERS, INC., NY

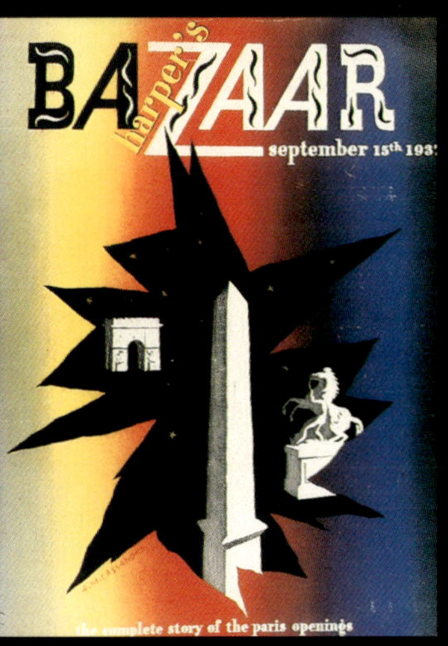

A.M. CASSANDRE

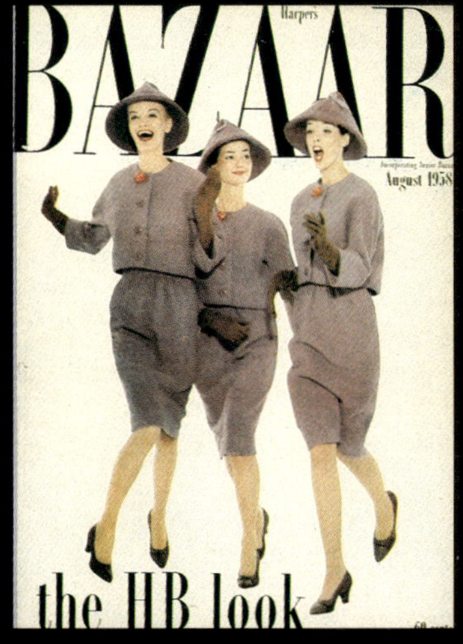

RICHARD AVEDON

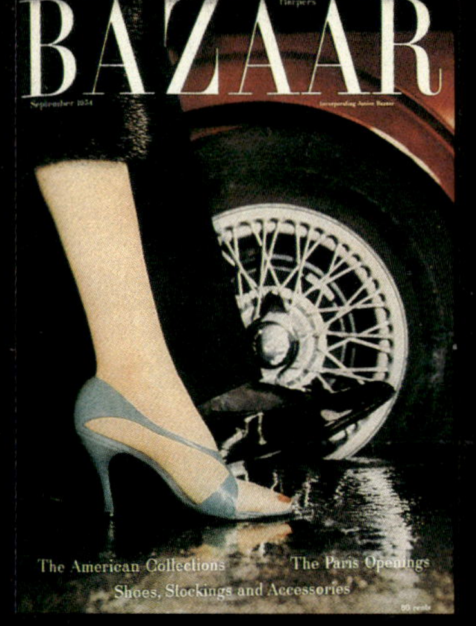

RICHARD AVEDON

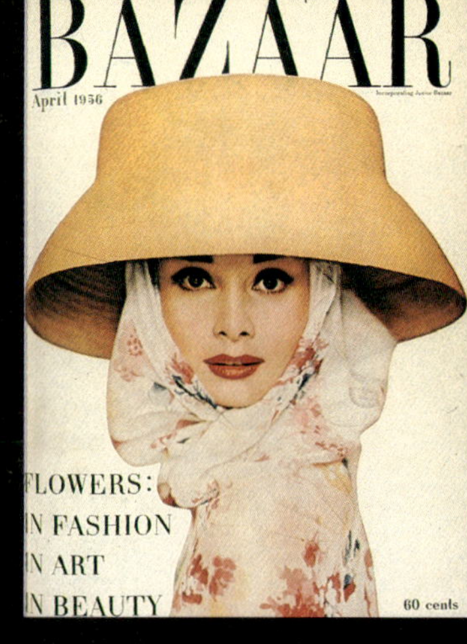

RICHARD AVEDON

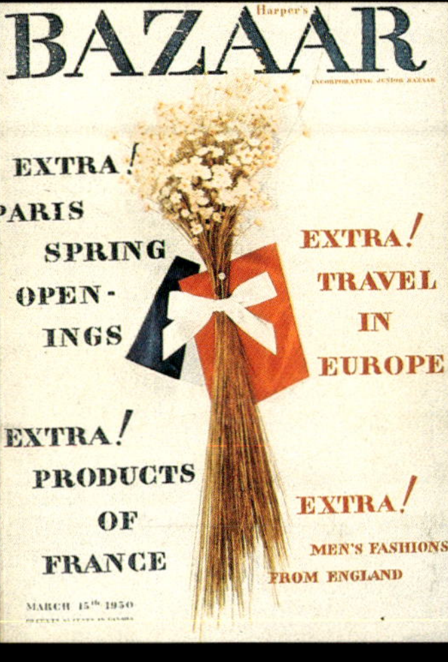

LESLIE GILL

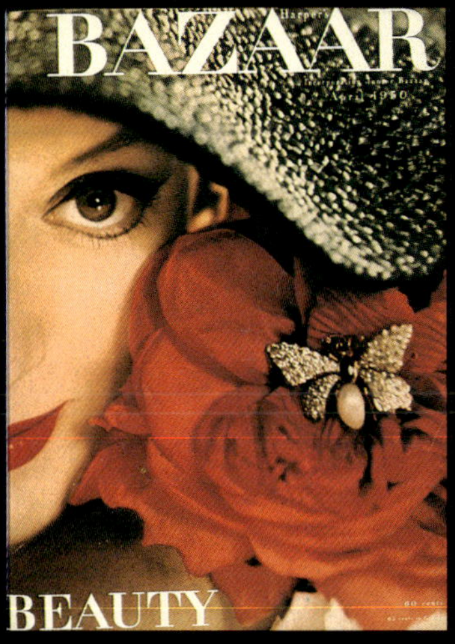

RICHARD AVEDON

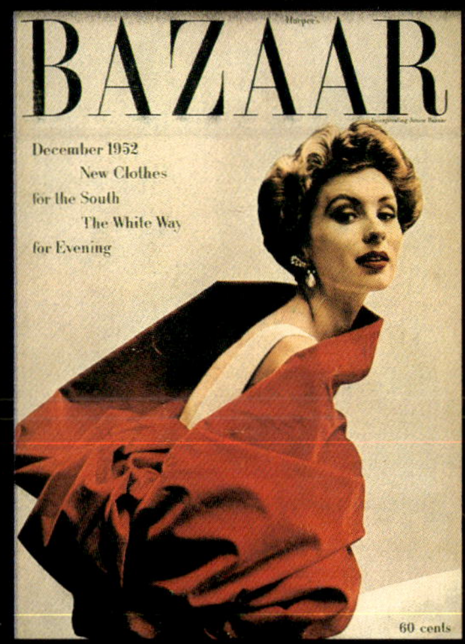

RICHARD AVEDON

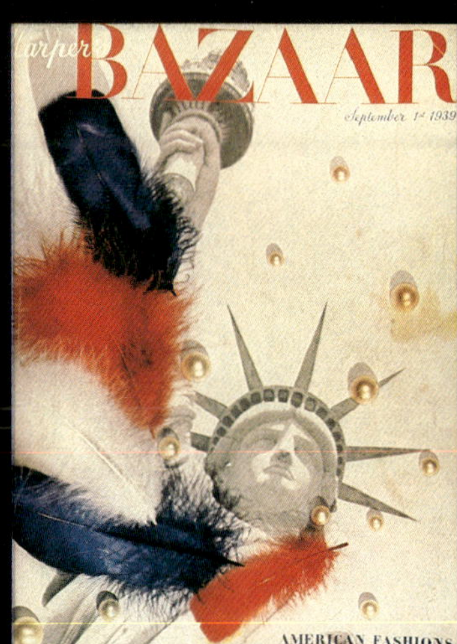

LESLIE GILL AND IRVING PENN

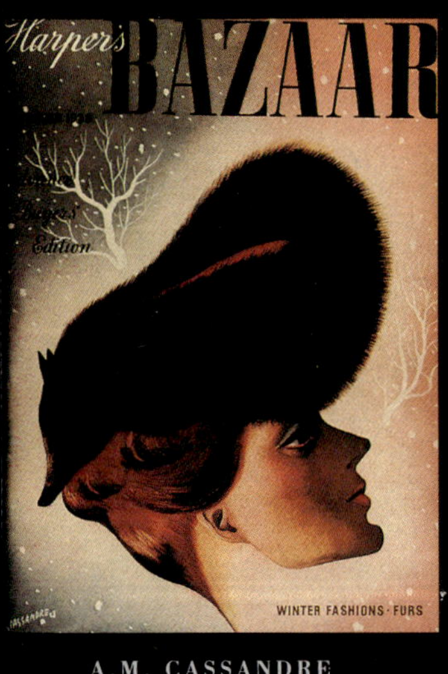

A.M. CASSANDRE

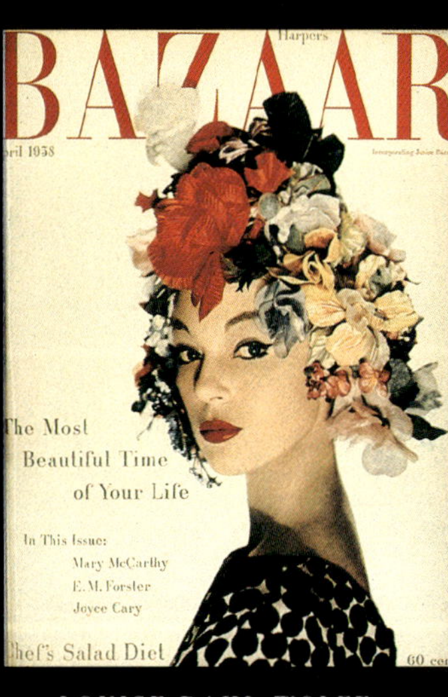

LOUISE DAHL-WOLFE

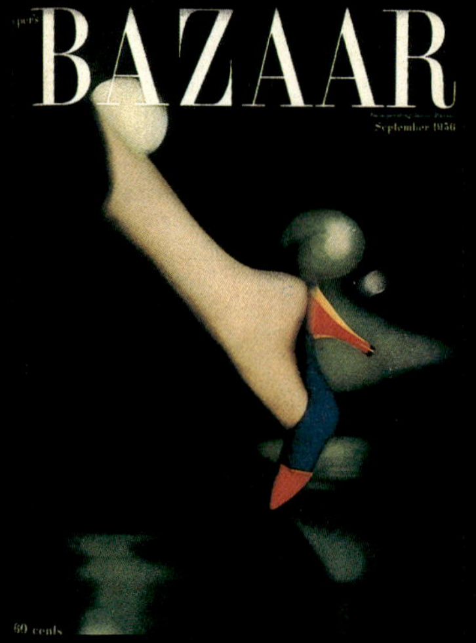

RICHARD AVEDON

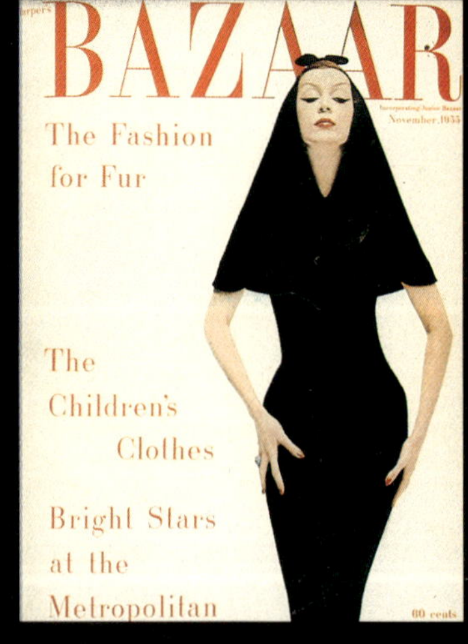

RICHARD AVEDON

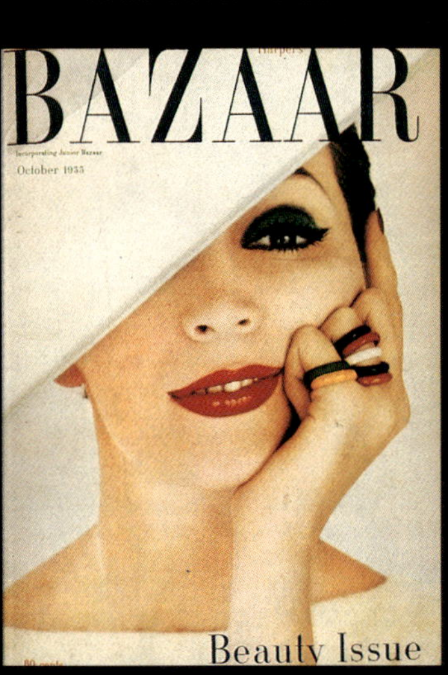

RICHARD AVEDON

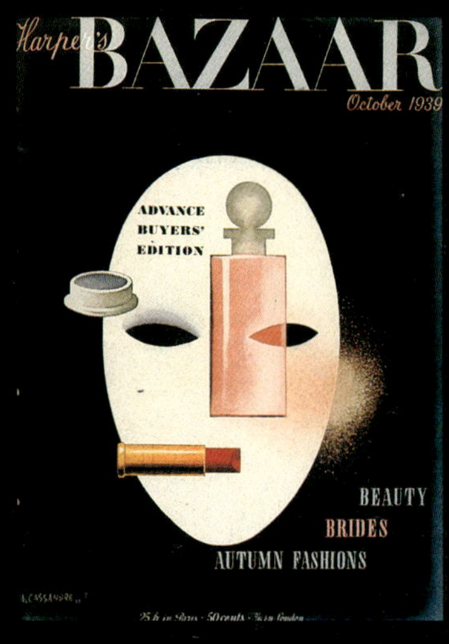

A.M. CASSANDRE

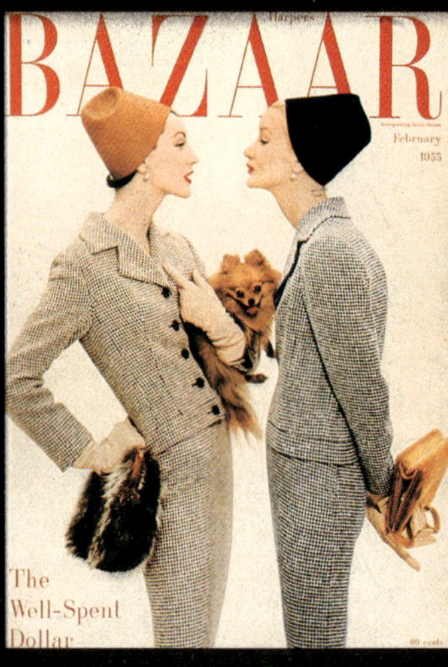

RICHARD AVEDON

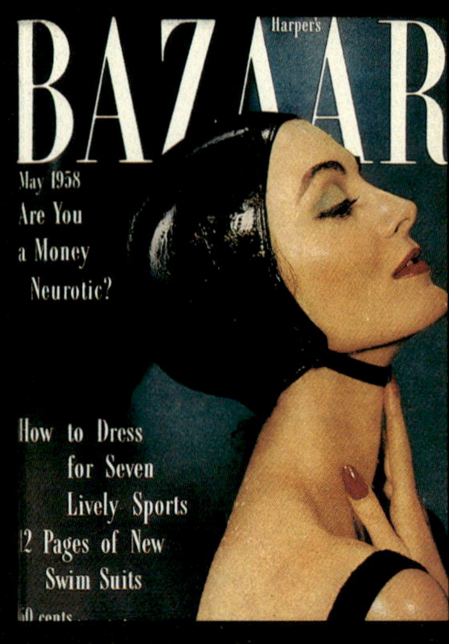

DERUJINSKY

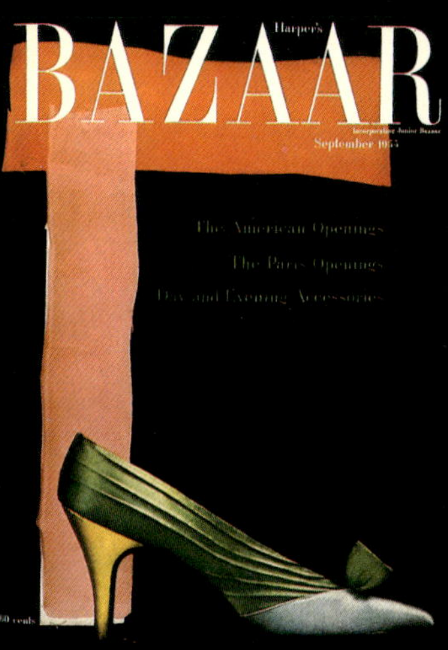

RICHARD AVEDON

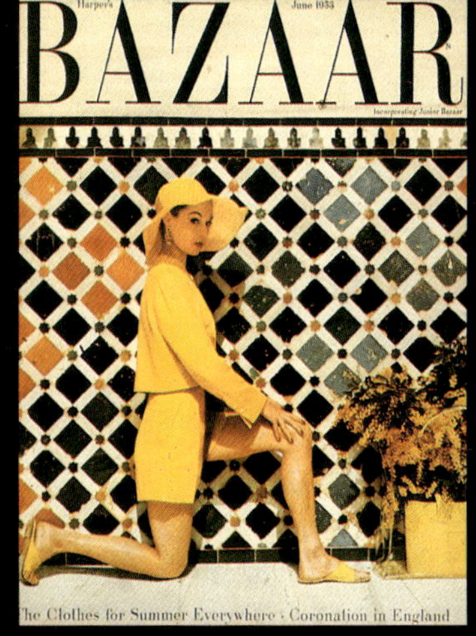

LOUISE DAHL-WOLFE

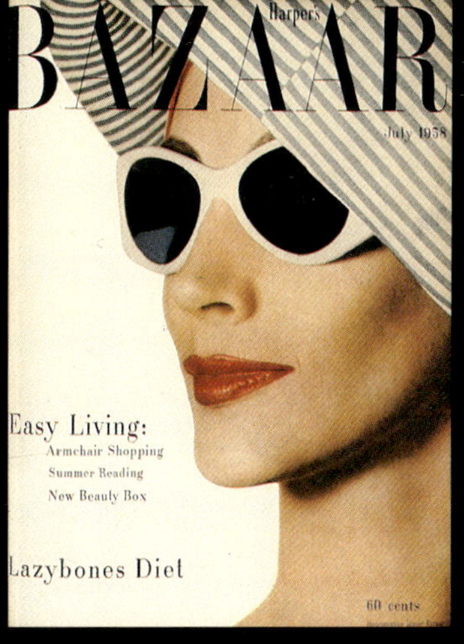

DERUJINSKY

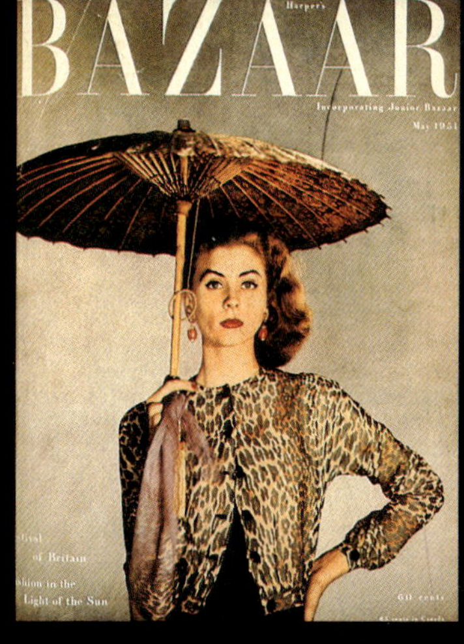

LOUISE DAHL-WOLFE

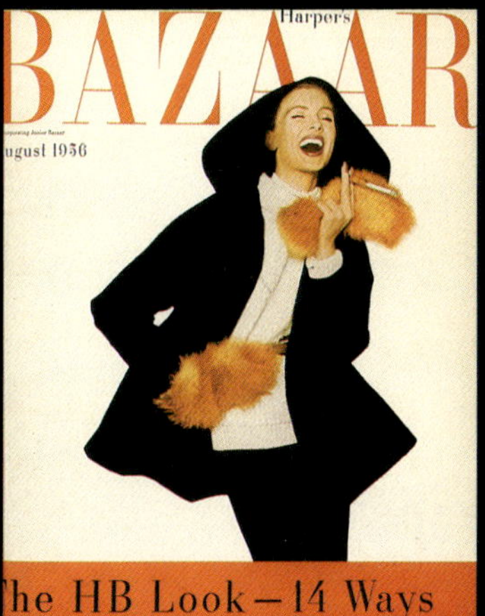

RICHARD AVEDON

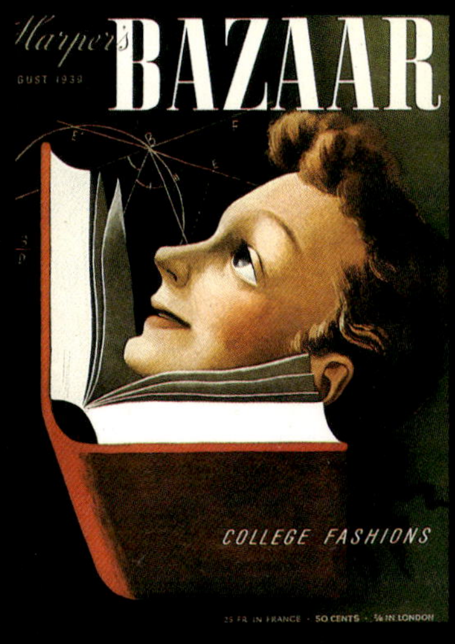

A.M. CASSANDRE

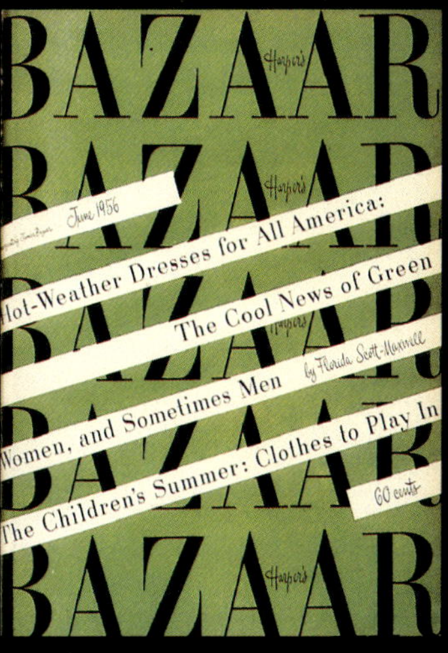

ALEXEY BRODOVITCH

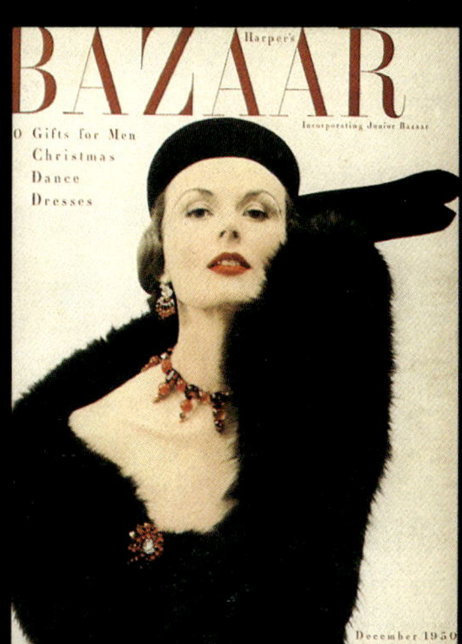

RICHARD AVEDON

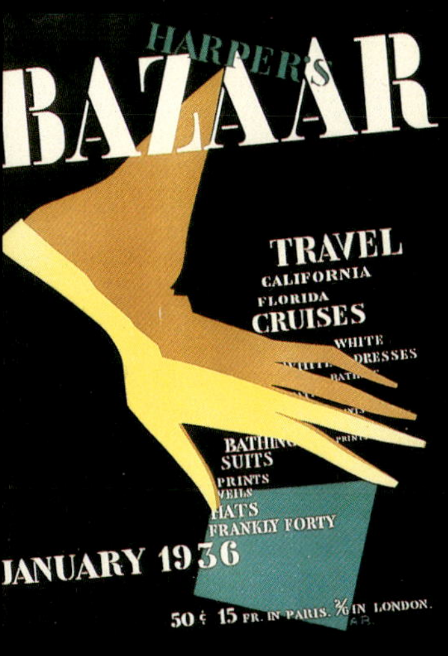

ALEXEY BRODOVITCH

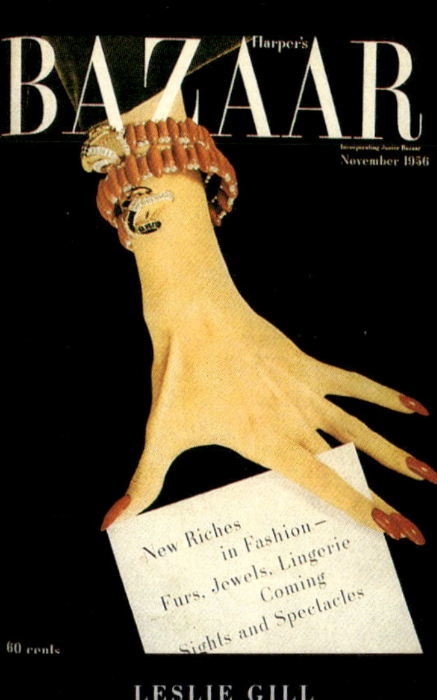

LESLIE GILL

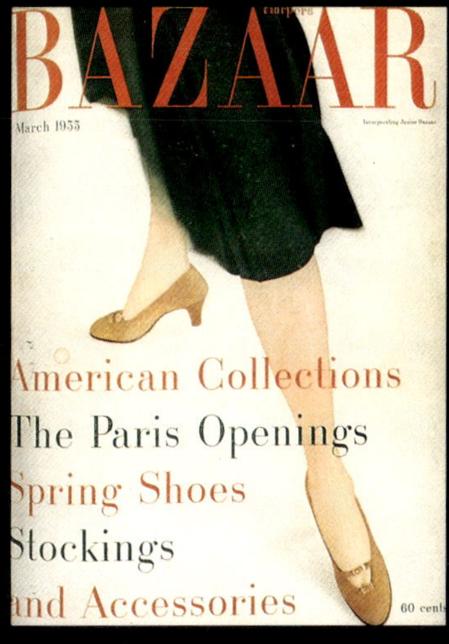

RICHARD AVEDON

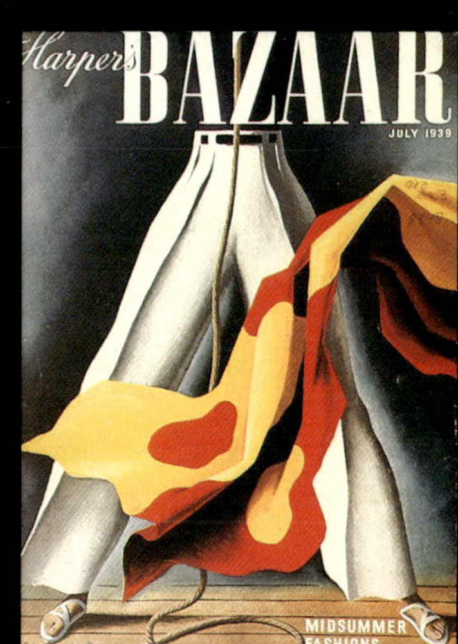

A.M. CASSANDRE

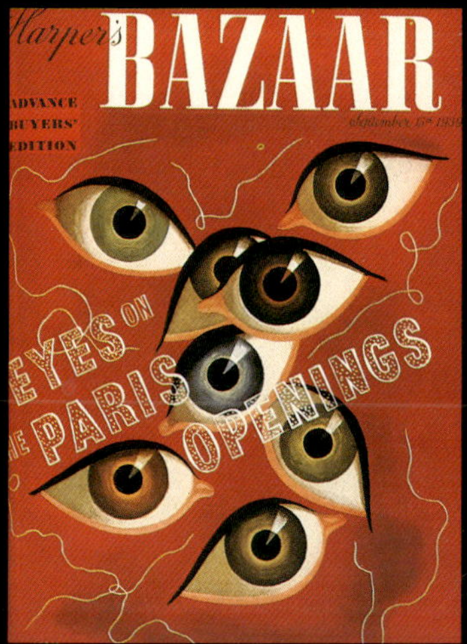

A.M. CASSANDRE

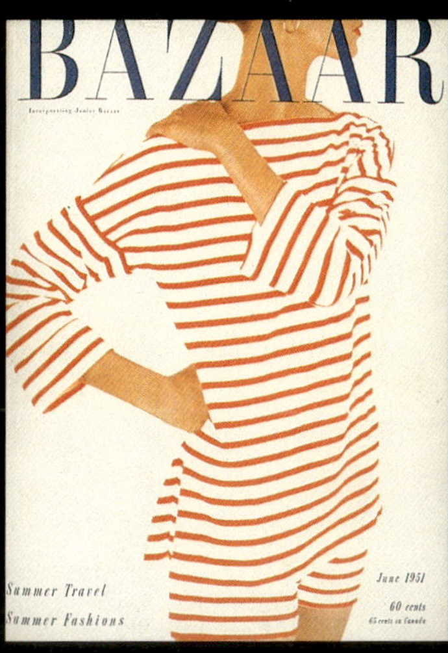

RICHARD AVEDON

LOUISE DAHL-WOLFE

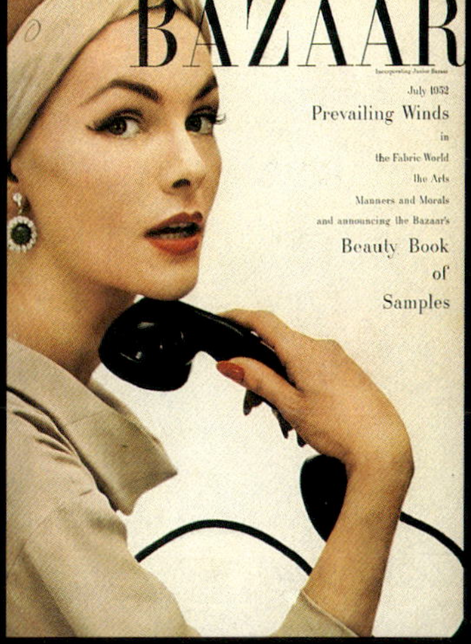

RICHARD AVEDON

FOR DOCUMENTS OF AMERICAN DESIGN:
PROJECT MANAGER: WILL HOPKINS
EDITOR: SARAH BODINE
DESIGNER: RAY KOMAI
ASSISTANT TO THE DESIGNER: JOSEPH LEE
GRAPHIC PRODUCTION: KATHY CORRIGAN, MICHAEL SARIDIS
TIME LINE DESIGN: PEG PATTERSON, PATTERSON AND WOOD

FOR HARRY N. ABRAMS, INC.:
EDITOR: ERIC HIMMEL
GRAPHIC PRODUCTION: DORIS LEATH STRUGATZ
JACKET DESIGN: SAMUEL N. ANTUPIT

LIBRARY OF CONGRESS CATALOGING-IN-PUBLICATION DATA

GRUNDBERG, ANDY.
ALEXEY BRODOVITCH/ ANDY GRUNDBERG.
P. CM.—(MASTERS OF GRAPHIC DESIGN)
BIBLIOGRAPHY: P.
ISBN 0-8109-0724-0
1. BRODOVITCH, ALEXEY. 1898–1971. 2. DESIGNERS—UNITED STATES—BIBLIOGRAPHY.
3. GRAPHIC ARTS—UNITED STATES—HISTORY—20TH CENTURY.
I. TITLE.
II. SERIES.
NC999.4.B76G78 1989
741.6'092'4—DC19
[B]

PUBLISHED IN 1989 BY HARRY N. ABRAMS, INCORPORATED, NEW YORK

A TIMES MIRROR COMPANY

PRINTED AND BOUND IN JAPAN

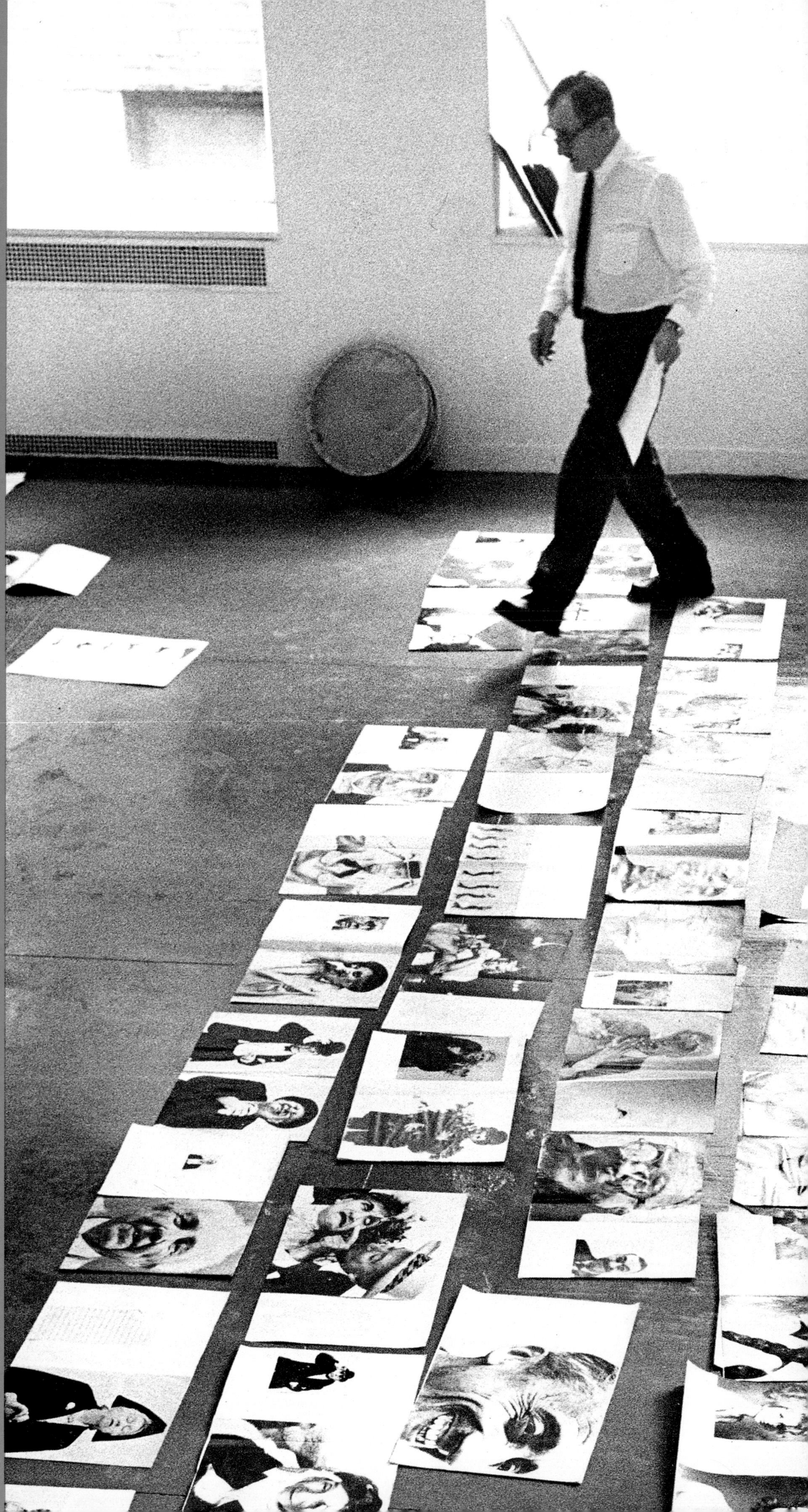

Right:
ALEXEY BRODOVITCH IN RICHARD AVEDON'S STUDIO, WORKING ON THE LAYOUTS FOR *OBSERVATIONS*, 1958. PHOTOGRAPH BY RICHARD AVEDON

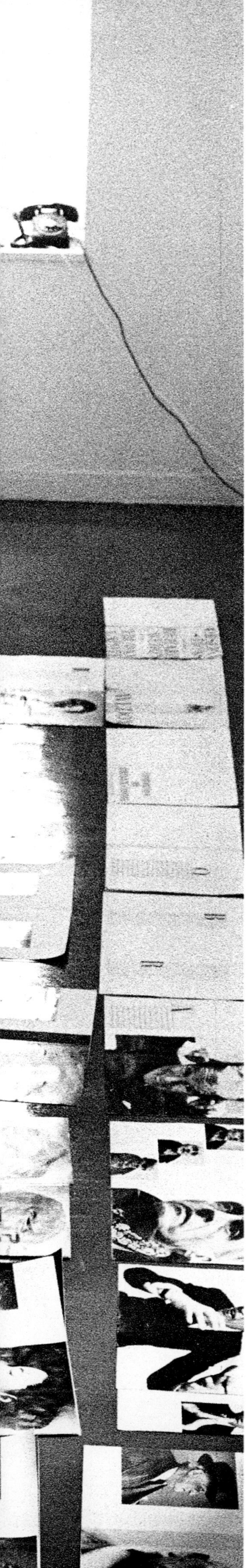

CONTENTS

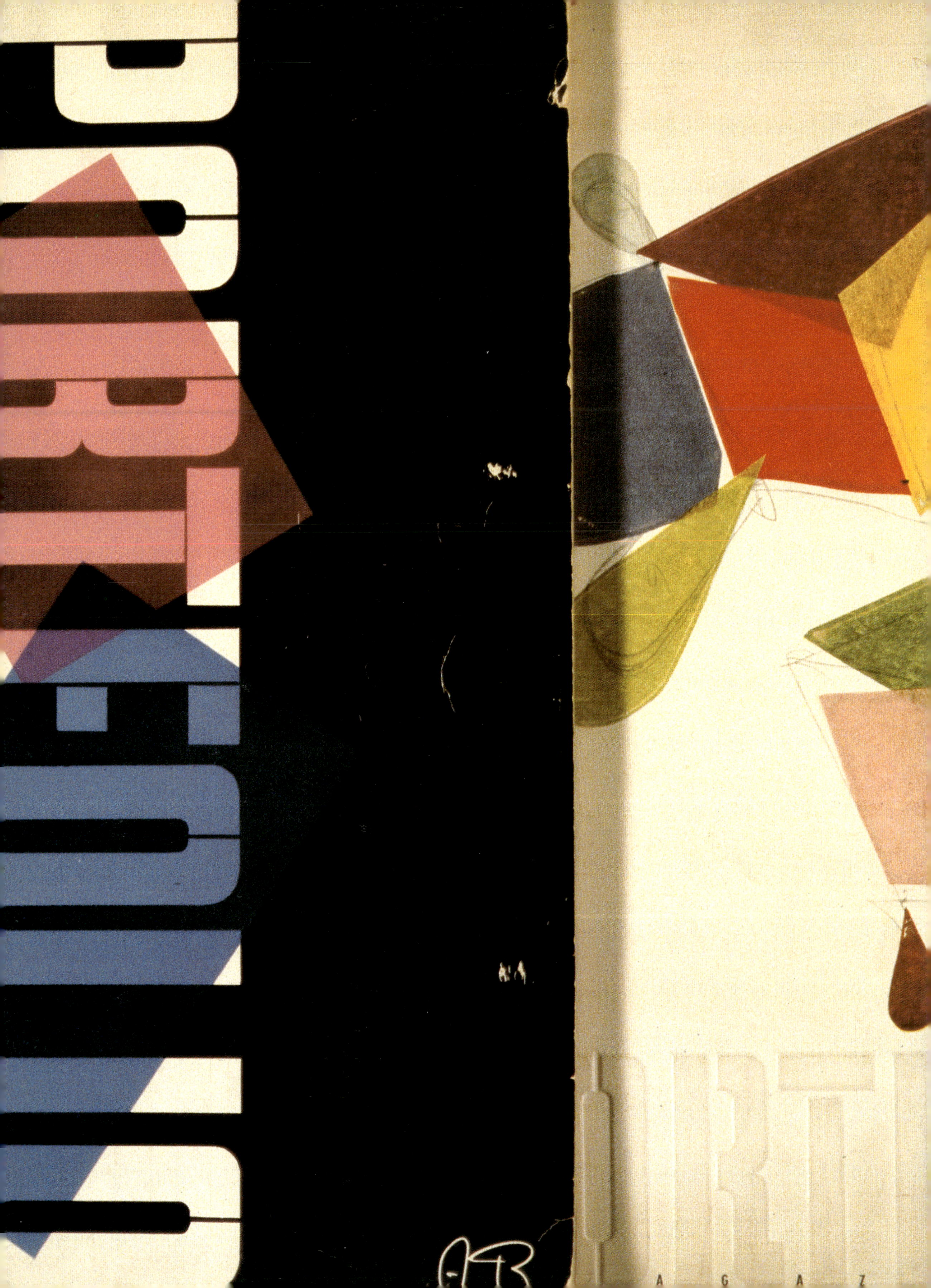
PORTFOLIO

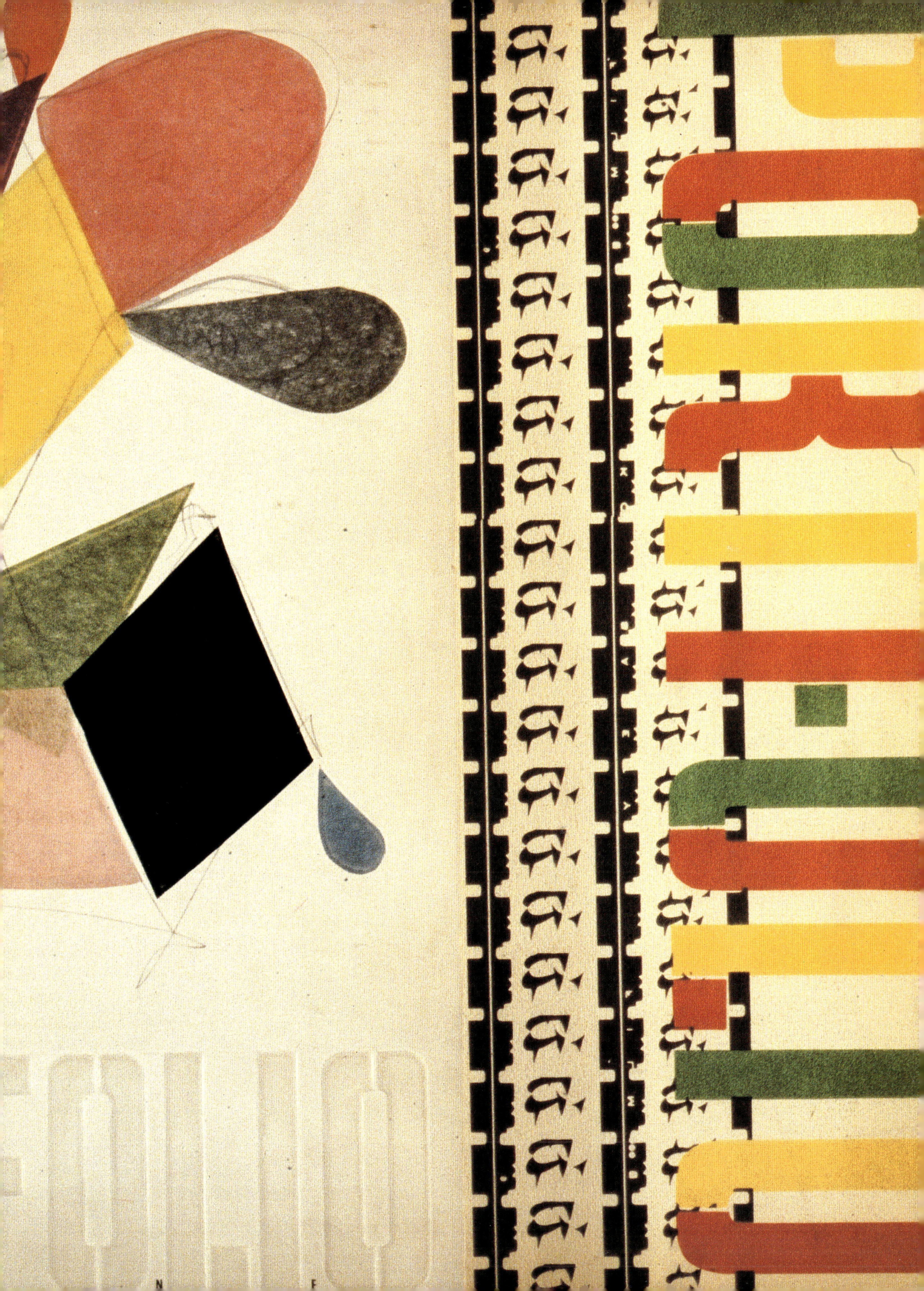

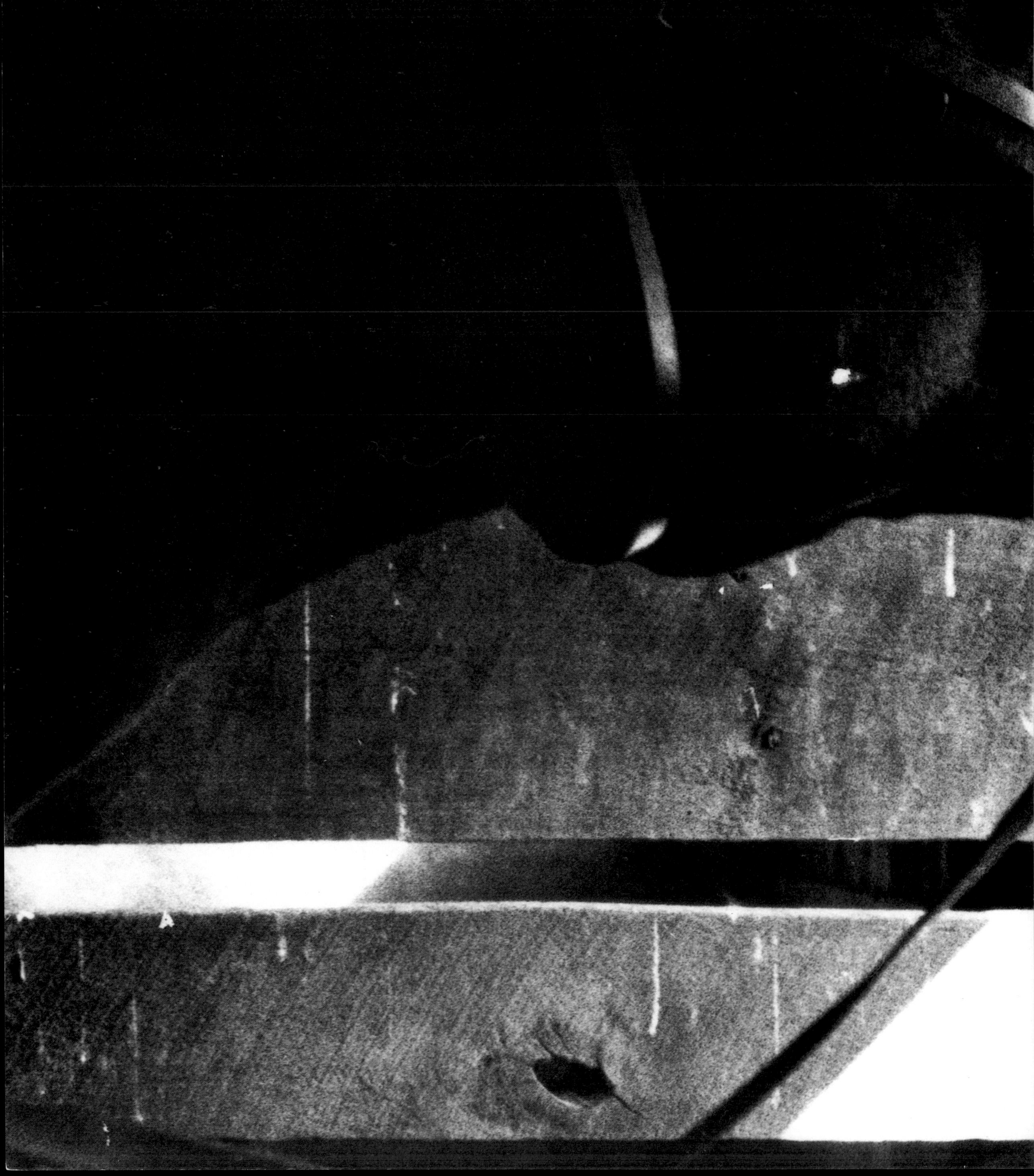

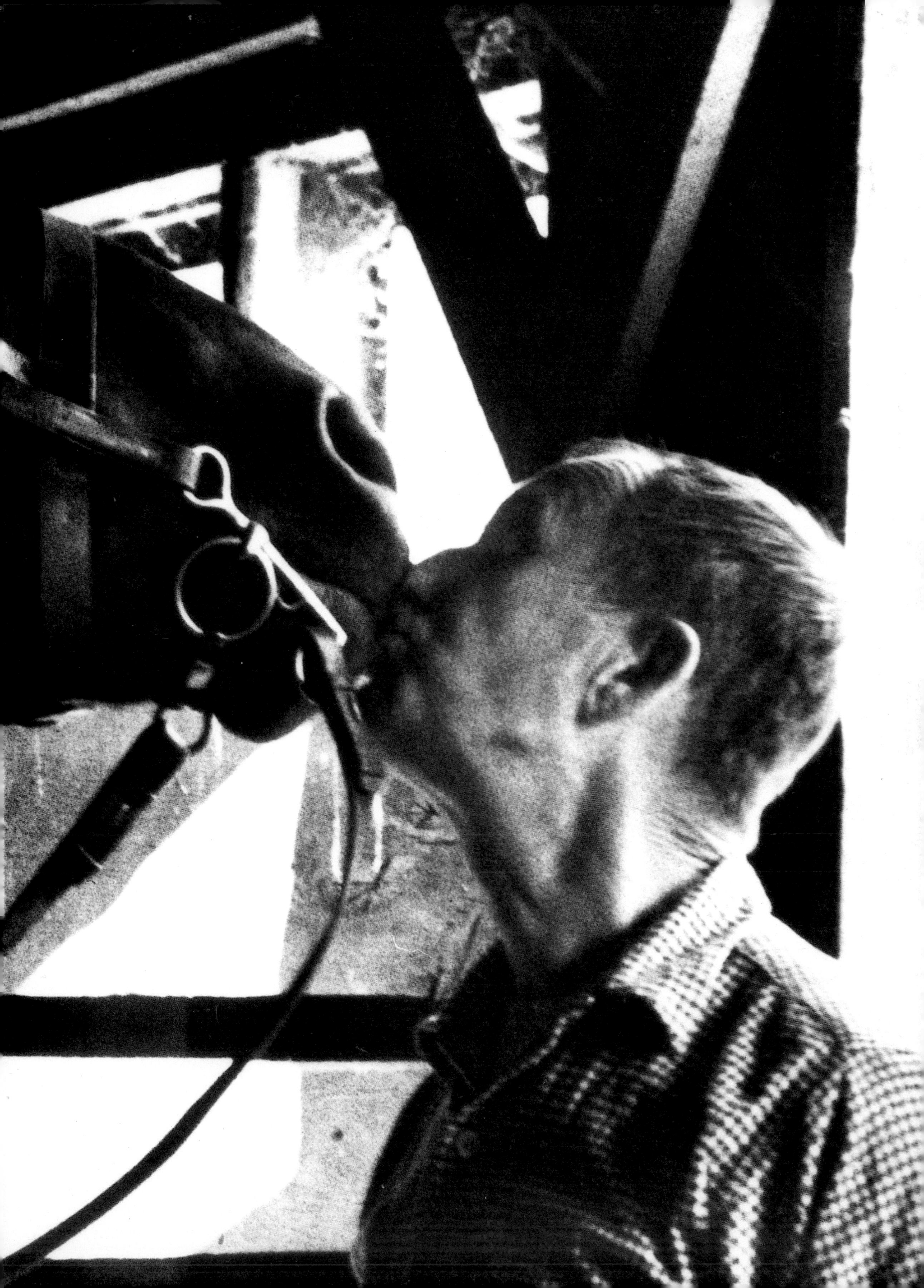

Right:
RICHARD AVEDON.
ZAZI, IN ITALY. 1946.
FROM *OBSERVATIONS*

Below:
ALEXEY BRODOVITCH.
DESIGN FOR THE SLIPCASE
OF *OBSERVATIONS*
BY RICHARD AVEDON. 1959

Pages 10 and 11:
ALEXEY BRODOVITCH.
THREE COVERS FOR
PORTFOLIO MAGAZINE.
1950-1951

Pages 12 and 13:
PHOTOGRAPHER UNKNOWN.
ALEXEY BRODOVITCH.
C.1950

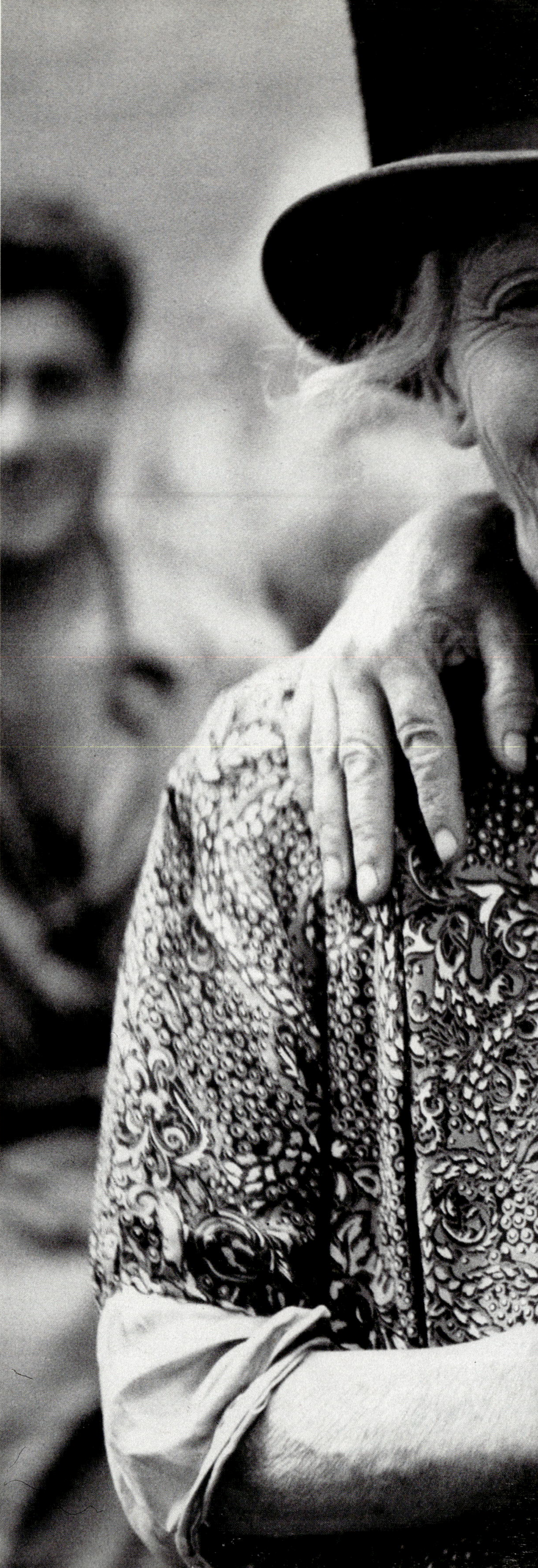

OBSERVA
-TIONS
PHOTOGRAPHS BY
RICHARD
AVEDON
COMMENTS BY
TRUMAN
CAPOTE

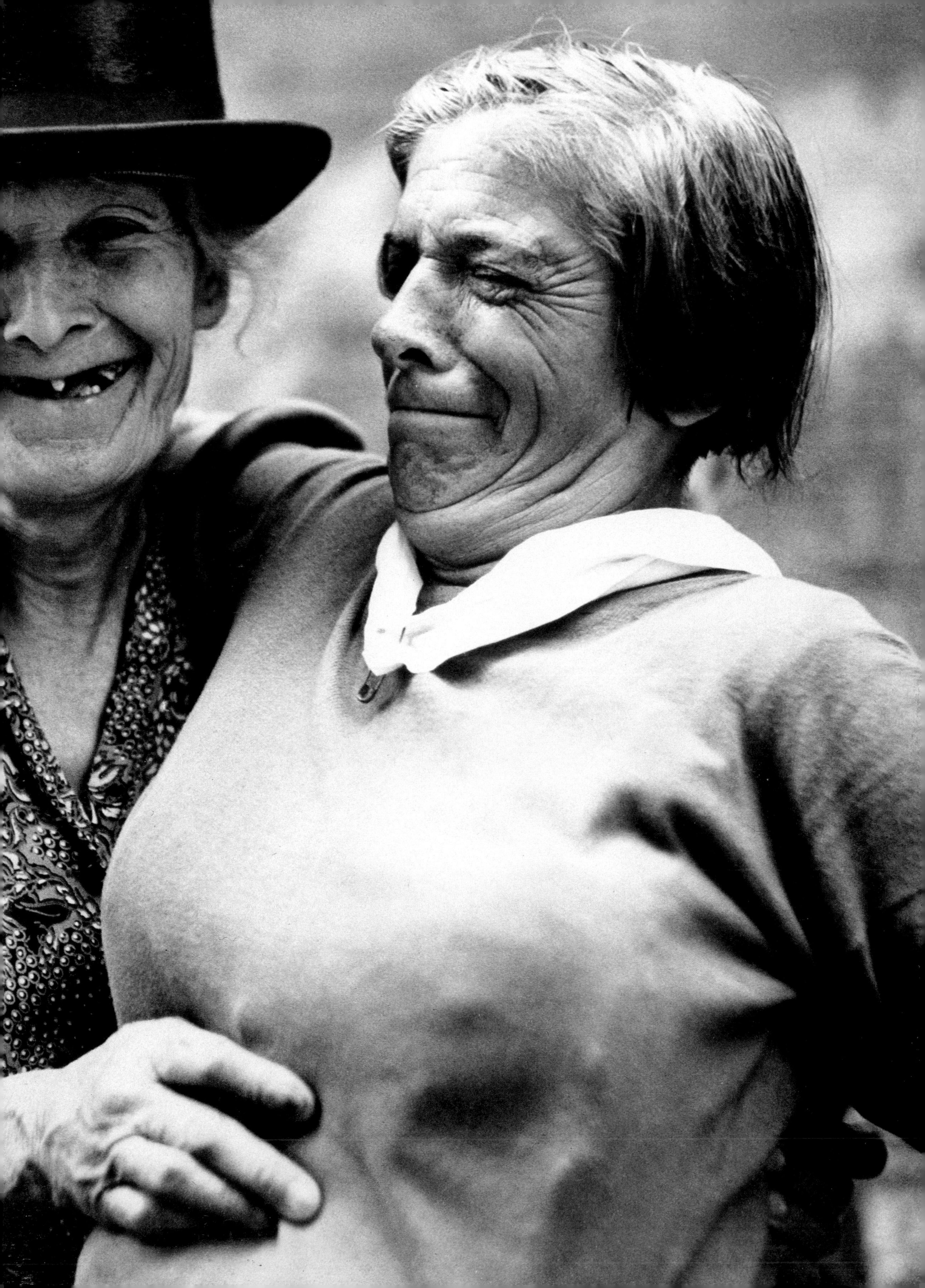

ALEXEY BRODOVITCH

A THOROUGHLY MODERN MAN

1

"Why to eat bacon and eggs every day?"
—ALEXEY BRODOVITCH

In the 1930s, forties, and fifties, Alexey Brodovitch was the very model of the modern art director. He played a central role in introducing into the United States an unabashedly modern graphic style forged in the 1920s from an amalgam of vanguard movements in European art and design. Out of these elements, and his own idiosyncratic interpolations, he fashioned a distinctively American design look, characterized by its energy, elegance, and economy of means. His illustrations, advertisements, posters, and magazine and book designs helped transform American graphic design between the wars and, in the postwar years, continued to serve as exemplars of invention and innovation.

As one of the first designers to devote himself to teaching graphic design as a professional discipline, he fostered a younger generation of designers sympathetic to his notions of modernity. Even before he was hired as art director of *Harper's Bazaar* in 1934, he had introduced a new, experimental design curriculum into the American system of higher education, and he continued to train graphic designers, illustrators, and photographers well into the 1960s.

Brodovitch was a tireless advocate of photography's powers of communication. Fascinated with the medium's potential to go beyond everyday reality, he made it the backbone of his design technique, using photographs to cue his layout decisions. Seeking new ways of depicting clothes, he prominently featured the innovative fashion photographs of Martin Munkasci, Man Ray, and Richard Avedon, among many others. Seeking to expand the scope of *Harper's Bazaar* and to give it more seriousness, he introduced the documentary-style photographs of Bill Brandt, Brassaï, Henri Cartier-Bresson, and Lisette Model to the American public.

For young and aspiring photographers in New York, he was an arbiter of style and success. A nod of approval or a passing suggestion from this patrician, paternal Russian émigré was enough to set impressionable image makers off in search of new and unexplored territory. By insisting on originality, and by scornfully dismissing imitation and habit, he created a climate favorable to an expressive, impressionistic approach to photography. This new style found its apotheosis on the pages of *Harper's Bazaar*, and for a time in the 1950s it became the dominant aesthetic of creative photography.

For those in the fashion world, Brodovitch represented the epitome of taste. Working under Carmel Snow, whose tenure as editor of *Harper's Bazaar* coincided almost exactly with his years as art director, Brodovitch made the *Bazaar* the most visually exciting publication of its day. His increasingly spare but always dynamic layouts, enlivened by blurred and stop-action photographs, played a role in the transformation of fashion from an essentially aristocratic enterprise devoted to clothes manufactured in Paris into a more broad-based (if no less narcissistic and hierarchical) preoccupation with personal and cultural "life-styles."

To the general public, he remained a cipher, a man behind the scenes. Like all good designers, he was successful in attracting attention to the page without attracting attention to himself. He remained a shadowy background figure even after he was satirized, in the guise of an art director named Dovitch, in the popular film *Funny Face*. Nevertheless, at *Harper's Bazaar* Brodovitch labored on the front lines of celebrity, and he was in large part responsible for the public recognition achieved by many artists and photographers, from A. M. Cassandre to Hiro.

To his family and close friends, and probably in his own mind, he was the permanently exiled Russian aristocrat, an erstwhile soldier for the czar, the last of a noble breed condemned to toil in the degraded world of commerce. He even complained that the world of fashion was beneath him. And while Brodovitch was not a genuine aristocrat, he was a true snob, perennially disappointed with the world, with his circumstances in it, with his wife and only child, and ultimately with himself. It was this dissatisfaction, which tended towards self-destructiveness, that accounts for Brodovitch's impatience with convention, his urge to make visual experience always new, and his insistence on the highest standards of performance from those around him, and from himself.

With his halting, Russian-accented English, his cigarette holder, and his punctilious manner, Brodovitch seemed to many the incarnation of fashionable elegance, a designer whose work and life were parallel, if not inseparable.

His need for visual excitement was tremendous. He was always waiting for that one step forward that would juice him up a little bit.

His assistants and students fell almost immediately under the spell of his powerful personality. But as those who knew him well readily recognized, his life and his work were profoundly at odds. From close range, he seemed a tragic, Dostoyevskian character, a compulsive worker and heavy drinker whose appetite for gin gradually became insatiable. Eventually, alcoholism would ravage his physical and mental health, ending his productive career soon after he turned sixty. At turns he could be charming or tyrannical. "To some people he was like a god, but to me, he was a bastard," recalls Ben Fernandez, one of his last students.[1]

He was addicted throughout his life to the allure of the new, the unexpected, the unconventional. He yearned for visual stimulation, to be transported from everyday life into a realm filled simultaneously with clarity and surprise. "He was such a bored man, one of the real Russian souls," remembers Lillian Bassman, one of his assistants at the *Bazaar* and an art director of the short-lived *Junior Bazaar*. "His need for visual excitement was tremendous. He was always waiting for that one step forward that would juice him up a little bit. His favorite line in class was, 'Why to eat bacon and eggs every day?' "[2]

Given this need for change in his creative life, it is paradoxical that Brodovitch tried to be a conventional husband and parent. But his home life could be charitably characterized as disorderly and acutely unhappy. He had married the woman who had nursed his wounds in the waning moments of the Russian Revolution, and the marriage lasted from 1920 until she died in 1959. Nevertheless, by all accounts their relationship was frequently contentious and bitter; while he worked in the center of the sophisticated cultural life of New York City, she stayed outside, running the family's country house as if it were a dacha on the Russian steppes. Their only son, Nikita, was born with what apparently was hydrocephalus, and although the exact nature of his illness was never discussed, his behavior showed unmistakable signs of mental and emotional retardation. Brodovitch's disappointment and sense of failure over Nikita's learning and psychological disabilities may account for the patently paternalistic way in which he treated the young

He had no theories or systems to guide him in creating a magazine spread; no modules or grids lie beneath his characteristically spare pages.

men who became his apprentices. He turned to them, and to his female co-workers, to compensate for the conflicts in his family life.

Yet despite what in retrospect seem major, unresolved tensions in his personality, Brodovitch's graphic design is unfalteringly precise, balanced, and majestic. His work undoubtedly was, to an extent, a reprieve from the upsets and upheavals of daily life, at once a solace and an ideal. Brodovitch stayed at *Harper's Bazaar* for twenty-four years, from 1934 to 1958, during bad times and good, weathering the infighting and power struggles within both the Hearst Corporation, the *Bazaar*'s corporate parent, and the magazine's own editorial staff. One can speculate that some part of him craved the stability that the job offered—the same part of him, perhaps, that urged him to be a conventional husband and father. Once he lost his position, in the same shift of personnel and editorial focus that forced the departure of Carmel Snow, his health fell apart as quickly as his career.

Some who knew Brodovitch have suggested that the pristine elegance of his graphic design grew out of a nostalgia for the more simple times of his childhood. Diana Vreeland, who began her career in fashion at *Harper's Bazaar* in the 1940s, suggested as much in a statement written shortly after his death in 1971:

He loved white paper, the more the better, and it was very hard indeed for him to allow even the most beautiful blow-up of a Cartier-Bresson photo to spoil the immaculate clarity and whiteness . . . one felt that when he was alone with his white paper, he was resting in the snows of his native Russia, and finding a purity and cleanliness he could not find elsewhere.[3]

Whether this white space stood as a metaphor for snow, or whether it simply served as an island of calm perfection within the stormy sea of Brodovitch's life, it became the distinguishing hallmark of his magazine design. By the 1950s, the *Bazaar*'s design was emulated and imitated by scores of American magazines, from *Vogue* to *Look*.

Brodovitch did much more than design *Harper's Bazaar*, however. In the 1920s, which he spent in Paris, he designed posters, furnishings, jewelry, print ads, and interiors. Even while working at the magazine, he continued to work

It is largely due to Brodovitch that the responsibilities of an editorial art director were expanded to include almost total control of a publication's visual contents.

as a free-lance designer and illustrator, creating ads for Saks Fifth Avenue and other clients, posters for the Red Cross, and knock-down furniture. He was art director and art editor of the pioneering graphic-arts magazine *Portfolio*, published in 1950 and 1951, and he designed a number of books, including *Observations*, with photographs by Richard Avedon and text by Truman Capote, in 1959. He devoted what spare time he had left to painting and photography.

As a consequence of his exposure to European Modernism in the formative stages of his career, he refused, like André Breton, Jean Cocteau, and Man Ray, to be inhibited by notions of specialization or professionalism. He never felt the need to seek training as a designer; he simply worked at it. It is ironic, then, that his career coincides exactly with the development of graphic design as an independent, specialized profession—especially since in Brodovitch's hands it more closely resembled an art. He had no theories or systems to guide him in creating a magazine spread; no modules or grids lie beneath his characteristically spare pages. Although esteemed as an inspirational teacher, and despite having taught hundreds of design classes over a span of thirty years, he never developed a way of talking about the decisions he made regarding the position and proportion of images and type on the page. He never sought a principle or method to explain to students how to design to his standards. Perhaps this is why he professed not to be a teacher, but a "can opener"—someone whose role, as an art director and as a teacher, was to encourage creativity, not to codify it.[4]

Brodovitch's nonverbal, essentially intuitive approach to the practice of design allowed for a maximum of hands-on discovery and flexibility during the design process. While his editorial design at *Harper's Bazaar* is recognizable, it is by no means all of a piece; his approach varied according to the materials at hand, the nature of the assignment, and the tenor of the times. Starting with a disjunctive combination of Art Deco and Purist influences, he distilled them into a unique, flexible syntax that proved ideal for the American fashion audience of the 1930s. At the same time, he incorporated aspects of European Surrealism into his work, prizing its ability to shock and surprise; its presence gave

Bazaar readers the privileged feeling of peeking into the precincts of the international avant garde. During the war, responding to the social mood of austerity, Brodovitch's work was characterized by an almost minimalist restraint; when postwar conditions encouraged American self-sufficiency and a return to hedonism, his layouts were enlivened by photographs that spoke of youth, vigor, and high spirits. During the ascendency of Abstract Expressionism in the art world, he featured blurry, out-of-focus images on the pages of the magazine, and encouraged photographers to use their cameras as expressive tools.

Brodovitch's reliance on taste in lieu of theory differentiates him from other important designers, such as Jan Tschichold and Paul Rand, who sought to codify the elements of design and the tasks of the designer. Brodovitch put words to paper very reluctantly. When he did, as in his prospectus for the first Design Laboratory at the Pennsylvania Museum School of Industrial Art, he characteristically borrowed from someone else.[5] But if he was not a designer interested in explicating design principles, in the mold of Tschichold and Rand, he certainly was part of their tradition. The ways in which he used type reflect the modern principles elucidated by Tschichold in his 1928 book *Die Neue Typographie*. Rand's ideas about design, elaborated in *Thoughts on Design*, were in turn influenced by Brodovitch's early practice in the United States.[6]

What ultimately distinguishes Brodovitch from most of his contemporaries, however, is his conception of what graphic design, and the role of the designer, should be. He refused to consider himself a mere practitioner of a fixed set of skills—skills which could be applied, in nearly mechanical fashion, to whatever project came to hand. As a magazine art director, he broadened the definition of his profession to include much more than designing pages. He insisted on, and for the most part got, control of the process of assigning illustrators and photographers, and of selecting which of the resulting images would appear on the magazine's pages. While we may consider this degree of involvement standard procedure for an art director today, it is largely due to Brodovitch that the responsibilities of an editorial art director were expanded to include almost total control of a publication's visual contents.[7]

Equally important, Brodovitch refused to consider style as the ultimate goal of design. Instead, he advocated a continual renewal of visual stimulation, avoiding the dreaded pitfalls of boredom and habit. Though he was not the first person to adopt Ezra Pound's dictum, "Make it new," as gospel, he was one of the most insistent in putting the idea into practice. If his design work at *Harper's Bazaar* sometimes failed to live up to this directive, sliding temporarily into familiar territory, it most likely was because Brodovitch himself was so prone to boredom. In looking back at the more than three-hundred issues of the *Bazaar* that he designed, one finds not one Brodovitch "look" but several. As a believer in the vitalizing power of continual change, he embodied, more than any other designer, the underlying ethos of Modernism. ■

PARIS OF THE TWENTIES

During the ten years he lived in Paris, Brodovitch became acquainted with a variety of vanguard art movements and styles. Of these, Art Deco, Purism, and Surrealism had an especially potent influence. As can be seen on these pages, the young designer quickly absorbed their distinct graphic tendencies.

Brodovitch's poster for a 1924 artists' ball won first prize in a competition; this was his first public notice as a designer.

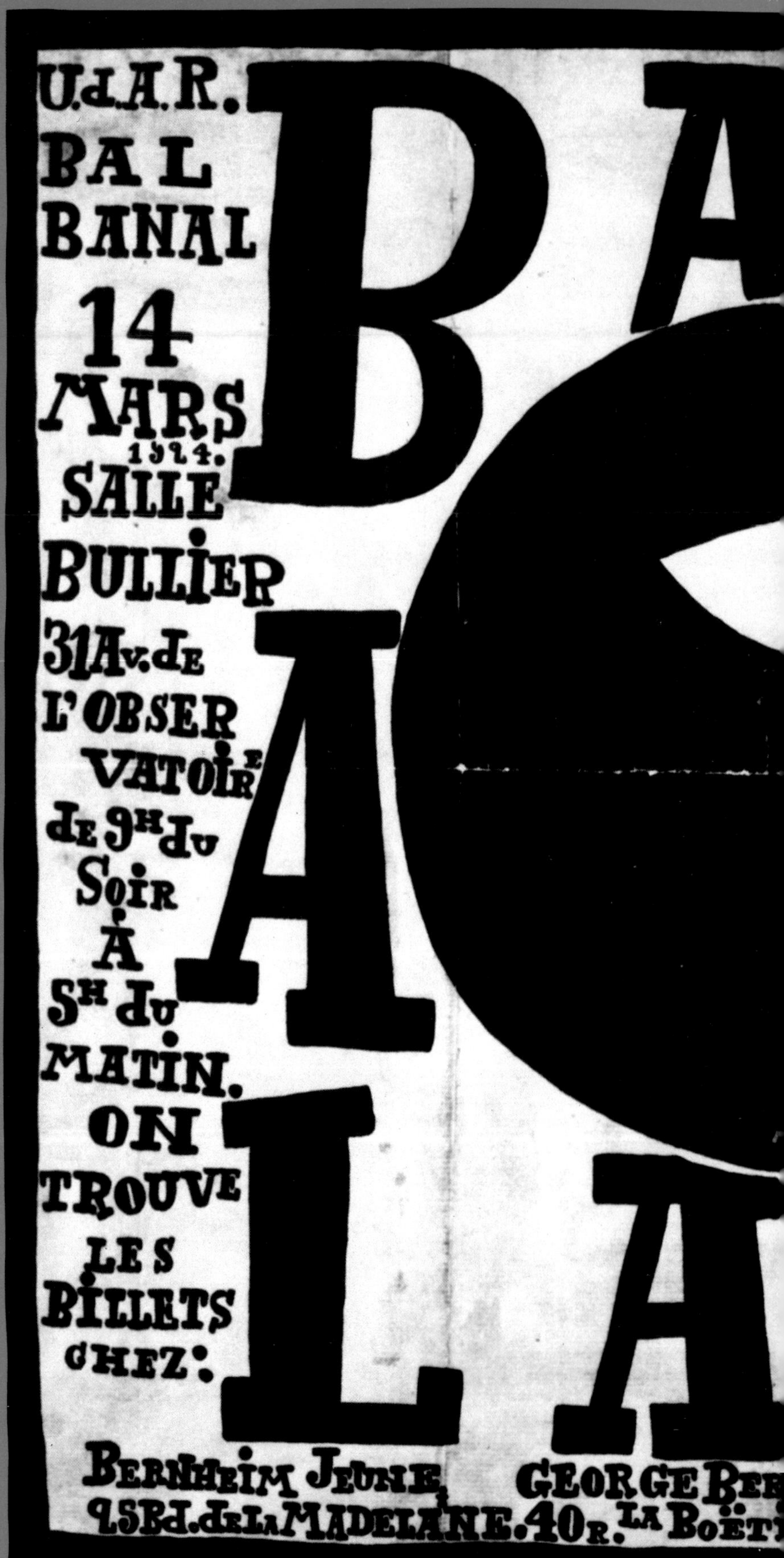

ALEXEY BRODOVITCH.
BAL BANAL POSTER. 1924

A. Brodovitch
1924

NAL.

NAB

POVOLOTSKY
13 R. BONAPARTE

GEORGE PAUL GUILLAUME.
56 R. LA BOETIE. 59 R. LA BOËTIE.

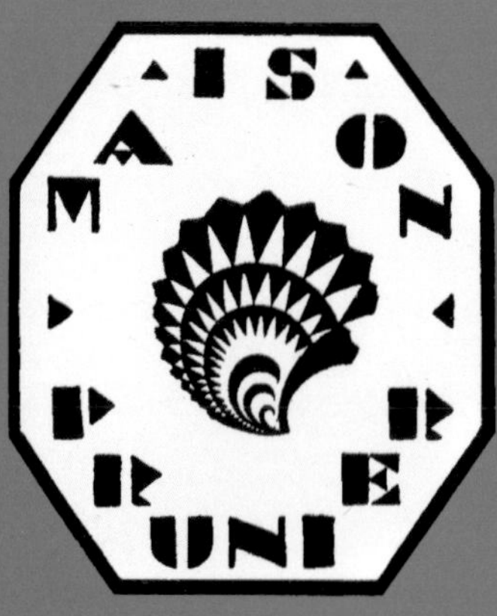

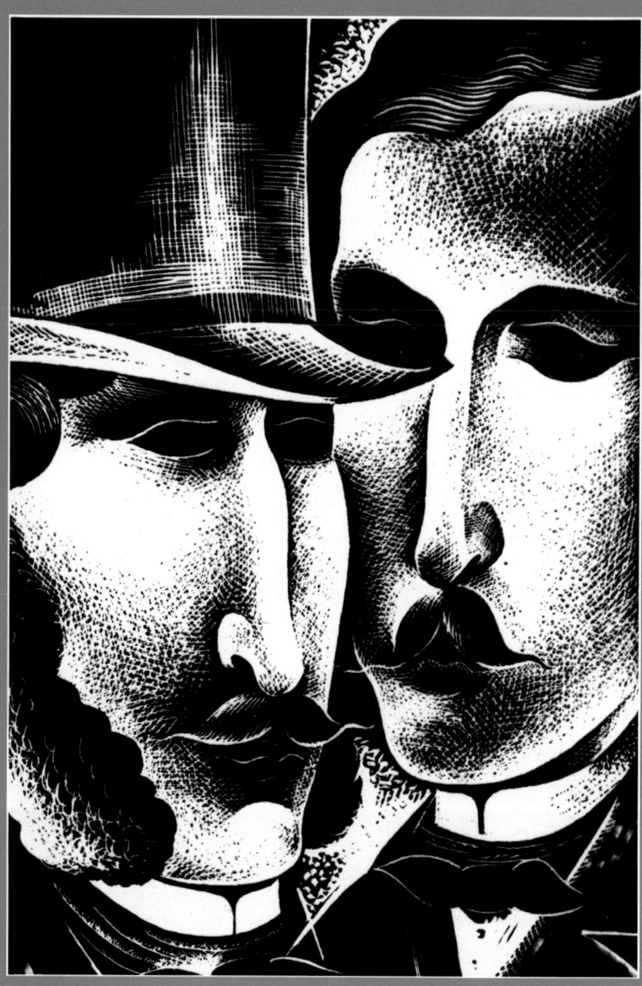

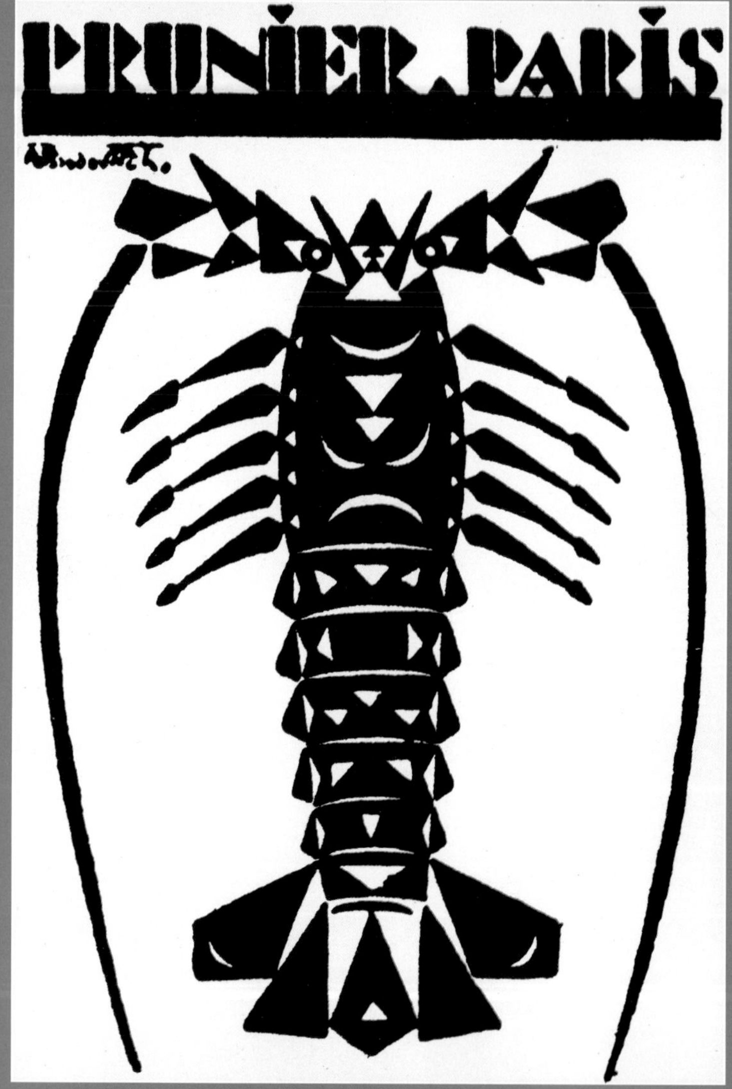

Left:

ALEXEY BRODOVITCH.
ILLUSTRATION FOR
MONSIEUR DE BOUGRELON
BY JEAN LORRAIN. 1928

Above:

ALEXEY BRODOVITCH.
LOGOTYPE AND MENU COVER
FOR PRUNIER RESTAURANT.
1927

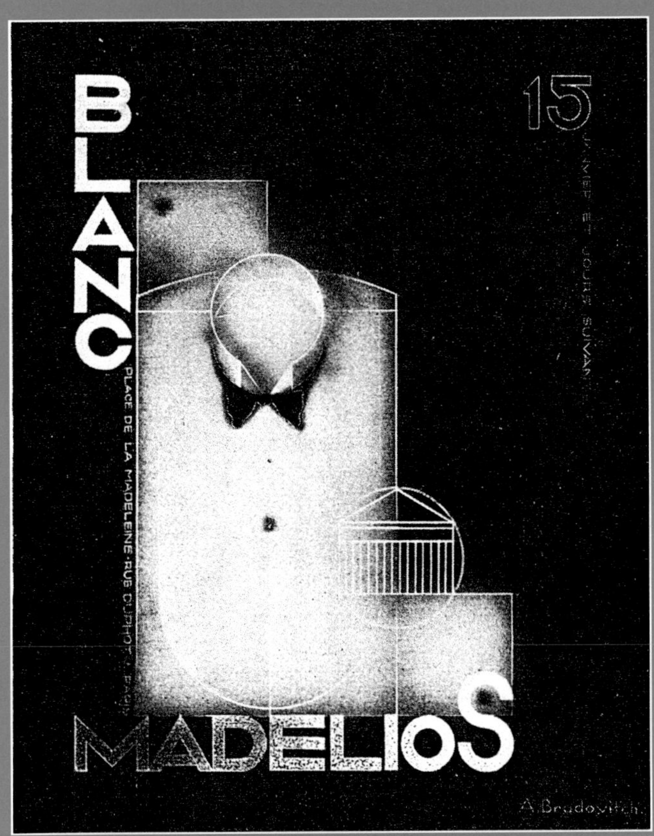

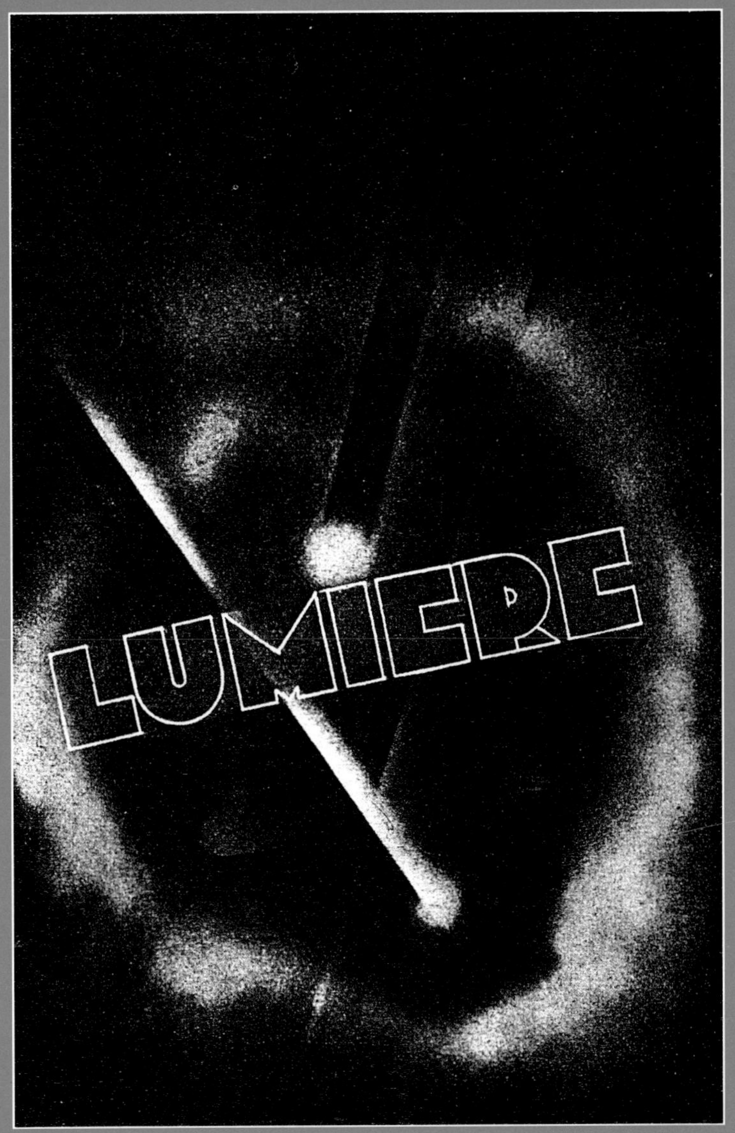

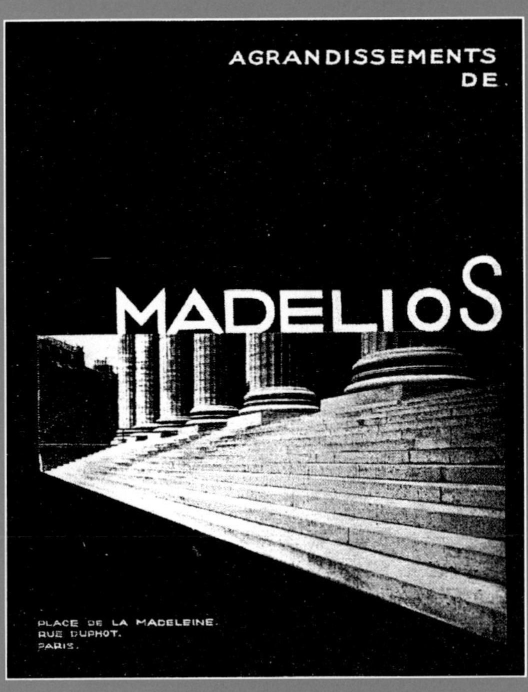

ALEXEY BRODOVITCH. ADVERTISEMENTS FOR MADELIOS, THE MEN'S BOUTIQUE OF THE PARISIAN DEPARTMENT STORE AUX TROIS QUARTIERS. 1928–30

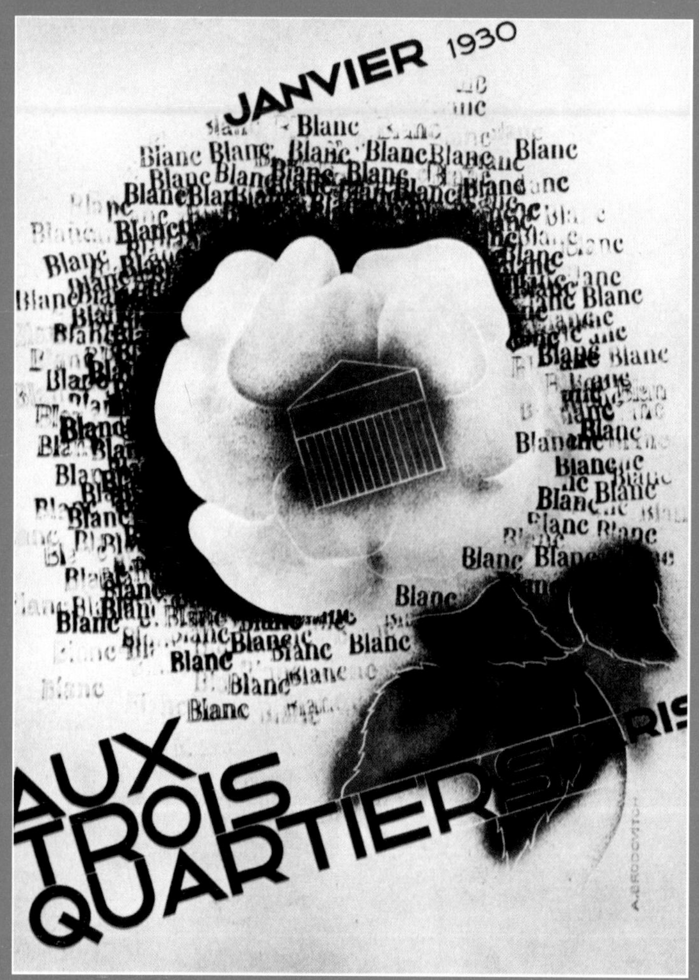

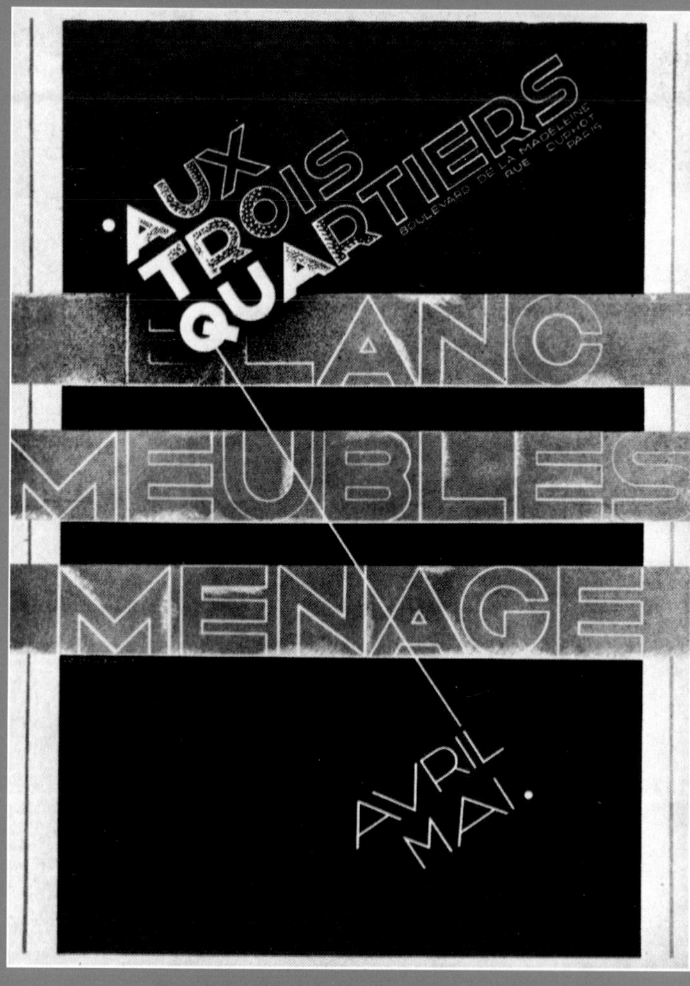

Above and opposite:
ALEXEY BRODOVITCH.
THREE ADVERTISEMENTS FOR
AUX TROIS QUARTIERS.
1929-30

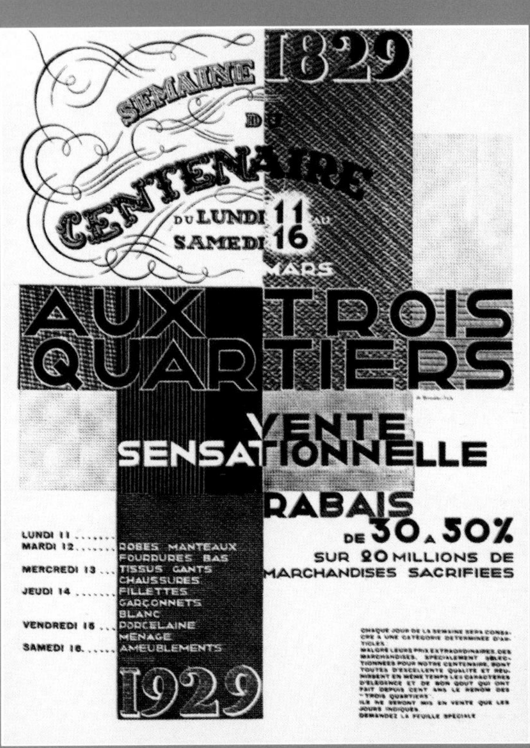

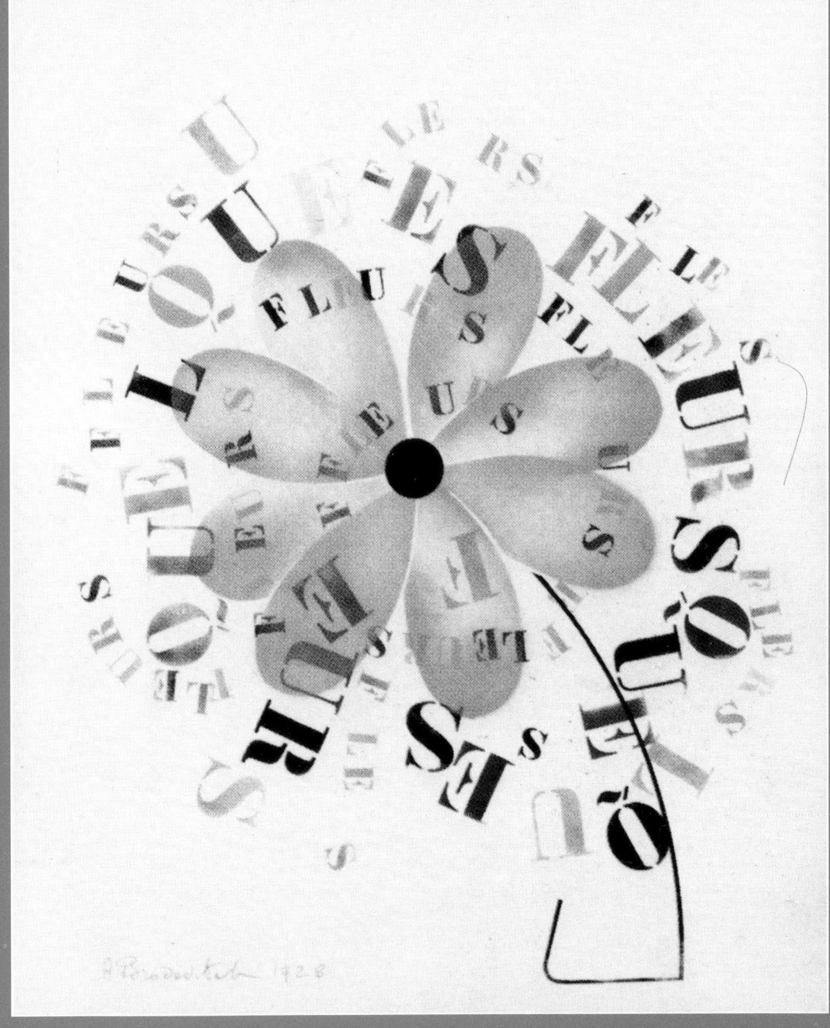

Above:

ALEXEY BRODOVITCH.

POSTER DESIGN. 1928

THE EMIGRE MIND

2

"Etonnez-moi!"
—SERGEI DIAGHILEV

"Astonish me!"
—ALEXEY BRODOVITCH

For someone transplanted from his native soil, the ability to adapt is more than a knack that can come in handy. If one is to achieve any kind of security and stature in a place where one is destined always to be an outsider, it is essential. Not surprisingly, then, a chameleonlike adaptability is the most important, obvious, and determining characteristic of Brodovitch's early work as a designer—and, to a somewhat lesser degree, of his entire career. Forced to invent his own identity, he became a master of the art of assimilating a variety of influences and forging from them a style of his own. Adaptability is a necessity for all graphic designers, of course, but Brodovitch made it his hallmark.

In the United States, Brodovitch was an émigré twice over. He was born in Russia in 1898, by his own account, the son of a well-off doctor sympathetic to the czar. By the age of twenty, however, the doors of his native land slammed shut. An officer in the White army defeated by the Bolsheviks, he emigrated to France, spending the decade of the 1920s immersed in the avant-garde atmosphere of Paris. In 1930 he sailed to the United States, where he would spend the rest of his working life. While some immigrants never make a successful adjustment to their new environment, Brodovitch thrived on what was foreign to him. He had a nose for the new, and he was adept at incorporating it into his design work. Long before pastiche became recognized as a characteristic impulse of twentieth-century art, Brodovitch was employing it in *Harper's Bazaar* to masterful effect.

Having grown up in pre-revolutionary Russia, where his teens were spent as a student at the imperial military school and as a cavalry officer in Eastern Europe, Brodovitch was a man whose native land was forever locked in the past tense. If France and the United States quickly recognized his prodigious talent, it was in part because he just as quickly grasped, in his intuitive, wordless way, what they expected of him. Unable to return to the stability of his childhood, he cultivated the one aspect of life that had taken its place: change.

Just how adaptable he could be can be seen by comparing two books of photographs he designed for the New York publisher J.J. Augustin at the end of World War II. *Ballet*, a volume of the designer's own photographs of the Ballets Russes

ALEXEY BRODOVITCH ON THE SOIL OF HIS NATIVE RUSSIA, C. 1915

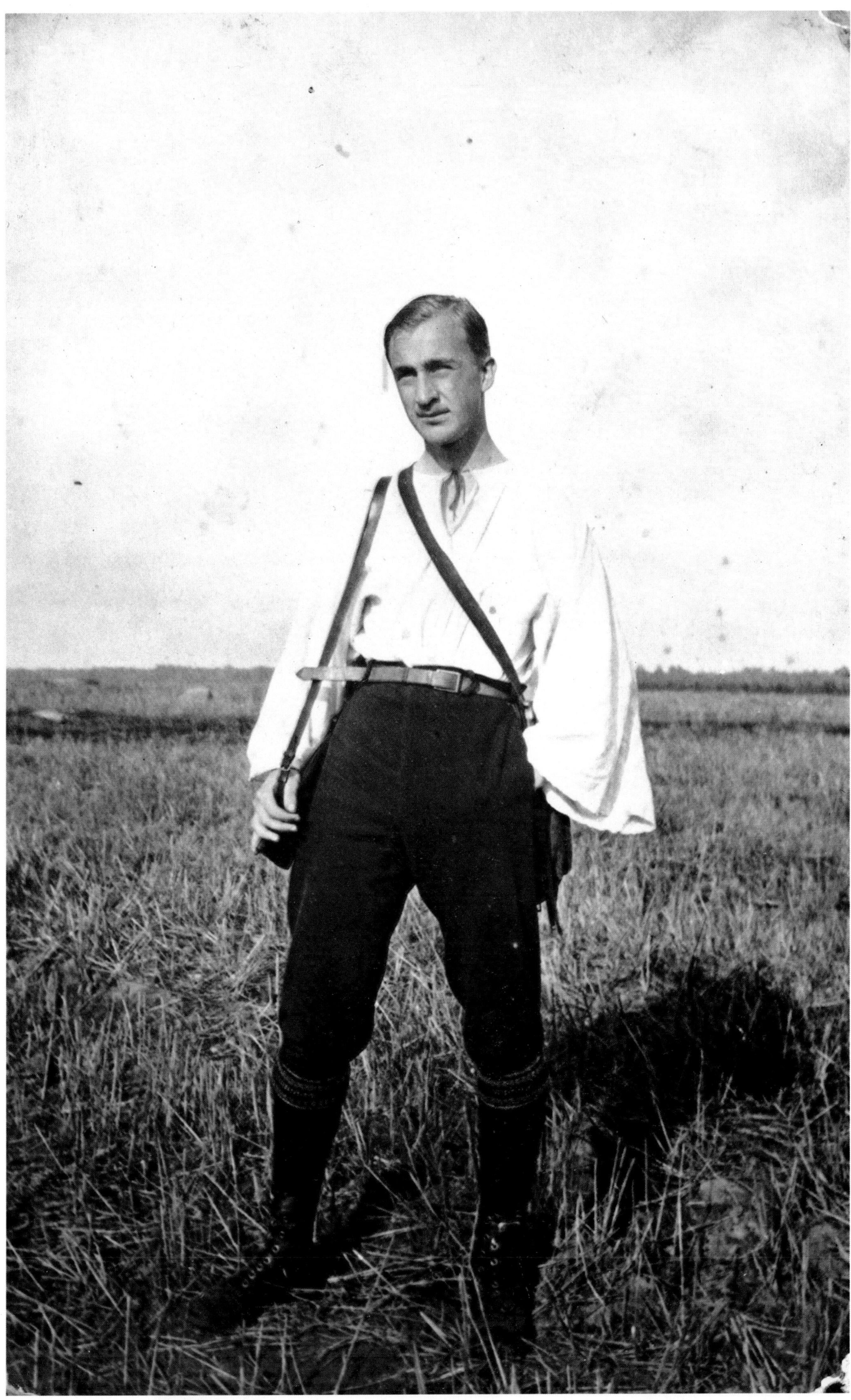

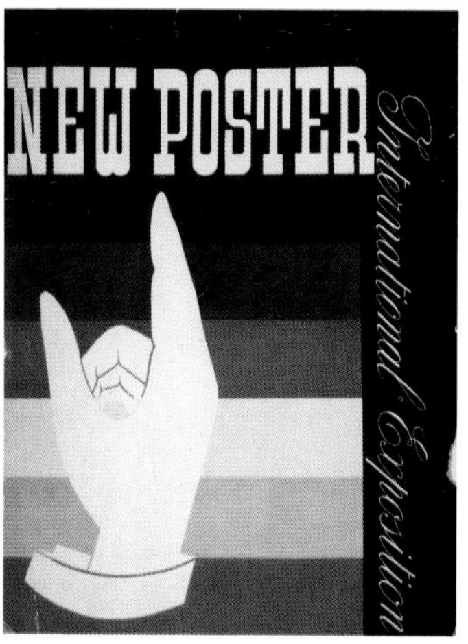

The 1937 "New Poster" show at the Franklin Institute in Philadelphia introduced modern European poster design to the United States. Brodovitch organized the exhibition, selected the works, and designed its installation and catalogue.

(pages 48–53), was entirely his own creation. The already blurred and grainy pictures of ballet dancers are enlarged to bleed off the pages on all four sides; their sequence is broken only by white chapter pages used to indicate the different ballets being performed. The typeface of each chapter page is different, and the faces range in style from baroque to Western barroom. In several places, two separate photographs are matched on facing pages to give the effect of one single, continuous panorama of dance.

The other book, *Day of Paris* by André Kertész, with a text by George Davis, is a model of circumspection by comparison (pages 44–47). Most of its pictures are presented as rectangular inserts within the white borders of the page, in the conventional style of European illustrated magazines of the 1920s and thirties. The type is unassuming; the design as a whole exudes quiet and restraint. Brodovitch clearly did not want the design to overshadow Kertesz's lyrical and rather delicate images, so he created an environment in which the pictures could get their messages across slowly and sympathetically. The design of *Day of Paris* is as inobtrusive as *Ballet*'s is bold and startling.

What he brought to the United States in the way of modern design ideas can be seen especially vividly in his advertising illustrations of the early 1930s, which were radical for his new land but in fact were allied with European poster styles of the time. The catalogue to a 1937 show called "New Poster," which Brodovitch organized for the Franklin Institute in Philadelphia, makes this influence clear. Illustrated alongside contributions by Brodovitch and by such early students as Nelson Gruppo and Mary Fullerton (later Faulconer) are posters by Herbert Bayer, A.M. Cassandre, E. McKnight Kauffer, Herbert Matter and other established designers of the time. While the posters of Brodovitch and his students are in no way copies of the European contributions, they reflect the European aesthetic.

Similarly, Brodovitch's first layouts for *Harper's Bazaar* strongly echo the work of Mehemed Fehmy Agha, the Russian émigré art director of *Vogue* and *Vanity Fair* who preceded Brodovitch to New York by several years. But Brodovitch rarely was slavish in his design borrowings; indeed, often he improved on the original model. His *Bazaar* layouts using a

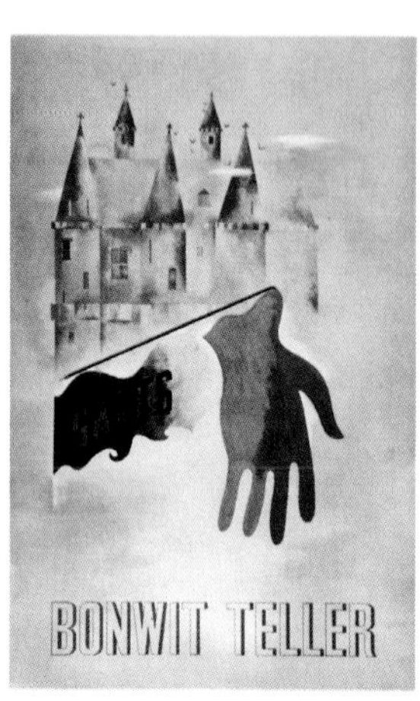

Top:
ALEXEY BRODOVITCH. "NEW POSTER" EXHIBITION CATALOGUE COVER, 1937

Above:
MARY FULLERTON. BONWIT TELLER POSTER, FROM THE "NEW POSTER" EXHIBITION CATALOGUE

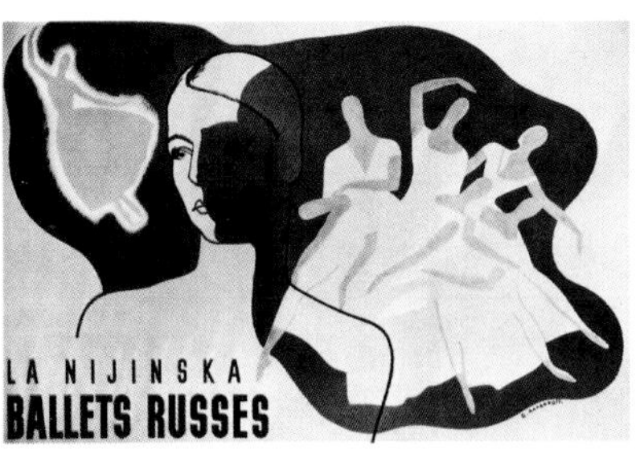

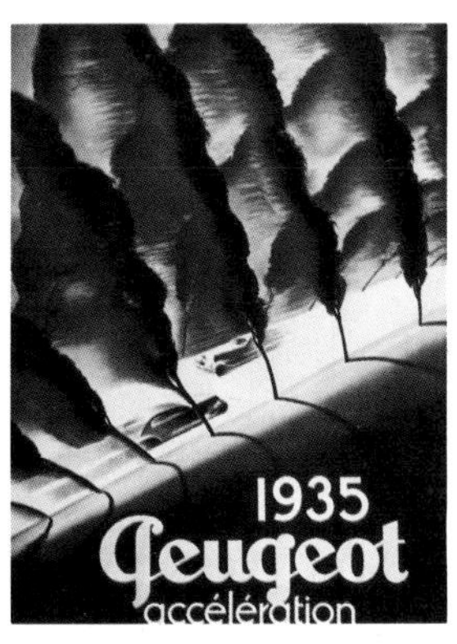

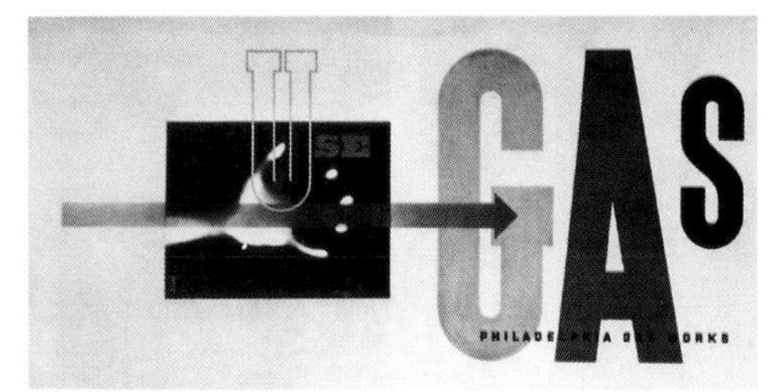

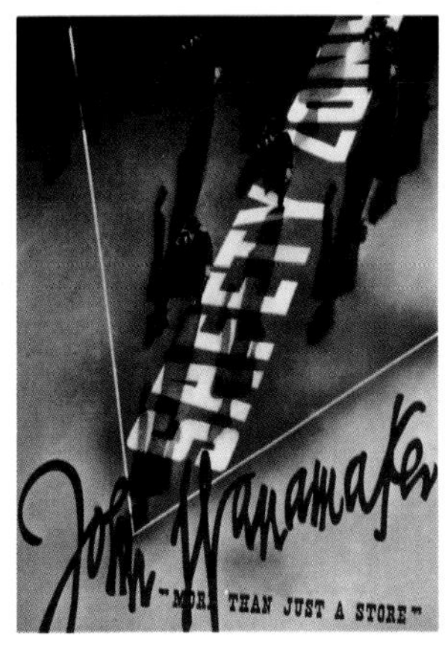

"fan" of small photographs across a spread, for example, were usually more coherent and pleasing than Agha's, even though Agha had established the technique at *Vogue*.

Brodovitch's former assistants at the magazine recall that he was not shy about appropriating their work, either. Lillian Bassman, who started as one of his workshop students, remembers an early "collaboration" she did with Brodovitch for a poster contest at the Museum of Modern Art. "Lillian, why not to do it together?," she remembers Brodovitch urging, after which he added, "So think of something." Bassman came up with a concept, took the photograph it needed, and dummied up the poster, which she presented to Brodovitch. "Brodovitch said 'The "i" should be closer to the "b," ' or something," but otherwise left the poster unchanged, she recalled. Yet when it was exhibited at the museum, Bassman found to her surprise that the credit read "Poster by Alexey Brodovitch."[8]

His verbal appropriations could be even more bald—presumably because language was never one of his strong suits. His widely quoted admonition to students, "Astonish me," is simply a translation of Diaghilev's earlier refrain, "Etonnez-moi."

Paris in the Twenties

When Alexey Brodovitch arrived in Paris as a young man in his twenties, with the wounds of war still fresh, he stepped into the center of the greatest period of artistic ferment in modern times. A new sense of freedom and possibility prevailed in the wake of World War I, an optimism generated and inspired in part by a new industrial age that promised to revolutionize transportation, communication, culture, and life itself. This excitement spilled over into all areas of artistic life. Painters, poets, novelists, sculptors, architects, photographers, designers, choreographers, composers—many of them French, but also including a host of émigrés from other European countries and America—filled Paris with a sense of limitless possibility that helped mitigate the memories of a devastating war.

It was not merely that these artists were each developing their own disciplines, picking up the pieces from the decade before the war and cementing the

Clockwise from left:
POSTERS FROM THE "NEW POSTER" EXHIBITION CATALOGUE:

HERBERT MATTER. JOHN WANAMAKER POSTER

YURI ANNENCOFF. BALLETS RUSSES POSTER

PAUL COLIN. PEUGEOT POSTER

LESTER BEAL. PHILADELPHIA GAS WORKS POSTER

Below:
JEAN COCTEAU. *HARPER'S BAZAAR* COVER, NOVEMBER 1946

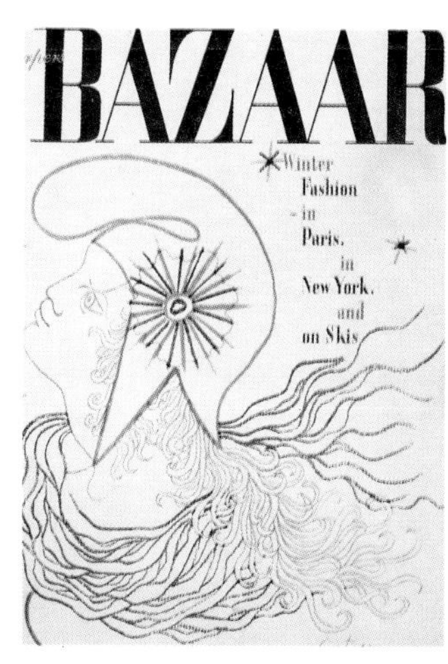

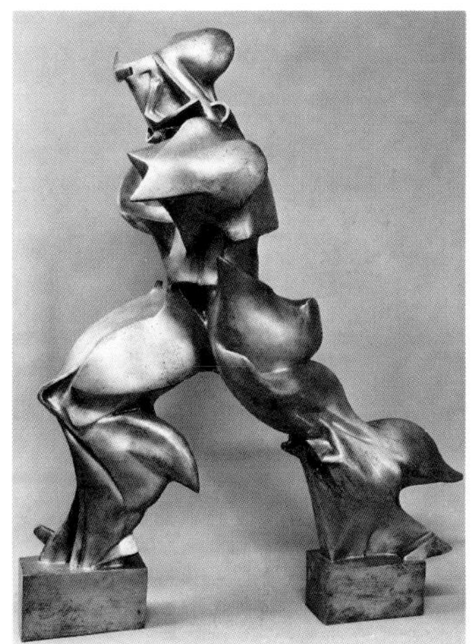

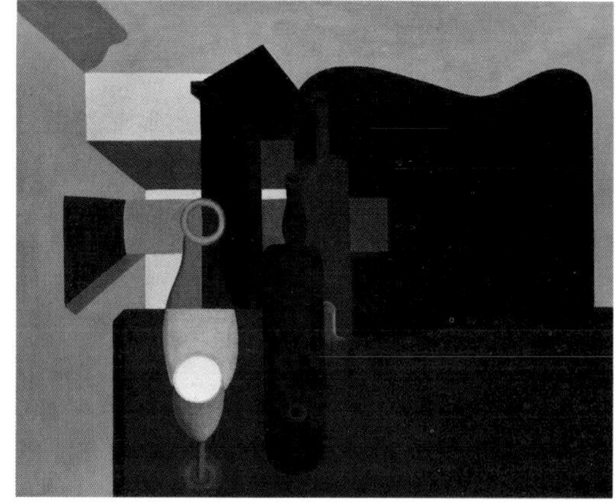

uniquely twentieth-century style of Modernism. There also was an unprecedented degree of interchange among them. The most striking example of this, in the decade Brodovitch was to spend in the French capital, revolved around the Surrealists. Their devotion to chance and the adventures of the subconscious was expressed in poetry, fiction, painting, and photography, as well as in such untested and as-yet-unnamed forms as performance art.

This cross-pollination of the arts allowed relatively unsung fields of expression, such as photography, to develop alongside those that were more valued, such as painting. As in our own times, the distinction between what was "fine art" and what was "commercial art" was narrowed, if not erased. What mattered was the possibility for new forms of expression, forms that would deal in a direct and meaningful way with the conditions of contemporary life brought on by the Machine Age. In such a climate, graphic design flourished in close association with the other arts, and drew copiously from them. Brodovitch adopted this approach as his own.

He arrived in Paris without any formal art training, but presumably with some education in the French language. His parents are said to have wanted him to attend art school, but the onset of World War I forced a change of plans, and he went to the Russian equivalent of West Point instead. The Russian Revolution effectively ended his career as an officer and gentleman. In Paris, he first found work as a house painter, but he soon was painting sets for Sergei Diaghilev's Ballets Russes, a Russian émigré in the employ of other Russian émigrés.

The city was a cosmopolitan depot through which the world's artists and art movements passed. It became filled with radical ideas and revolutionary aesthetic notions from abroad: Dada from Zurich and Berlin, Suprematism and Constructivism from Moscow, Bauhaus design from Germany, Futurism from Italy, De Stijl from Holland—all flowed into Paris and mingled with the native strains of Cubism, Fauvism, Purism, and Surrealism. From out of this potpourri of artistic influences, Brodovitch found his beginnings as a designer.

Within this diversity of movements there were certain similarities and certain polarities. There was, for example, a belief in form as

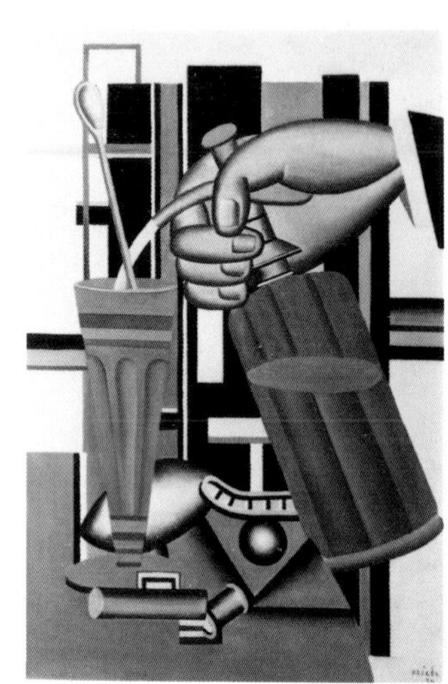

Left to right:

UMBERTO BOCCIONI. *UNIQUE FORMS OF CONTINUITY IN SPACE*. 1913

AMEDEE OZENFANT. *STILL LIFE*. 1920

FERNAND LEGER. *THE SIPHON*. 1924

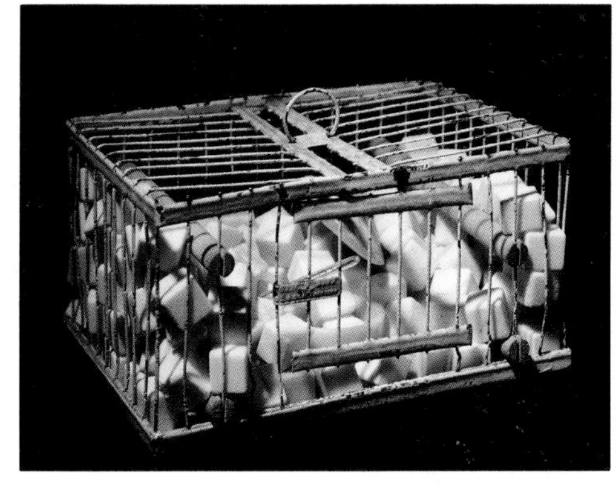

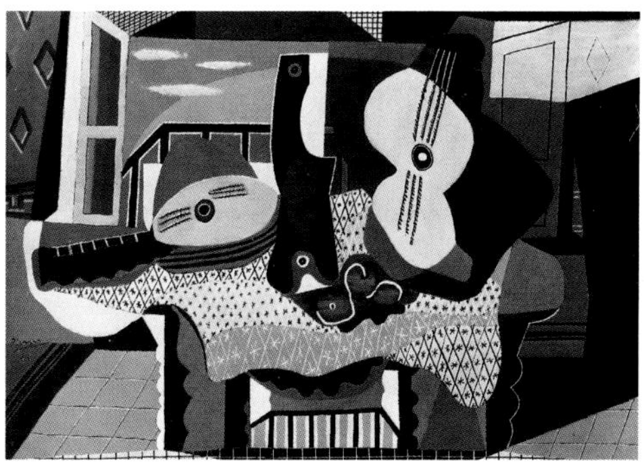

Post–World War I Europe was awash with new ideas about art and its role in modern life, in an awakening brought on in part by advancing technology. Brodovitch, like many others, was seized by the sense of possibility that this experimental climate engendered.

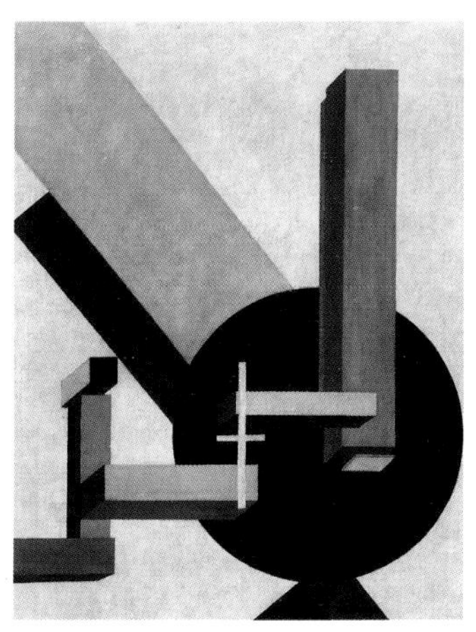

an ideal—that geometric forms represented the modern world more accurately and purely than any organic manifestations. At the same time, however, there was a strong impulse to make art that was socially useful, if not instrumental to social revolution. Much of the best new art from between the wars stems from a combination of these apparently contradictory impulses; it aspires to achieve both a purity of graphic means, usually geometrically expressed, and a wide audience.

Beginning in the 1920s, there arose a renewed interest throughout Europe in posters, placards, and other forms of graphic display, as well as in photography and film, since these were visual forms intended for mass audiences. They were all part of the dawning new age—proclaimed by Walter Benjamin, in 1936, as the Age of Mechanical Reproduction. For Brodovitch, with an unfulfilled childhood ambition to be an artist and a need to support himself and his family, it was an age of opportunity.

First Designs

Brodovitch's design career began during the time he was painting ballet sets for the Ballets Russes, some of which Diaghilev had commissioned such artists as Pablo Picasso, Henri Matisse, and André Derain to design.[9] When not painting sets, he drew designs for fabrics, crystal, and china, which he sold to fashionable shops. He soon gave up set painting and began to work part-time doing layouts of pages for *Cahiers d'Art*, an important art journal, and *Arts et Métiers Graphiques*, an influential design magazine published by the innovative type house Deberny-Peignot. As a layout man, as the job was then called, he was responsible for fitting together type, photographs, and illustrations on the pages of the magazines before they were sent to the printer. There was no art director to oversee or direct this process. He would have had the opportunity, rare by today's practice, of influencing the design of the pages he was preparing. But there is no way of positively determining which of the magazine's pages were created by the young designer.

The other design work Brodovitch is said to have done at this time has not survived. Nor is there any compelling evidence that he took classes in design, or came under the tutelage of one specific designer. (It is

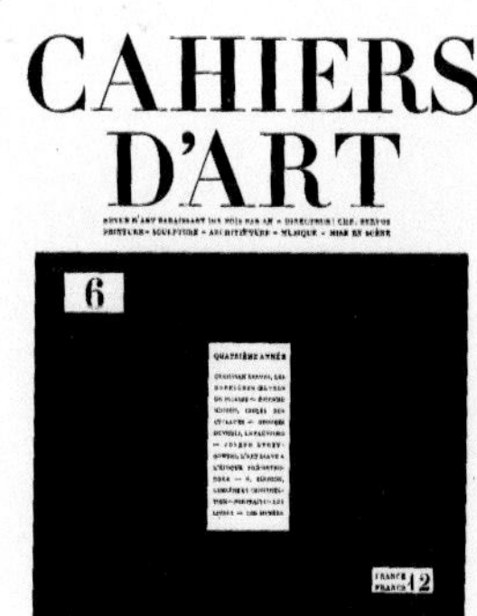

Left to right:

EL LISSITZKY. *PROUN ID*. 1919

MARCEL DUCHAMP. *WHY NOT SNEEZE ROSE SELAVY?* 1921

PABLO PICASSO. *MANDOLIN AND GUITAR*. 1924

COVER OF THE MAGAZINE *CAHIERS D'ART*, NO. 6

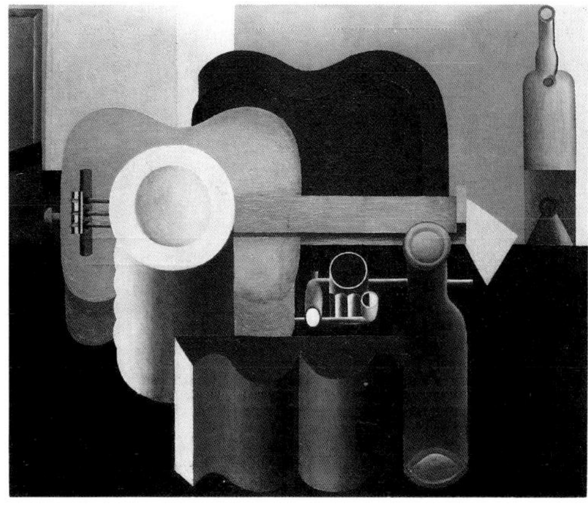

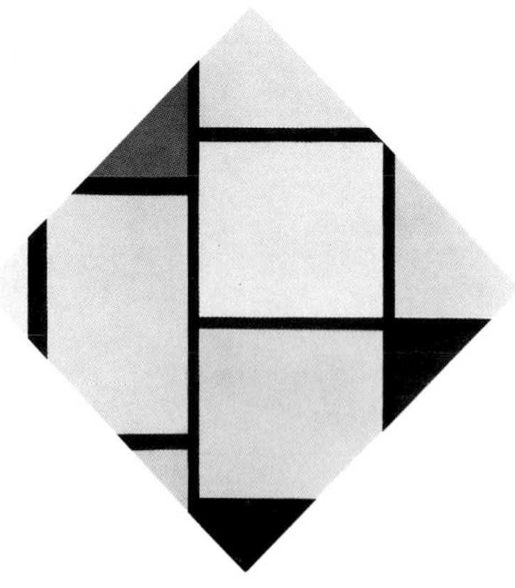

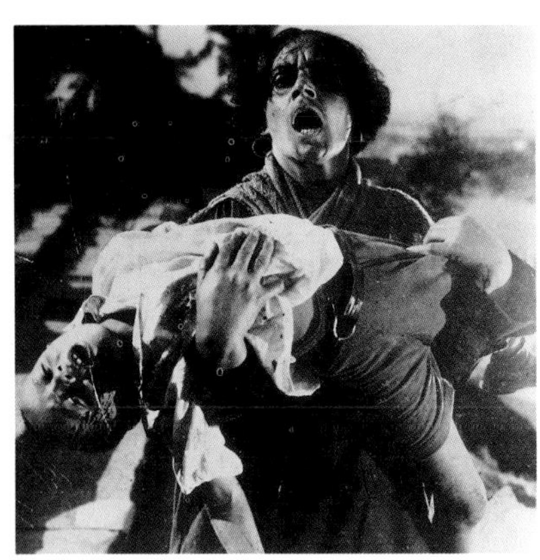

possible that he may have studied at Fernand Léger and Amédée Ozenfant's Academie de l'Art Moderne, the center of the Purist movement, or that he might have worked at Le Corbusier's atelier, as some biographical material suggests, but facts are lacking.) Yet judging from his output later in the decade—including posters, advertisements, and book illustrations (pages 24–29)—and the number of clients seeking his work, it did not take him long to develop an eclectic, iconoclastic graphic style of considerable appeal.

Essentially adaptive, Brodovitch's design work of the 1920s reflects three main influences. These include the decorative, dynamic manner of Art Deco, the geometric stolidity and force of Purism, and the unexpected imagery and discontinuous surfaces of Surrealism. Each of these influences remained an important element of the design style he brought to the United States in the thirties, although his tendency to rely on Surrealism's stylistic conventions and spatial illusionism gradually diminished over the years.

From all appearances, Brodovitch seems to have been familiar with the practices, if not the theories, of Le Corbusier and Sergei Eisenstein. Le Corbusier's ideas concerning the module—what he saw as the fundamental building block of the human form and its environment—may have helped Brodovitch find the sense of structure and proportion that are hallmarks of his graphic design.[10] Eisenstein's theory of film, emphasizing the principle of montage, may account in part for Brodovitch's innovative combinations of type, illustration, and photography on the pages of *Harper's Bazaar* (see Chapter 4, pages 98–107).

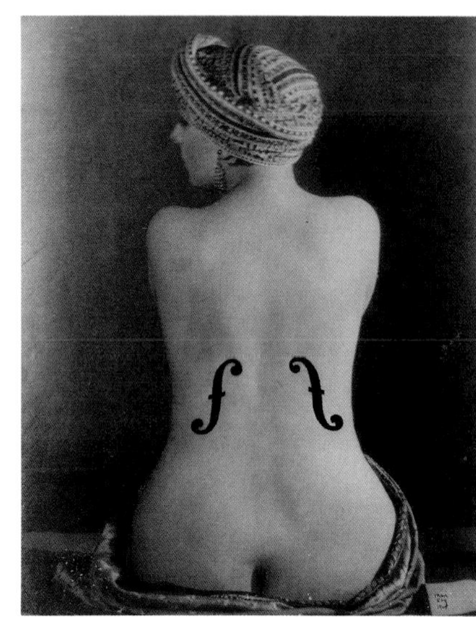

One needs to be cautious, however, in attributing any theoretical ideas to Brodovitch, since by all indications he was neither a reader nor a follower of theory. In addition, the urge to use geometric forms as models of universal first principles, and to adopt film as the most "modern" of media, was widespread during Brodovitch's formative years. Arranging photographs as if they were frames of a film, for example—something Brodovitch did repeatedly at *Harper's Bazaar* in the thirties—was something of a graphic cliché in the European illustrated press of the twenties, signifying speed, newness, and the Machine Age. It is more likely that he

Both pages, left to right:
FILM STILL FROM SERGEI EISENSTEIN'S *BATTLESHIP POTEMKIN*

LE CORBUSIER. *STILL LIFE.* 1920

PIET MONDRIAN. *LOZENGE IN RED, YELLOW AND BLUE.* C. 1926

MAN RAY. *LE VIOLIN D'INGRES.* 1924

A. M. CASSANDRE. POSTER, FROM THE "NEW POSTER" EXHIBITION CATALOGUE

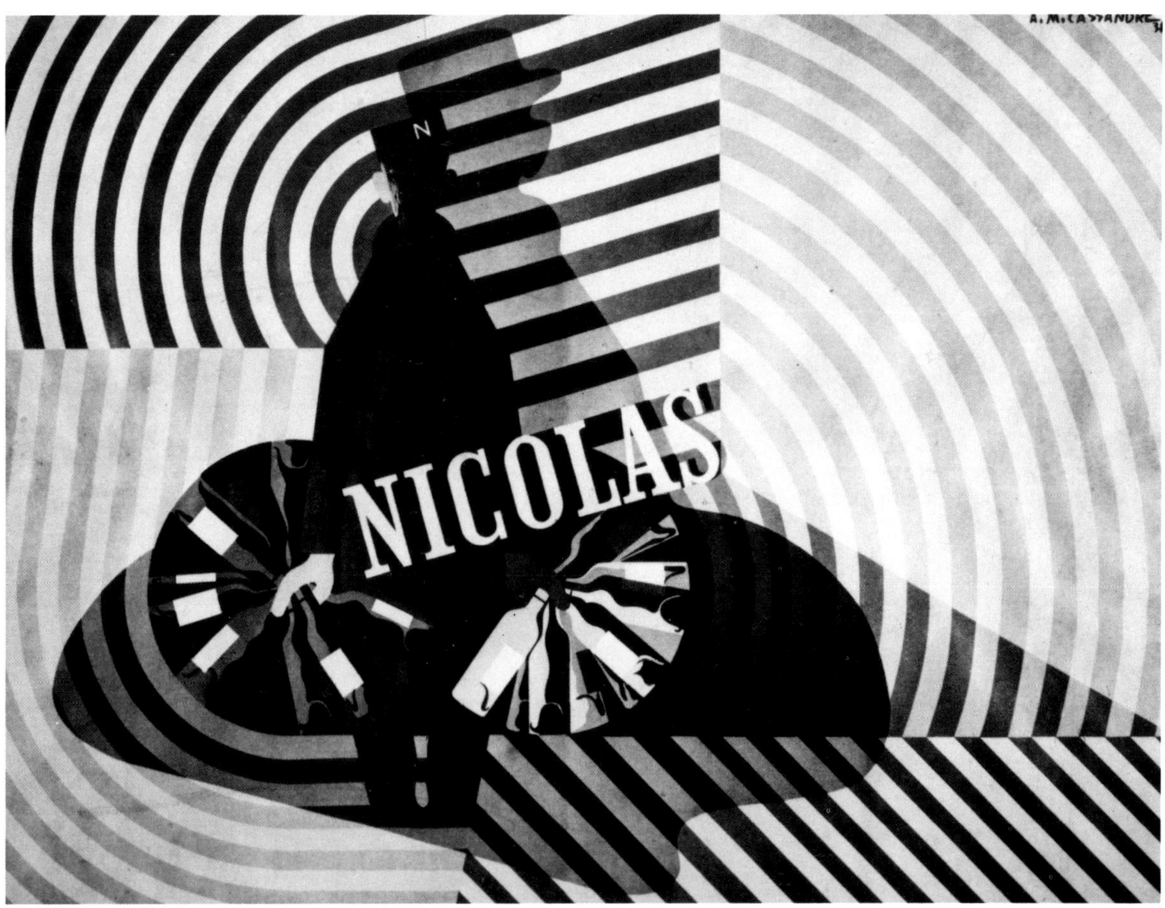

came under the broad influence of Le Corbusier's and Eisentein's theories, which had a certain currency in Paris of the twenties, than that he encountered their ideas directly.

Brodovitch's first public success came in 1924, when he entered and won a poster design competition for an artist's soiree called Le Bal Banal. The poster (page 24), besides being the oldest documented work by Brodovitch known to survive, is suggestive both of the influences on him and of his own future directions. The graphic, light-to-dark inversion of its mask shape, type, and background not only suggests the positive-negative process of photography, but also symbolically represents the process of masking: one trades one's identity for another, contrary one. In Brodovitch's case, the masquerade was in a sense real: he was a Russian living in France, a cavalry officer disguised as a designer.

The attention he received increased the next year when the landmark Exposition des Arts Décoratifs et Industriels Modernes took place in Paris. At the exhibition—which spawned the name Art Deco and brought the style to wide public attention—Brodovitch won five medals for his designs, including the top award for best designer pavilion. While, once again, there is no documentation of the work he displayed at the show, the reception he received suggests that it was in tune with the Art Deco style that swept the exhibition.

Indeed, his poster for the Bal Banal is essentially Art Deco in appearance and, like the work of the famous poster artist A. M. Cassandre, unites typogra-

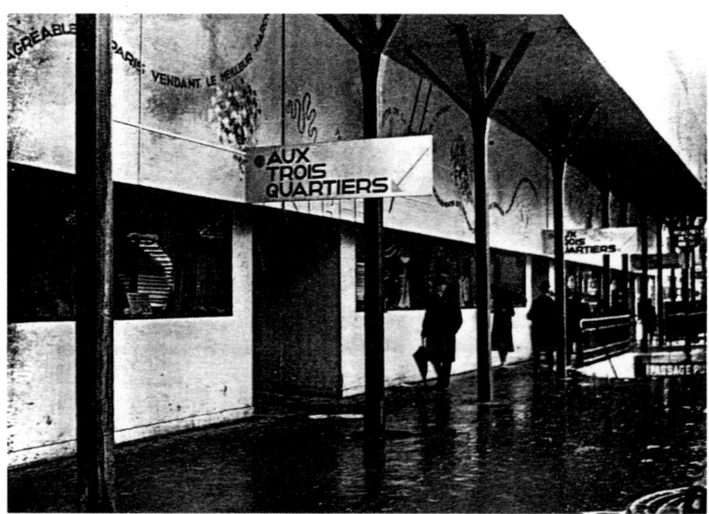

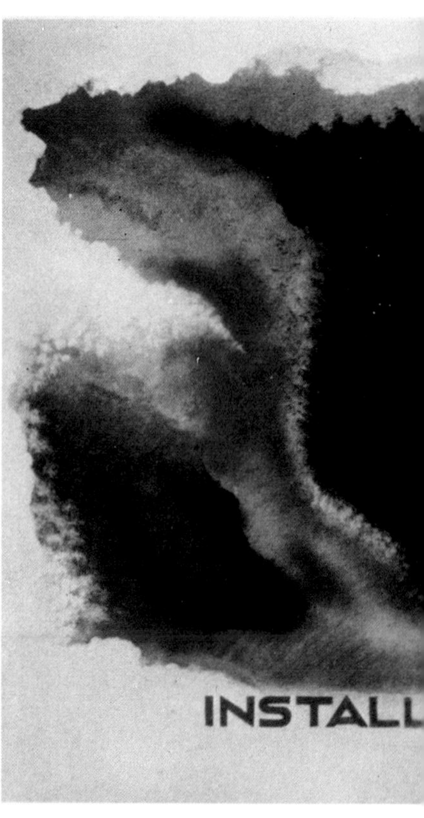

Right:
ALEXEY BRODOVITCH. TEMPORARY FACADE, AUX TROIS QUARTIERS, PARIS. 1928–30

Opposite:
ALEXEY BRODOVITCH. DESIGN FOR THE FACADE OF ATHELIA, THE DESIGN STUDIOS OF AUX TROIS QUARTIERS. 1928–30

Brodovitch's most public work of the twenties was his decoration of Aux Trois Quartiers' false front, erected during renovation. Geometric and decorative elements derived from Purism and Art Deco, respectively, can be discerned in his graphic elaboration of the facade.

phy and simplified representational forms in an overall pattern. Cassandre's posters had begun appearing in Paris a year earlier, and Brodovitch greatly admired them. (One of his first moves at *Harper's Bazaar* would be to dismiss Erté, who had been illustrating most of the magazine's covers, and hire Cassandre in his place.) Unlike Brodovitch, Cassandre had an academic training as a painter, at the Ecole des Beaux-Arts; his simple, graphic forms and bold typography show the influence of Constructivism, albeit with a decorative edge. Cassandre's combination of geometric rigor and decorative line provides the closest parallel to the style of Brodovitch's own illustrations of the time.

Brodovitch's work that followed the Art Deco exposition is by no means unified, and he felt free to work in a variety of styles. His scratchboard-style engravings for the 1928 book *Monsieur de Bougrelon*, by Jean Lorrain (page 26), have an ornateness that recalls turn-of-the-century Art Nouveau, but which is tempered by a Léger-like simplification of the figures. On the other hand, his menus, napkins, and window treatments for the restaurant Prunier, the Four Seasons of its day, employ thickly inked, symbolic representations of shellfish together with beefy, geometric, hand-lettered type, in a manner that is much more indebted to the masculine Purist style (page 26).

At Aux Trois Quartiers

In 1928 the by-then-fashionable graphic artist and illustrator was hired by a Parisian department store, Aux Trois Quartiers, to work in its fledgling design

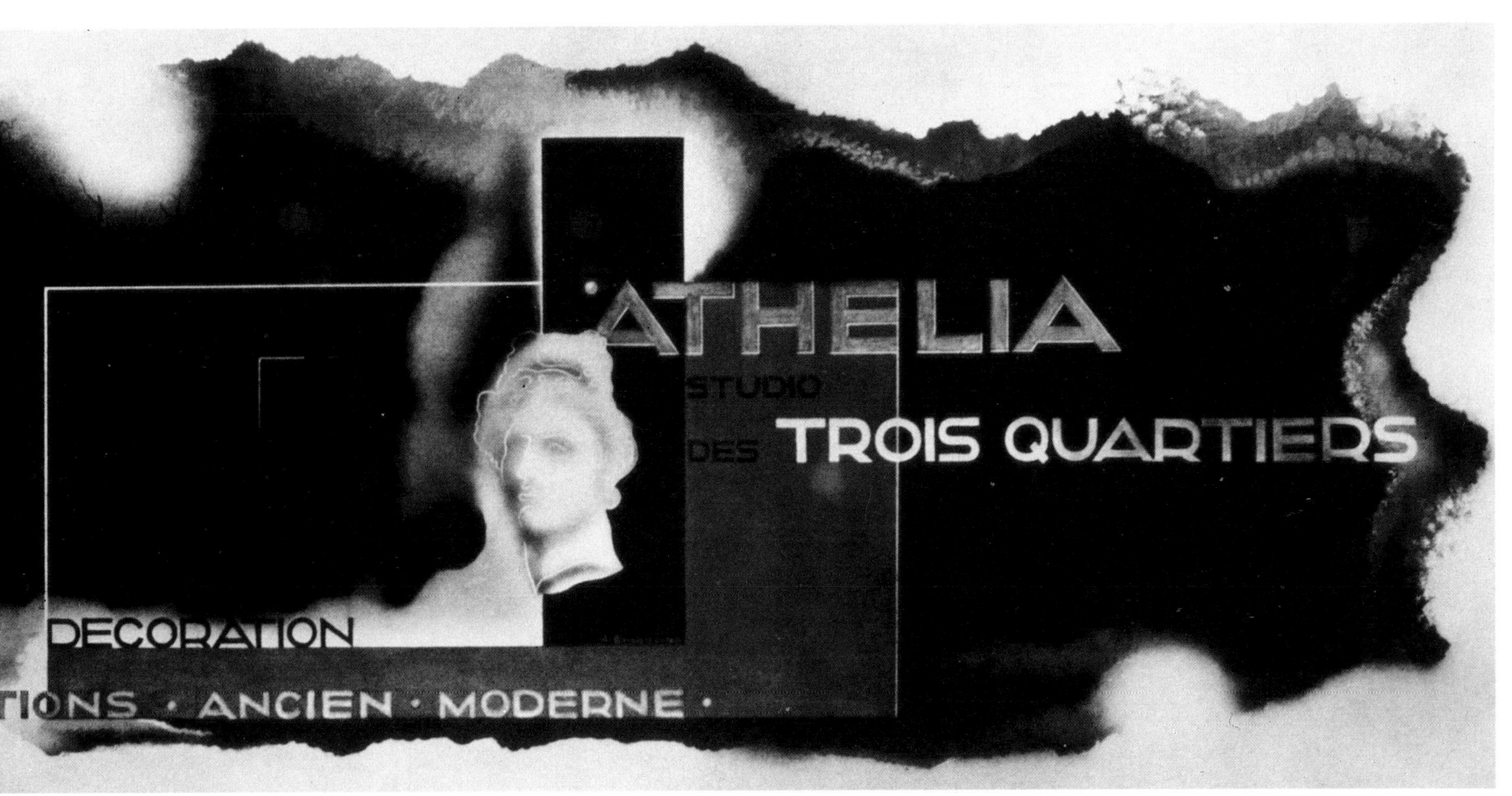

studio. Given the classical-sounding name Athelia, the studio was under the direction of Robert Block, an architect who had lived in America for many years. Block gave Brodovitch responsibility for a number of internal design projects, including the design and illustration of catalogues and advertisements for Aux Trois Quartier's luxury men's boutique, Madelios (so named because it was on the Place de la Madeleine). These, as well as Brodovitch's temporary facade for the main store, erected during an extensive renovation, were widely reproduced in European magazines, including *Arts et Métiers Graphiques*.[11]

Brodovitch's advertisements for the department store Aux Trois Quartiers are essentially Art Deco in conception (pages 25–27). While consisting primarily of type and the sort of broad, geometric planes typical of Cassandre's and other French posters of the time, they often are embellished with Brodovitch's own illustrations, done with ink and airbrush, or, more innovatively, with photographs. The page space usually is divided into rectangles, sometimes given a dynamic tilt, and as the type crosses one of the internal dividing lines it reverses from black to white, or goes from solid to stencil. His ingenuity is most obvious in the series of print ads for Madelios, in which he utilized images of the neighboring Madeleine's famous portico. The portico neatly functions both as a kind of logotype for the store and as a signpost of its location.

More attention-getting, at least in terms of its audience, was his temporary facade for Aux Trois Quartiers itself, which ran the length of a block beneath a protective overhang held up by posts. The covering Brodovitch designed was unified by flowing lines of type, which snaked across the separate sheets of the overhang, and it was embellished with decorative, abstractionist swirls and flourishes. A section devoted to the store's Athelia design studio, where Brodovitch was employed, combined a representation of a classical bust with a schematic diagram of a room, both set on an amoebalike oval of color. Since one of Athelia's purposes was to provide interior-design services to the store's customers, Brodovitch's choice of figurative elements had both a symbolic and commercial rationale.

The two tendencies revealed in these designs—the one fluid, organic, and ornamental, the other geometric, spare, and "rational"—come from a blending of two of the major design influences on

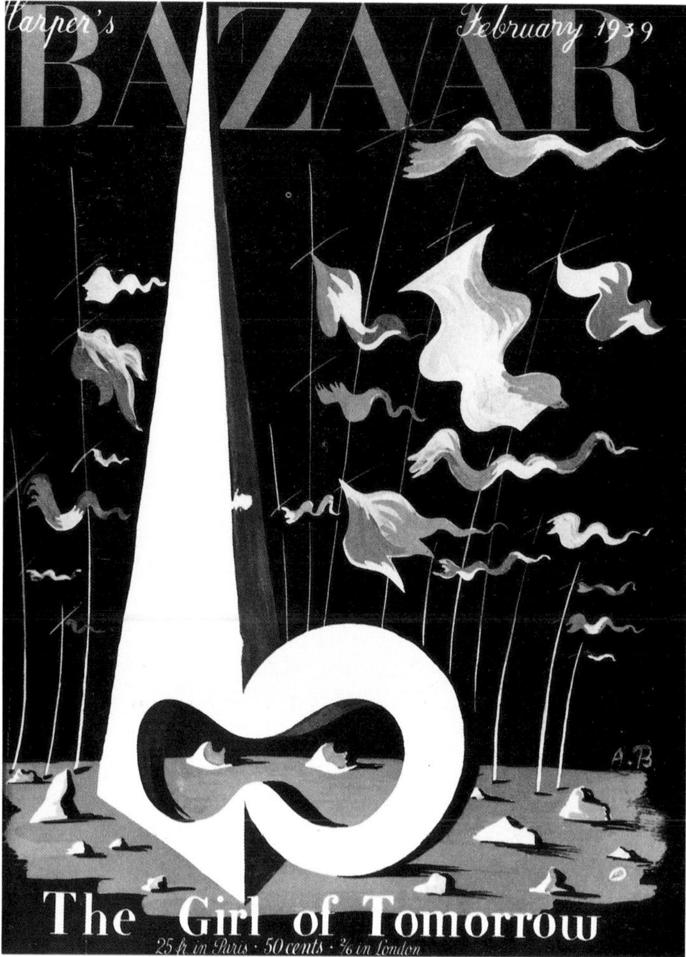

Brodovitch illustrated several *Bazaar* covers during his twenty-four years as the magazine's art director. This one, using the Trylon and Perisphere, symbols of the 1939 World's Fair, shows most clearly the influence of Surrealism on his work of the late thirties and early forties. The use of the mask recalls his first success, the poster for the Bal Banal. Besides borrowing graphic ideas from others, Brodovitch also recycled his own work.

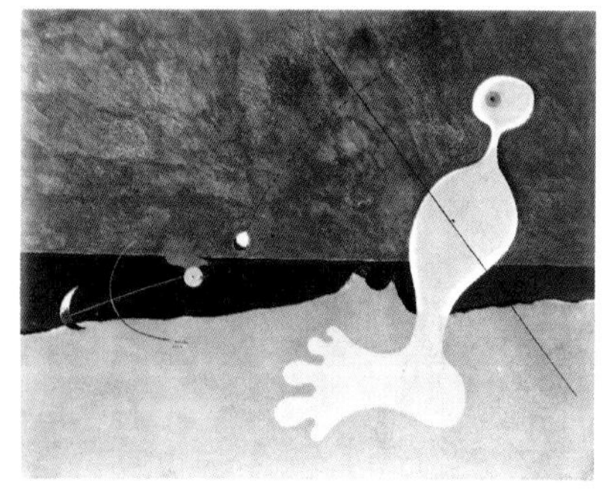

Brodovitch: Art Deco and Constructivism. While Art Deco was not directly in opposition to the rectilinear reductivism and diagonal dynamics of Constructivism, Brodovitch's best work in the 1920s makes the tension between them explicit. It also can be seen on the pages of *Harper's Bazaar* as late as the forties—where, for example, the precisionist, still-life photographs of Leslie Gill can be found alongside the nervous, flowing ink sketches of Saul Steinberg.

The influence of Surrealism can also be seen in the drawings and designs Brodovitch executed for Aux Trois Quartiers and its design studio, especially in the illusionary landscapes and interior spaces he inserted within his otherwise geometric compositions. Brodovitch is known to have admired the paintings of Surrealists Max Ernst, Joan Miró, and Salvador Dalí—especially their floating, biomorphic forms and unexpected, jolting juxtapositions. Brodovitch's Bal Banal poster has an aspect of Surrealist dream state about it, and its use of a mask echoes a frequent Surrealist theme, derived from Freud—that ordinary life is but a disguise. From an obsession with masking to a fascination with fashion is but a small step.

Brodovitch's later use of Surrealist themes and Surrealist artists at *Harper's Bazaar* shows how profoundly he understood the connection of fashion and the subconscious mind. Fashion, like Surrealism, has an irrational, irresistible appeal; both depend on an initial unfamiliarity to create an independent

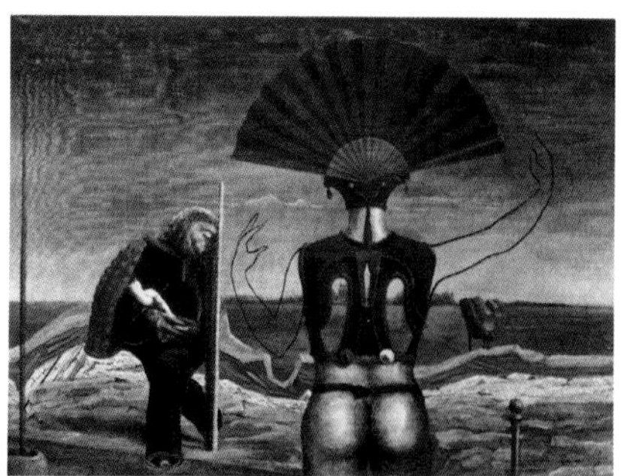

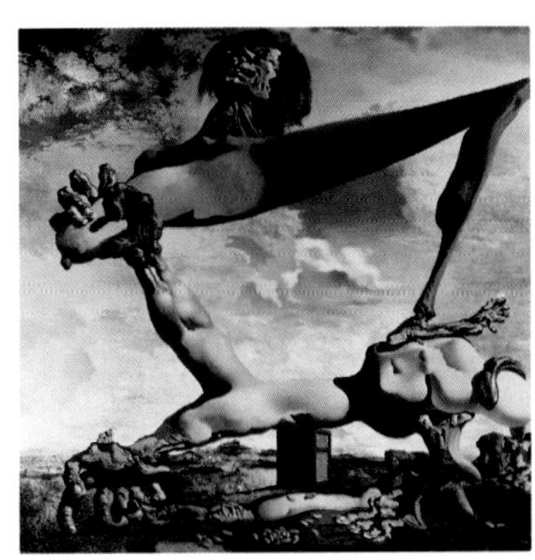

dream world. One of his infrequent covers, an illustration for the February 1939 issue, shows a tall pyramid in a barren, rocky landscape; the pyramid's base opens into the form of a mask, with two rocks where eyes should be. Also in the thirties he introduced the work of Dalí and Man Ray to readers of the *Bazaar*, using their disjunctive visions to capture the attention of the audience and to signal the arrival of a new, vanguard spirit in fashion. Brodovitch's use of Surrealist art was not willful or arbitrary, however, for it coincided with the use of Surrealist images in contemporary dress design. Elsa Schiaparelli, especially, loved Surrealist surprises, designing, for example, a woman's hat shaped like a high-heeled shoe.[12]

Brodovitch's 1939 *Harper's Bazaar* cover is illustrative of another characteristic aspect of his career. Besides drawing from a diverse range of styles in fashioning his work, adopting and adapting them with the flair of a master of pastiche, he also appropriated his own work. In this case, the cover is reminiscent not only of Dalí's forlorn dreamscapes but also of Brodovitch's own Bal Banal poster of fifteen years earlier. This kind of creative recycling, often the result of deadline pressures, can be found in the work of many designers, but Brodovitch reused himself with a particular zeal. The examples are innumerable and amusing. His illustration of a stylized dressmaker's form, originally used in a 1937 brochure for the dressmaker Elizabeth Hawes, reappears in slightly altered form in a 1940 ad for Saks Fifth Avenue (he was then the store's designer), and still later in *Harper's Bazaar*. Obviously Brodovitch's voracious appetite for the new was supplemented by—and in part supported by—a lifelong penchant for the slightly used.

The Climate in America

When Brodovitch arrived in Philadelphia in 1930, having been invited to establish a department of advertising design at the School of Industrial Art of the Pennsylvania Museum, American graphic design was in its infancy. At magazines and in advertising, people still spoke of "commercial artists" and "layout men," not of "graphic designers" and "art directors." Those who considered themselves professional designers worked mainly in and for

Both pages, left to right:

JOAN MIRO. *PERSON THROWING A STONE AT A BIRD*. 1926

ALEXEY BRODOVITCH. *HARPER'S BAZAAR* COVER, FEBRUARY 1939

MAX ERNST. *WOMAN, OLD MAN AND FLOWER*. 1923–24

SALVADOR DALI. *SOFT CONSTRUCTION WITH BOILED BEANS: PREMONITION OF CIVIL WAR*. 1936

ALEXEY BRODOVITCH. BROCHURE FOR ELIZABETH HAWES. C. 1937

Brodovitch designed this brochure for Elizabeth Hawes, a prominent American dress designer of the thirties. He was so attracted to the idea of the dressmaker's form as a symbol of fashion that he later used it editorially in *Harper's Bazaar* and again, as advertising, for Saks Fifth Avenue. Coincidentally, Man Ray had used the same sort of dressmaker's form to Surrealist ends in a 1919 drawing, *La Volière*.

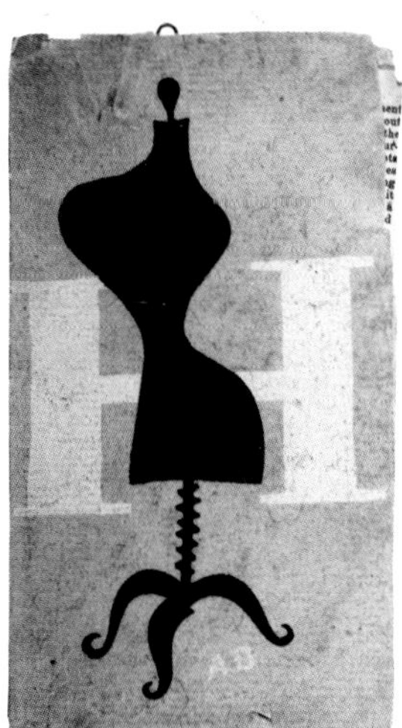

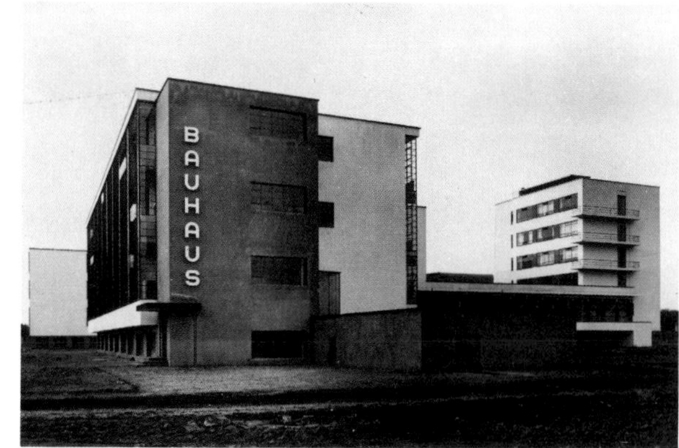

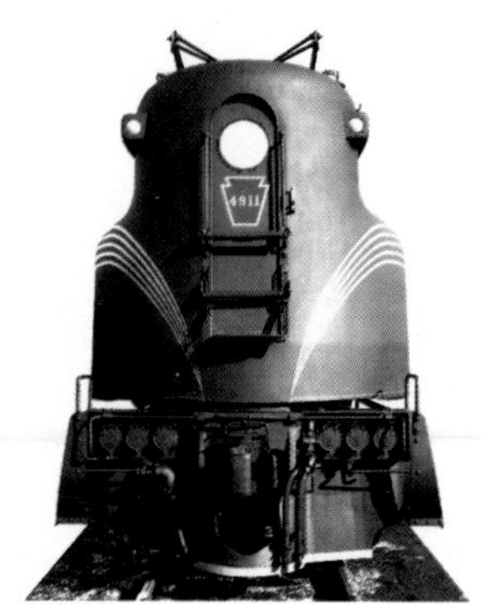

In the United States, industrial designers were the first to gain professional status for their work, in large part due to the pioneering efforts of Norman Bel Geddes, Raymond Lowey, and Walter Dorian Teague. Professional recognition came to graphic designers only after the emigration of Brodovitch and other Europeans.

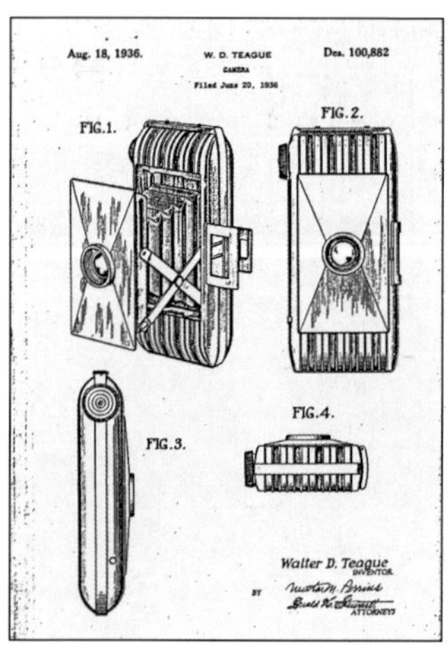

industry—men like Norman Bel Geddes, Raymond Loewy, and Walter Dorwin Teague, whom we know today as industrial designers.

Modern European painting, typography, illustration, photomontage, and photography had not yet made an impact on the design of American magazines, which with few exceptions continued to separate the text and illustrations into discrete boxes on the page, and to treat each page as an independent unit with no relation to those before or after it. From today's vantage point, the commonly used type faces seem dowdy, and headlines frequently seem too thin to support their own weight. Confined to boxes on the page, photographs and illustrations look static, even prissy. Advertising was no more advanced, with an emphasis on blocks of text that explained the product to the reader, rather than on type as a graphic element with which to seize attention. Most often, the illustration, headline type, and text were centered on the page, their bilateral symmetry suggesting a placid acceptance of the existing order of things.

Signs of change were on the horizon, however. In introducing the *9th Annual of Advertising Art*, published in 1930 by the Art Directors Club of New York, Henry Eckhardt wrote, "This annual, more than any of its predecessors, proclaims that modern advertising art is growing decidedly decorative in style; that it is growing decidedly dramatic in subject." To Eckhardt, the trend was away from realism and toward a more graphic, less literal style. In looking at this annual today, though, the shift seems more wished for than real; one sees not so much a new bold graphic sense as a continued reliance on the conventional and myth-laden—a condition perhaps best exemplified by a Steinway ad, executed in the style of Thomas Hart Benton, that invokes the spirit of Paul Bunyon. But by mid-decade, the work reproduced in the advertising annuals does indeed reflect a new spirit in advertising.

American graphic design in the early 1930s was transformed by a simultaneous process of modernization and professionalization. Brodovitch's teaching, and the example of his work, played an important role in this transformation. But he was by no means the only source of access Americans had to European Modernist design. An entire generation of émigré designers, artists,

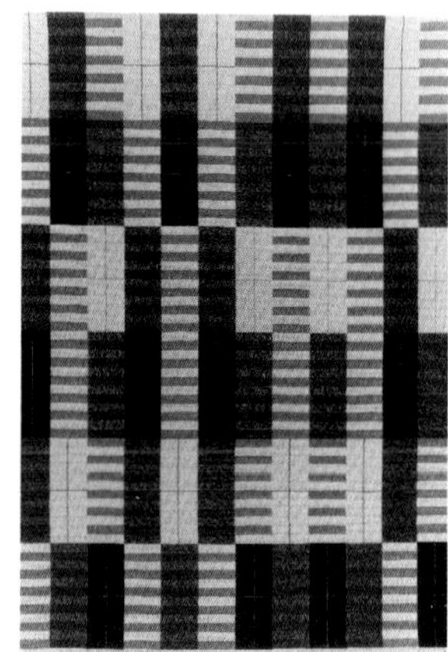

Clockwise from left:

WALTER DORIAN TEAGUE. DESIGN FOR A CAMERA. 1936

RAYMOND LOEWY. GG-1 LOCOMOTIVE. 1934

WALTER GROPIUS. BAUHAUS, DESSAU, GERMANY. 1925–26

ANNI ALBERS. *TAPESTRY*. 1926

A prewar influx of Europeans schooled in the principles of modern art and design helped create a new visual climate in the United States—one in which underlying structure would become more important than surface decoration. Many of the émigrés of the thirties were veterans of the Bauhaus, where they had learned an experimental and experiential approach to design problems. Some, like Herbert Matter, did free-lance work for *Harper's Bazaar*. Others, like László Moholy-Nagy, Mies van der Rohe, and Josef and Anni Albers, found teaching positions.

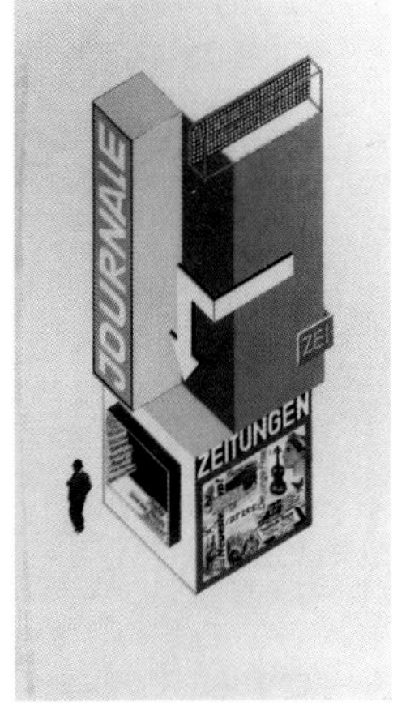

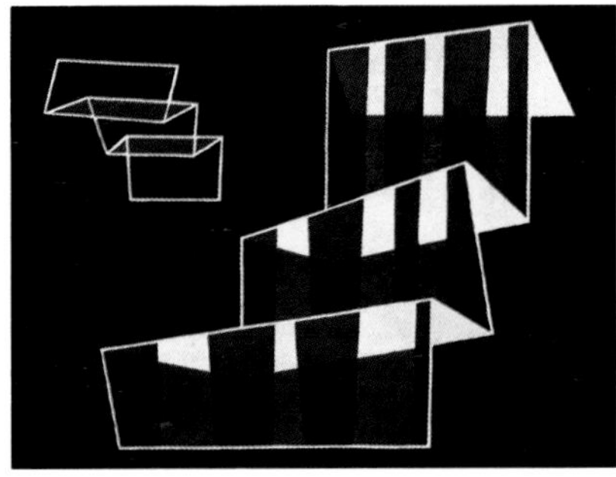

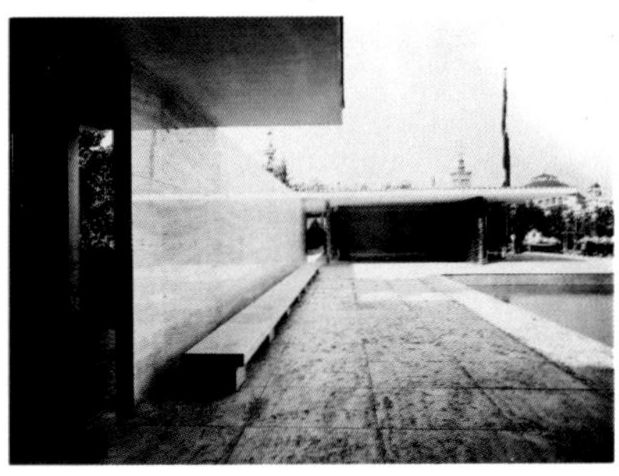

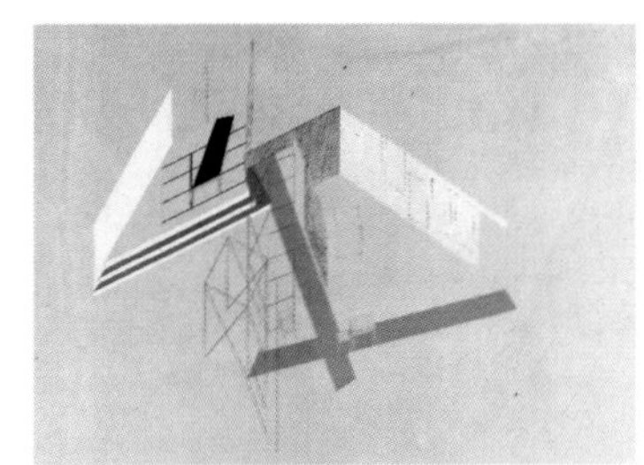

Left to right:

MIES VAN DER ROHE. GERMAN PAVILION, BARCELONA EXPOSITION. 1929

HERBERT BAYER. *DESIGN FOR A NEWSSTAND*. 1924

JOSEF ALBERS. *STEPS*. 1935

LASZLO MOHOLY-NAGY. *STAGE DRAWING FOR TALES OF HOFFMANN*. 1929

and architects landed on these shores during the decade. Josef and Anni Albers began teaching at Black Mountain College in North Carolina in 1933; László Moholy-Nagy established the New Bauhaus (later the Institute of Design) in Chicago in 1937, with designer Gyorgy Kepes on the faculty; Walter Gropius was appointed a professor at Harvard in 1937; Mies van der Rohe began teaching at the Illinois Institute of Technology a year later. The designers Herbert Matter, in 1936, Will Burtin, in 1938, and Herbert Bayer, in 1939, also came to the United States. Most came from Germany, where they had been connected to the Bauhaus either as teachers or as students; the exceptions—Burtin studied in Cologne, Matter in Paris—were certainly influenced by Bauhaus principles.

In terms of graphic design in the United States, this influx had a decisive effect, introducing what might be termed a holistic approach to design problems and processes. Instead of thinking of illustration, type, and layout as means to embellish or amplify a text, these designers used design as an autonomous means of expression. Their design theory held that content does not exist separately from form, but rather that the two are interdependent. As a result, their work in magazines, architecture, furniture, advertising, and packaging had a conceptual basis that was new to American eyes. As graphic-design historian Lorraine Wild has written, "It is the expansion of the designer's task from a craft to a method of thought that represents the professionalization of graphic design."[13]

Unlike many of the Bauhaus émigrés, Brodovitch never had been a party to the fierce aesthetic battles waged between those who wanted their work to have a direct social impact and those who believed art best served the cause of human freedom by transcending politics. With no scruples about betraying either political or artistic ideals, he adapted more readily than most émigrés to the realities of American business practice—particularly advertising—and to the role of design within this structure. Although as a teacher he adopted the Bauhaus rhetoric about the "new vision" and the modern mission of design—rhetoric most likely "borrowed" from Moholy-Nagy—his conception of design's revolutionary function was as unformed as his politics generally.

This is not to say, however, that Brodovitch's work had no politics. By refusing to acknowledge that the Modernist ideal of design as a force for social betterment might become in practice an instrument to promote the consumption of goods, he in effect served the latter. Whether this was a conscious decision we cannot know, but it is consistent with his background. His attachment to the old regime in Russia was no more overtly political than his design work, but it too was a vote in favor of the existing order. If the combination of a love of change with a devotion to things as they are seems patently contradictory, it served Brodovitch well in his professional life. And, seen in terms of his émigré mind, which valorized adaptability at the same time that it longed nostalgically for stability, it makes perfect sense. ■

In Focus:

DAY OF PARIS

As a designer, Brodovitch was less interested in establishing a recognizable style than in matching his design to the materials at hand. Two books he designed for the New York publisher J. J. Augustin—*Day of Paris*, with photographs by André Kertesz, and *Ballet*, a book of Brodovitch's own photographs (both published in 1945)—show how wide his design vocabulary was. *Day of Paris*, shown on these and the following two pages, is more conventional, treating Kertesz's lyric and poetic images as if they were pictures on a gallery wall. The economical design uses white space to give the photographs the breathing space they seem to require.

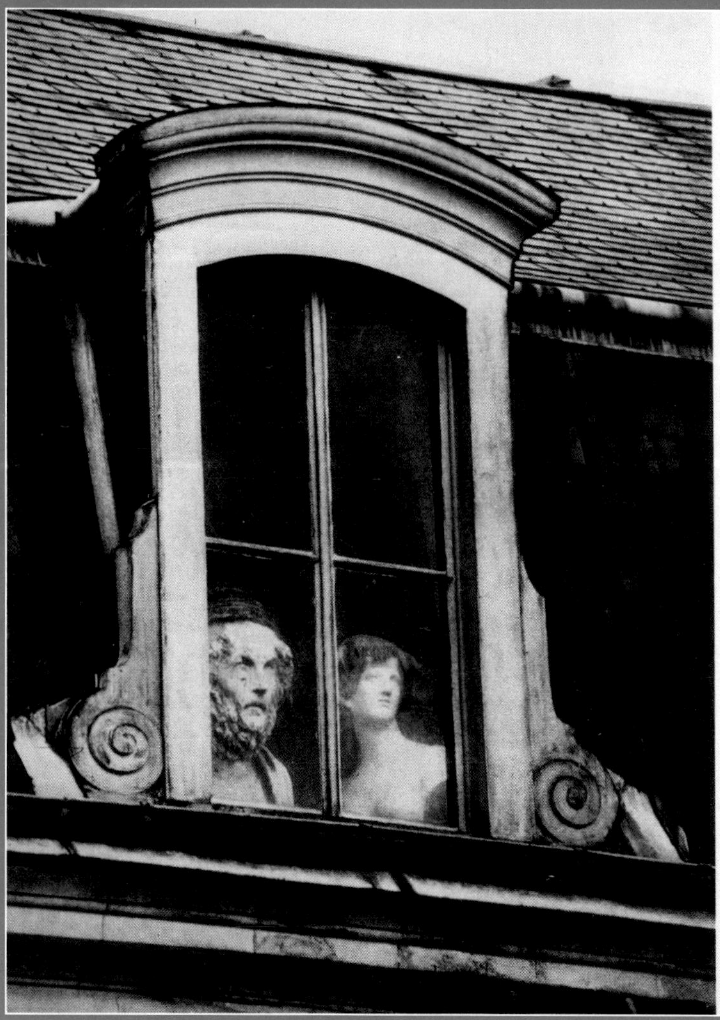

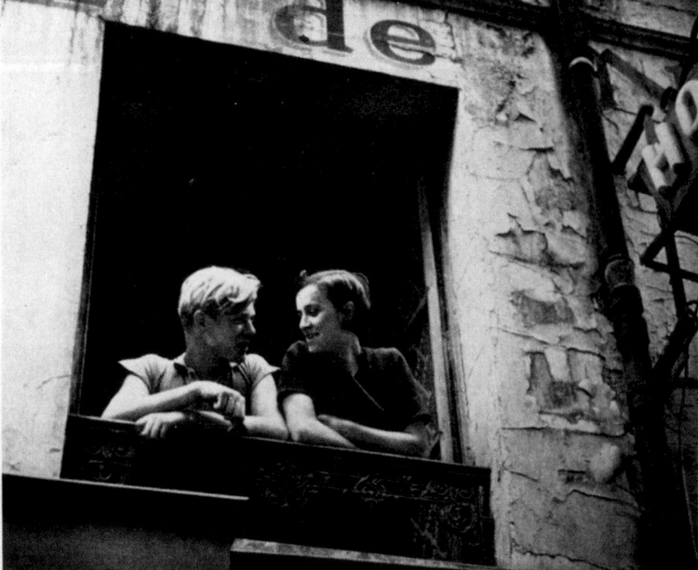

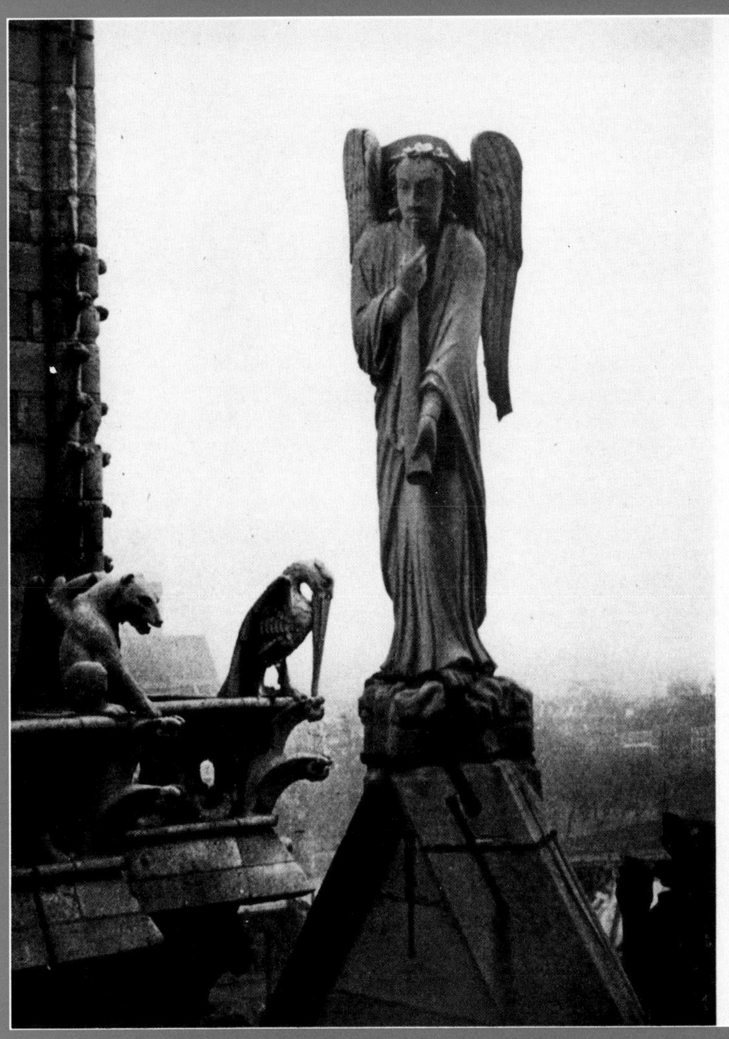

From the towers of Nôtre Dame, the strong angel sounds the hour of dawn. Now the noctambulist slinks toward his door. Under the bridge, the beggar knotted in sleep mumbles a name. The poet moves his futile torment from his table to the window. Already the life of the day has begun. A wagon piled high with vegetables creaks across the square. Workmen head toward the *métro*. But the gargoyles continue to stare in ironic horror at the city below. Only the angel, absorbed in his chore, stares blankly into space.

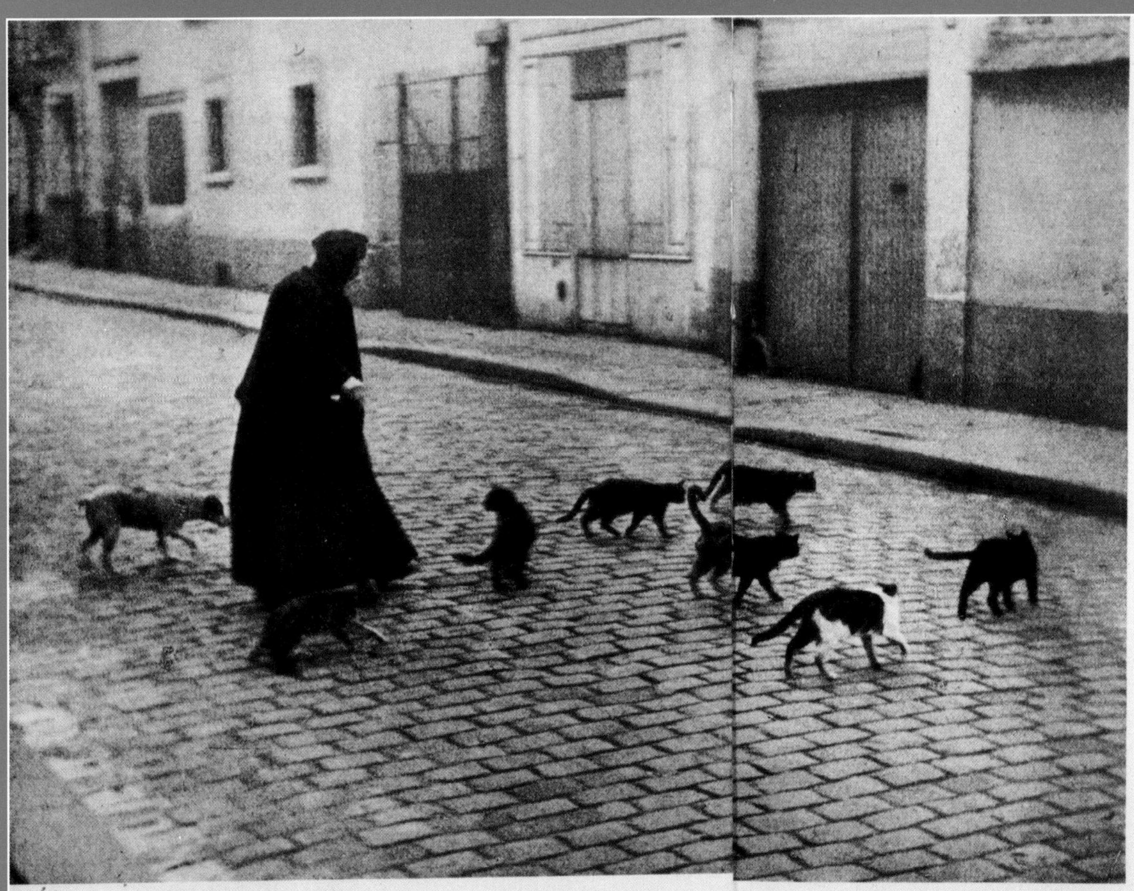

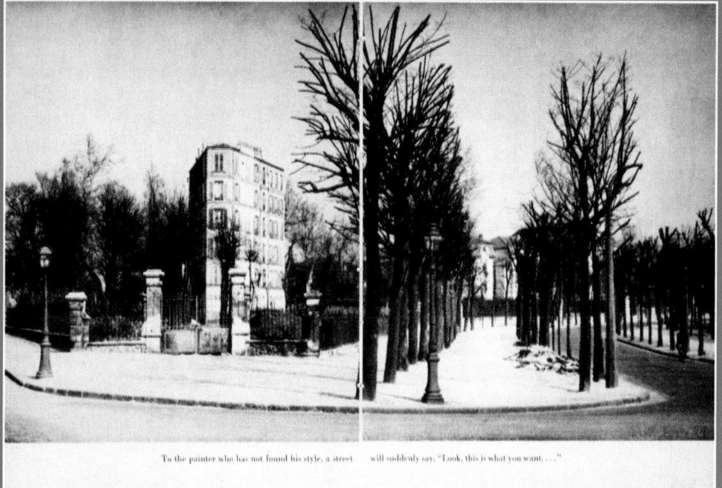

To the painter who has not found his style, a street will suddenly say, "Look, this is what you want. . . ."

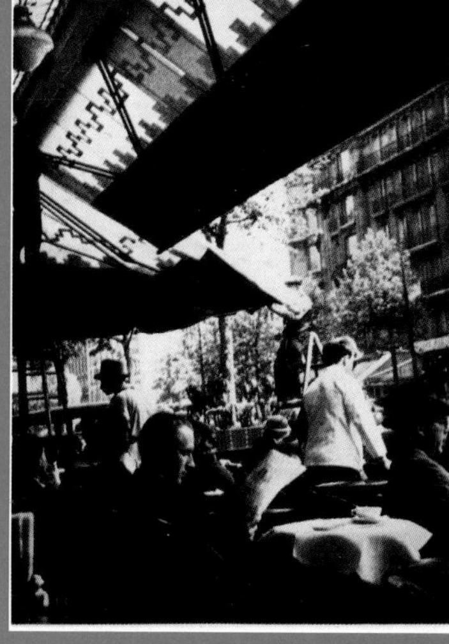

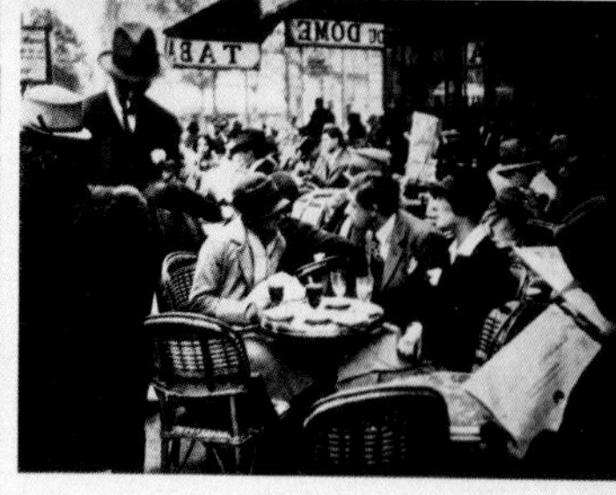

By noon, the terraces of the Montparnasse cafés have filled up. From now until long after midnight the crowds face each other like hostile armies. There is a fierce *snobbisme*: each café has its customers who have never set foot on the terrace across the street. Lady school teachers from Evanston stare at a stalwart Tyrolean lad and say how clean and like *us* the Germans really are (he is off to Crete to draw maps). Oh, and that funny old artist over there with the wild haircut (in exactly one year, eighty days, five hours and twenty minutes he will assassinate a prime minister). *La vie de bohème*. . . .

61

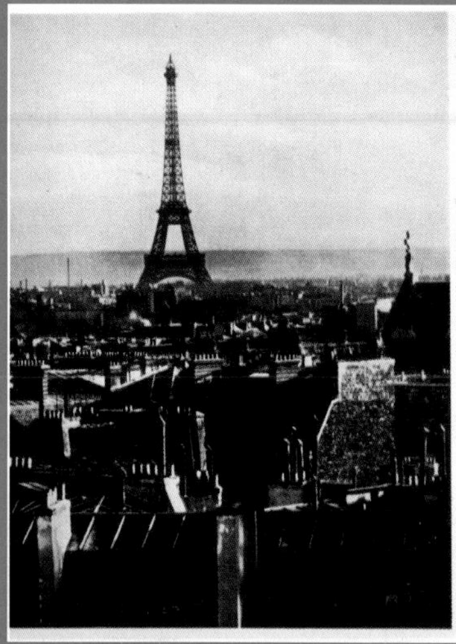

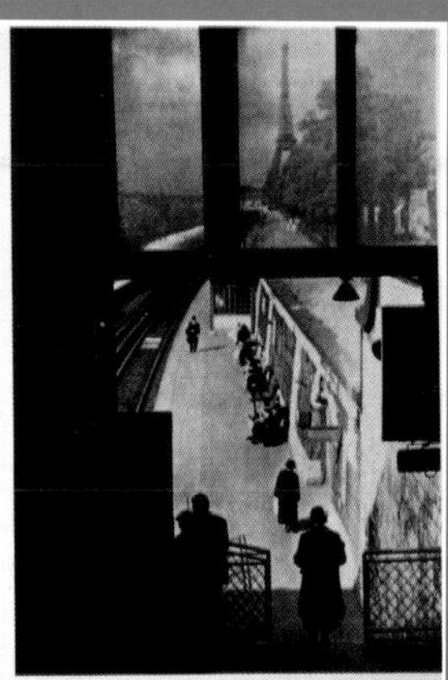

The poet writes: "O Eiffel Tower, shepherdess, your flock of bridges are bleating this morning. . . ." The roofs of Paris reflect the clear morning light at a thousand angles. Behind the horizon of crowded chimney pots, the dome of Sacré-Coeur rises like a bubble.

7

Paris pauses to breathe. Shops close, offices are deserted. In the soft shadows of Larue's a waiter brings in a sole with truffles on a silver dish. In the bistro at the corner the workman sits down to a loaf of bread, a bottle of wine and a steaming tripes *à la mode de Caen*.

Behind the shutters, the old countess is not hungry. She waves in time as her two ugly griffons get feebly on their hind legs and waltz to a tune from a music box.

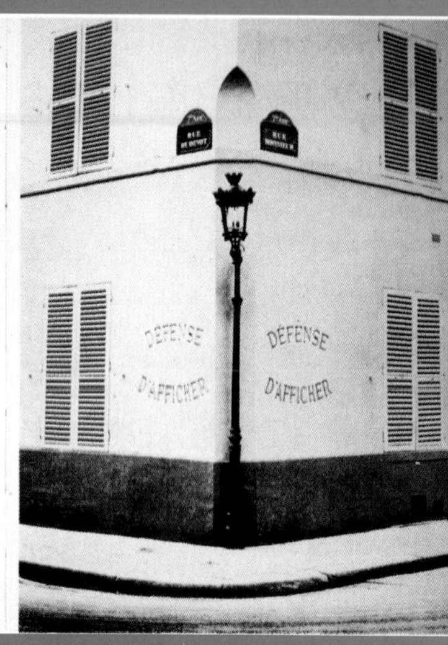

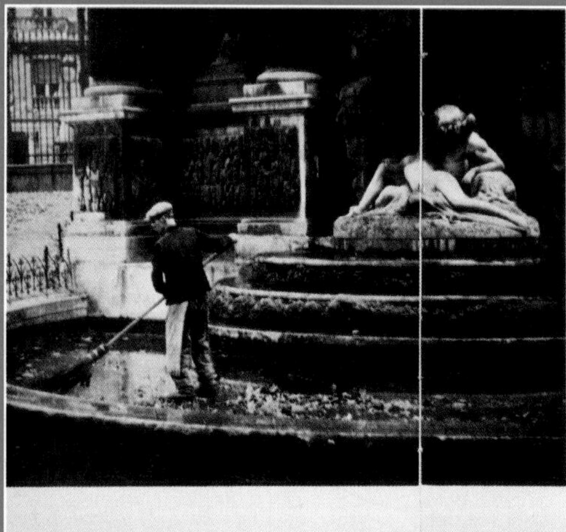

For thirty years he has overheard the reflection that never is the Luxembourg Gardens as beautiful as in autumn. It never fails to fill him with bitterness—if they had to swab out those filthy leaves!

54 55

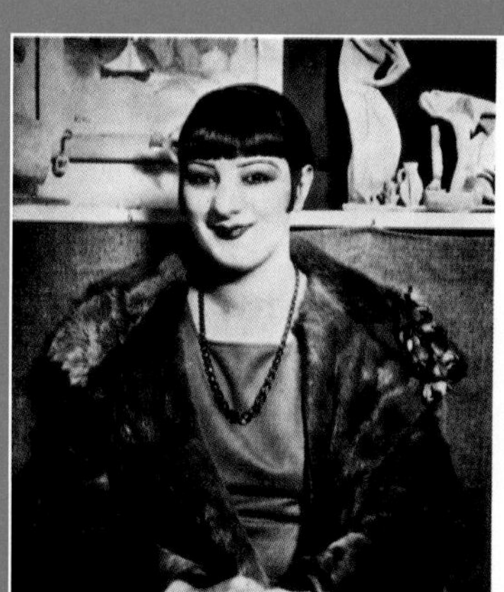

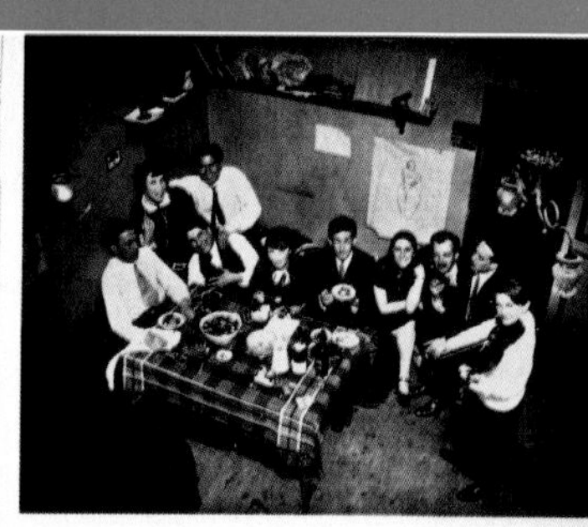

She is proud that her fame has spread all over the world as Kiki of Montparnasse, model, mistress and crony of artists; she is even prouder that she has never grown pubic hair. She has, like the celebrants above, the innocence of the classic bohemian.

137

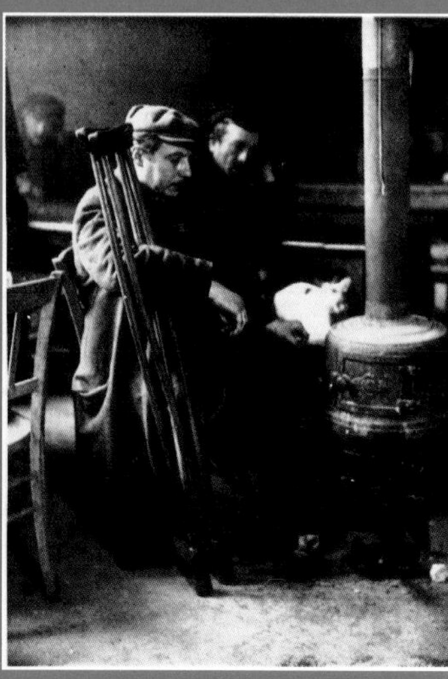

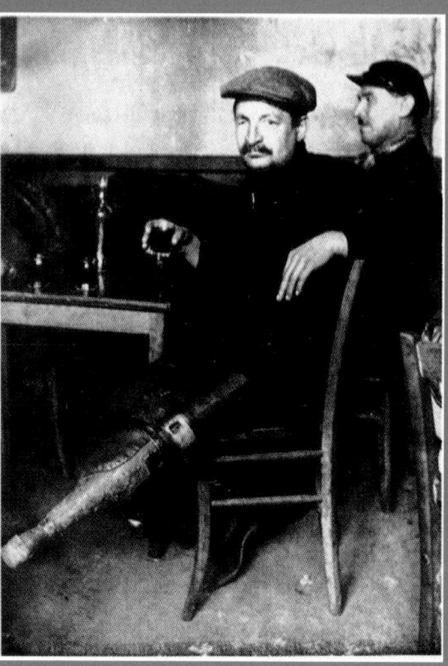

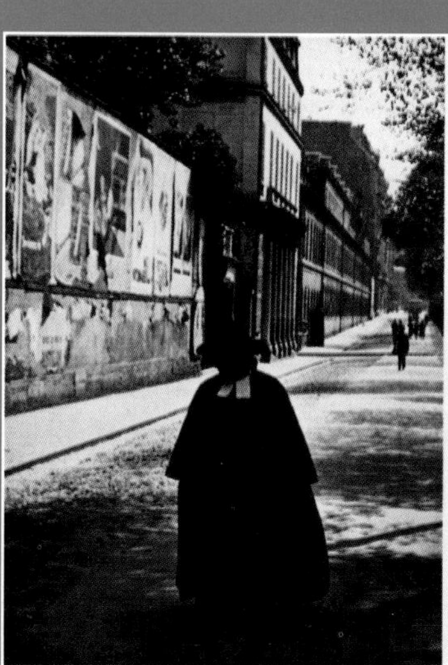

The hour of vespers; of release from work; of the evening apéritif in the café.

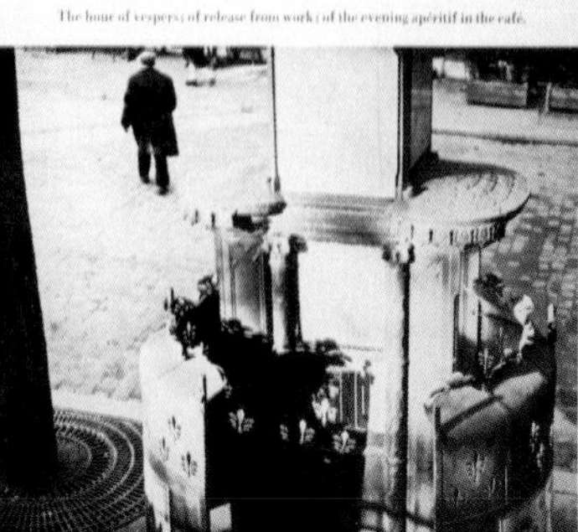

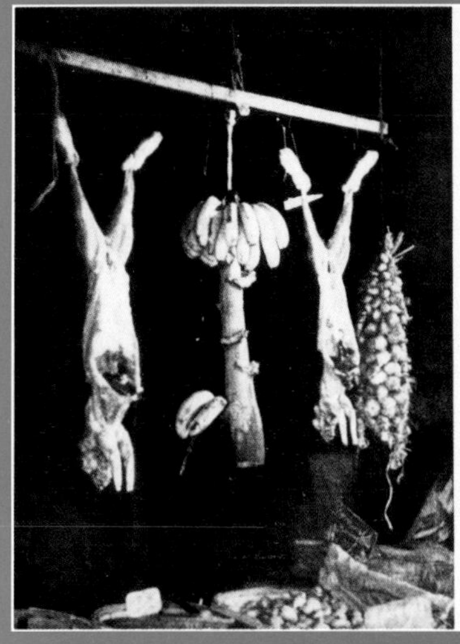

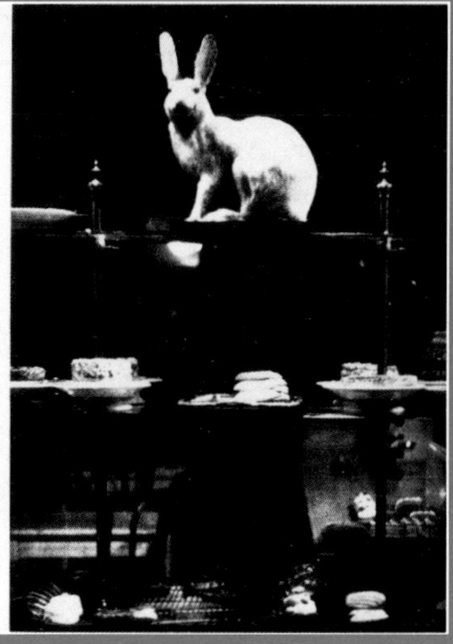

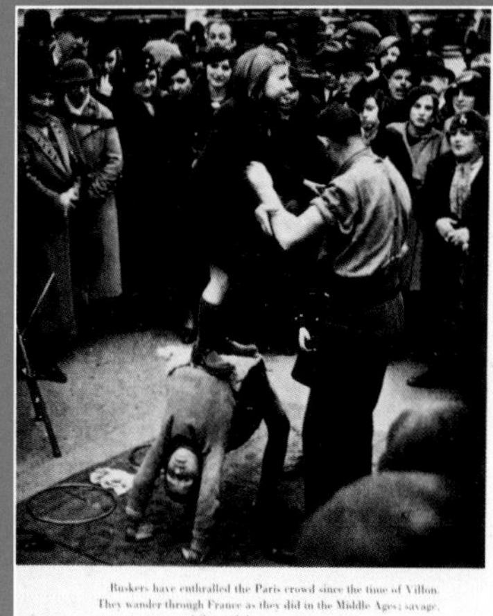

Buskers have enthralled the Paris crowd since the time of Villon. They wander through France as they did in the Middle Ages; savage, mysterious, strangely beautiful.

06

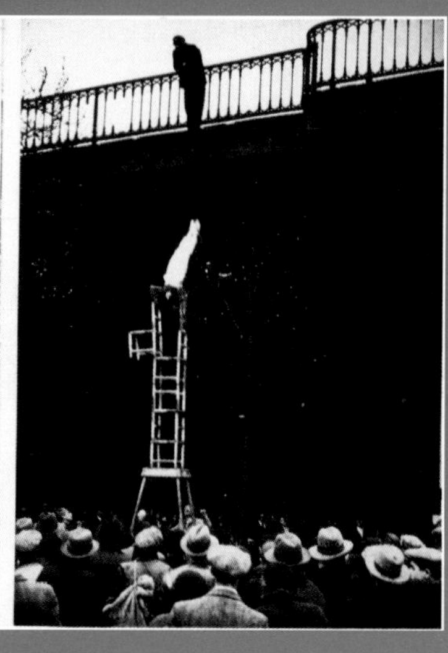

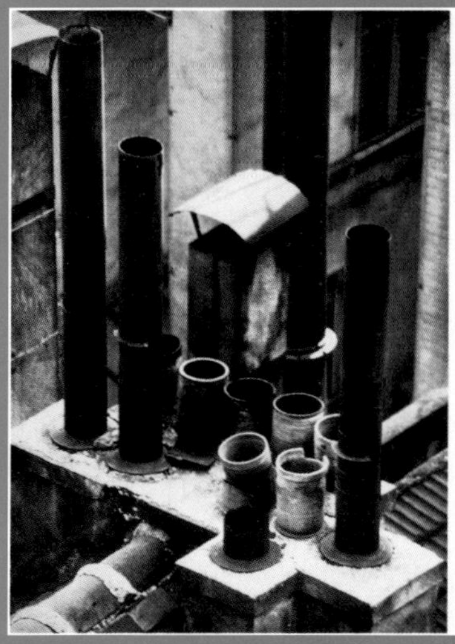

The bourgeois still sleeps, comfortably aware that he will walk down swept stairs, drink fresh milk. In the hotel, the lover withdraws a cramped arm and turns away. Under a Latin Quarter roof, the concierge scrubs briskly, muttering about the tenant who rouses her every night with his raucous *"Cordon, s'il vous plait!"* In the street, old Madame Durand goes through her matinal rite of feeding a select group of neighborhood cats.

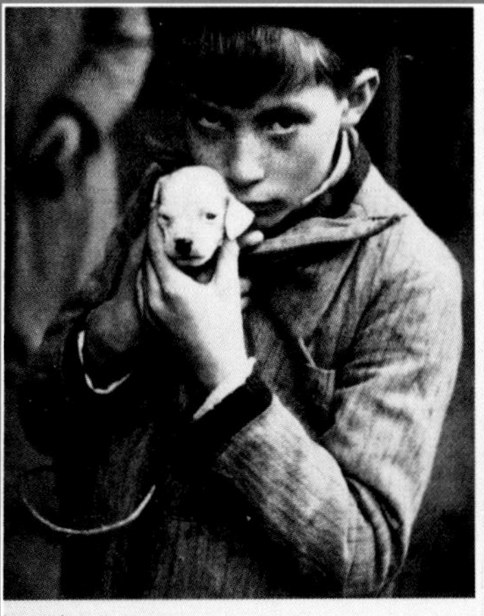

hese eyes ask a question.

10

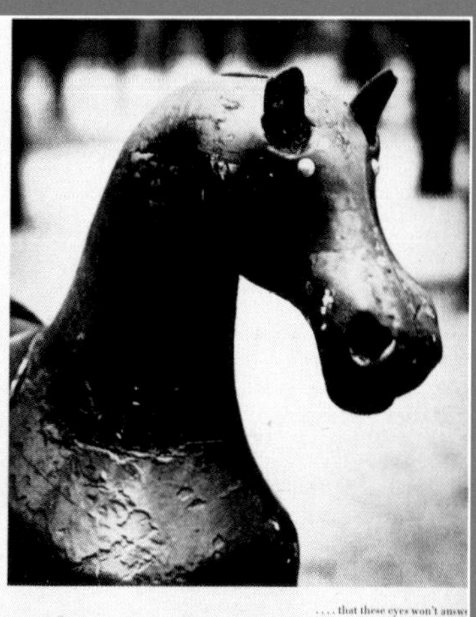

. . . . that these eyes won't answ

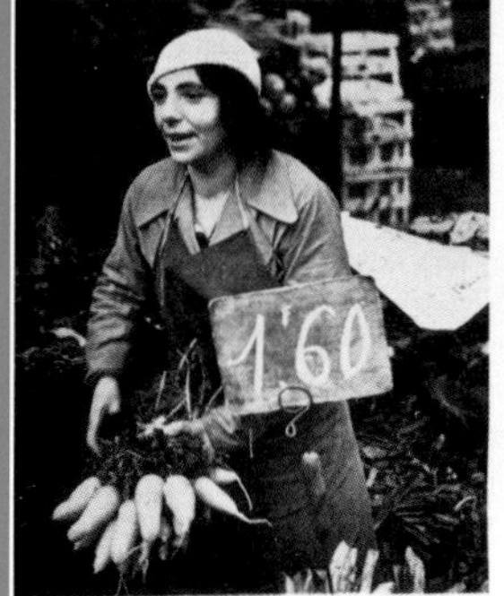

See that old priest headed this way? He may be a saint in his religion, but he's a devil when it comes to a bargain.

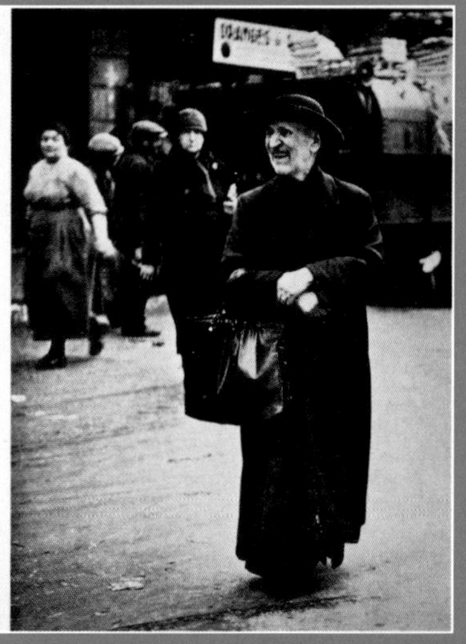

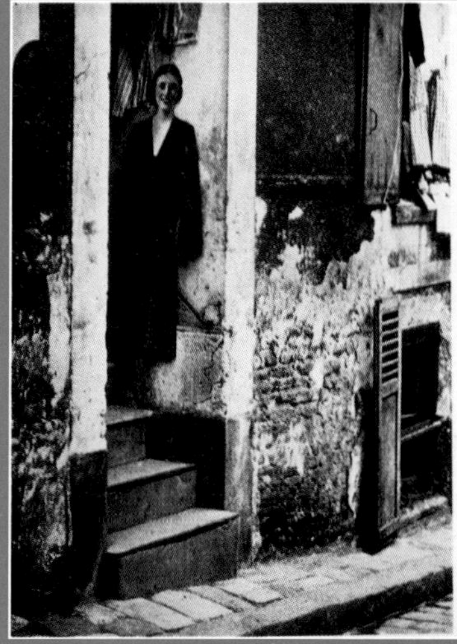

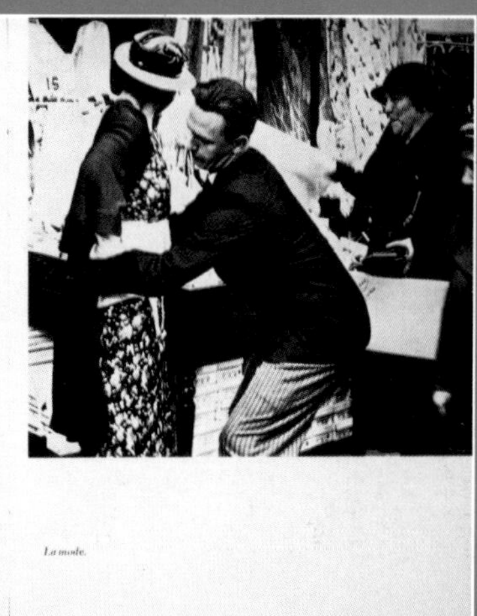

La mode.

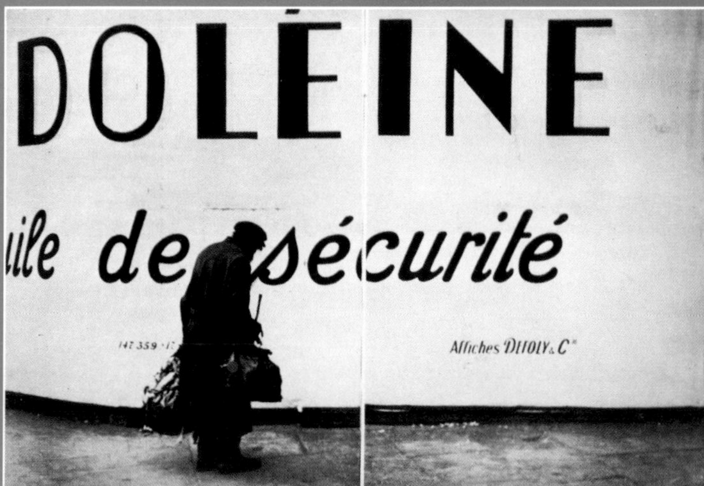

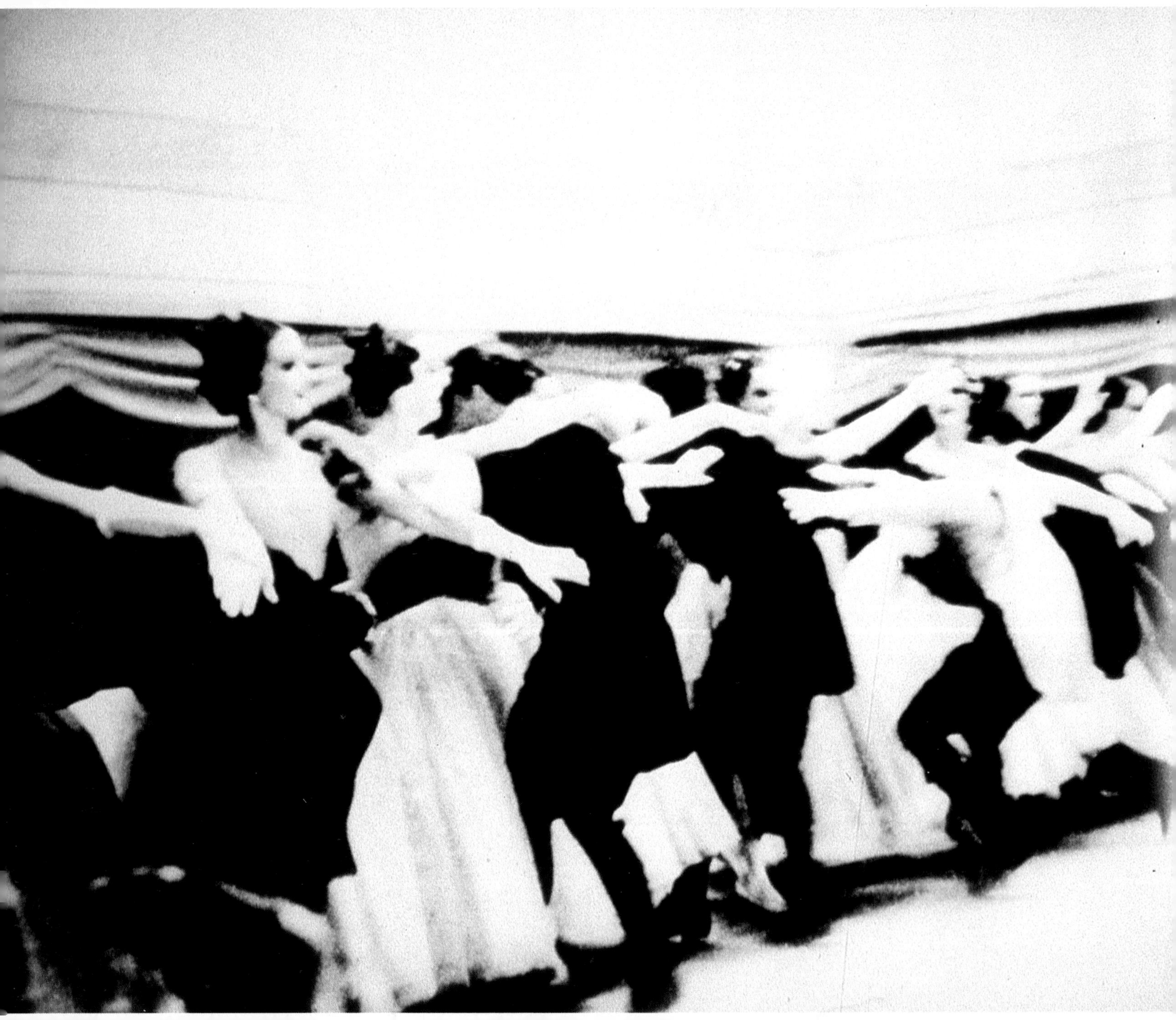

Ballet, designed by Brodovitch using photographs he had taken in the late thirties while standing backstage at performances of the Ballets Russes, is both a tour de force of graphic creativity and a precursor of the photographic style the art director promulgated in the years after World War II. By bleeding the blurred, grainy pictures off the sides of the pages and into the gutter of the book, he communicated the emotional impact of dance directly, rather than literally describing it. In several places, photographs on facing pages seem to blend into one seamless panorama. The *Ballet* photographs, taken without flash using long shutter speeds, recall the style of Martin Munkacsi's early work. *Ballet* was the most sustained project of Brodovitch's career—perhaps because the subject matter recalled to him his Paris years—and was enormously influential among photographers of the forties and fifties.

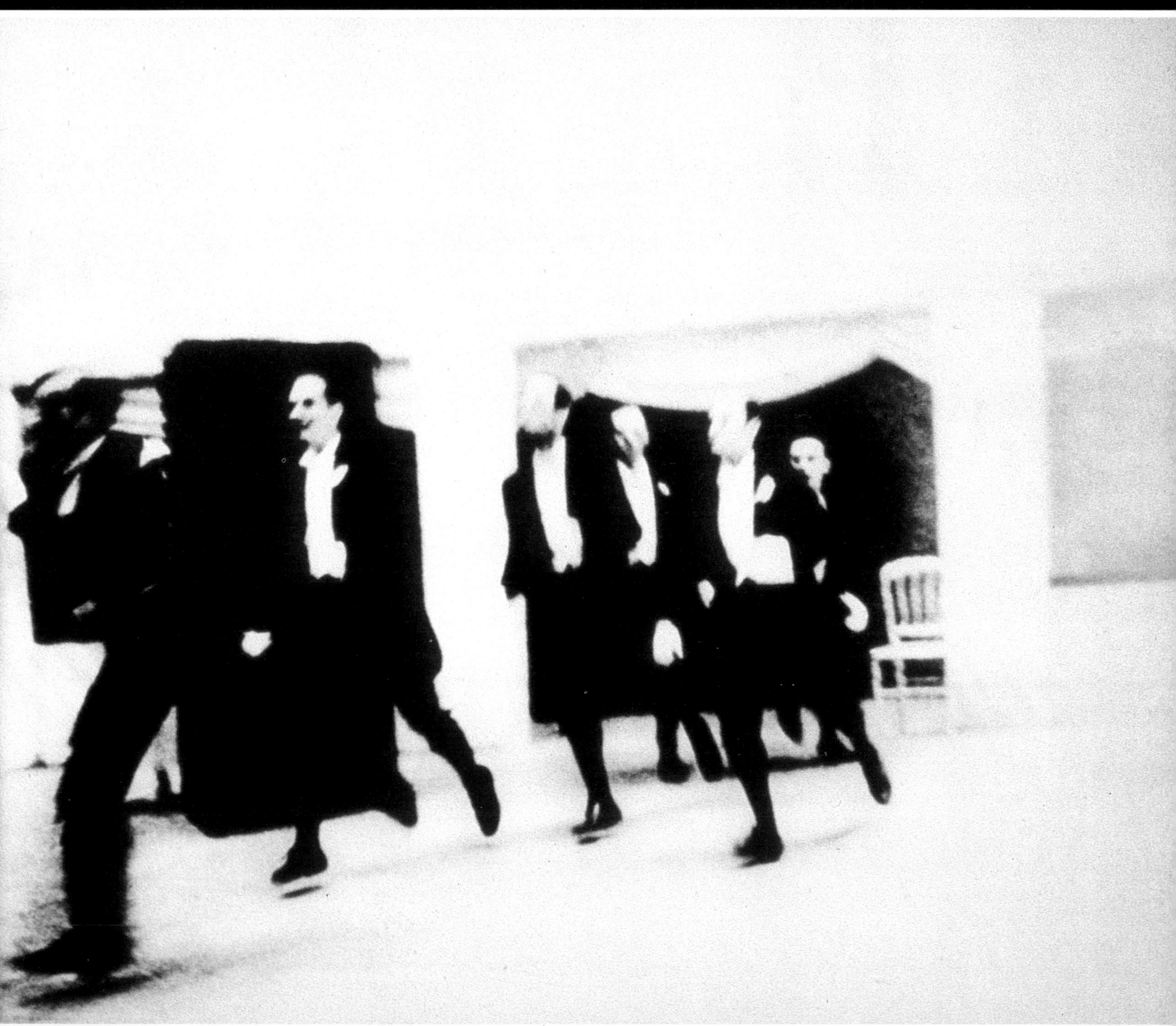

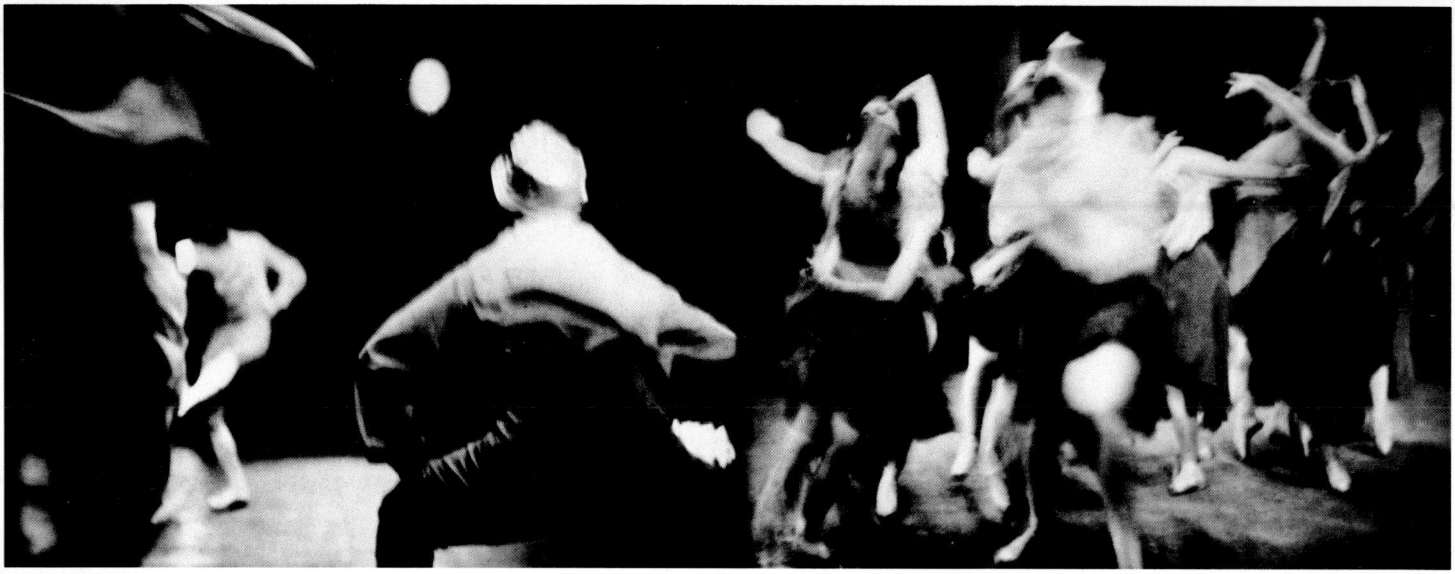

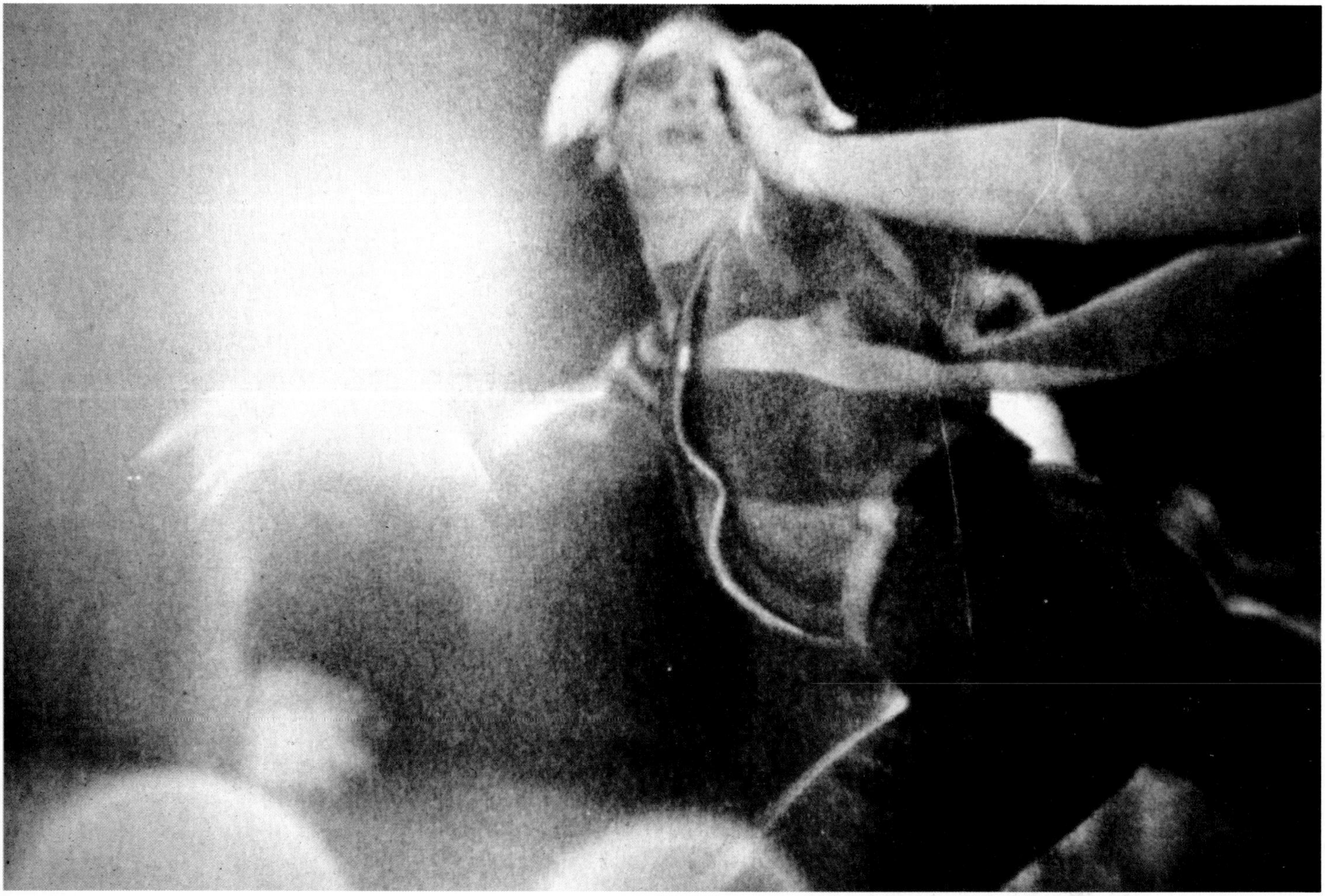

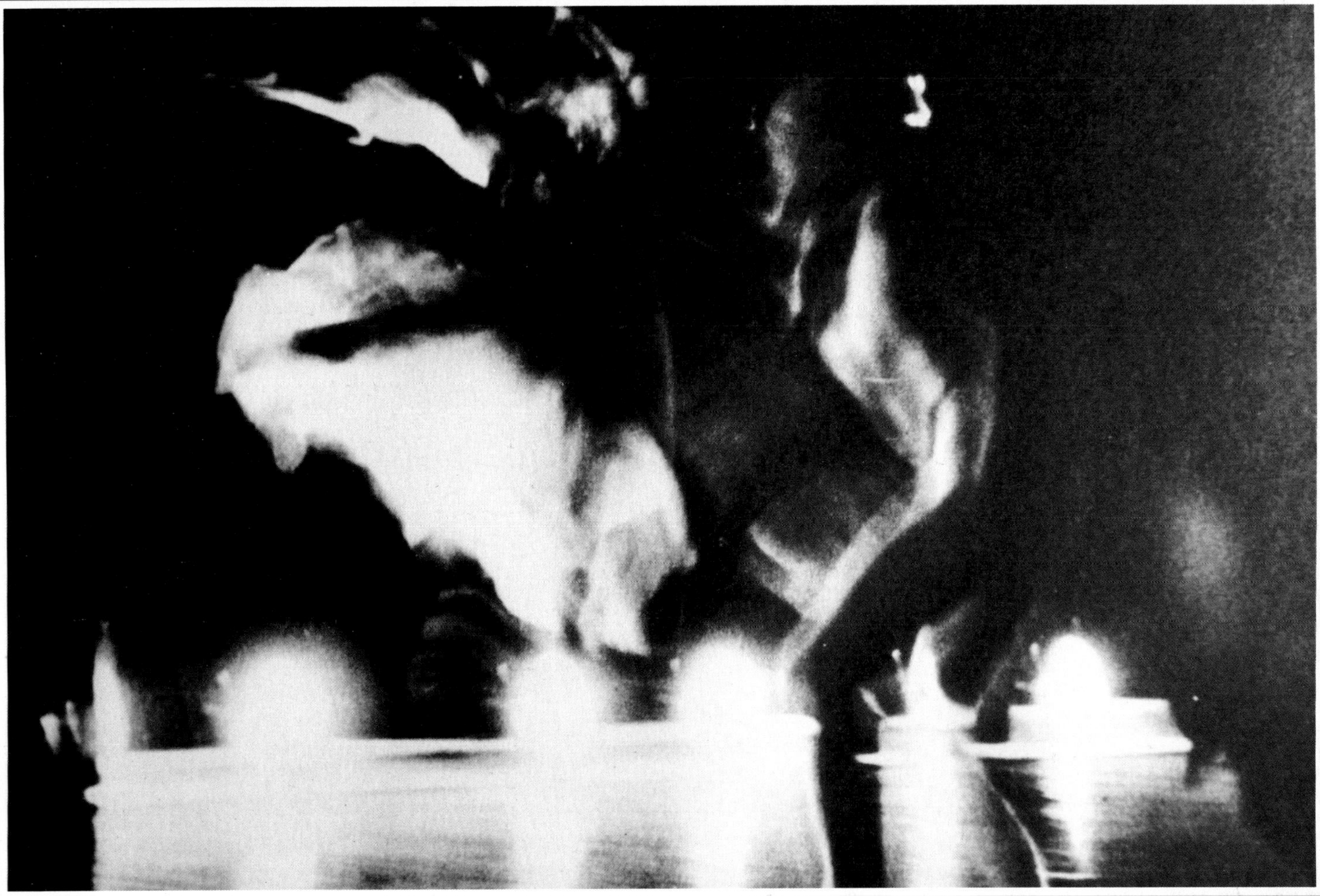

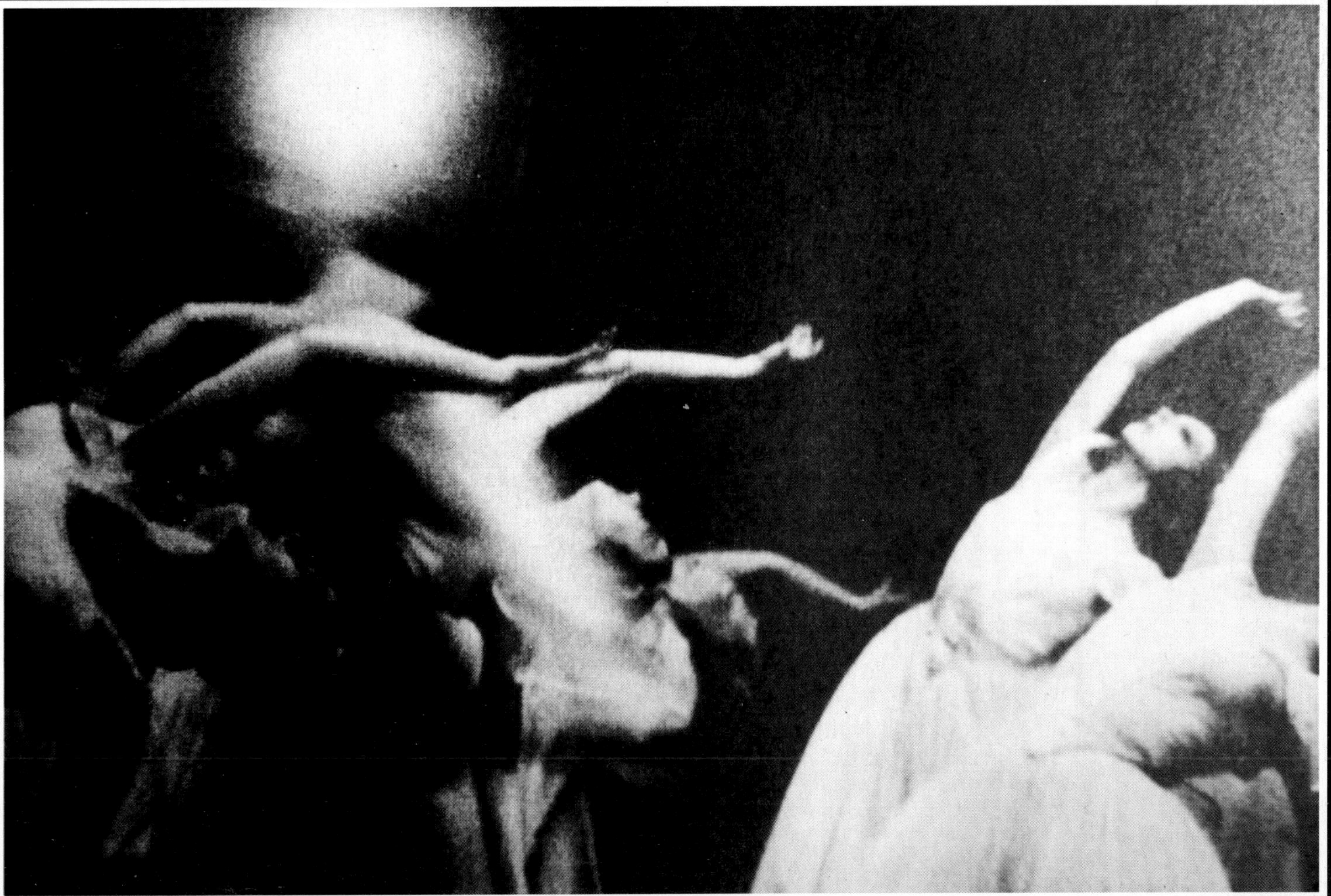

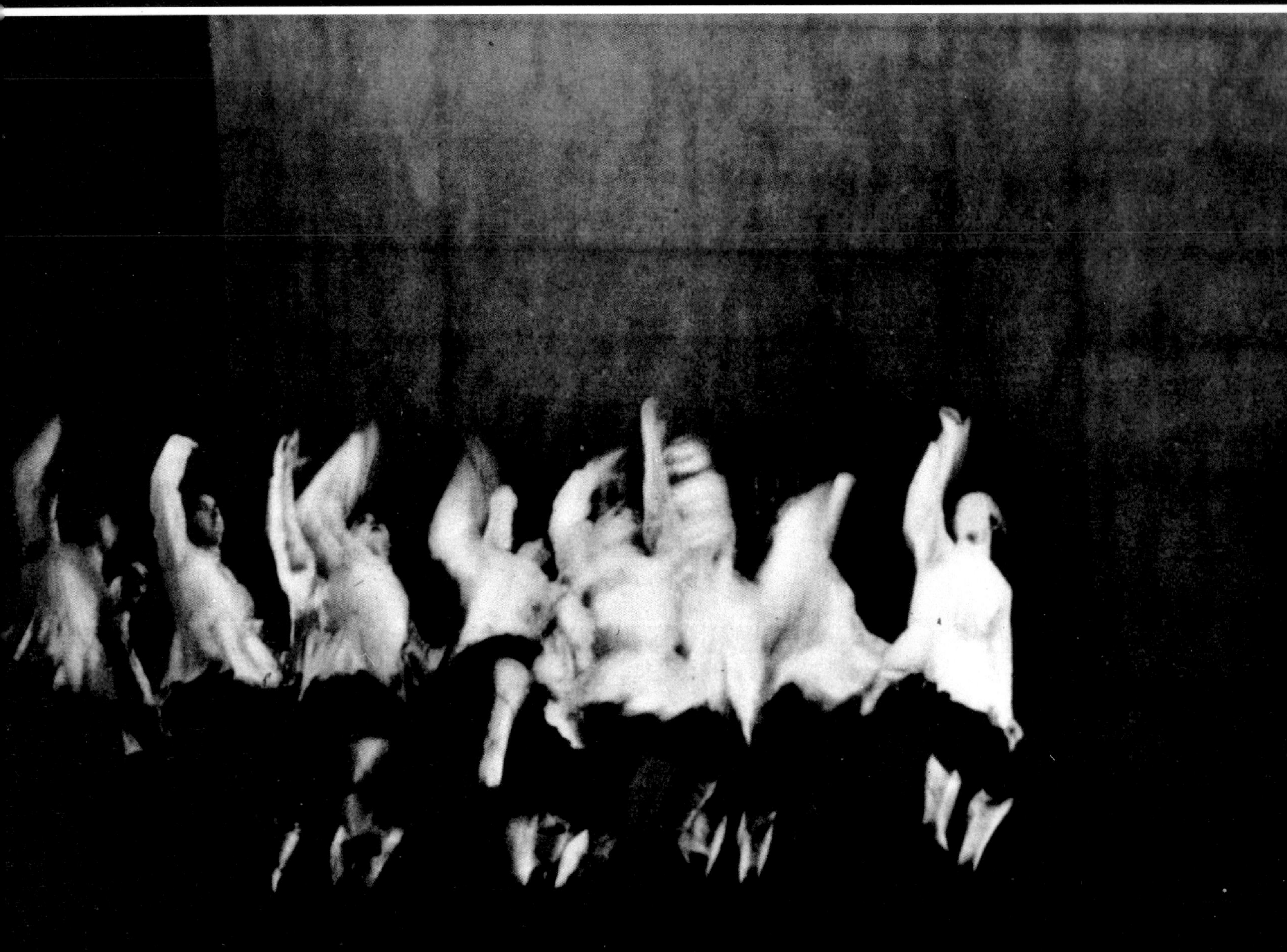

Right:

CONTENTS PAGE, *BALLET*

LES NOCES
LES CENT BAISERS
SYMPHONIE FANTASTIQUE
LE TRICORNE
BOUTIQUE FANTASQUE
COTILLION
CHOREARTIUM
SEPTIEME
SYMPHONIE
LE LAC DES CYGNES
LES SYLPHIDES
CONCURRENCE

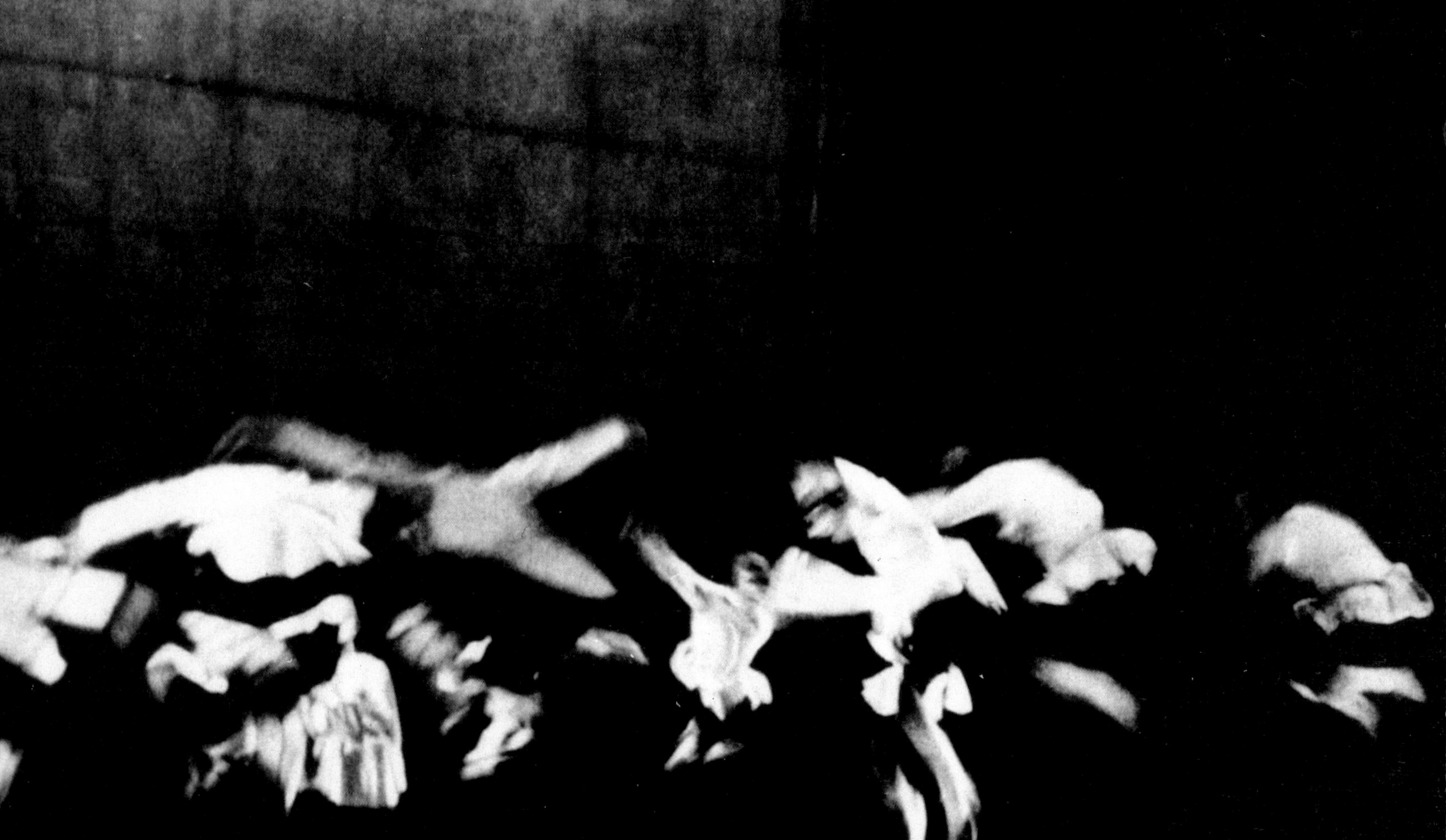

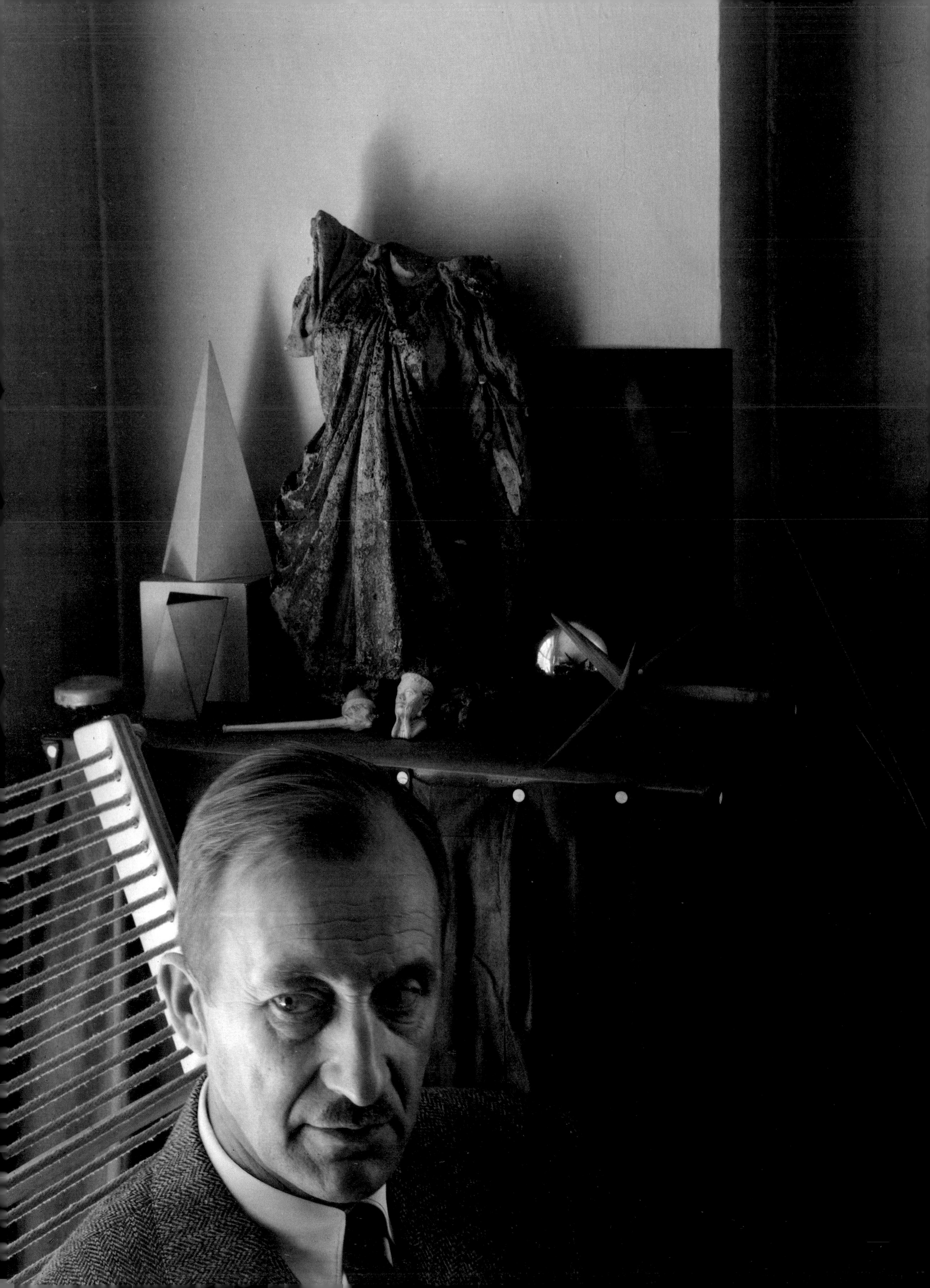

THE GOSPEL OF THE NEW

3

Brodovitch was thirty-two when he arrived in Philadelphia with his wife and son. Although sufficiently cosmopolitan to have learned at least rudimentary English, he must have felt a surge of coltish excitement about encountering the new world. Here, in the United States, was where modern life was most advanced, where industry and the arts flourished unhindered by the constraints of tradition. This, at least, was the prevailing fantasy about America among European émigrés. But he quickly discovered that advertising design—the subject he had been hired to teach at the Pennsylvania Museum School of Industrial Art (now the Philadelphia College of Art)—lagged far behind its European counterpart. Brodovitch's first task in the United States, therefore, was to create a climate receptive to the modern spirit of graphic design.

He accomplished this in several ways. He started by instilling in his students his own thirst for newness, showing them examples of his work and that of his European contemporaries. Once he had trained them in the modern style, he set about publicizing their work on behalf of his design program. He organized the

ARNOLD NEWMAN.
ALEXEY BRODOVITCH. 1946

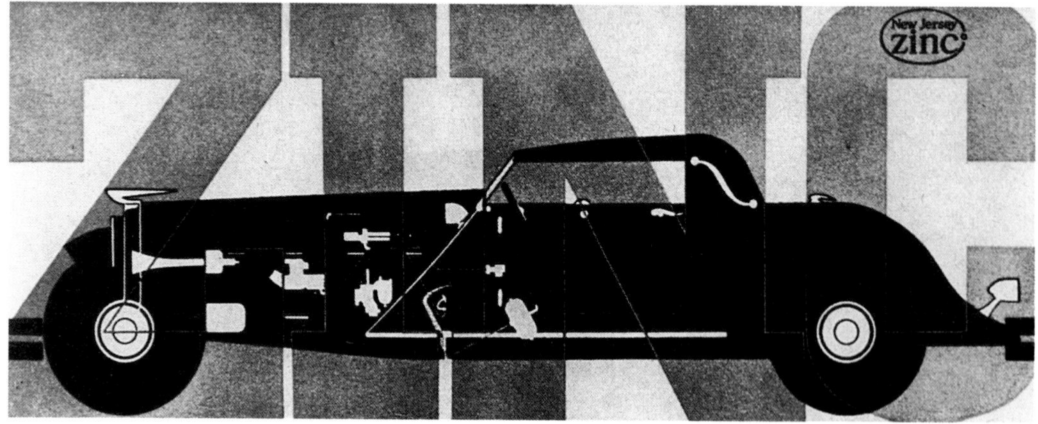

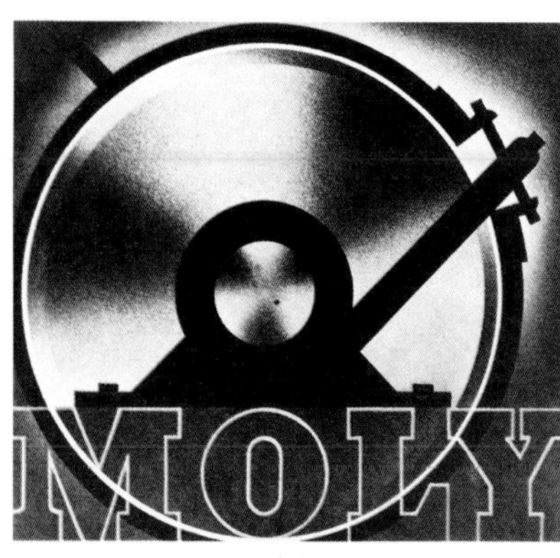

"New Poster" show placing his students' work alongside that of well-known artists and designers (page 32). He made sure that newspapers and magazines covered his program; they obliged by printing articles extolling the accomplishments of his students. For example, *The Art Digest* of March 1, 1936, reported that forty-two Brodovitch students included in a show at the school had earned "in excess of $125,000" by doing advertising assignments. The publicity apparently worked; among his students in Philadelphia were Mary Faulconer, Nelson Gruppo, Sol Mednick, Irving Penn, Raymond Ballinger, and Ben Rose, all of whom later became well-known in New York editorial and advertising circles.

At the same time, Brodovitch established a free-lance career of his own, doing advertising illustration for clients ranging from DuPont to Climax Molybdenum. He primarily used an airbrush for these ads, a technique that at the time was considered daringly innovative. (The airbrush had been around for decades, but it was used primarily as a retouching tool, not as a drawing instrument.) Many of his assignments came from the N. W. Ayer agency, which, not coincidentally, had hired his student Nelson Gruppo as one of its art directors. These ads attracted a great deal of attention, thanks to the Art Directors Club's annual exhibitions. Between 1931 and 1935, Brodovitch received five medals, four honorable mentions, and a first prize for his advertising work, according to a résumé Brodovitch prepared shortly after 1935.[14] While he did most of his work at his studio in downtown Philadelphia, he found himself frequently riding the train to New York.

Since he was teaching advertising design as well as practicing it, Brodovitch attempted to codify his notions of its place in the modern world. In a typewritten manuscript titled "Ideas on Advertising," he wrote:

We are living in the age of industry and mechanisation [sic] . . .

The tempo of life is fast—new achievements open new horizons—our psychology and taste are in constant evolution.

The best medium to persuade [someone] to buy is to appeal to the common-sense of the consumer, knowing his weaknesses . . . .

With all our weakness for sex and admiration for old-timers, no longer can we sell

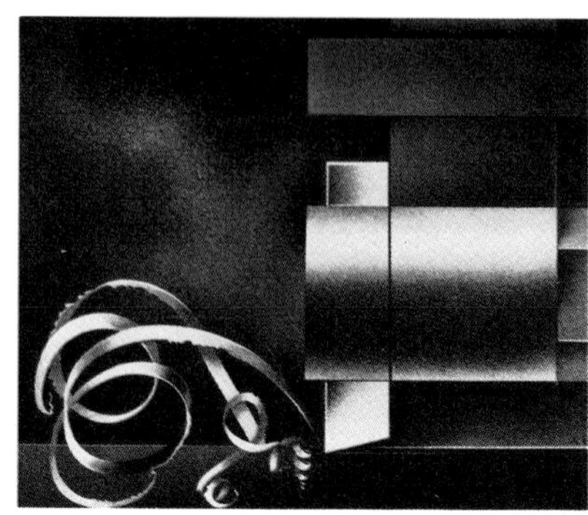

In the 1930s Brodovitch produced advertising illustrations for a number of companies, most of them clients of the N. W. Ayer advertising agency, which had its offices in Philadelphia. These illustrations, for Van Raalte hosiery, International Printing Ink, New Jersey Zinc, Steinway & Sons pianos, Climax Molybdenum, and others, reflect the stylistic heritage of his Paris years. Most were done with an airbrush, and several received awards in the annual Art Director's Club competitions.

Both pages, left to right:

ALEXEY BRODOVITCH. ILLUSTRATION FOR CLIMAX MOLYBDENUM. ART DIRECTOR: NELSON GRUPPO, N. W. AYER & SON. 1934

ALEXEY BRODOVITCH. ILLUSTRATION FOR NEW JERSEY ZINC

ALEXEY BRODOVITCH. ILLUSTRATION FOR CLIMAX MOLYBDENUM. ART DIRECTOR: NELSON GRUPPO, N.W. AYER & SON. 1934

ALEXEY BRODOVITCH. PENNSYLVANIA STATE POLICE PUBLIC SERVICE POSTER, FROM THE "NEW POSTER" EXHIBITION CATALOGUE

ALEXEY BRODOVITCH. ART DIRECTOR'S CLUB EXHIBITION POSTER. 1934

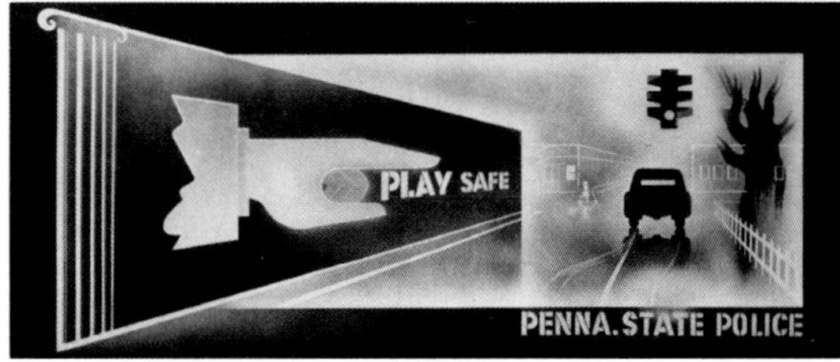

the cigarette, the liquor, or the perfume by announcing that "They are milder" and showing a nice-looking picture of a beautiful girl, or the traditional Colonel of Kentucky . . .

The Advertising idea of today must be prepared and presented in a dramatic, new, unusual, direct and logical manner.[15]

For all his appeal to the new, however, Brodovitch maintained an affection for tradition. During his years in Philadelphia, he painted in his spare time. While he had gained a reputation in the design world for using the airbrush, dentistry drills, and other instruments of the industrial age, when it came to "fine art" he favored the conventional brush and canvas. His paintings, which were exhibited by the Crillon Gallery in Philadelphia in 1933, are remembered by Irving Penn as gray, leaden scenes evocative of factories and steel mills.[16] Unfortunately, all that remains to document them is the gallery brochure listing their titles; the paintings themselves apparently were destroyed in a fire at the Brodovitchs' country house.

Carmel Snow and *Harper's Bazaar*

Carmel Snow first laid eyes on Brodovitch's work in the spring of 1934, when the photographer Ralph Steiner took her to Rockefeller Center to see an exhibition of advertising design sponsored by the Art Director's Club of New York. Snow, who was to prove one of the century's most innovative and influential magazine editors, had only recently been named editor of *Harper's Bazaar* and was eager to transform it into a real rival of *Vogue*, the Condé Nast magazine where she had started her career. She would later write in her autobiography, *The World of Carmel Snow*, of her first impressions that day:

I saw a fresh, new conception of layout technique that struck me like a revelation: pages that "bled" beautifully cropped photographs, typography and design that were bold and arresting. Within ten minutes I had asked Brodovitch to have cocktails with me, and that evening I signed him to a provisional contract as art director.[17]

But before Mrs. Snow could add Brodovitch to the talented staff she was assembling for *Harper's Bazaar*, she had to seek the approval

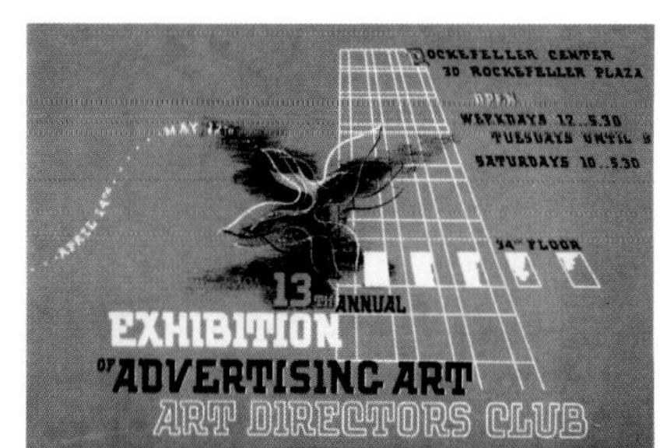

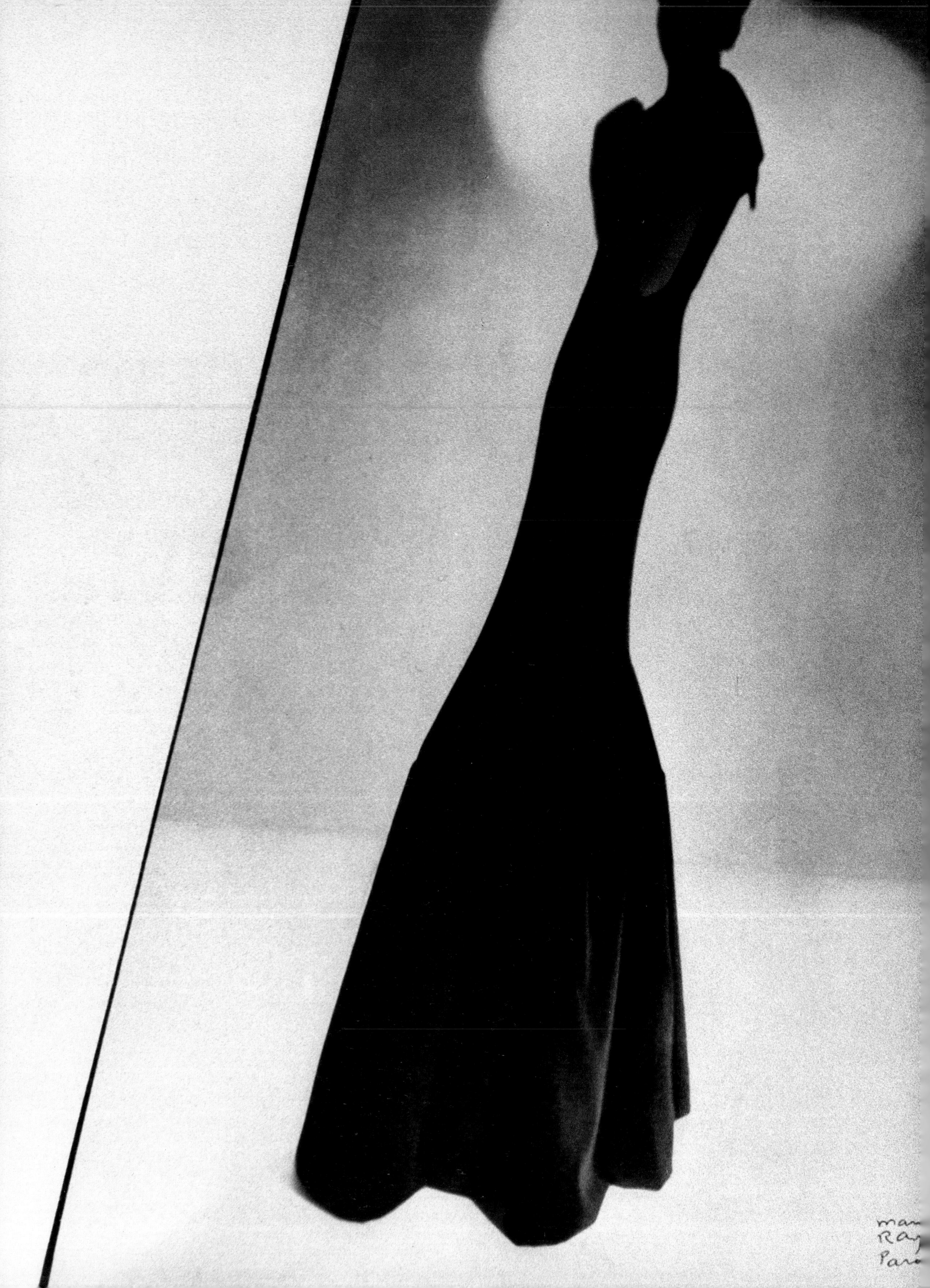

From the very first issues he designed for *Harper's Bazaar*, Brodovitch was sensitive to photographs as no other art director had been. He was especially attentive to the shapes within the frame and used them, as is evident here, to cue the placement of text and headlines.

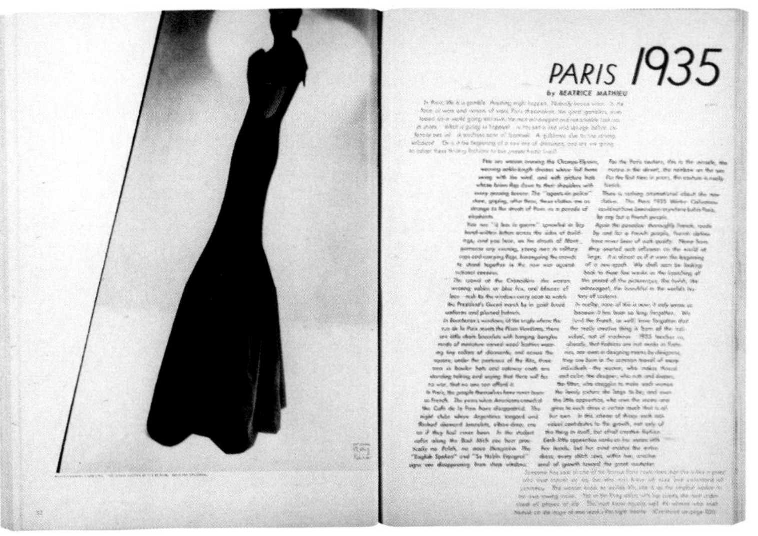

PARIS 1935

by BEATRICE MATHIEU

HARPER'S BAZAAR, OCTOBER 1934. PHOTOGRAPHER: MAN RAY

of the *Bazaar*'s owner, William Randolph Hearst. To get it she asked Brodovitch to create some sample page layouts and, acting as her own courier, flew with them to Hearst's castle in Wales, where the publisher was staying. After dining with Hearst and his entourage, she approached him about hiring Brodovitch as *Bazaar*'s art director, showing him the samples of the designer's work.

To Hearst, accustomed to the conventions of American graphic design, Brodovitch's layouts must have seemed brash, unruly, and foreign, being imbued with the strange flavor of the European avant garde. The layouts themselves are now lost, but we can imagine that they were radically unlike the restrained, symmetrical style that dominated American books, magazines, and advertising of the time. In the hands of someone like W. A. Dwiggins, the respected book designer, this style was capable of refinement and elegance, but in contrast to what was being done in Europe it could look staid, ornate, and dainty. By the twenties American designers had adopted the embellishments of Art Nouveau, but in 1934 they had yet to assimilate the graphic dynamism of Art Deco and Constructivism.

Despite Hearst's apparent lack of enthusiasm for Brodovitch's sample pages, Snow prevailed.[18] Thus began an incredibly creative collaboration of editorial and design talents that would last a quarter of a century, and that would transform *Harper's Bazaar* from a fashion also-ran into one of the most admired, respected, and prestigious magazines of the 1940s and fifties. Brodovitch's contribution to the magazine was not merely to inject it with the design ideas he had acquired in Europe and begun to propagate, mainly in advertising, in the United States. Consistent with his devotion to newness and spontaneity, which dovetailed remarkably with fashion's own first principles, he reshaped and renewed the magazine throughout his tenure. By maintaining a high level of refinement throughout at the same time, he had bestowed upon him what is perhaps fashion's ultimate accolade: he was said to have "good taste." Although he was known to complain that *Harper's Bazaar*'s ultimate function was merely to promote fashion, in reality his temperament and the magazine's mission made a perfect match.[19]

What might the sample layouts that Carmel Snow carried to Hearst have looked like? We can guess that they closely resembled the kinds of pages that Brodovitch began designing almost immediately for *Harper's Bazaar*. One of the first issues he was responsible for (October 1934) opened with a story on the new Paris collections. On the left-hand page of the spread is a photograph by Man Ray. The elongated shape of the model (most likely one of Man Ray's darkroom stunts) leans dramatically to the right, and the photo itself is cut on a diagonal in repetition of her tilt. On the right-hand page are two columns of type set to mimic the slant of the photograph on the opposite page, together with the simple, sans-serif headline "Paris 1935." What makes this design so characteristic of Brodovitch is its simultaneous boldness and economy. Simply by duplicating the elements within the photograph and using them as keys to his overall design, he was able to achieve what to American audiences were unprecedented effects.

To those who worked with him at the *Bazaar*, the hallmark of Brodovitch's career as a designer was the unfailing elegance of his pages. Indeed, even today there is no magazine that consis-

THE BEAUTIFUL INDIVIDUALIST

• An Englishman touring America by car reports that he had a strange illusion—for weeks he thought he was traveling one jump behind a bus load of beauties because at every town where he stopped he saw the same pretty girls with the same pretty hair and the same dazzling smiles. An Irishman has the same reaction; he labels American girls Kate and Duplicate. And a mother tells us that she sent a real girl off to boarding school and got back a carbon copy of a thousand others. The more we hear, the more we are sure that the high standard of American good looks is not only our pride but our dilemma. How can a woman today stand out from the masses of other pretty women who cross her path? It seems to us that the clue to the beautiful individualist is EMPHASIS. The face you never forget is the one that knows its best features and deliberately accents them. Your beauty may be in your eyes—then remember that the difference between pretty eyes and unforgettable eyes is determined by make-up. It may be your hair—then lavish time and money on its care, tint it and coif it in wonderful ways. Your beauty may lie not in your facial contours but in your quality—ethereal, vivid, or polished as porcelain. Or—and don't struggle to hide it—your very irregularity may be what you've got that *she* hasn't got: an erratic eyebrow, a bold nose or, like the lady opposite, a neck long and curving as a swan's.

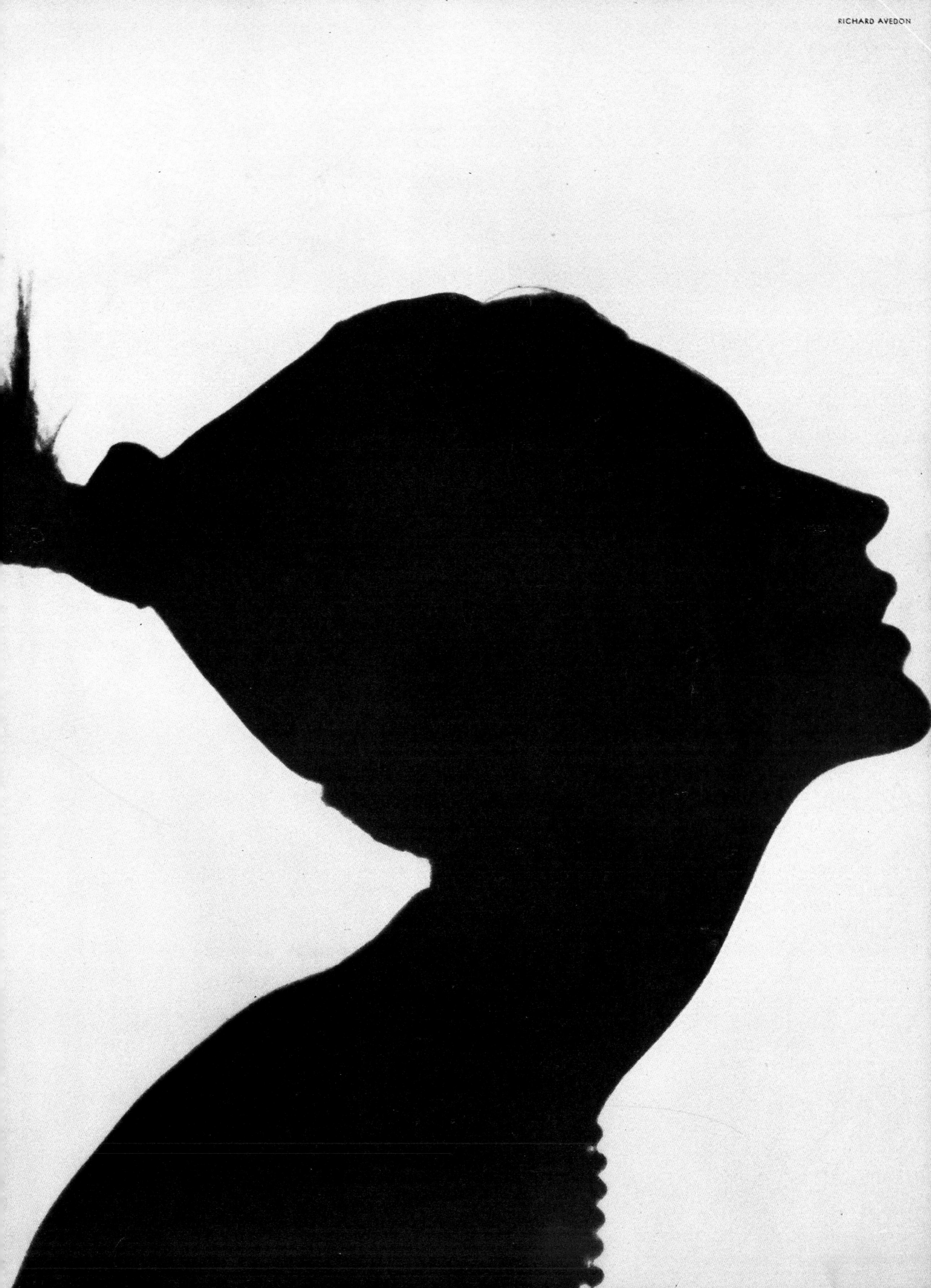

RICHARD AVEDON

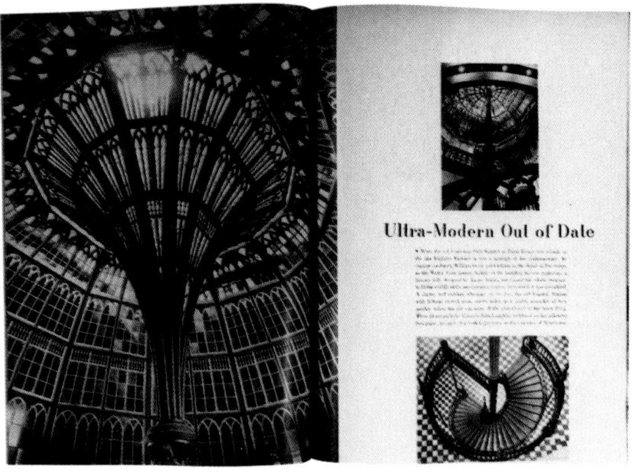

Left and opposite:
HARPER'S BAZAAR, MARCH 1956. PHOTOGRAPHER: CLARENCE JOHN LAUGHLIN

Previous pages: When Brodovitch arrived at *Harper's Bazaar*, the underlying idea of fashion was relatively narrow and aristocratic: a woman's clothes were an indication of her social position. But in the quarter century he was the magazine's art director, fashion became both more diffuse and more democratic. No longer defined solely by clothes and class, it came to represent not so much a manner of dressing as a style of living. Consequently, Brodovitch could use pictures like this virtually featureless silhouette by Richard Avedon, which appeared as the opening spread of the annual *Bazaar* beauty issue. The model is rendered as almost a cutout figure, and readers are encouraged to see themselves in her glamorous profile.

Previous pages:
HARPER'S BAZAAR, OCTOBER 1950. PHOTOGRAPHER: RICHARD AVEDON

tently achieves the distinction of design that was standard during his tenure there. One could argue, however, that the quality that guaranteed his success was his devotion to the new, to unending surprise and vitality. In practice there was no conflict here: Brodovitch's combination of elegance and innovation was an ideal mix for a fashion magazine. The former meant that his layouts were admired as classics in their time. The latter meant that he developed no rigid traits that would be susceptible to becoming dated. Although his *Bazaar* layouts were and are distinctive, the means by which we can identify them is not so much a matter of any design "signature" as of an unmistakable coherence of design and content.

Enlarging Fashion

Brodovitch's arrival at *Harper's Bazaar* coincided with a fundamental change in the mission of fashion magazines and, even more important, in the very definition of fashion. When *Bazaar* and *Vogue*, its competitor, were founded in the nineteenth century, they were essentially devoted to dispensing and preserving the values of the "smart set," which consisted of old-moneyed, aristocratic American families. What was then called *Harper's Bazar* proclaimed itself "A Repository of Fashion, Pleasure and Instruction." It was, editorially, much like the "women's magazines" of today, covering housekeeping and gardening along with its ration of poetry, novelettes, self-help articles, and other amusements. "Fashion" was conceived of largely in terms of society—as what the New York and Newport sophisticates were wearing—and tips were offered about how to appear fashionable.

Only after World War I did the idea of fashion as clothing, independent of social status, gradually begin to take root. Dress designers—especially in Paris, the fashion capital, where they were most professionalized—sought to expand their markets. The fashion magazines, in turn, wanted to expand their circulation. Rather than use the wealthy as models of what one should aspire to in life, the fashion industry and the fashion press began to sell to women the notion that fashionable garments by themselves could bestow some of the glamour and self confidence displayed so flamboyantly by the rich. Like Cinderella's slipper, clothes were presented as

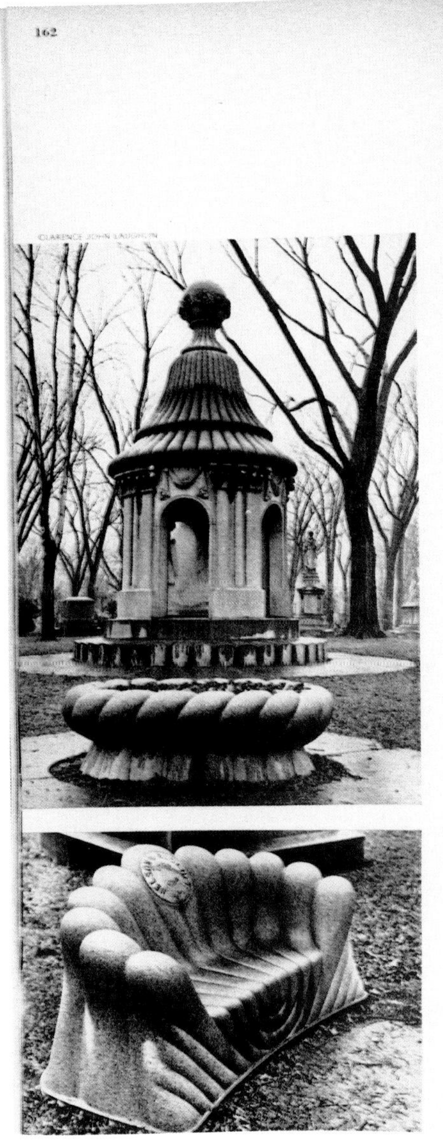

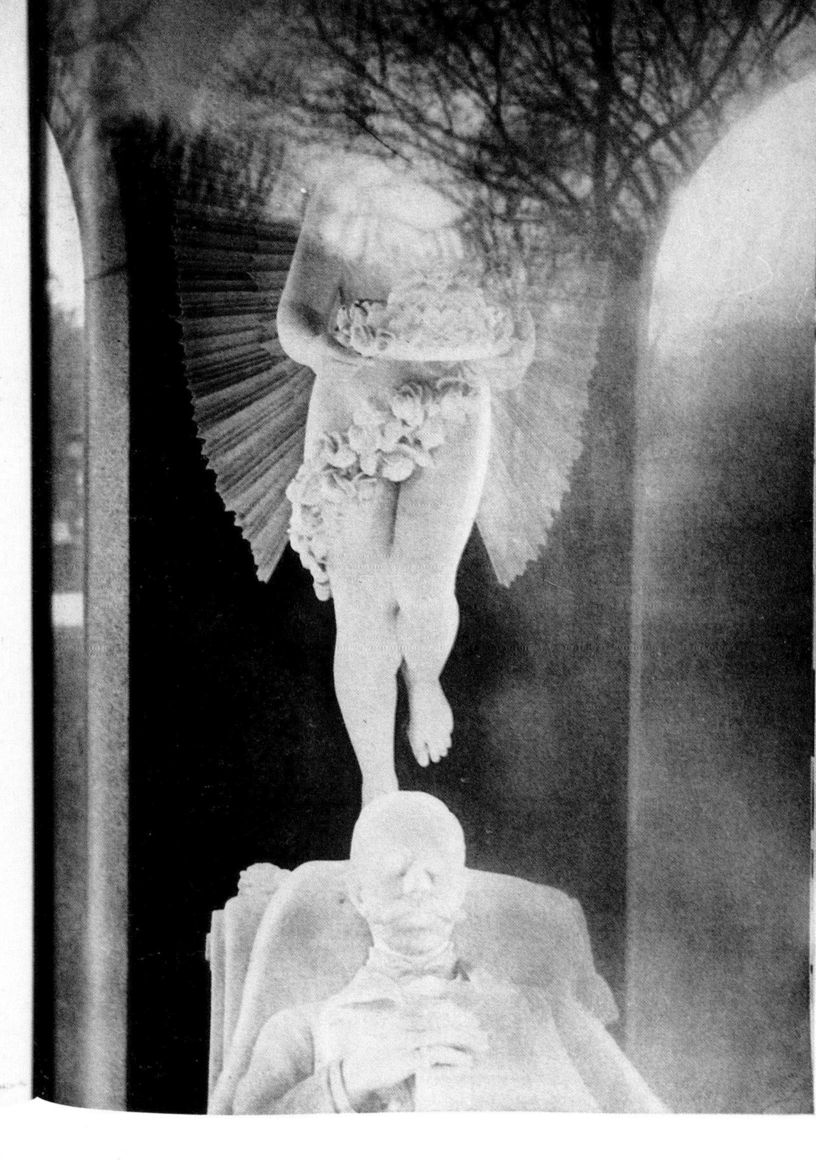

talismans that could release one from the drudgery of ordinary life. Together with *Vogue*, *Harper's Bazaar* was an important element in this paradoxical redefinition of fashion as an aristocratic pursuit arrayed on a democratic field.

At the same time, the *Bazaar* and other fashion magazines increasingly emphasized traditional high culture as one of the concerns of well-dressed women. Thus pages of clothes modeled by mannequins were interleaved with the words, images, and portraits of renowned novelists, painters, photographers, dancers, and actors. In the 1930s, Diana Vreeland's imaginative but entirely fatuous "Why Don't You" column might be followed by a two-page spread of Clarence John Laughlin photographs or by a Eudora Welty short story. If such combinations are taken for granted today, it is because the formula proved so successful. When Condé Nast stopped publishing *Vanity Fair* in 1936, its cultural aspirations were folded into *Vogue*, the Condé Nast fashion magazine.

The guiding genius behind the *Bazaar*'s editorial transformation from a clothes magazine to a clothes-and-culture magazine was Carmel Snow, whose impact on Brodovitch's career is difficult to overestimate. Snow was a savvy and tenacious woman, but what most marked her tenure as editor was her yen to be admired as a person of culture as well as of fashion. While neither aristocratic nor cosmopolitan by background, she soon developed an appreciation for the cultured life. Her first fashion job was at Condé Nast's *Vogue*, where she worked in the late twenties. There she specialized in fashion, and was seen as the heir apparent to Edna Woolard Chase, then *Vogue*'s editor.[20] But she really wanted to work for *Vanity Fair*.

Having learned from Edward Steichen, Condé Nast's chief photographer at the time, both the rudiments of fashion photography and an appreciation for modern art and design, she knew that the *Bazaar* could not progress with a steady diet of Baron de Meyer pictures. De Meyer, who had come to the *Bazaar* after he was replaced at *Vogue* by Steichen, made mannered, spun-sugar fashion photographs within the confines of the studio. Snow shunted him aside and brought in Martin Munkacsi, a Hungarian-born photographer already well known in Germany for his candid action pictures.

Although Brodovitch is

The "new" *Harper's Bazaar*, under Carmel Snow's editorship, emphasized culture for its own sake. Taking advantage of Brodovitch's contacts in Europe and his wide knowledge of photography, the magazine introduced the work of many artists and photographers to its American audience. Some, like Clarence John Laughlin (pages 62 and 63), were unlikely candidates for the pages of a fashion magazine, but Brodovitch ensured that the *Bazaar* presented his images with a sense of dignity. The magazine's cultural coverage increased markedly during and immediately after World War II, when new fashions were in short supply.

Spreads from HARPER'S BAZAAR, *clockwise from top right:*

AUGUST 1954. PHOTOGRAPHER: WERNER BISCHOF

SEPTEMBER 1957. POEM BY THEODORE ROETHKE

MARCH 15, 1950. PHOTOGRAPHER: BRASSAI

APRIL 1942. PHOTOGRAPHER: WALKER EVANS

DECEMBER 1957. ILLUSTRATOR: FELIKS TOPOLSKI

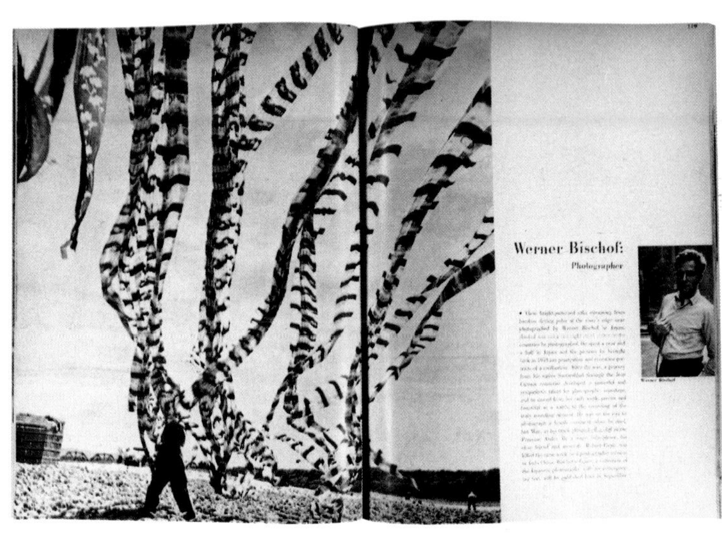

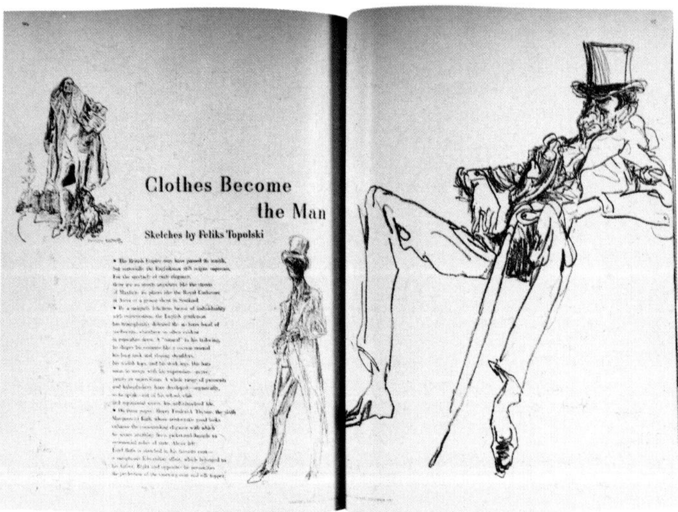

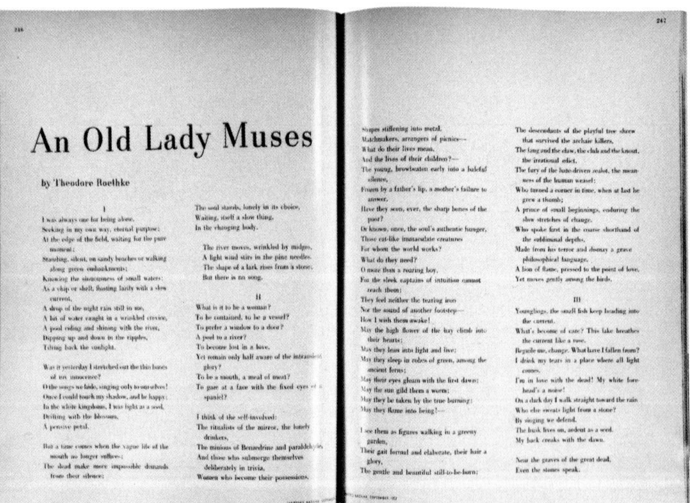

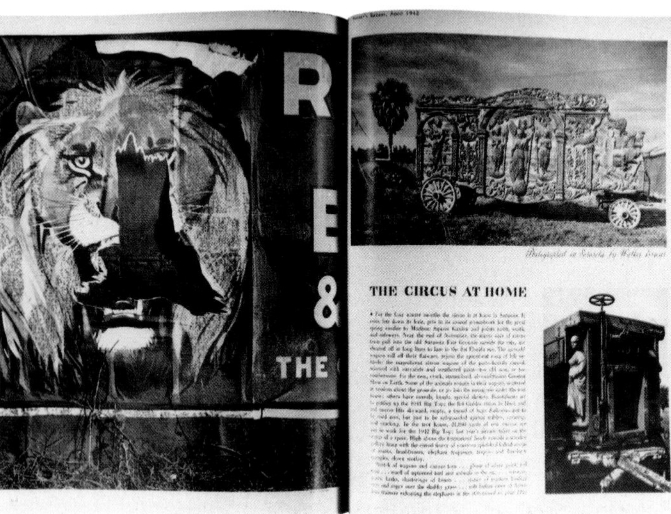

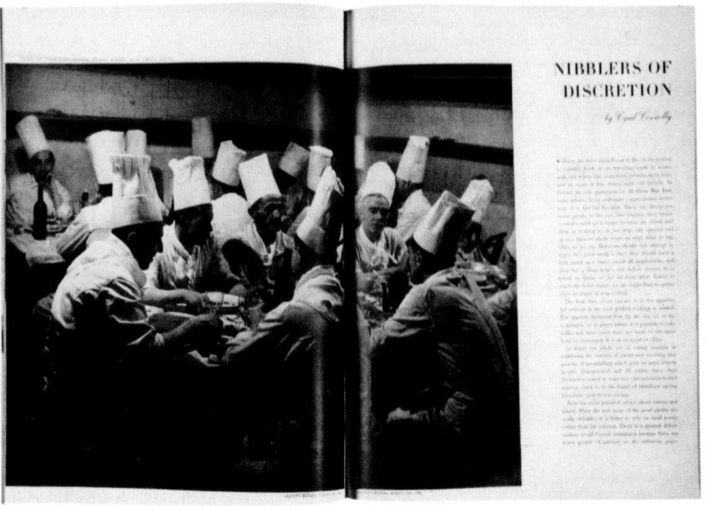

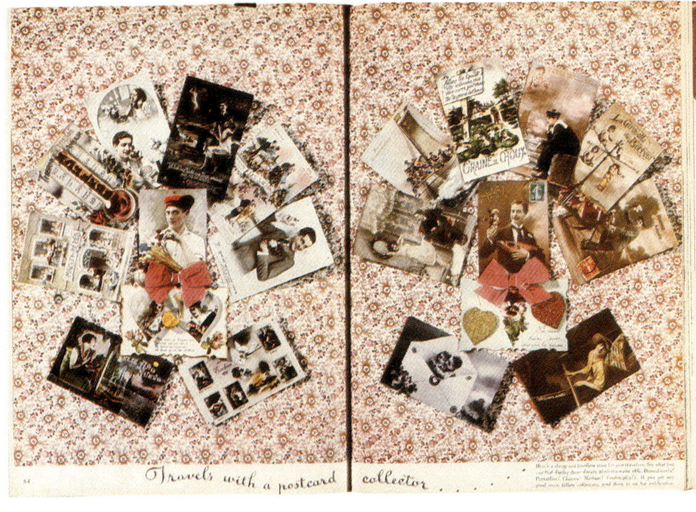
Travels with a postcard collector . . .

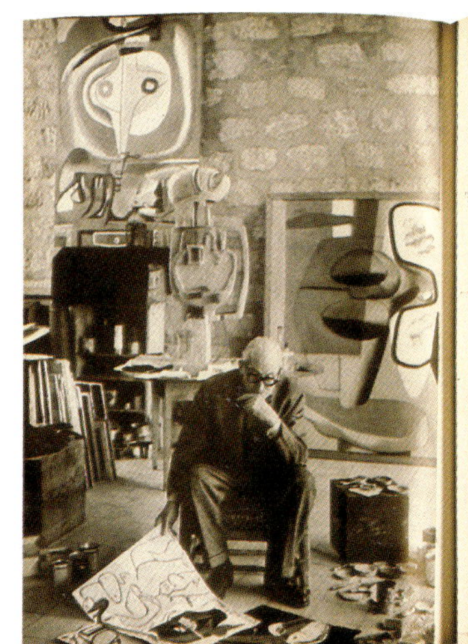

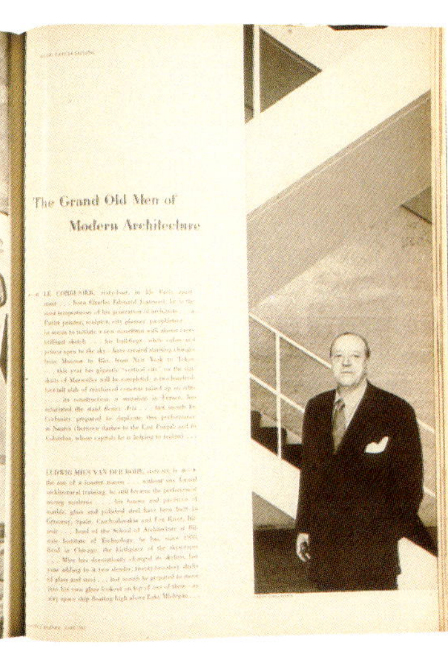
The Grand Old Men of Modern Architecture

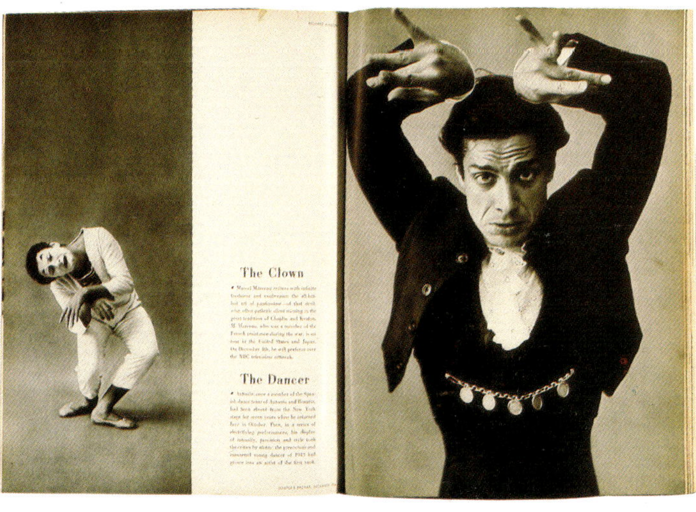
The Clown

The Dancer

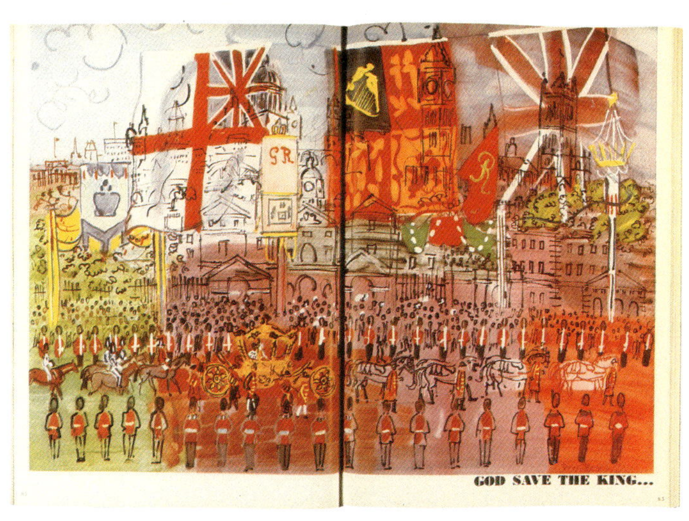
GOD SAVE THE KING...

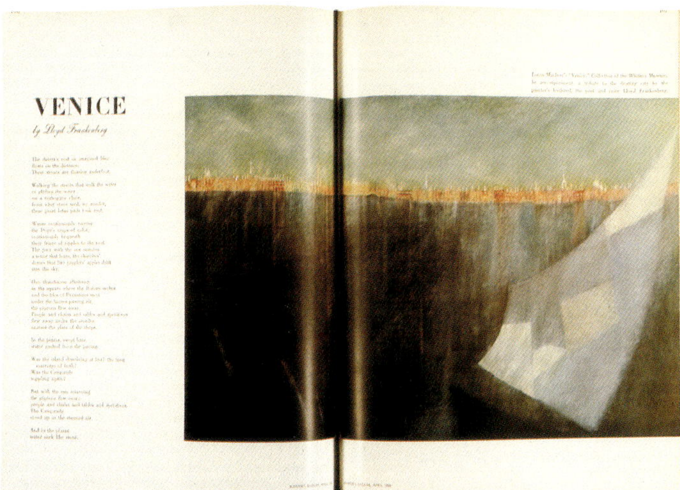
VENICE

by Lloyd Frankenberg

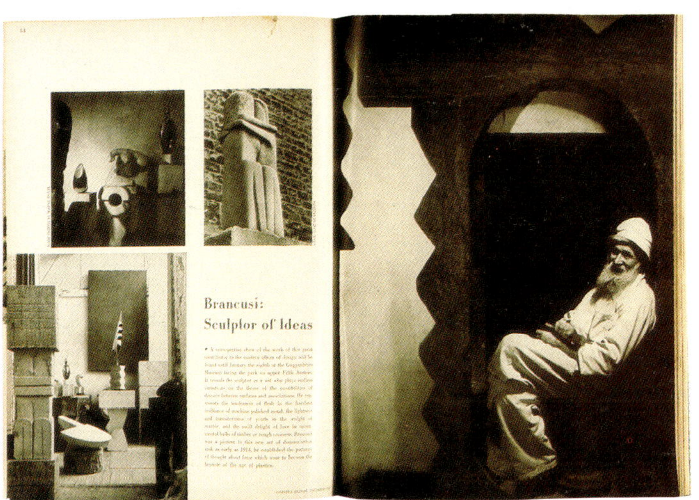
Brancusi: Sculptor of Ideas

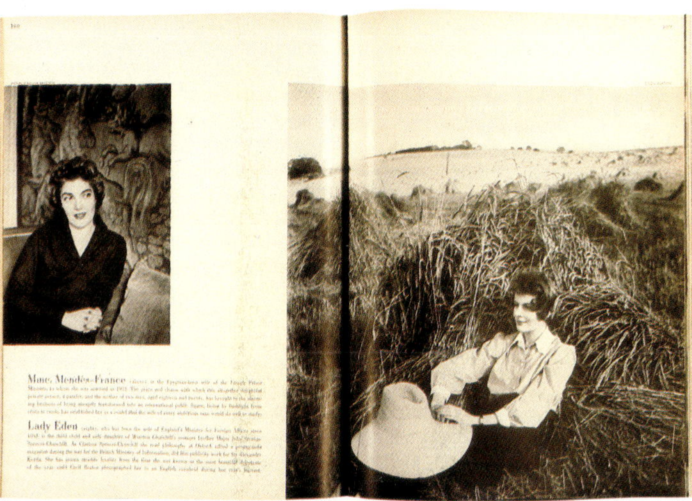
Mme. Mendès-France

Lady Eden

Spreads from HARPER'S BAZAAR, *clockwise from top left:*
JUNE 1936. POSTCARDS

JUNE 1952. PHOTOGRAPHERS: HENRI CARTIER-BRESSON AND HARRY CALLAHAN

MAY 1937. ARTIST: RAOUL DUFY

DECEMBER 1955. PHOTOGRAPHERS: WAYNE MILLER AND HENRI CARTIER-BRESSON

FEBRUARY 1955. PHOTOGRAPHERS: HENRI CARTIER-BRESSON AND CECIL BEATON

APRIL 1950. ARTIST: LOREN MACIVER

DECEMBER 1955. PHOTOGRAPHER: RICHARD AVEDON

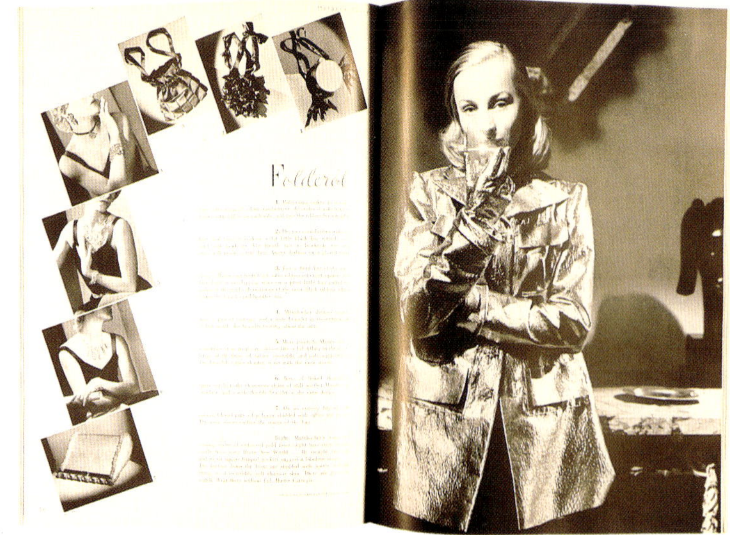

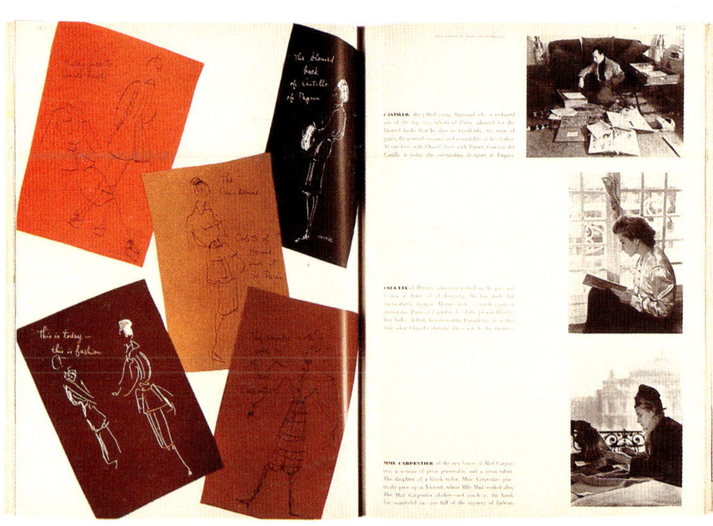

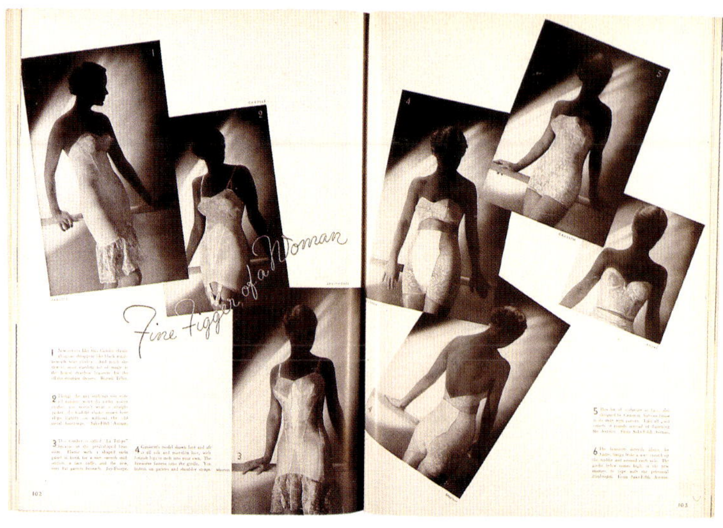

Clockwise from top right:

HARPER'S BAZAAR, SEPTEMBER 15, 1939. PHOTOGRAPHER: GEORGE HOYNINGEN-HUENE

HARPER'S BAZAAR, NOVEMBER 1934

HARPER'S BAZAAR, APRIL 1945. PHOTOGRAPHER: HENRI CARTIER-BRESSON

often assumed to have "discovered" Munkacsi, it was Snow who first saw that his ability to capture action in a dynamic, spontaneous way could be used to express the new sense of American fashion: one of movement, excitement, and casual flair. Munkacsi's first published picture in *Bazaar*—of the model Lucille Brokaw running along a beach in a bathing suit and cape—appeared in December 1933. Snow later would call Munkacsi's candid style, "the first big innovation I introduce into *Harper's Bazaar*." The image was so successful, at least in the editor's estimation, that Munkacsi repeated it, with a different model and swim suit, a year later (page 118).

Snow also set about revitalizing the magazine's design as early as 1933. The masthead at the time lists no art director, but seems clear that the shift to a more modern look was instigated by Snow, who was no doubt inspired by the changes being wrought at *Vogue* by its innovative art director, Mehemed Fehmy Agha. Dr. Agha (the title is traditional, if apocryphal) had become the art director of *Vogue* in 1928.[21] A cosmopolitan Turk who had studied at the Academy of Fine Arts in Kiev and later with Le Corbusier in France, Agha was working in Berlin at the

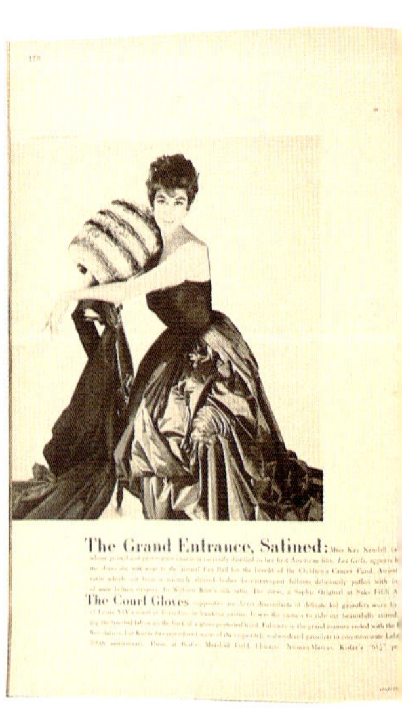

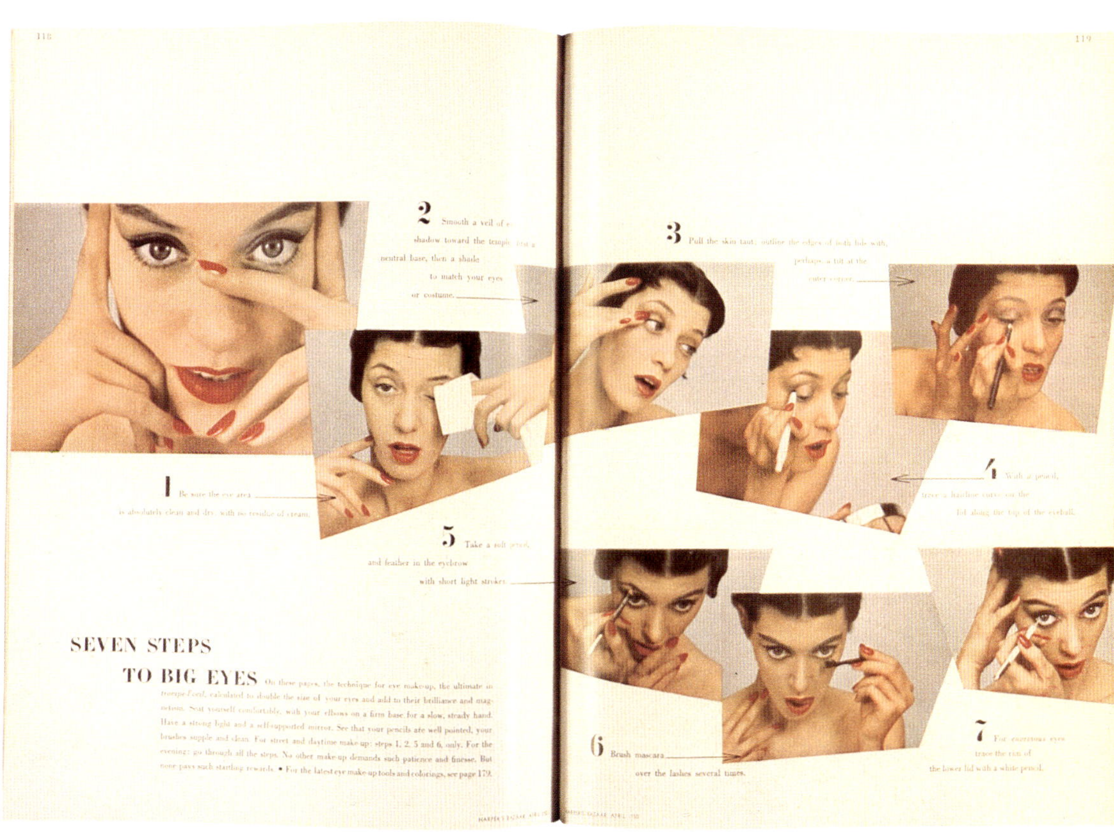

2 Smooth a veil of

shadow toward the temple

neutral base, then a shade

to match your eyes

or costume.

3 Pull the skin taut; outline the edges of both lids with,

perhaps, a tilt at the

outer corner.

1

is absolutely clean and dry, with no residue of cream.

4 With a pencil,

lid along the top of the eyeball.

5 Take a soft

and feather in the eyebrow

with short light strokes

SEVEN STEPS

TO BIG EYES On these pages, the technique for eye make-up, the ultimate in trompe l'oeil, calculated to double the size of your eyes and add to their brilliance and magnetism. Seat yourself comfortably, with your elbows on a firm base for a slow, steady hand. Have a strong light and a self-supported mirror. See that your pencils are well pointed, your brushes supple and clean. For street and daytime make-up: steps 1, 2, 5 and 6, only. For the evening: go through all the steps. No other make-up demands such patience and finesse. But none pays such startling rewards. • For the latest eye make-up tools and colorings, see page 179.

6 Brush mascara

over the lashes several times.

7 For

trace the rim of

the lower lid with a white pencil.

Arranging photographs like playing cards, splayed out on the page or in the shape of a fan, was a technique already in use when Brodovitch began designing *Harper's Bazaar* in 1934. But in Brodovitch's layouts, overlaps or positions rarely seem arbitrary. Nevertheless, by the fifties he had virtually abandoned using pictures in this way; instead of looking as if they had been dropped on the page, the photographs in effect became the page.

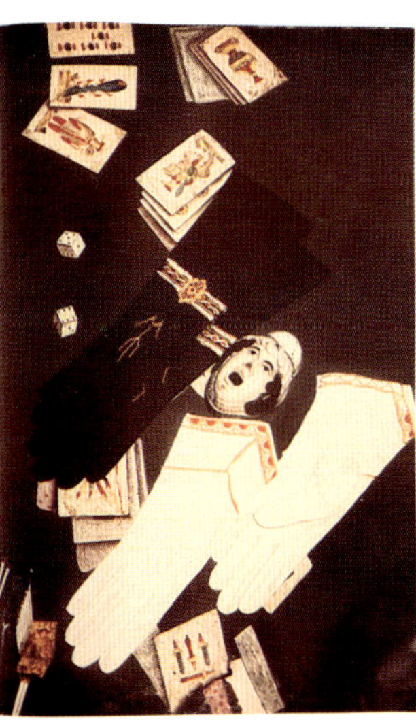

German edition of *Vogue* when he was spotted by Condé Nast. During the first years of his fifteen-year tenure at the flagship American *Vogue*, Agha revolutionized its layouts and, with the assistance of Steichen, the magazine's chief photographer, expanded photography's role in the design. According to Snow, who was then working there,

[Agha] was trained in the new European style of layouts, which was a complete departure from the static, stilted look of all American magazines at the time . . . . Dr. Agha wanted bigger photographs (vigorously supported by Steichen and me), more white space, and modern typography.

Thus, with Snow's encouragement, *Harper's Bazaar* began to display photographs in coherent groups, with their edges overlapping. Sometimes they ran across a spread, fan fashion, a technique "borrowed" from Agha. Color photographs began to be used editorially for the first time. Pictures were silhouetted and combined with trompe l'oeil fabric backgrounds. Bodoni became the standard typeface for text throughout the magazine (and would remain so for all of Brodovitch's years there).

Top:
HARPER'S BAZAAR,
APRIL 1950

Left:
HARPER'S BAZAAR,
OCTOBER 1957.
PHOTOGRAPHER:
LOUISE DAHL-WOLFE

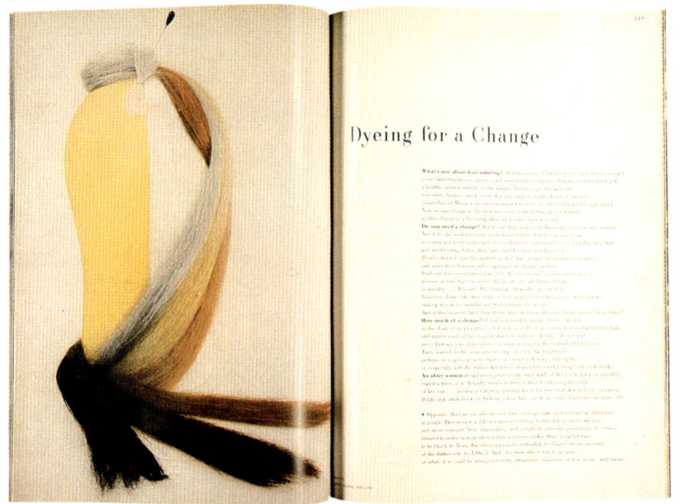

Dyeing for a Change

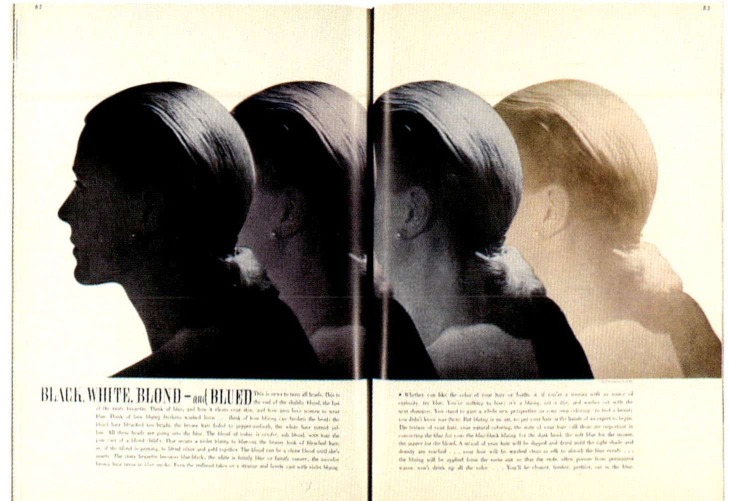

BLACK, WHITE, BLOND—and BLUED

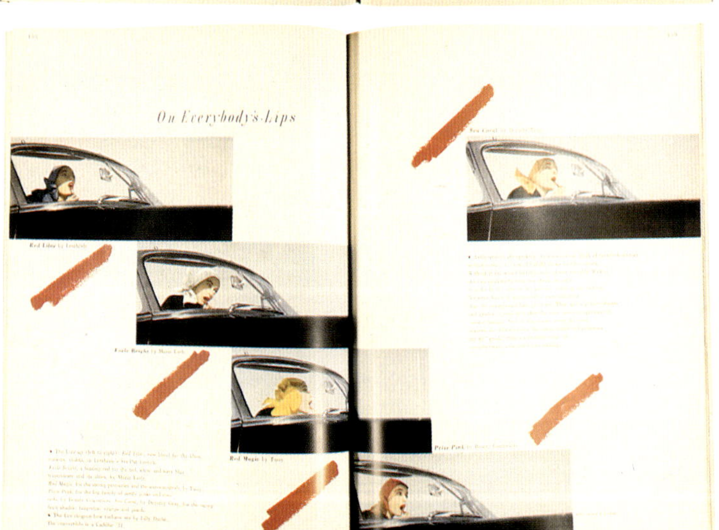

On Everybody's Lips

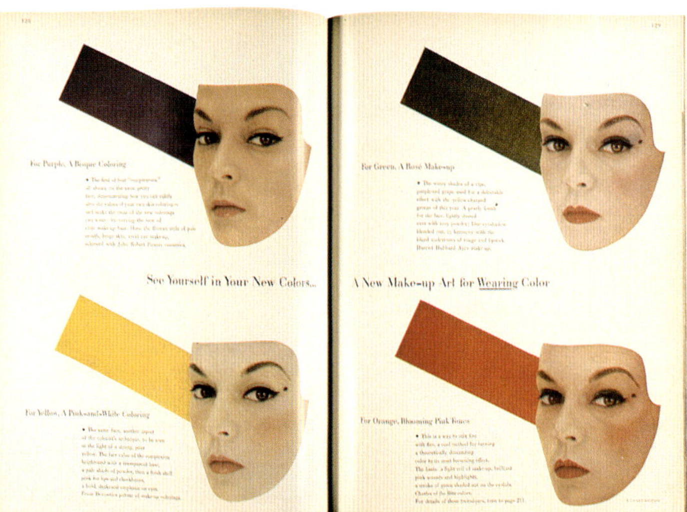

See Yourself in Your New Colors...

A New Make-up Art for Wearing Color

Color was relatively new in magazines of the 1930s, when full-color illustration required laborious preparation and long lead times. But by using process or second color inventively, Brodovitch was able to give the *Bazaar* an added sense of currency and luxury. Instead of seeking to duplicate colors as they exist in the world, he applied color to his layouts expressively and intuitively. Even when full-color reproduction became commonplace, he still used broad swaths of single colors as visual exclamation points. This use of color was especially evident in *Junior Bazaar*, which Hearst published as an independent magazine from 1945 to 1947. Brodovitch and Lillian Bassman, the magazine's other art director, always utilized color in an imaginative way on the covers.

Spreads from HARPER'S BAZAAR, *this page, from top:* APRIL 1957. PHOTOGRAPHER: LESLIE GILL

MARCH 1945. PHOTOGRAPHER: GEORGE HOYNINGEN-HUENE

APRIL 1951. PHOTOGRAPHER: PLUCER

APRIL 1953. PHOTOGRAPHER: RICHARD AVEDON

Opposite: *JUNIOR BAZAAR* COVER, JANUARY 1947. ART DIRECTORS: ALEXEY BRODOVITCH AND LILLIAN BASSMAN. PHOTOGRAPHER: ERNST BEADLE

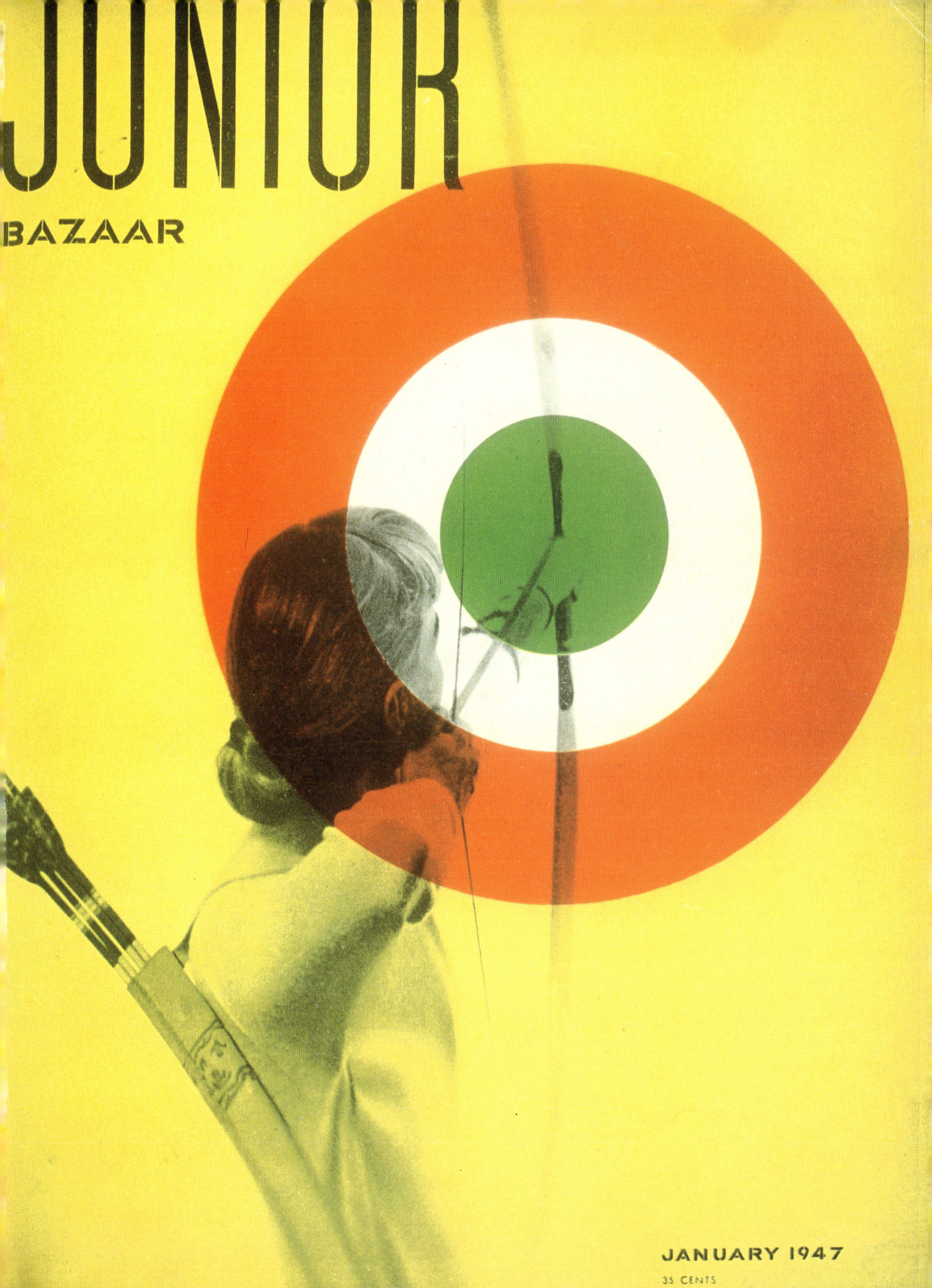
JUNIOR
BAZAAR
JANUARY 1947
35 CENTS

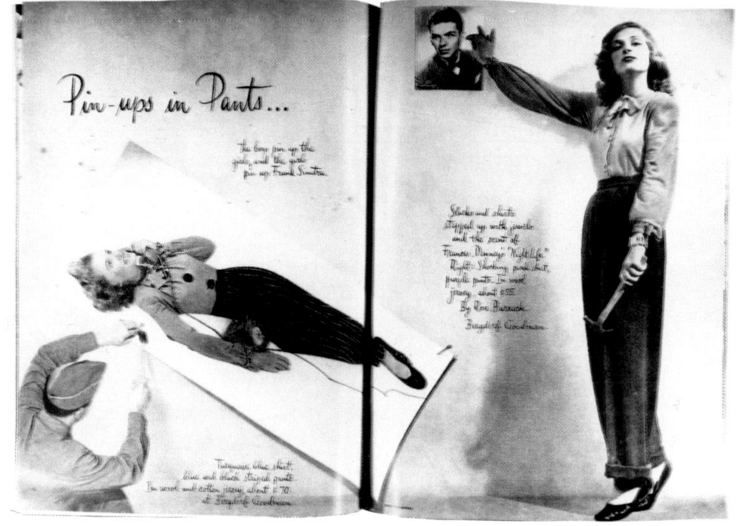

Influenced by Surrealism, Brodovitch emphasized mirroring and spatial illusion in many of his prewar page designs. For example, he used type and photographs together in ways that created multiple perspectives within a single space (left) or he combined separate photographs on facing pages to create the impression of a single, but doubled, scene (below). This latter technique he used to great advantage in his 1945 book *Ballet*. Brodovitch's dissatisfaction with literally descriptive photographs also can be seen in the blurred and unfocused photography that he promoted in the fifties.

These design changes, together with the introduction of Munkacsi's dynamic, active photographs and the chic Parisian illustrations of Christian Bérard, created the beginnings of a new look for the magazine before Brodovitch's appointment as art director.

Nevertheless, Brodovitch's impact is immediately apparent. While the issues previous to his arrival in mid-1934 contain a few pages designed to be seen as unified spreads, Brodovitch conceived the entire editorial section that way. Snow already had dispensed with the black rules that had funereally framed every photograph as recently as 1933, but Brodovitch went further and treated the photographs as collaborative elements in the total page design. He used Man Ray's photographs as the centerpieces of the magazine's new look. One led off the editorial section of September 1934—the first issue of the magazine to show evidence of Brodovitch's touch. His imaginative grasp of the materials given him extended to such uninspiring subjects as fabrics. In the same issue, Brodovitch laid fabric swatches across a color spread and enhanced them with the addition of airbrushed shadows, pen illustrations, and a hand-lettered headline.

Just how much Brodovitch borrowed from Agha is a matter of opinion. In the *Vogue Book of Fashion Photography: The First Sixty Years*, Polly Devlin ascribes to Agha at *Vogue* many of the innovations frequently attributed to Brodovitch at *Harper's Bazaar:*

Until Dr. Agha's arrival the look, layout and presentation of the pages were rooted in Vogue's beginnings as a society magazine, when text had been paramount and fashion drawings the only illustrations. Drawings and photographs alike were most often presented conventionally within frames. Words and pictures were not closely allied, and each page had the same wide margins. Agha removed the frames and sometimes the margins, and enlarged the photographs or filled whole pages with them, put together to tell one fashion story. He laced the pages with headlines, used bigger print, and gave them an enticing, accessible look . . . . He also turned the art director from a supporting character into a leading figure who could enormously influence a photographer's work and career. He could improve bad pictures, diminish great ones, and make average ones memorable, by the way he cropped them and positioned them in the magazine.[22]

Given Brodovitch's already well-developed tendency for pastiche, and the similarities in their backgrounds, it is in no way surprising that *Bazaar*'s new art director, whose magazine experience consisted of pasting up pages of *Arts et Métiers Graphiques* and *Cahiers d'Art*, should look to Agha's designs as models for his own. There are, however, significant differences in the design styles of the two art directors, and differences of temperament as well. Agha leaned more toward the decorative than Brodovitch, even though both shared Art Deco roots. He understood photographs as elements on the page but often without any regard for what they contained, whereas Brodovitch's designs often seem molded to the contours of a photograph's internal forms. His "fan" spreads, for example, are much more sensitive to the subject matter of the individual pictures than Agha's; instead of the overlaps hiding important details or forms, Brodovitch's "fans" accentuate the content of the pictures (pages 66–67).

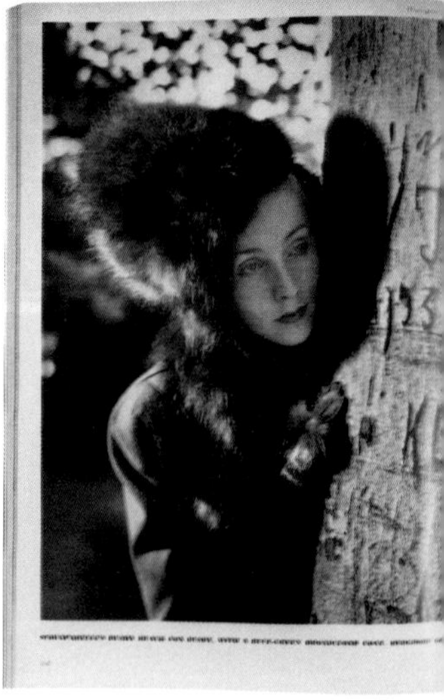

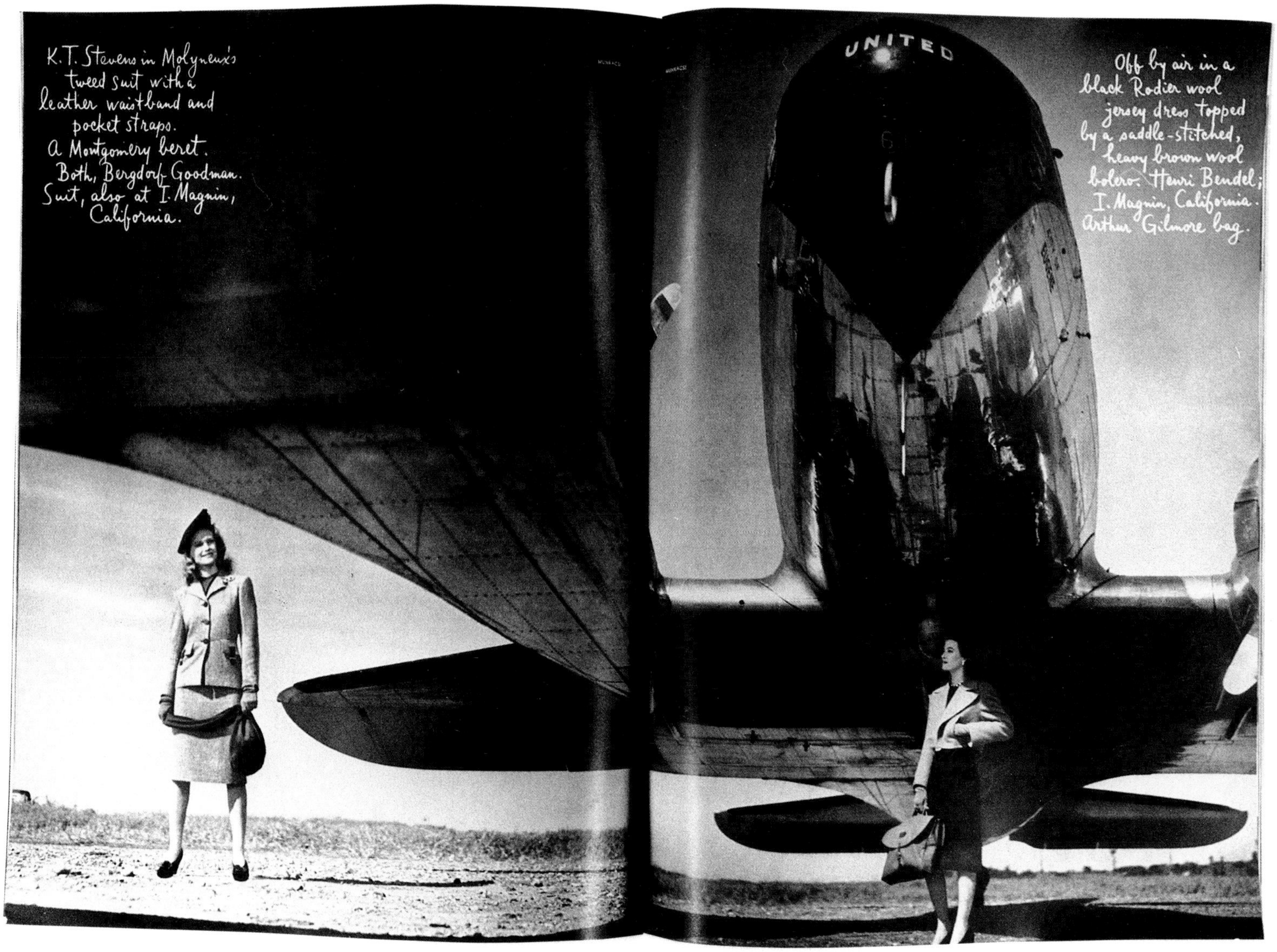

K.T. Stevens in Molyneux's tweed suit with a leather waistband and pocket straps. A Montgomery beret. Both, Bergdorf Goodman. Suit, also at I. Magnin, California.

Off by air in a black Rodier wool jersey dress topped by a saddle-stitched, heavy brown wool bolero. Henri Bendel; I. Magnin, California. Arthur Gilmore bag.

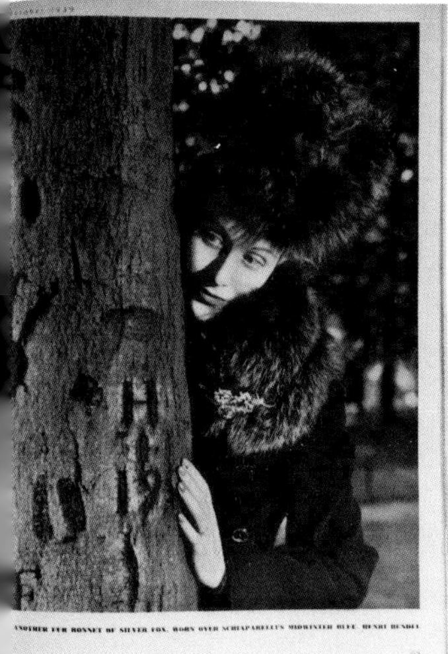

The Thirties: Surrealism's Influence

Although Brodovitch had immediately made his design presence felt at *Harper's Bazaar* on his arrival, he did not revolutionize it overnight. Still, his repertory of layout concepts and design devices was prodigious from the start. One of the first of the innovations he brought to American magazine design was to begin casting the text in a shape that mirrored the photograph across from it. Done across two pages, this produced repeat or mirror images. Brodovitch found other ways to double forms. In a two-page layout from 1936, two models appear within what seems a single framed mirror—although in actuality Brodovitch paired two separate photographs, neatly joining them at the gutter. This fascination with doubling and reflections is part of the Surrealist heritage he was gradually to discard.

He fostered illusionism in other ways. He ran type across photographic images in a way that altered the photographs' inherent perspective; at times he put the type itself in perspective, as if it had its own depth. In this way he made the page visually active not only from side to side and top to bottom; he gave it the illusion of

Opposite above:
HARPER'S BAZAAR, SEPTEMBER 1943. PHOTOGRAPHER: ERWIN BLUMENFELD

Above:
HARPER'S BAZAAR, OCTOBER 1944. PHOTOGRAPHER: MARTIN MUNKACSI

Left:
HARPER'S BAZAAR, OCTOBER 1939. PHOTOGRAPHER: ERWIN BLUMENFELD

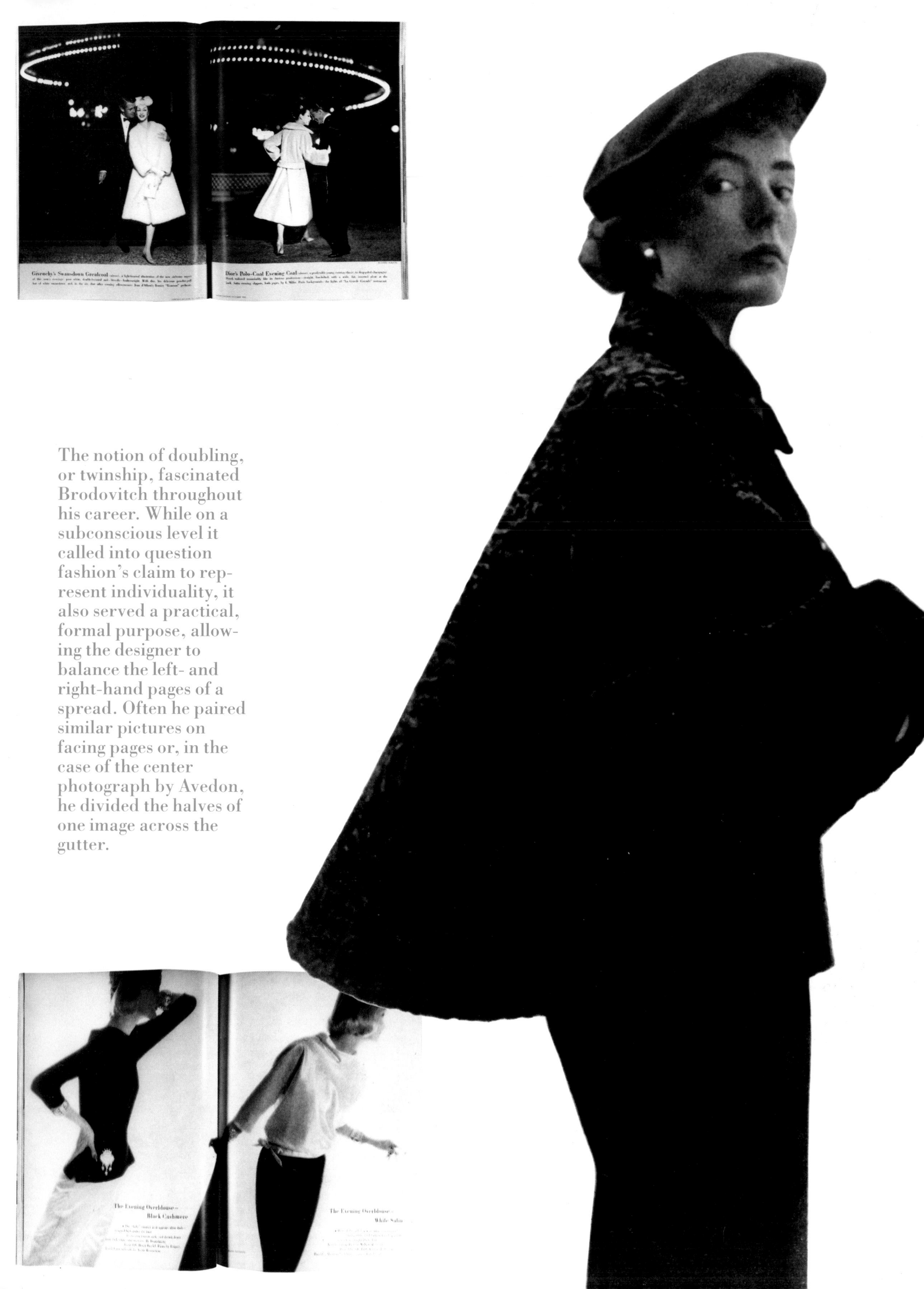

The notion of doubling, or twinship, fascinated Brodovitch throughout his career. While on a subconscious level it called into question fashion's claim to represent individuality, it also served a practical, formal purpose, allowing the designer to balance the left- and right-hand pages of a spread. Often he paired similar pictures on facing pages or, in the case of the center photograph by Avedon, he divided the halves of one image across the gutter.

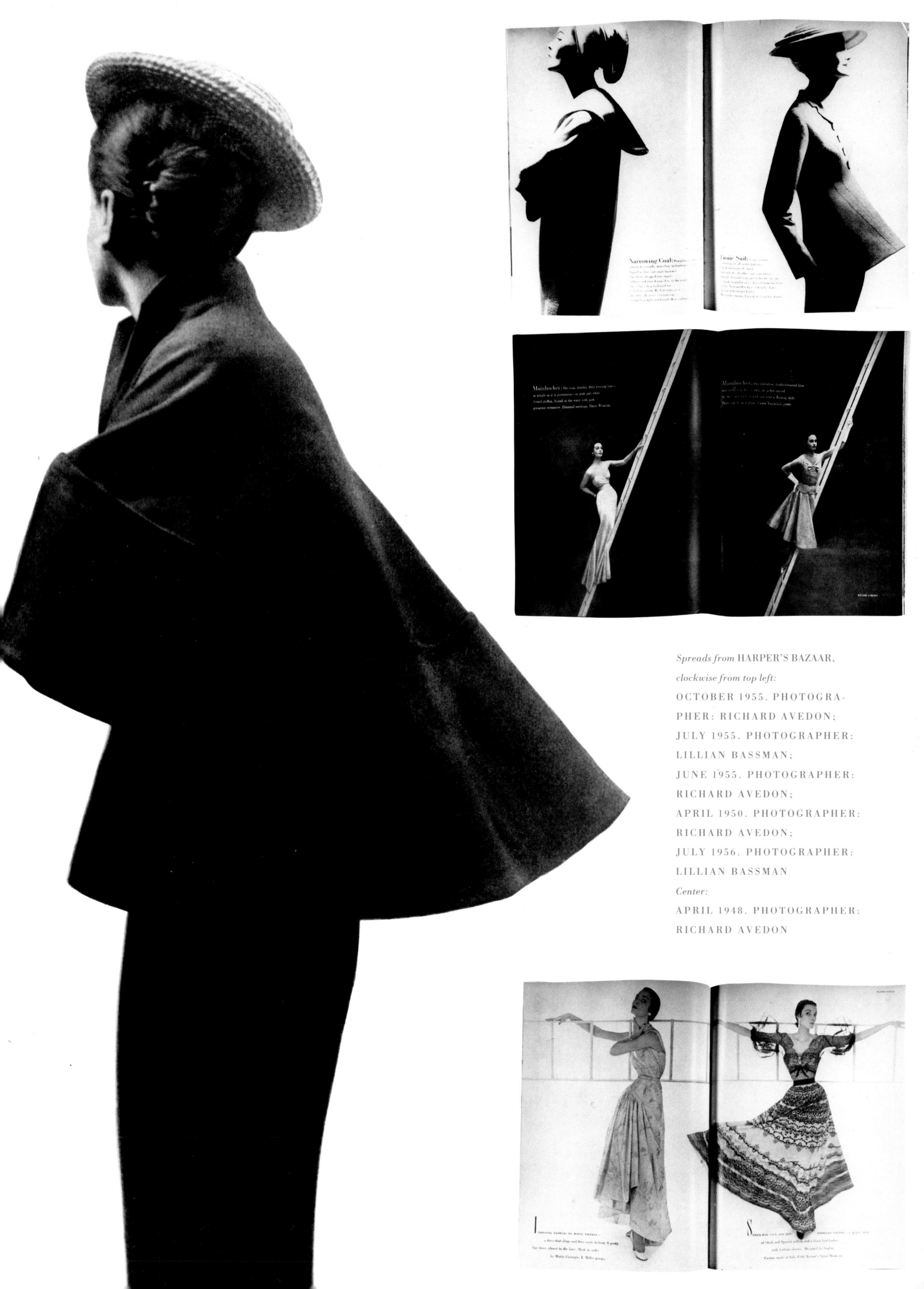

Spreads from HARPER'S BAZAAR, *clockwise from top left:* OCTOBER 1955. PHOTOGRAPHER: RICHARD AVEDON; JULY 1955. PHOTOGRAPHER: LILLIAN BASSMAN; JUNE 1955. PHOTOGRAPHER: RICHARD AVEDON; APRIL 1950. PHOTOGRAPHER: RICHARD AVEDON; JULY 1956. PHOTOGRAPHER: LILLIAN BASSMAN

Center: APRIL 1948. PHOTOGRAPHER: RICHARD AVEDON

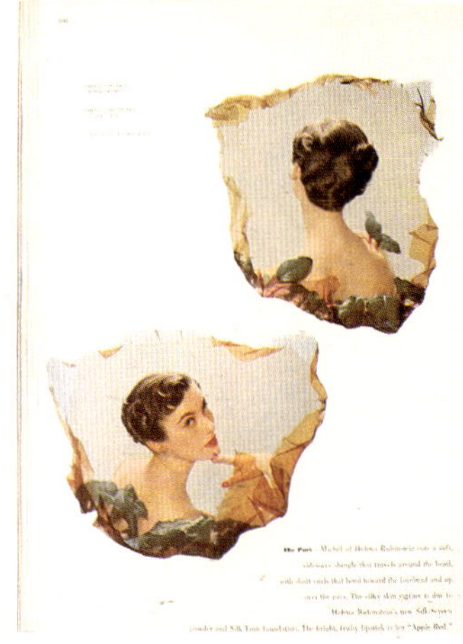

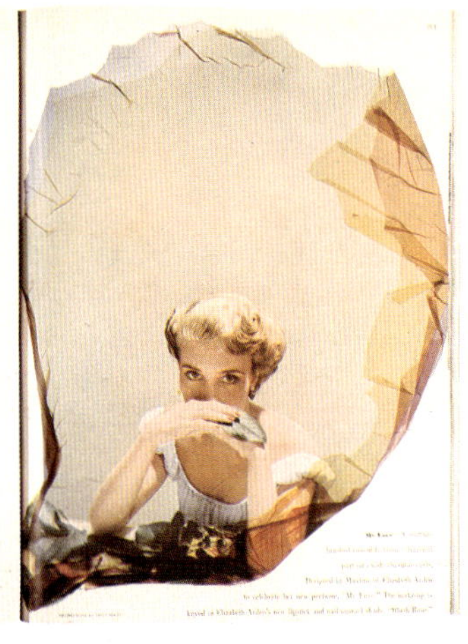

Surrealism made itself felt in *Harper's Bazaar* of the thirties both as a style and as an experimental, "unconscious" approach to subject matter. Brodovitch used pictures sent by radio, X-ray images from a medical lab, and irregularly shaped photographs with torn edges to enliven his pages. His designs also borrowed Surrealist themes, such as the fetishization of parts of women's bodies, particularly the lips. Compare, for example, the layout at right with Man Ray's 1932–34 painting *Observation Time— The Lovers* of a pair of lips floating in the sky above Paris (page 116).

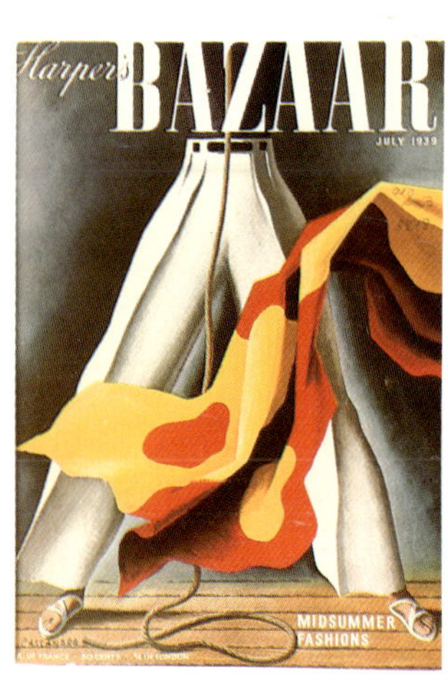

three dimensions. The idea of spatial illusion was carried further by the use of silhouettes, "torn" edges on images, airbrushed shadows, hand-drawn headlines, overlapped drawings, and photomontage. Some illustrations were made to appear pinned to the page with tacks, complete with their own shadows; sometimes a silhouetted photograph of a hand appears to "enter" the page, making the rest of the layout recede into the background. Not surprisingly, at the time Brodovitch was fabricating layouts such as these he was also reproducing paintings by Salvador Dalí, photographs by Man Ray, and such incongruous "anonymous" images as an X-ray image of cosmetic bottles, credited to the New York X-Ray Laboratory. In Paris, fashion itself was in the midst of a Surrealist craze.

Brodovitch's determination to mold *Harper's Bazaar* in this European image can be seen not only inside the magazine but also on its covers. Although he continued to rely almost exclusively on illustrations until the forties, he quickly jettisoned Erté, who had been the bread-and-butter *Bazaar* cover illustrator, and, beginning in 1937, installed Cassandre, a fellow Russian, in his place. Cassandre was to illustrate nearly every *Bazaar* cover for the next three years, until the renowned poster artist stopped coming to New York to solicit work. Although his covers are posterlike in conception, they bear little resemblance to the Art Deco style of his most brilliant Paris posters. Instead, they seem modeled on the Surrealism of Dalí, with its biomorphic shapes and intimations of landscape perspective. A similar style can be found in the covers Brodovitch illustrated before Cassandre's arrival—the first was in February 1935—and in Man Ray's photographic covers.

To the extent that printing technology would allow, Brodovitch used color in inventive ways. While full- or four-color pages rarely appeared until the 1940s—because the plates had to be laboriously prepared by a specialized printer, creating financial and deadline problems—he frequently utilized "second color" for his spreads (pages 68–69). He used it as a solid-color, rectilinear shape behind photographs or illustrations; as a screened, tinted shade across the entire page; or as a combination of solid color and tint. When he was able to, he would use two or

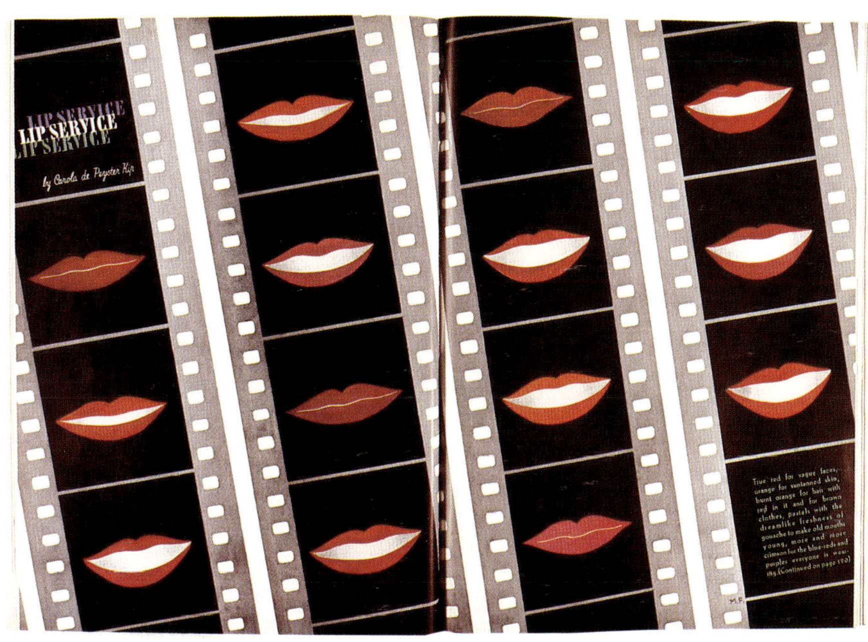

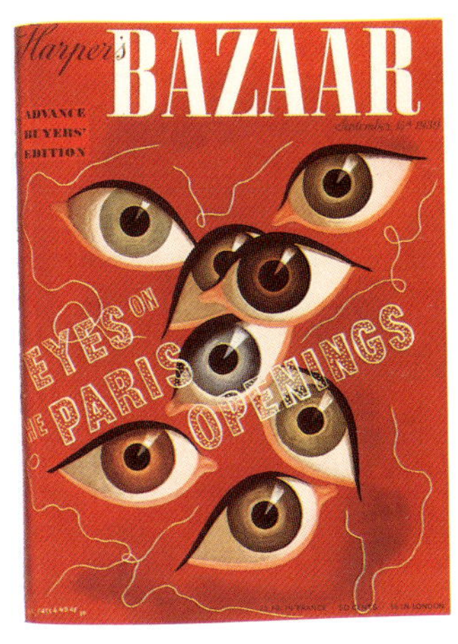

Both pages, left to right:
A.M. CASSANDRE. *HARPER'S BAZAAR* COVER, JULY 1939

HARPER'S BAZAAR, MAY 1949 PHOTOGRAPHER: ERNST BEADLE

A.M. CASSANDRE. *HARPER'S BAZAAR* COVER, SEPTEMBER 15, 1939

HARPER'S BAZAAR, JANUARY 1937. ILLUSTRATOR: MARY FULLERTON

sometimes three such colors, as in a January 1937 spread titled "Lip Service," in which "film strips" illustrated with a variety of red lips are enhanced by a combination of violet and green type.

At first Brodovitch made frequent use of the diagonal in his layouts, tilting photographs and type in a manner similar to what Agha was doing at *Vogue*. Often, he seems to have been attempting to energize photographs that would have looked static on their own. "If the image was good, he left it alone. If not, he did things to it," Richard Avedon has said.[23] And as Brodovitch himself remarked, "A layout man should be simple with good photographs. He should perform acrobatics when the pictures are bad."[24] But beginning in 1937, and increasingly thereafter, he began to adopt a more restrained and, from a photographer's perspective, more respectful manner of handling the *Bazaar*'s visual material. Skewed and cut-out photographs appear less frequently, the bold attempts at spatial illusionism fade, and the layouts become increasingly rectilinear and gridlike—more Constructivist and less Surrealist. Even his use of type changed; the headlines became thinner, quieter, less obtrusive. Perhaps Brodovitch sensed that the fashion climate was changing, and that Surrealism, for all its charms, was inappropriate in a world soon to be locked in a cataclysmic political struggle.

The Forties and Fifties: The White Style

World War II had a dramatic impact on the *Bazaar*. With the Nazi occupation of France in 1940, the Paris-based French fashion industry shut down almost completely. In the United States, the war effort was the first priority. Even the amount of fabric available for women's clothing was rationed by the government in order to insure adequate supplies for the military. Women, in the words of a *Bazaar* copywriter, had to "adjust [them]selves to ration cards, servantless houses, meatless Tuesdays, and manless everydays."[25]

Just how much the austerity of the war years influenced Brodovitch is not known, but by the beginning of his second decade at *Harper's Bazaar*, his layouts acquired an ever greater spareness and, because of it, a new sense of economy. Their most obvious feature is the use of white space. While the white, or "blank," areas—those parts of the layout without type, illustration, or photograph—were prominent even in his earliest designs (in his Bal Banal poster the "negative space" is as active as the "positive space"), now they became unmistakably the dominant feature.

Brodovitch used several techniques to achieve the "immaculate clarity" Diana Vreeland observed in his work. Often the fashion photographs were silhouet-

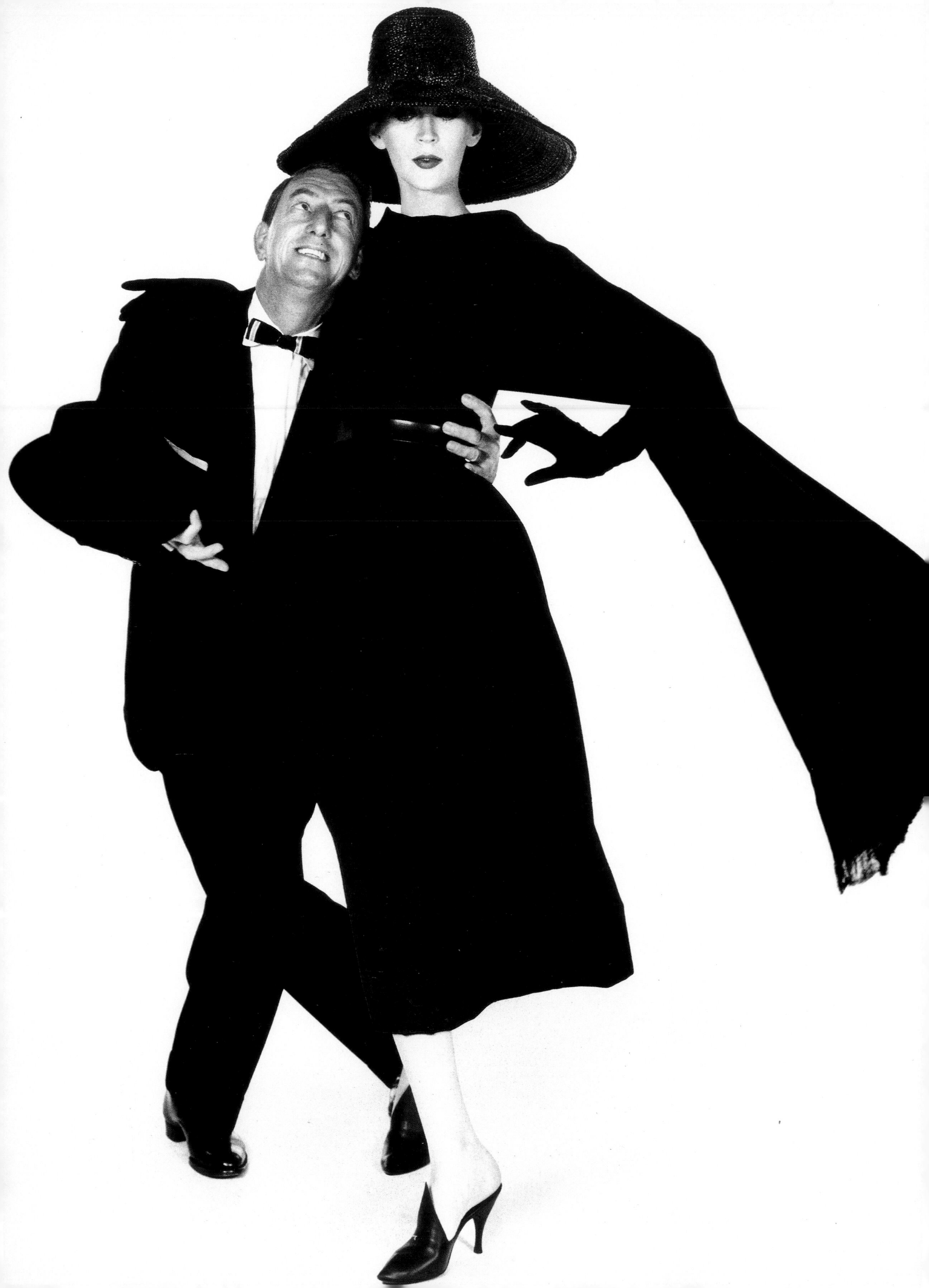

During the forties and fifties, Brodovitch largely forswore Surrealist illusionism, substituting a simplified, refined design rhetoric in its stead. No longer did he seek to give photographs graphic impact by cropping and tilting them radically, although he continued to exploit their formal relationships in the way he positioned them—and the accompanying copy—on the page. At the same time that Brodovitch's design began to verge on the transparent, the magazine began to merge the disparate domains of clothes and culture. The good-humored Avedon picture at left, showing actor Ray Bolger with the model Dovima, represents one of the first steps in the direction of conflating fashion, celebrity, and theater.

Opposite:
RICHARD AVEDON.
DOVIMA AND RAY BOLGER. 1957

This page, spreads from
HARPER'S BAZAAR,
clockwise from right:
NOVEMBER 1951.
PHOTOGRAPHER:
DERUJINSKY

SEPTEMBER 1956.
PHOTOGRAPHER: LOUISE
DAHL-WOLFE

SEPTEMBER 1952.
PHOTOGRAPHER:
DERUJINSKY

SEPTEMBER 1952.
PHOTOGRAPHER:
ERNST BEADLE

FEBRUARY 1957.
PHOTOGRAPHER:
RICHARD AVEDON

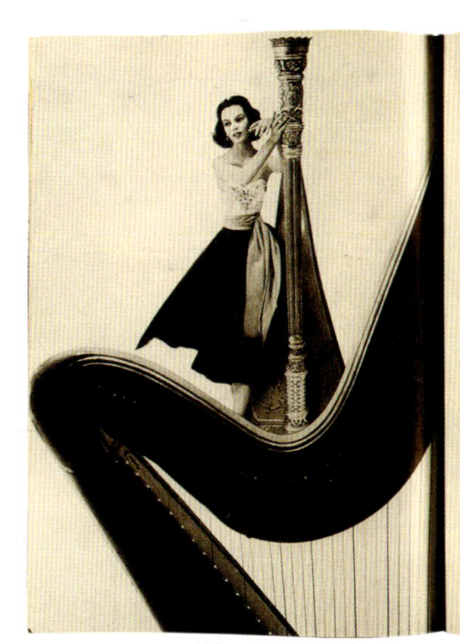

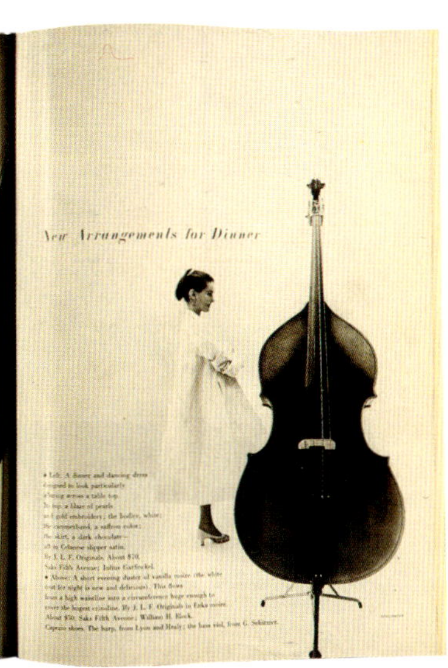

New Arrangements for Dinner

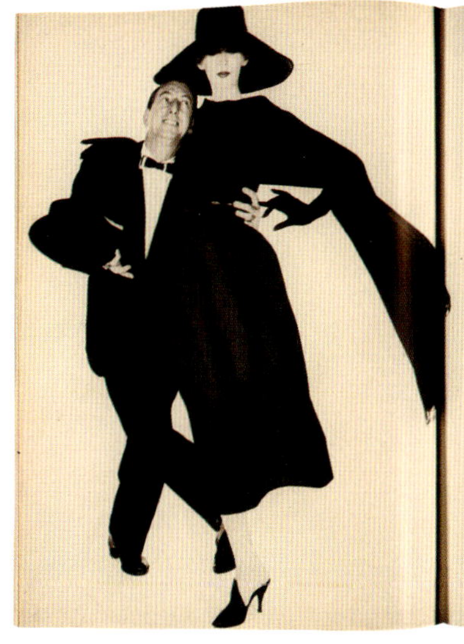

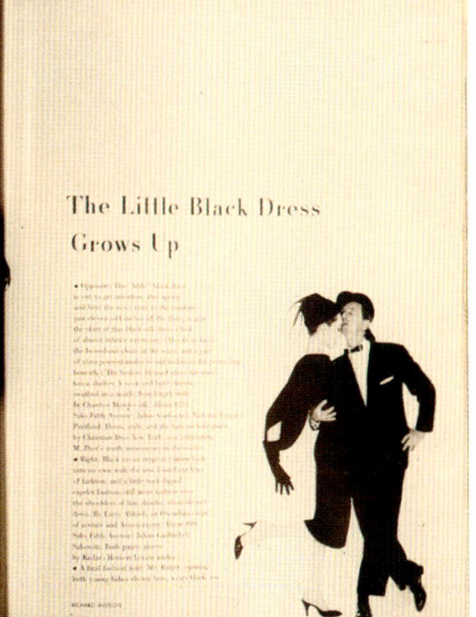

The Little Black Dress
Grows Up

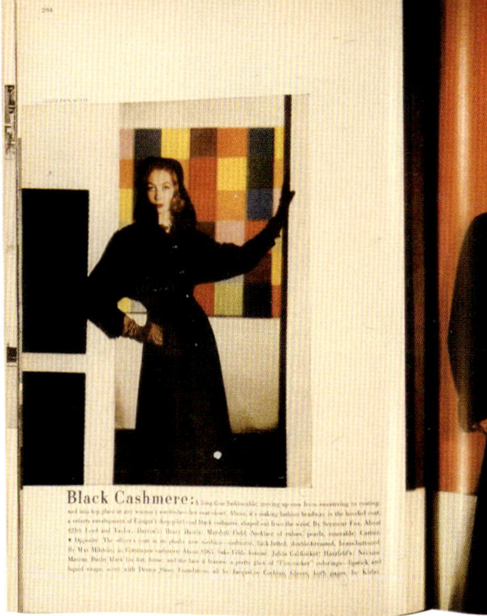

Black Cashmere:

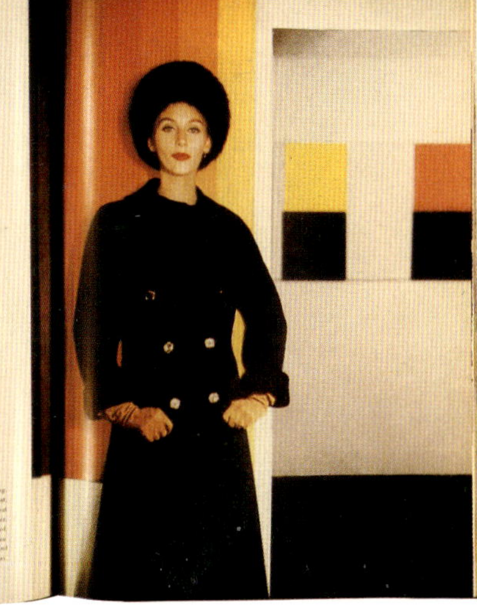

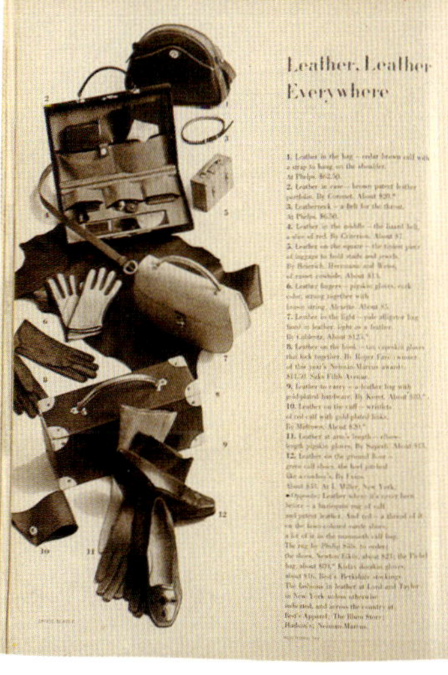

Leather, Leather
Everywhere

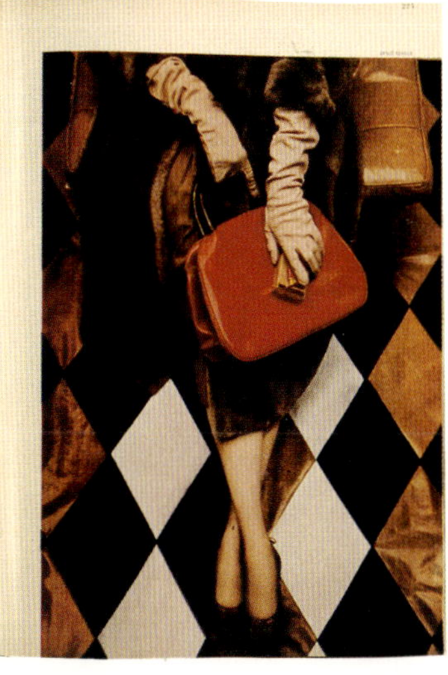

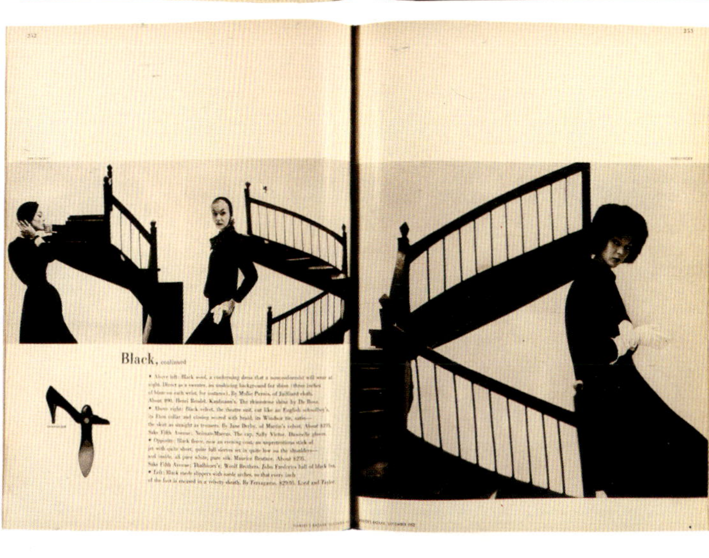

Black, continued

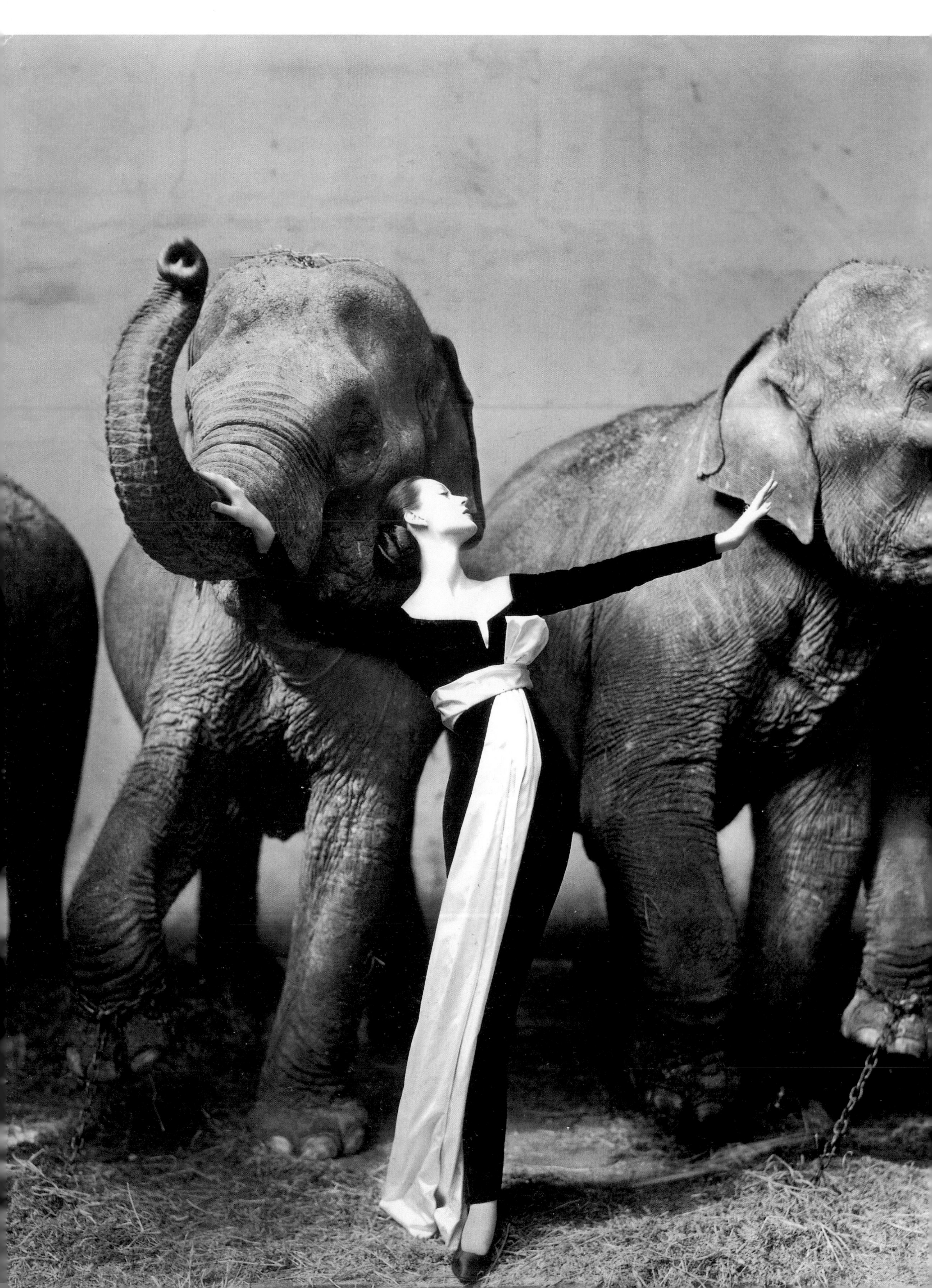

On-location fashion photography, pioneered by Munkacsi in the early thirties when studio photography was the norm, was used by Brodovitch throughout his career at *Harper's Bazaar*, with Carmel Snow's urging. As the designer's most obvious Surrealist devices faded in the postwar years, he encouraged photographers to find such surprising juxtapositions as the image at left. Taken by Richard Avedon in Paris, it shows the model Dovima striking a dancer's pose and wearing a Dior gown, in front of two circus elephants. The incongruity of the model's stately beauty and the elephants' earthy nonchalance gives the picture the kind of subliminal jolt that Brodovitch loved.

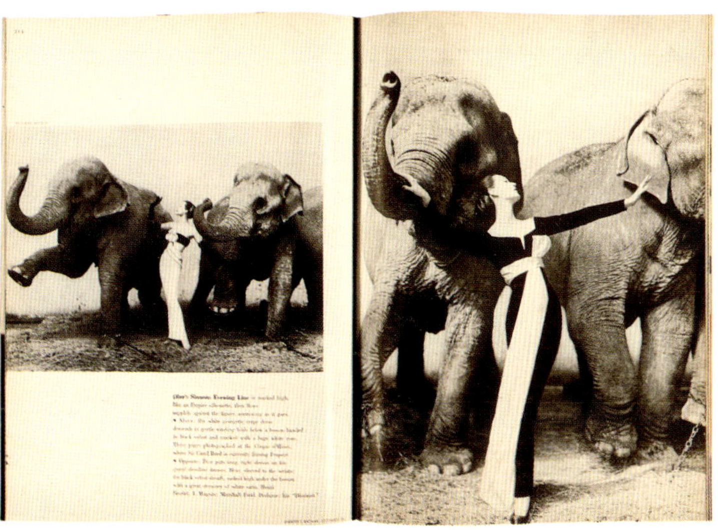

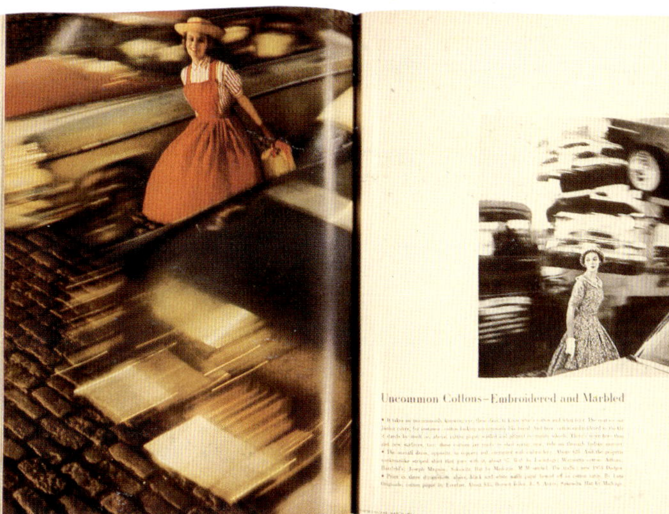

Uncommon Cottons—Embroidered and Marbled

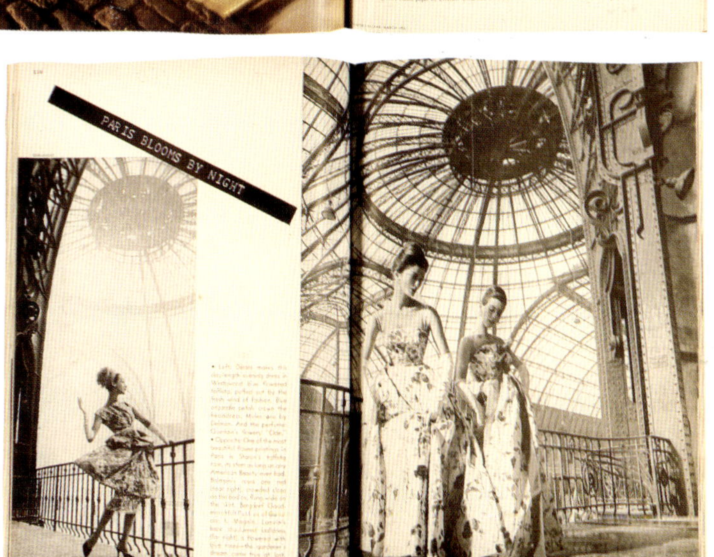

PARIS BLOOMS BY NIGHT

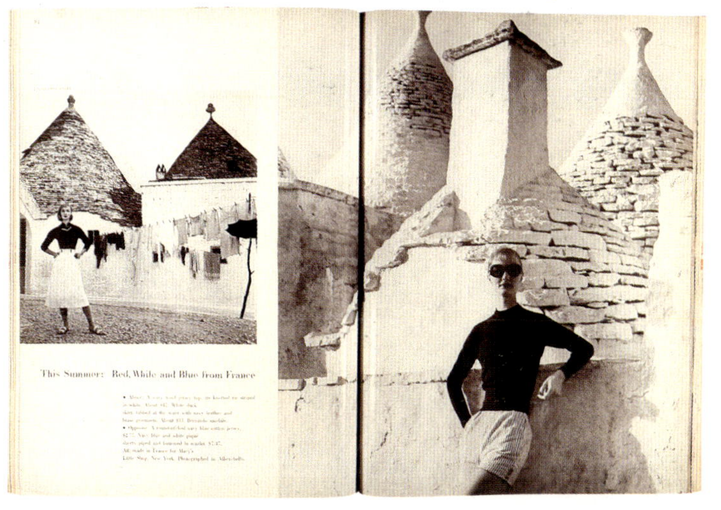

This Summer: Red, White and Blue from France

Opposite:
RICHARD AVEDON.
DOVIMA WITH ELEPHANTS.
EVENING DRESS BY YVES SAINT-LAURENT FOR THE HOUSE OF DIOR.
CIRQUE D'HIVER, PARIS.
AUGUST 1955

This page, spreads from
HARPER'S BAZAAR,
from top:
SEPTEMBER 1955. PHOTOGRAPHER: RICHARD AVEDON

MARCH 1955. PHOTOGRAPHER: DERUJINSKY

MARCH 1957. PHOTOGRAPHER: DERUJINSKY

MAY 1955.
PHOTOGRAPHER:
LOUISE DAHL-WOLFE

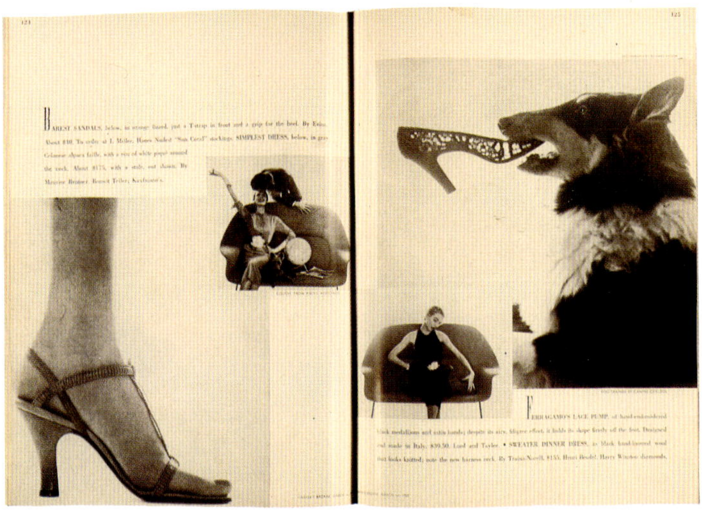

Like his counterparts at *Vogue* and other fashion magazines, Brodovitch constantly had to find new ways to present familiar subjects: cosmetics, perfumes, fabrics, and—perhaps the most mind-numbing in its repetitiveness—shoes. He often gave shoe assignments to students in his Design Laboratory classes to test their inventiveness; the photographer Hiro once labored for months to prove to Brodovitch that he could capture shoes in a way that was unprecedented. The designer, of course, had to "make it new" on the page. On these pages is a sampling of his layouts having to do with shoes, showing the range of his inventiveness.

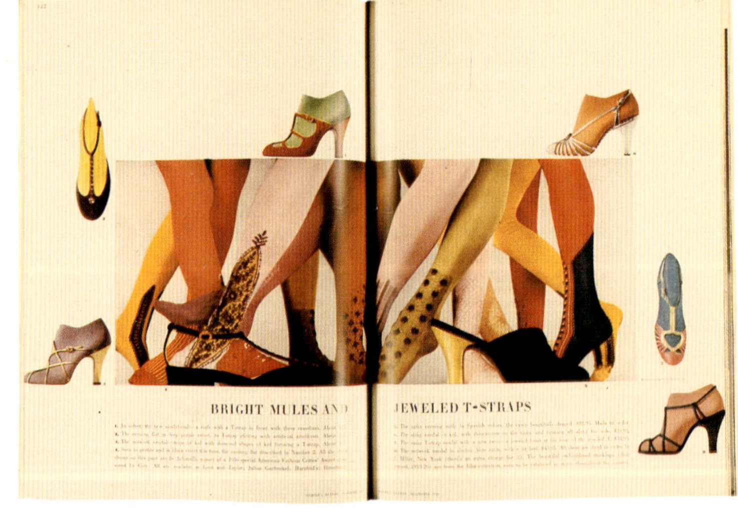

Spreads from HARPER'S BAZAAR, *clockwise from top:*
MARCH 1950.
PHOTOGRAPHER: RICHARD AVEDON

NOVEMBER 1950.
PHOTOGRAPHER: BEN ROSE

MARCH 1956. ILLUSTRATOR: ANDY WARHOL

DECEMBER 1956.
ILLUSTRATOR: THEA KLIROS

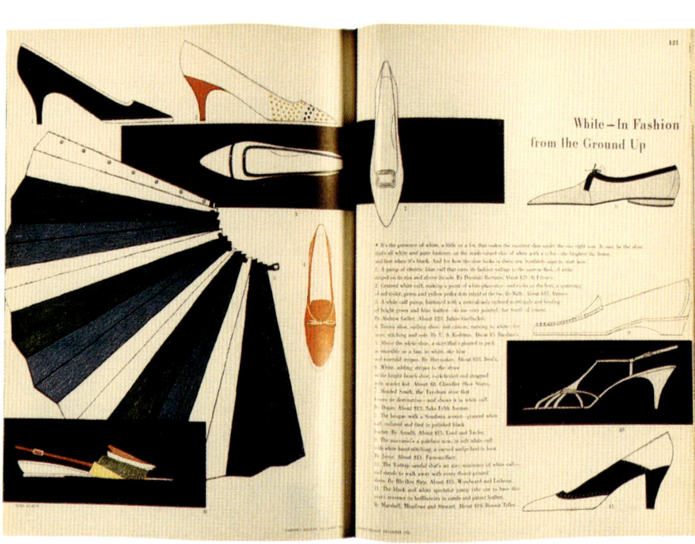

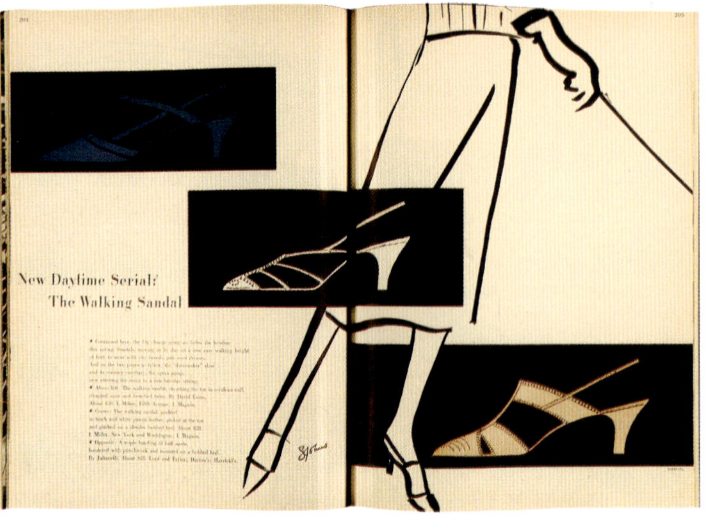

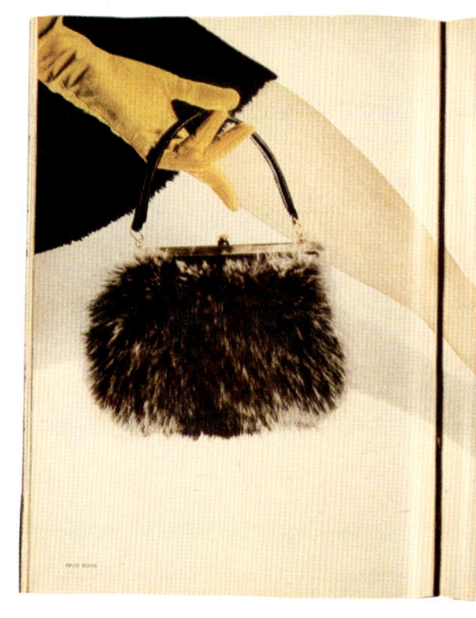

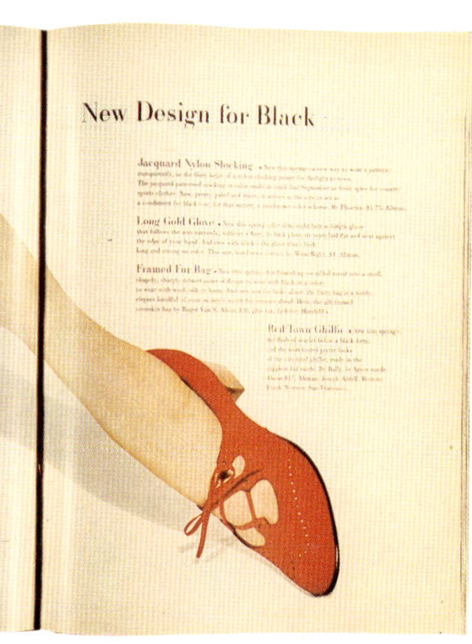

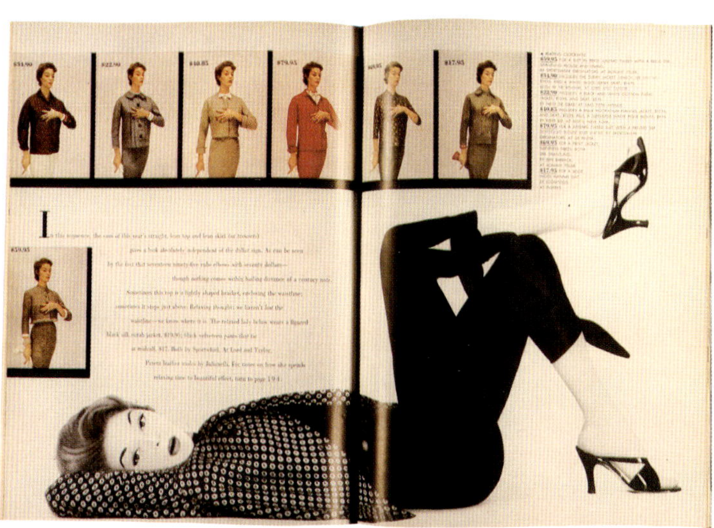

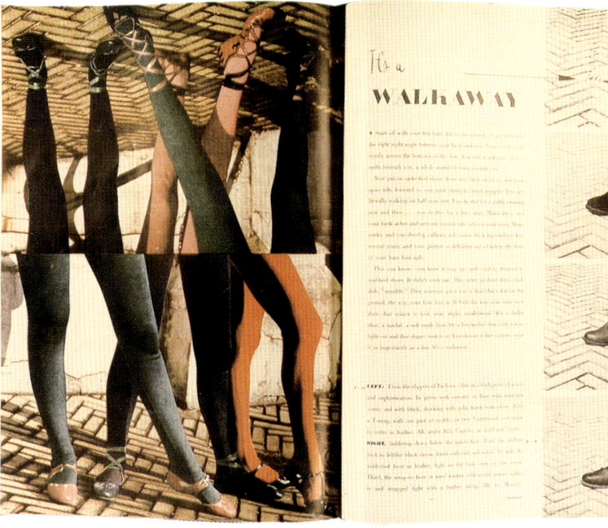

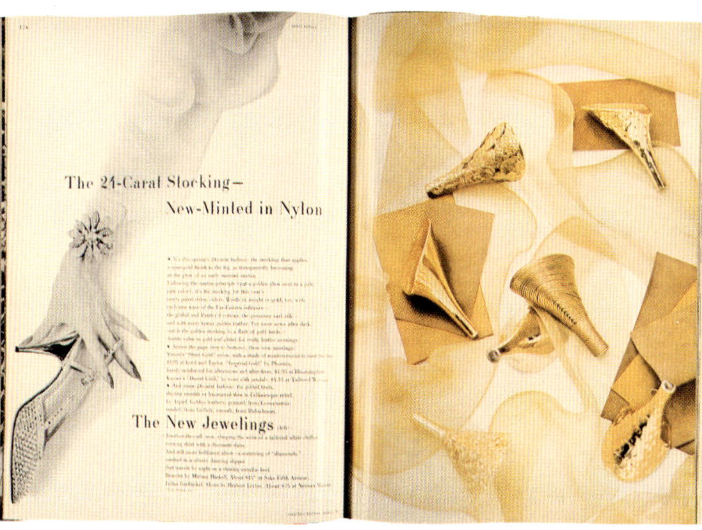

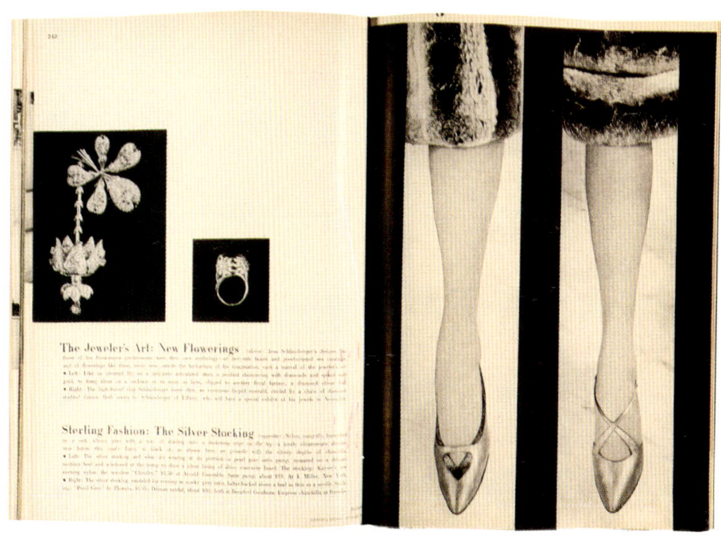

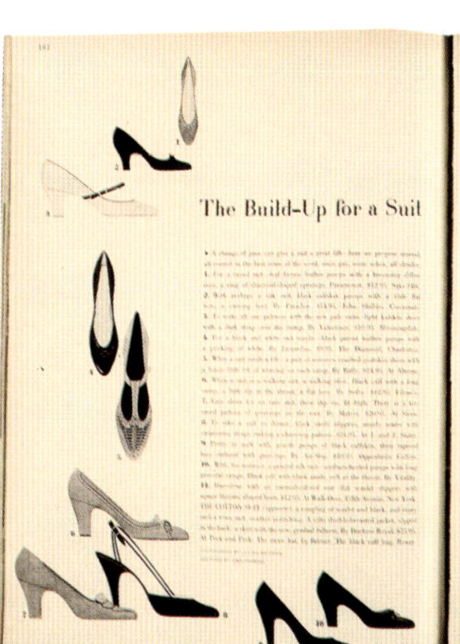

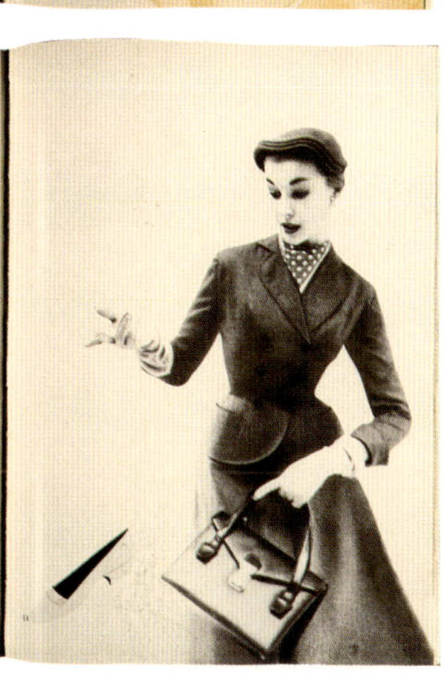

Spreads from HARPER'S BAZAAR, *clockwise from top right:* FEBRUARY 1955. PHOTOGRAPHER: ERNST BEADLE

AUGUST 1945. PHOTOGRAPHER: HERMAN LANDSHOFF

SEPTEMBER 1956. PHOTOGRAPHER: PELLEGRINO

FEBRUARY 1952. PHOTOGRAPHER: LILLIAN BASSMAN ILLUSTRATOR: ILMA HASKINS

MARCH 1956. PHOTOGRAPHER: ERNST BEADLE

FEBRUARY 1953. PHOTOGRAPHER: RICHARD AVEDON

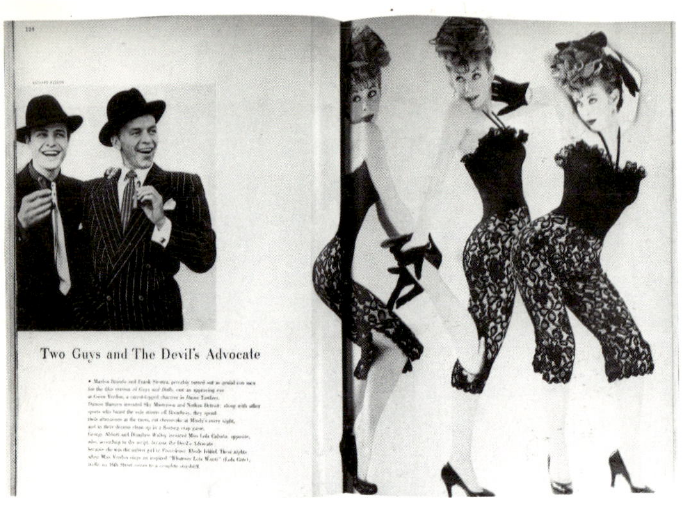
Two Guys and The Devil's Advocate

Above:
HARPER'S BAZAAR, AUGUST 1955. PHOTOGRAPHER: RICHARD AVEDON

Opposite:
HARPER'S BAZAAR, JANUARY 1946. PHOTOGRAPHER: RICHARD AVEDON

Right:
HARPER'S BAZAAR, AUGUST 1958. PHOTOGRAPHER: RICHARD AVEDON

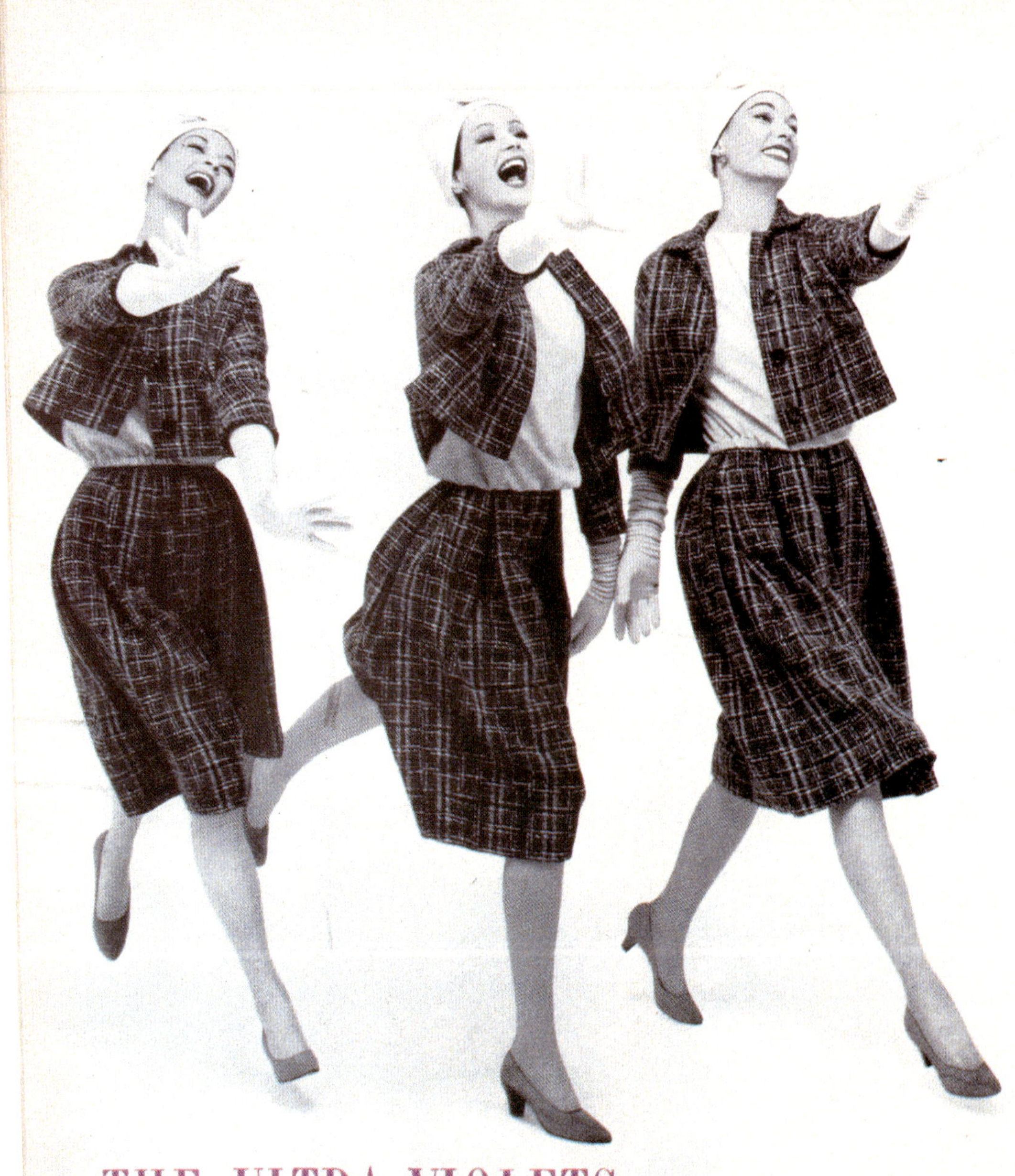
THE ULTRA VIOLETS

• Above: Nelly de Grab's wide swath of flecked Strong Hewat wool (a mix of violet with green, red, white) may be taken in part (the jacket, about $23, the skirt, about $25, and the beige wool overblouse for about $15), but we prefer the look of the whole, which is about $63. At Bloomingdale's; R. H. Stearns, Boston; Stix, Baer and Fuller, St. Louis.

• Opposite: Towncliffe has shaped magenta tweed into a particularly able exposition of the blouson-jacket suit, holds the waistline with elastic. At Bloomingdale's: Kaufmann's, Pittsburgh; Dayton's, Minneapolis; I. Magnin. About $80. Stockings, Van Raalte. Shoes, I. Miller. Madcaps hats, opposite and above, at Bloomingdale's.

RICHARD AVEDON

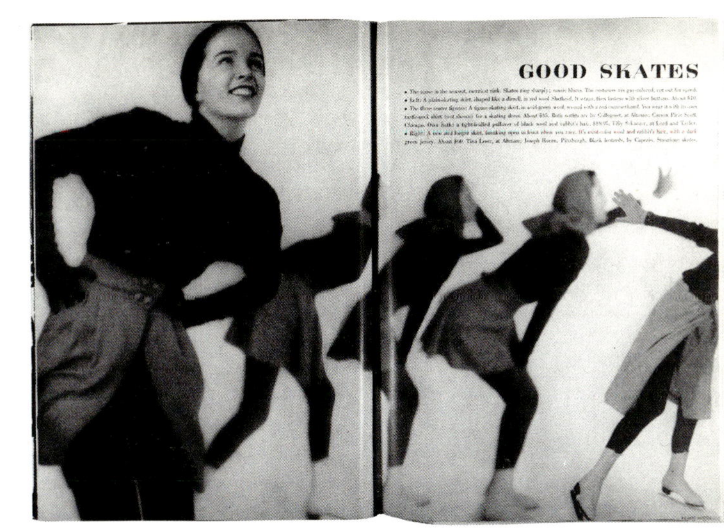

GOOD SKATES

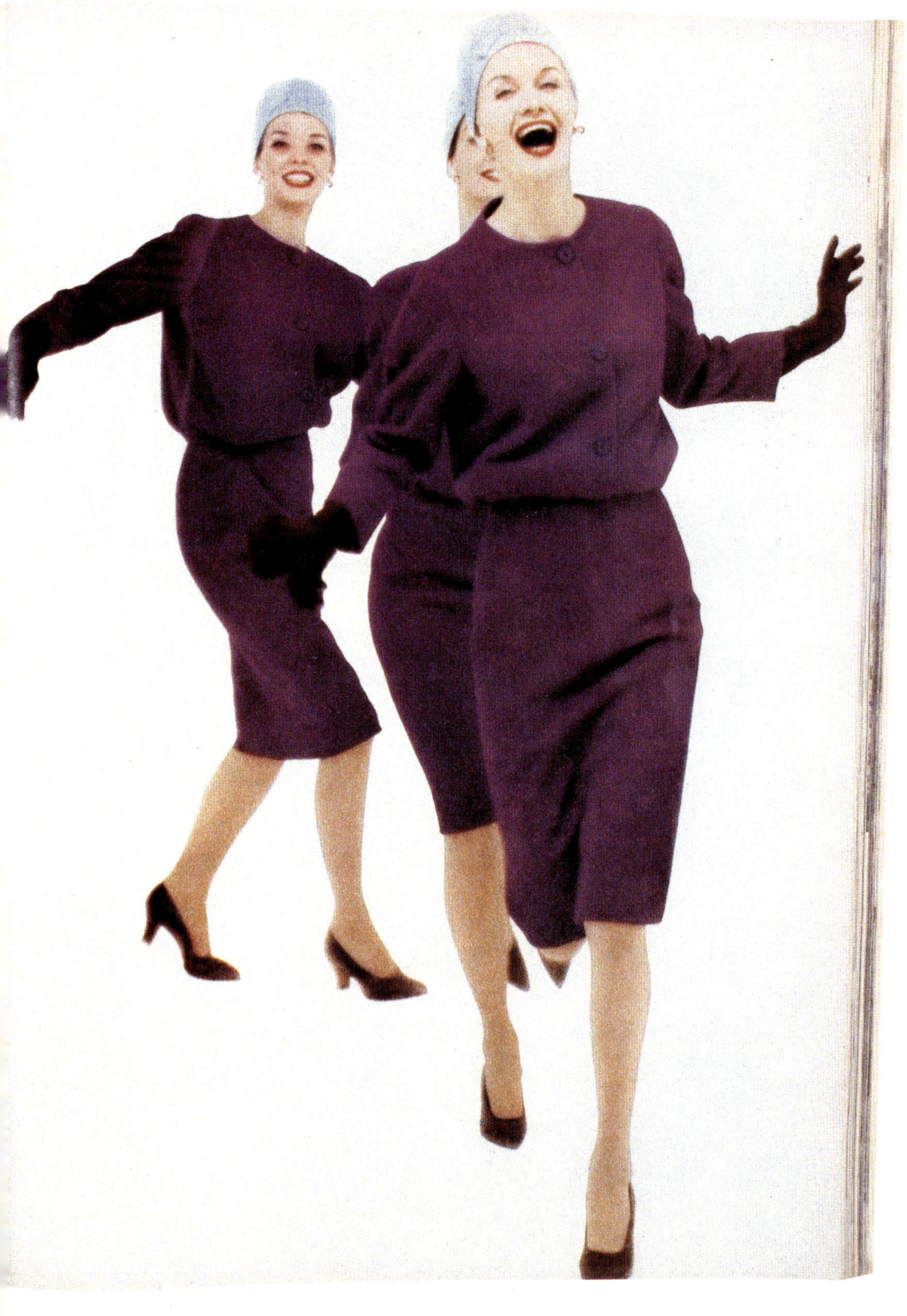

Brodovitch often used photographs as if they were frames in a film, repeating a pose or dress several times across the page to create a narrative, temporal feeling. Most of the time he achieved this cinematic effect by silhouetting individual photographs and re-combining them in the manner of photomontage (upper left and right). But in the case of "The Ultra Violets," he simply used Avedon's pictures straight. The replication of the dresses, worn by three similar-looking models, undercuts the magazine's usual message that every fashionable woman is an individual by virtue of her clothes. But since this entire issue of the *Bazaar* is full of such duplications, the editors must not have objected to the contradictions.

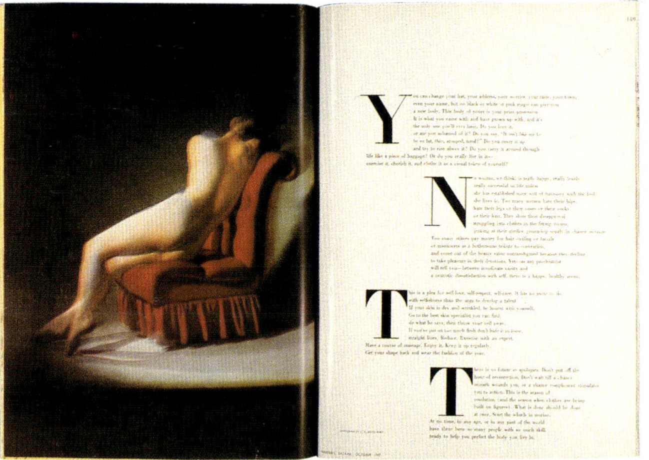

Left:
HARPER'S BAZAAR, OCTOBER 1947. PHOTOGRAPHER: E.P. REVES-BIRO

Opposite:
LILLIAN BASSMAN. *CARMEN MODELING A MERRY WIDOW*. c. 1949–51

ted, and then arranged across the all-white background of the page, like uncut paper dolls. But increasingly he relied on the photograph itself to provide the white, open feeling of his layouts. Starting in 1945, Brodovitch took advantage of the high-key, white backgrounds of Richard Avedon's pictures by bleeding them off the page on all sides. The text and captions were surprinted on the photographic backgrounds, where they appeared to be floating in empty space. With this apparently simple step, Brodovitch effectively merged the photograph into the magazine page itself, and reconciled it with his love of white space.

Scale and proportion are important in all of Brodovitch's layouts, but especially so when photographs are the primary visual elements on the page, as they are in the *Bazaar* of the late 1940s and fifties. He frequently paired pictures on a spread so that a large reproduction faced a small one. Usually the two sizes interact visually in a way that contradicts the scale of their subjects. He also would create a rhythm using similarly sized images—the silhouetted figure of a model jumping, for example—and then break it with the inclusion of a much larger figure. By changing sizes of reproductions and of the figures within them, he kept the reader off guard, trying to reconcile a variety of visual stimuli. If the method was not always unpredictable, the results were; Brodovitch in effect invented a new way of designing the page, in which the photograph and the page itself are interactive and synergistic.

What might be called Brodovitch's "white style" was accompanied by a new fondness on his part for blurry and out-of-focus photographs. While photographers such as Munkacsi, with his penchant for action, had earlier pointed the way, it was not until Brodovitch installed Richard Avedon as a major star in the firmament of the *Bazaar*, beginning in 1945, that he gave full vent to his taste for pictures that left practically everything to the imagination. For the rest of his years at the magazine, he encouraged photographers to abandon their traditional reliance on description and detail, in the name of creating more suggestive, impressionistic renditions.

For Brodovitch, the preference for blurred, action-filled photographs was a natural outgrowth of his own photography, as seen in his 1945 book *Ballet*. What seems unnatural is that Snow, and the *Bazaar*'s management, would allow him to use photographs that failed to show the models' clothes in any detail. But this presumes that they wanted the clothes to be shown clearly. In fact, it would appear that often they did not. When there were no clothes from Paris, and only inferior American designs to feature, the theory was that the less shown, the better. But there is another reason why Brodovitch could fill the *Bazaar* with unclear pictures of the latest fashions—a reason that explains why this design "strategy" lasted far beyond the postwar recovery: the clothes themselves were no longer the primary determinant of fashion. The emphasis of the fashion magazines had shifted from clothing to the image—or, to use today's less-than-felicitous term, life-style—of the fashionable woman, and this image specifically celebrated an attitude of freedom and spontaneity. The out-of-focus images of Avedon, as well as Herman Landshoff, Lillian Bassman, Karen and Paul Radkai, and others who worked regularly for the magazine, managed to suggest freedom and spontaneity even when their subject matter was corsetry. ■

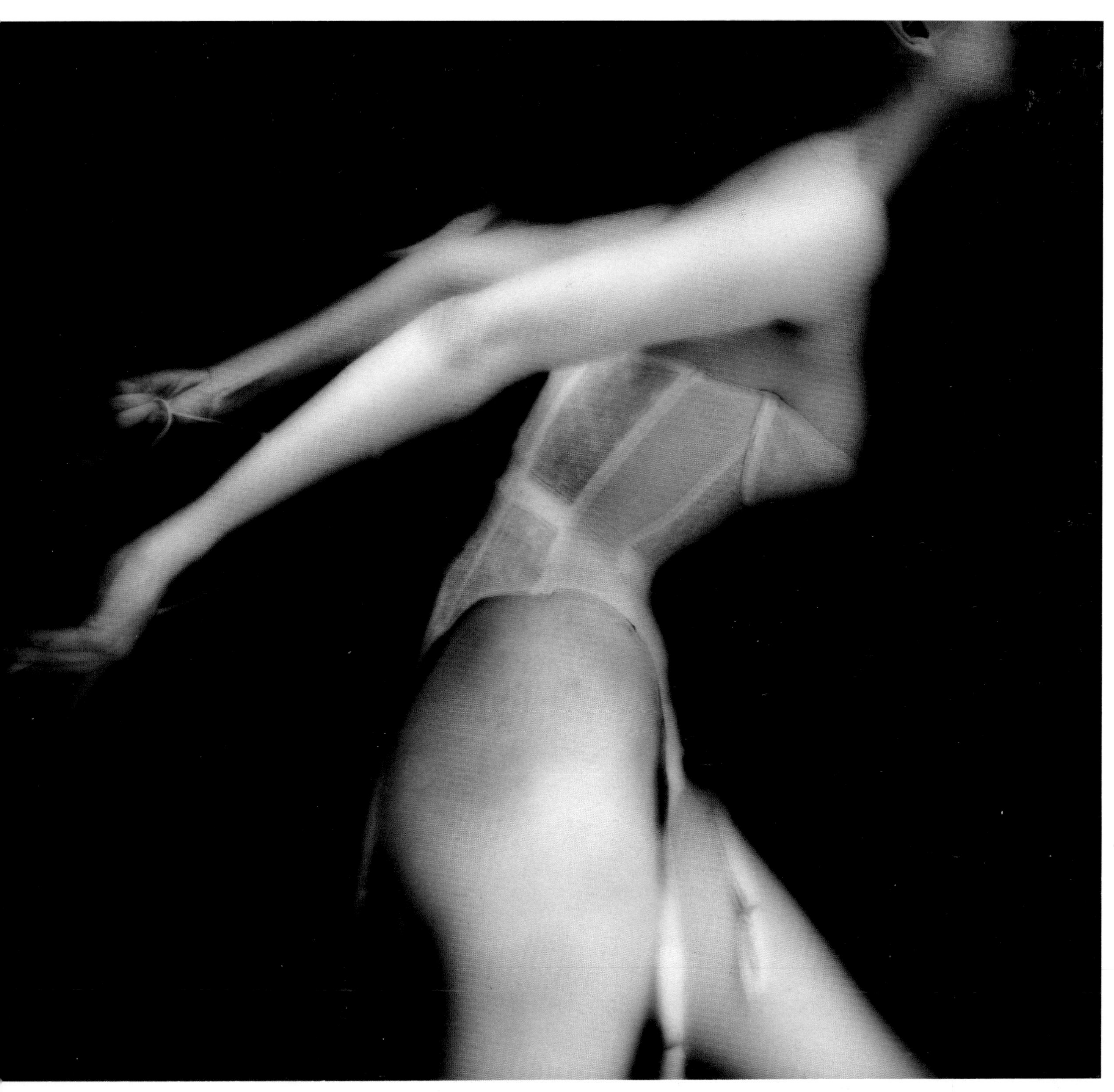

In Focus:
PORTFOLIO

The graphic-arts quarterly *Portfolio* lasted only three issues, but it has acquired legendary status among graphic designers. Brodovitch, its art director and art editor, worked on the magazine in 1949 and 1950, while he also was designing *Harper's Bazaar.* Momentarily freed from the practical and aesthetic restraints to which he had grown accustomed, he responded with a breathtaking design. He promoted features devoted to respected artists and designers (Saul Steinberg, Alexander Calder, Giambattista Bodoni), as well as articles on vernacular design (shopping bags, cattle brands), and he made layouts for them that are paradigms of imaginative, resourceful design. On the pages of *Portfolio*, Brodovitch demonstrated the assurance of a designer at the peak of his career. *Portfolio* encompassed a range of both subject matter and design styles, providing evidence not only of Brodovitch's broad taste and versatility as a designer, but also of the non-hierarchical way in which he treated visual material. For him, the difference between an Alexander Calder mobile and an image recorded by a Xerox machine was primarily one of sensibility, not of kind. He especially was sensitive to symbolic representations and typefaces, from Japanese calligraphy to Apollinaire's concrete poem "Il Pleut."

THREE SPREADS SHOWING THE NOTEBOOKS OF SAUL STEINBERG, *PORTFOLIO*, NO.1 (1950)

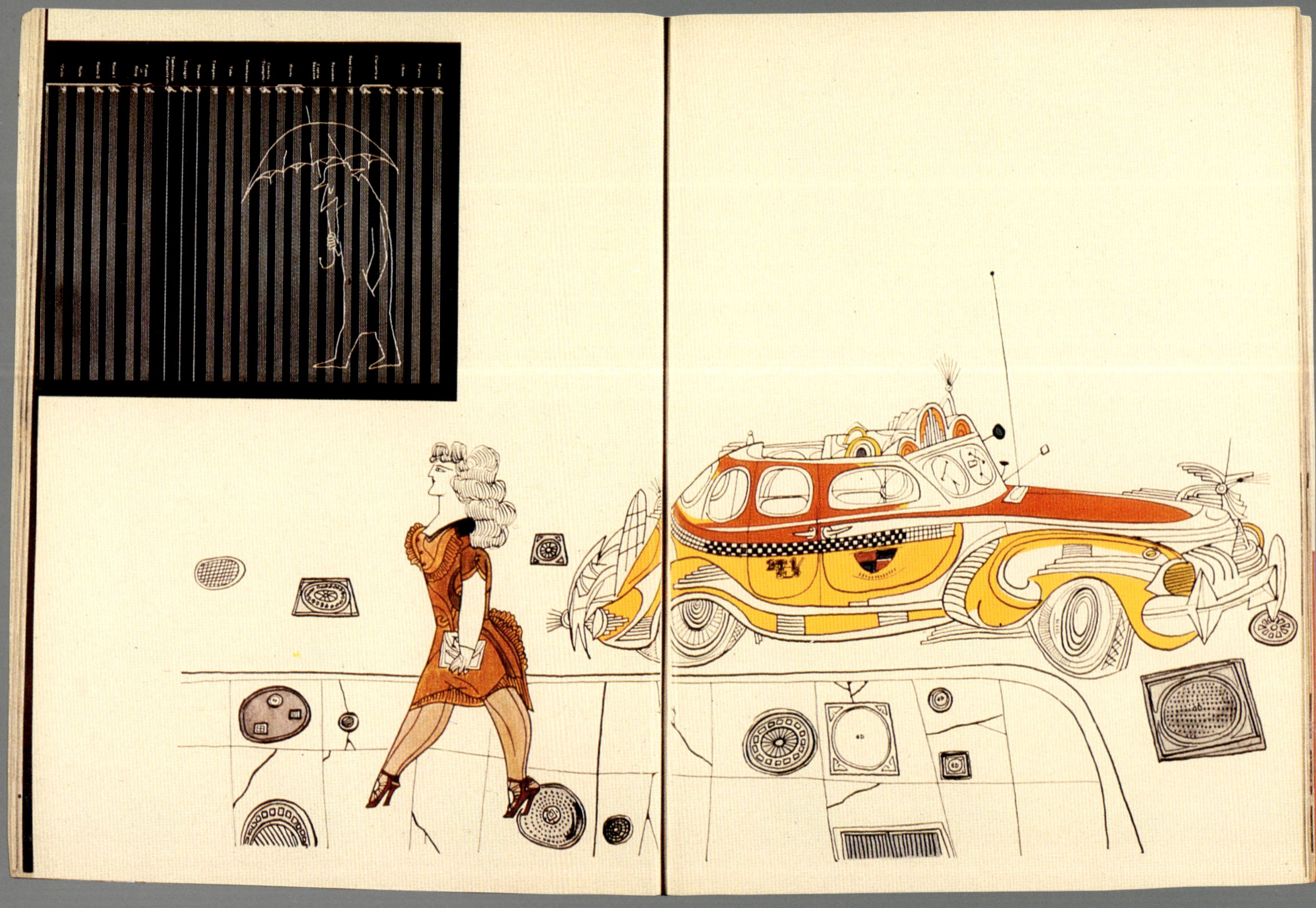

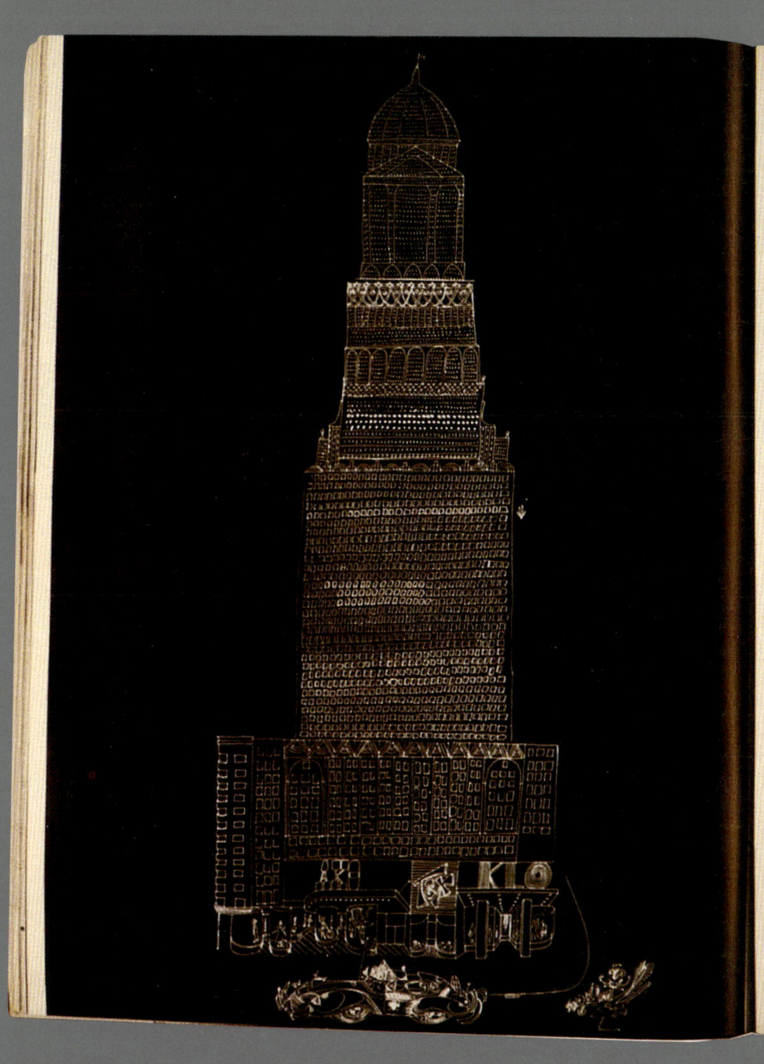

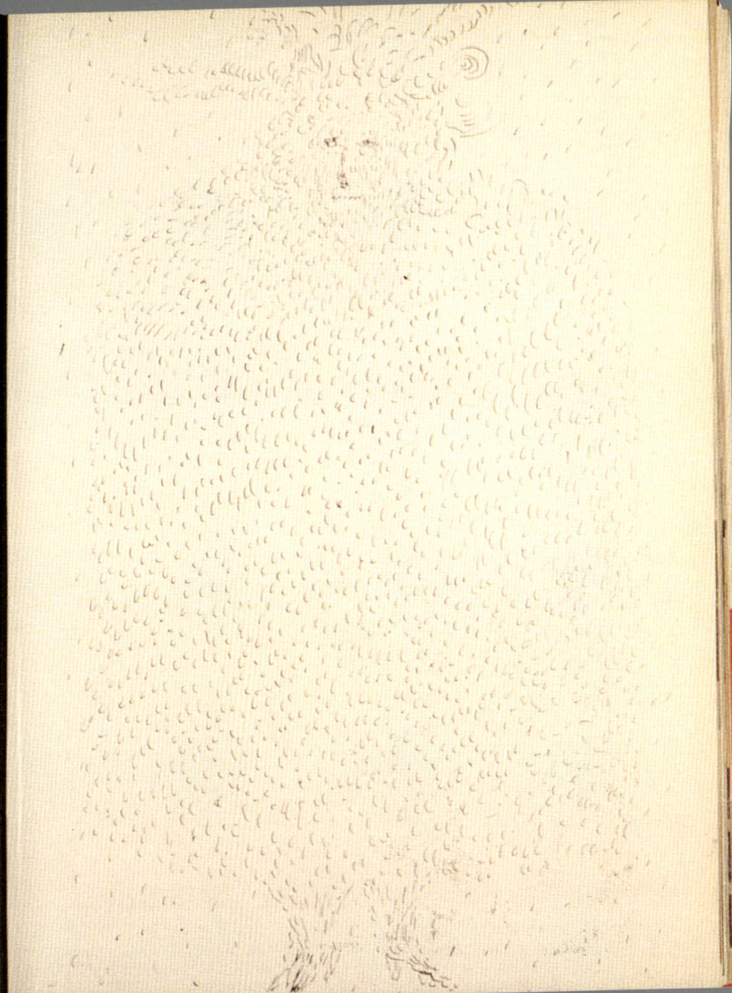

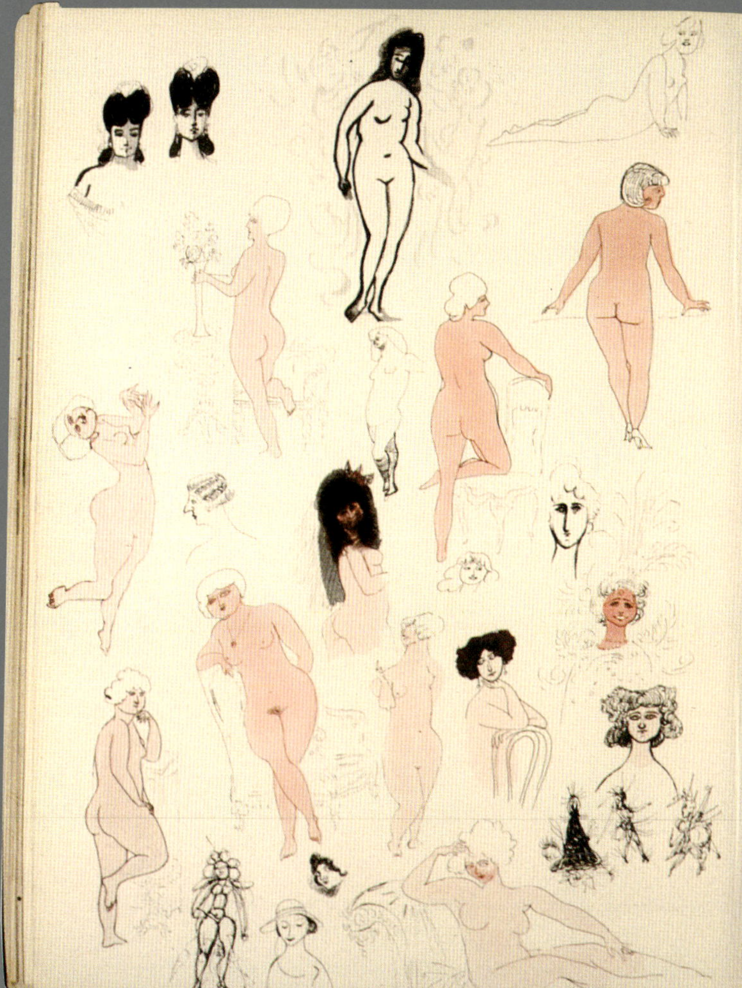

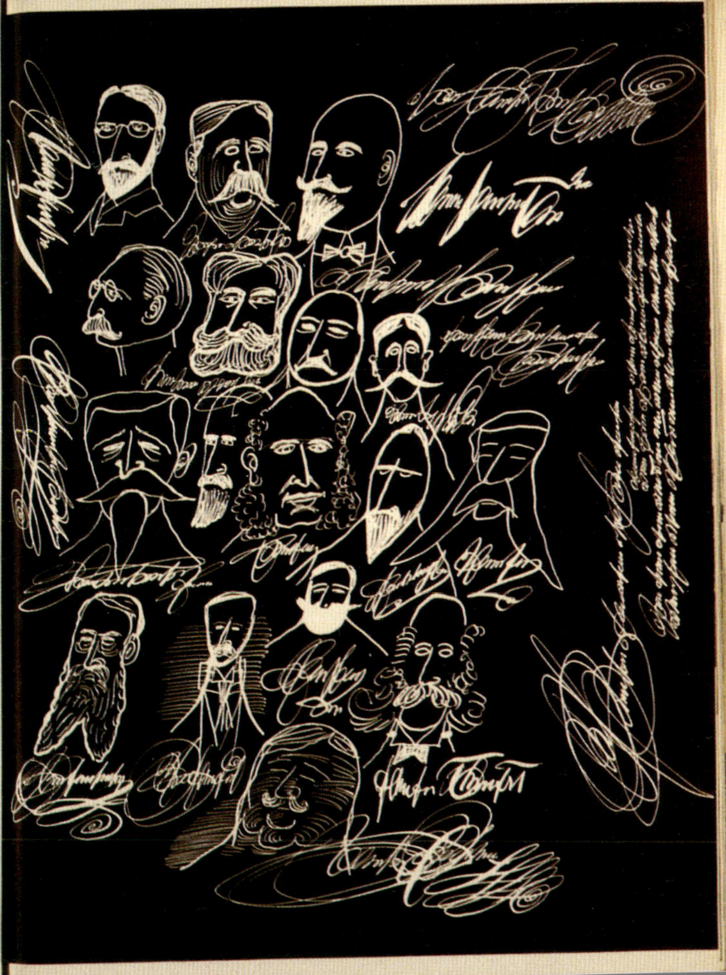

These and the following pages:
SPREADS FROM *PORTFOLIO*,
NOS. 1, 2, AND 3 (1950–51)

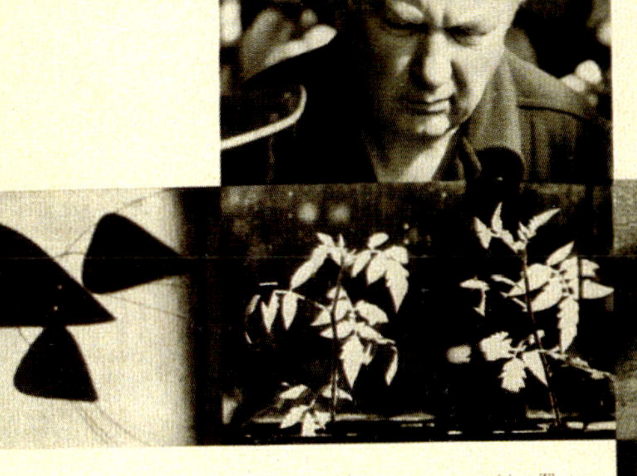

rod, but at the outermost extremities. That is the only way he can achieve the delicate balance on which the mobile depends. The necessity of achieving this balance also dictates the shape, size and weight of the counterpieces, so he cannot possibly tell when he starts exactly what the construction will look like when he is finished. This is like making a dog by starting with its tail.

Some mobiles look so complicated that a lady once asked Sandy if he would guarantee to service it after she bought it. Actually they are exceptionally sturdy, being based on sound engineering principles. A couple once had one—a flimsy looking thing made of wire and metal leaves—on the lawn of their home on Long Island. A hurricane came along, tore branches from oak trees a century old and wrecked the house. But when they went out to inspect the damage, they found the mobile, still upright, rotating languidly and uttering tinkling sounds.

The pristine quality of Calder's art is never liable to be spoiled by intellectualism or too much education. His friend Herbert Matter claims he is the most unintellectual artist he has ever met. Despite this—or be-

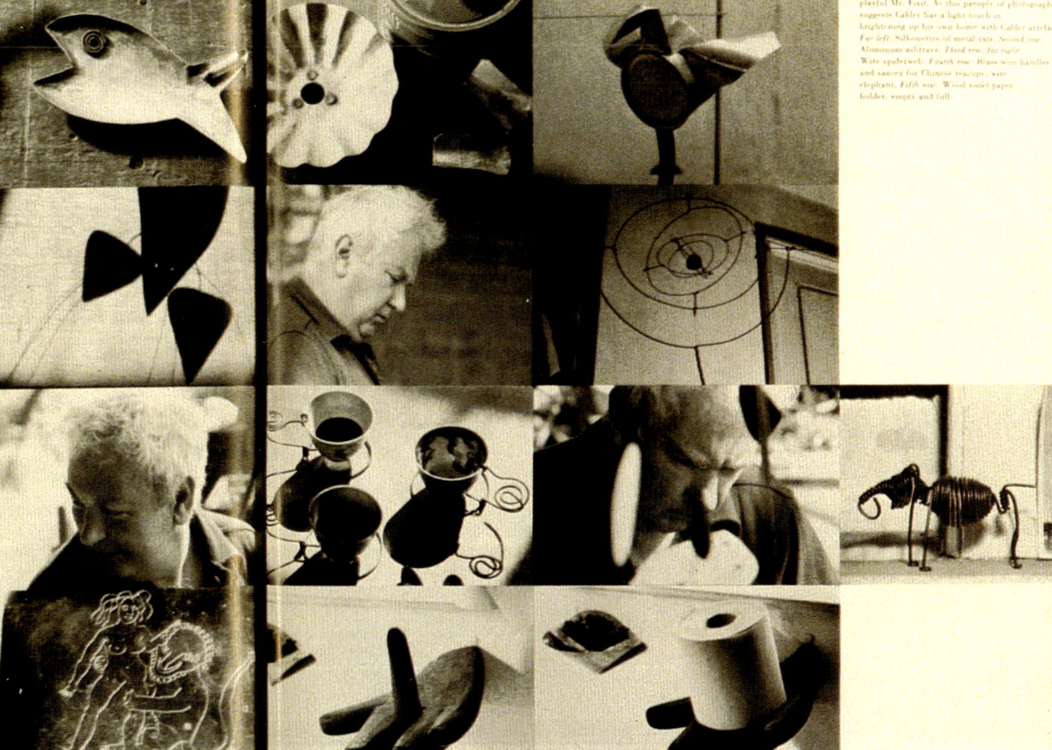

A faint line divides Calder the artist and Calder the playful Mr. Fixit. As this panoply of photographs suggests Calder has a light touch in brightening up his own home with Calder artefacts. *Far left:* Silhouettes of metal cats. *Second row:* Aluminum ashtrays. *Third row, far right:* Wire spiderweb. *Fourth row:* Brass wire handles and saucer for Chinese teacups; wire elephant. *Fifth row:* Wood toilet paper holder, empty and full.

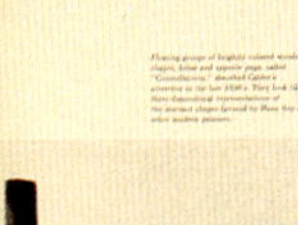

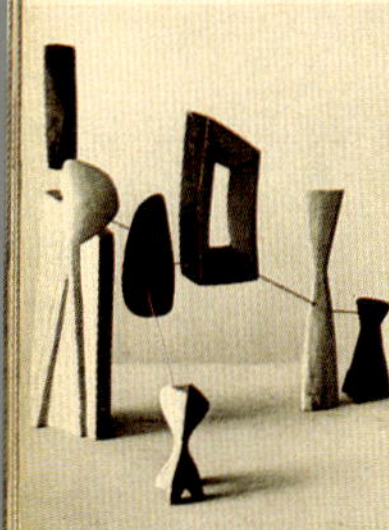

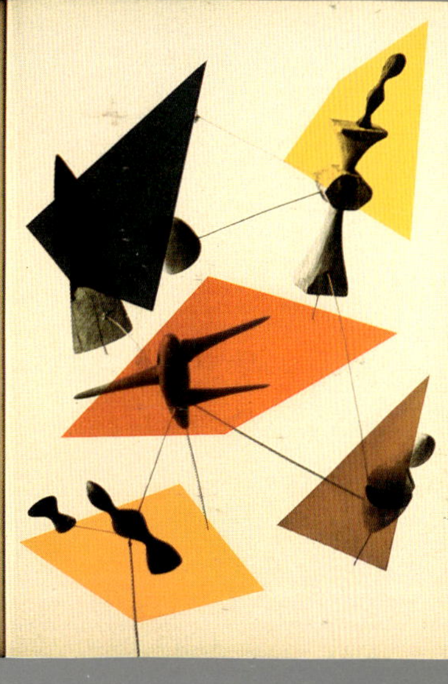

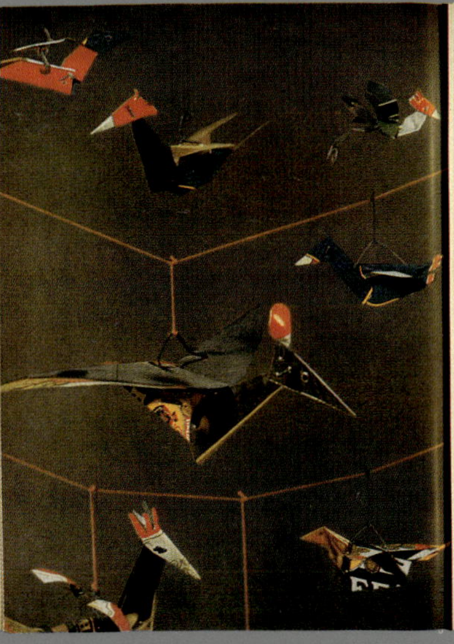

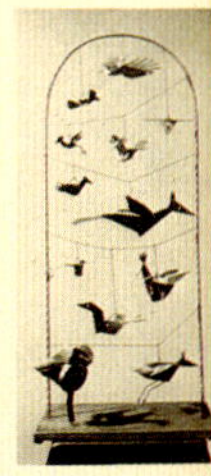

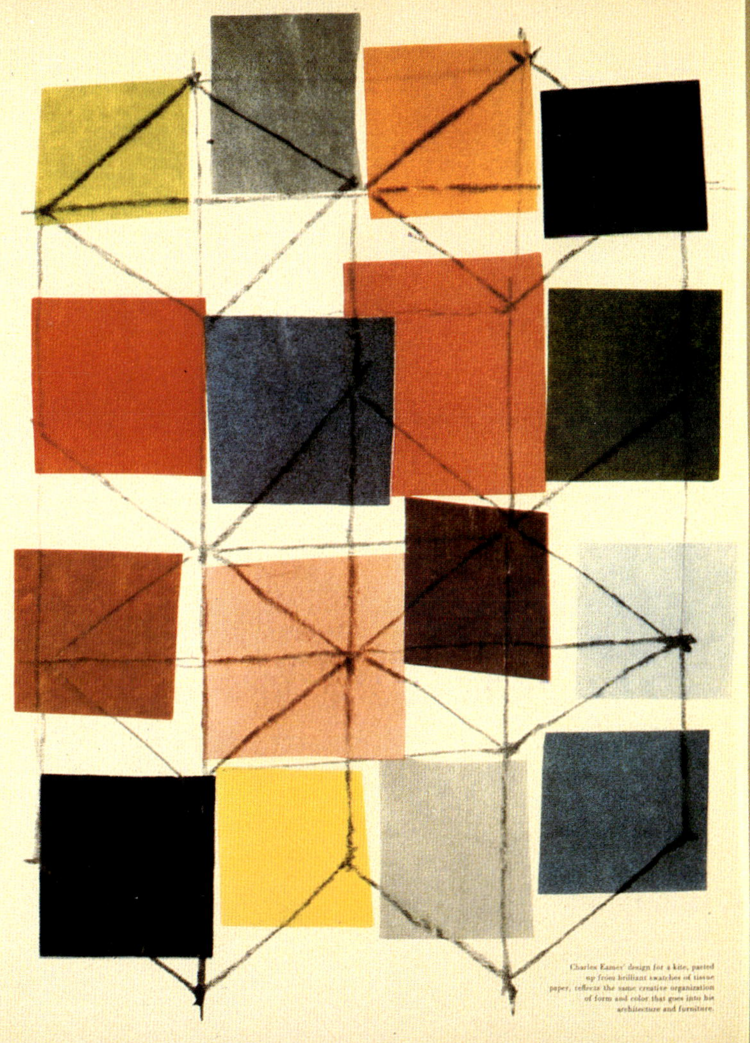

Charles Eames' design for a kite, pasted up from brilliant swatches of tissue paper, reflects the same creative organization of form and color that goes into his architecture and furniture.

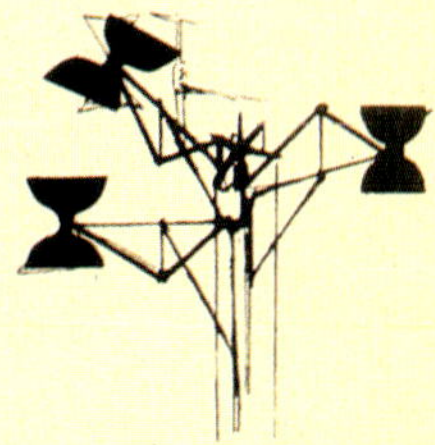

or accident, but previously nourished from many sources. In a strong individualist like Eames this sense of the value of eclecticism, of the combined wisdom and talents of a group, is somewhat unusual. He is more cooperative than many professional and theoretical co-operators, and has a great willingness to share and to accept ideas. Eames speaks more of "we" than "I", and is associated with a group activity unusual in both the business and the artists' world—a concept which borrows practically and consciously from the work shops and Guild concept of the Italian period when art seemed a more vital force in human lives.

The Eames' own house, built on the bluffs above the ocean in Santa Monica, is an unusual, but practical structure of steel and glass, with walls seventeen feet high. One side of Eames' house is, in the very descriptive words of Edgar Kaufmann, Jr., of the Museum of Modern Art, "a papery screen of factory sash and glass and transite combined with a neatness and gaiety that recalls the translucent membranes and reinforcing ribs of a young leaf". In designing the house Charles and Ray put themselves on record as having a passion for uncluttered space and breathing areas, and their desire to have a home that did not, like all too many homes, sit about like a fat idiot child and demand to be waited on. In describing the basic concept for the house, Eames said that they were "determined on the right and the necessity of privacy. To choose privacy from one another and anyone else." (With sound common sense, Eames considers two bathrooms for two people one of the secrets of a happy marriage.) "Basically apartment dwellers," he continues, "there is a conscious effort made to be free of complications relating to maintenance. The house must make no insistent demands of itself, but rather aid as a background for life in work, and as re-orientator and shock-absorber." The rather legal stiffness of this language (which may have been the sort of thing that gave rise to *Time*'s misleading description of "solemn, earnest, Charles Eames") is a thousand light years away from the true nature of Eames himself. Both Charles and Ray are people of more than considerable charm and humor and are without affectation or pomposity. More characteristic of the Eameses are the gay and

Lighting installations designed by Charles Eames, reproduced from his pencil drawings.

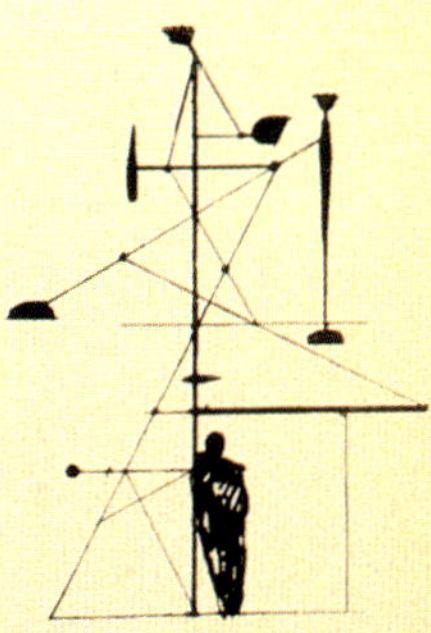

Molded plywood splint which Charles Eames developed for the U. S. Navy (*right*), and molded plywood parts for a child's chair shown stacked in the factory (*center*), have the plastic beauty of form that distinguishes the abstract plywood sculpture (*opposite page*) constructed by Charles' wife, Ray, with the same molding technique.

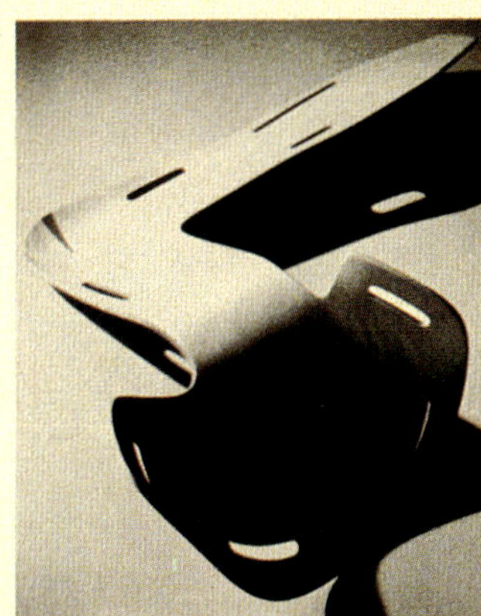

and Matthison of Finland and Sweden preceded the Eames chair, and the variety of modern plywood chairs today is infinite and confusing. But Eames has produced a chair that is unique in its beauty and in the mode of its manufacture. Eames' process of making furniture has been termed revolutionary in the sense that it has made possible the *molding* of plywood into involuted forms much as metal is stamped into shapes in industrial processes. To achieve this result, Eames has had to develop his own plastic binder and has created the machines that will press the plywood into the desired shape without shattering it. Briefly the process consists of taking the several laminations of wood individually as flat, thin sheets; cutting them into the required shape and laying them one atop the other, their wood grain running in opposite directions for greater strength, with the plastic binder sandwiched between each ply of wood. The whole is set onto the

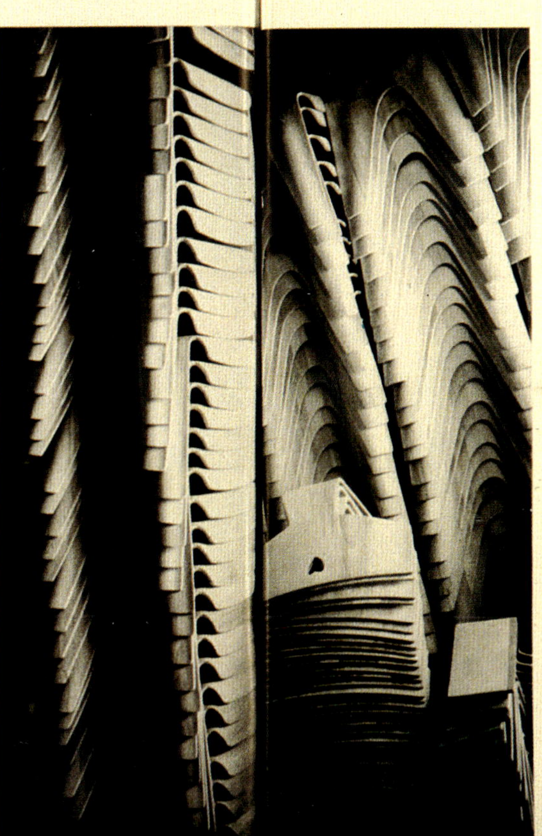

matrix and is slowly pressed into the shape by an inflatable rubber member. The use of compressed air, which inflates the rubber and presses the plywood gently into the mould, makes a process slow enough to bend the wood into multiple and opposing curves without breaking it. While the pressure is molding the wood, heat coils embedded into the rubber heat it to the point where the plastic binder fuses the plys and forms an almost impervious surface. The seat, legs, and back of the chair are joined to each other by rubber pads which give the structure a feeling of living mobility. The process involved in *this* fusing of member to member savors somewhat of electrocution, but with the end result more like that of horticultural grafting.

The basic Eames chair, which resembles somewhat a tough and graceful water lily pad with a formal bud on a stout stem, is pleasing because the shape is arrived at through the materials and processes in a natural manner. It has

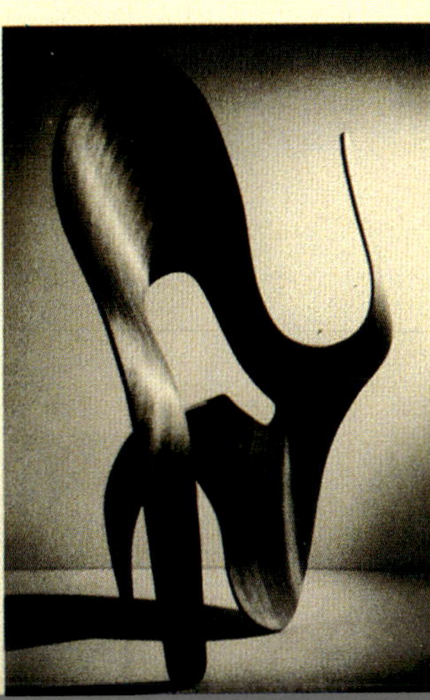

A la lueur de la guerre
Au refus des condamnés
Toutes les prisons de verre
L'Amour les a refermées

Pierre Reverdy, Le Chant des Morts,
with illustrations by Pablo Picasso.
Teriade, Paris, France, 1948
Courtesy Pierre Berès, Inc.

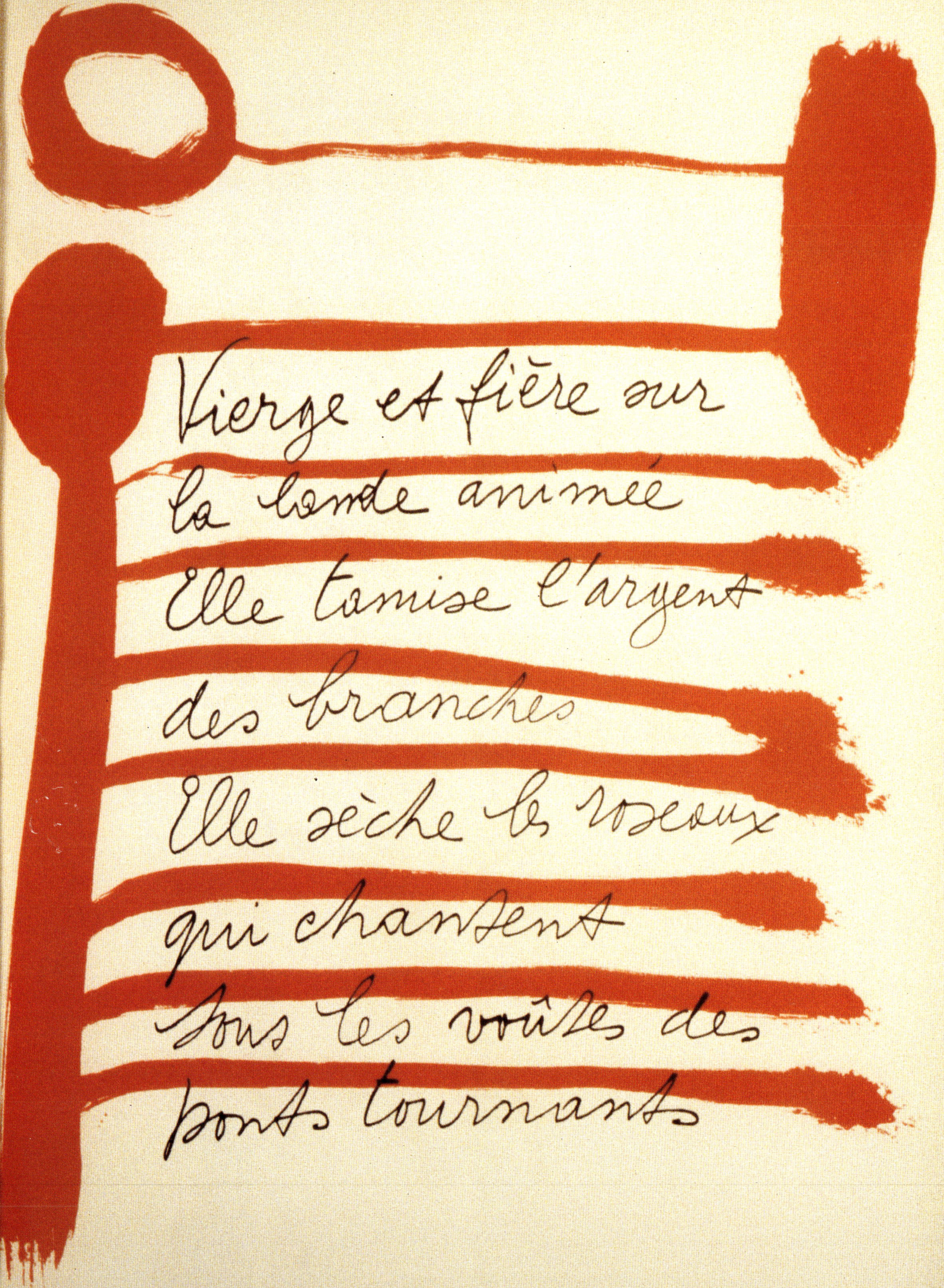

Vierge et fière sur
la lande animée
Elle tamise l'argent
des branches
Elle sèche les roseaux
qui chantent
Sous les voûtes des
ponts tournants

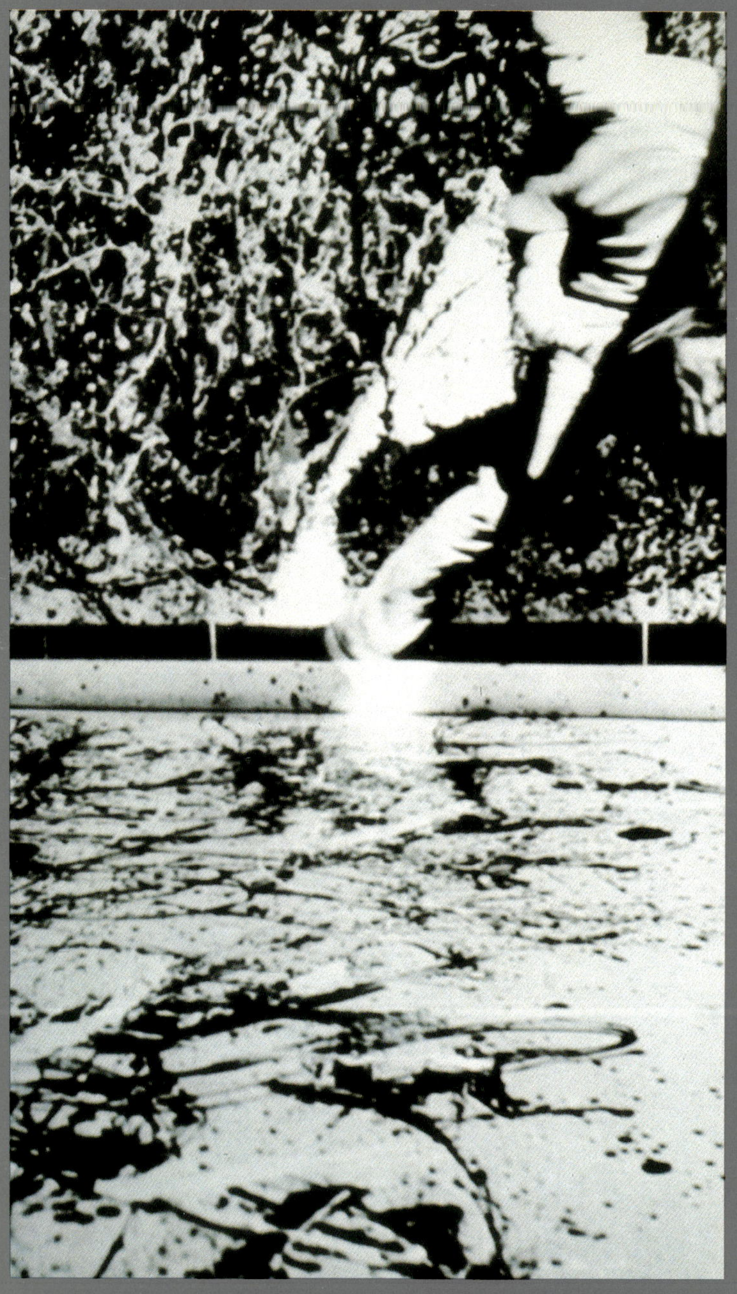

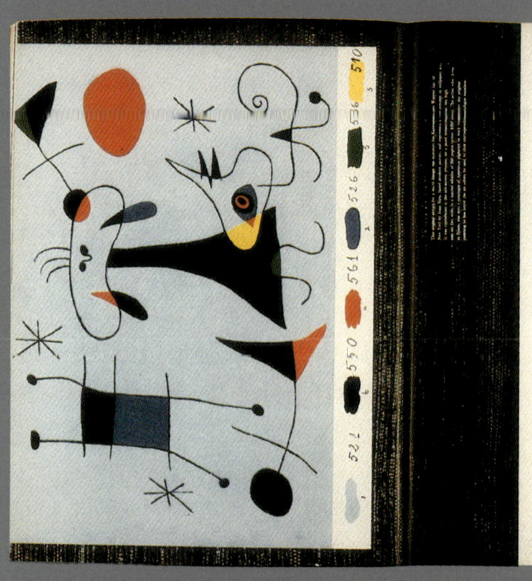

MIRO ON
THE WALL

The word "wallpaper" is no longer a synonym for the musty floral patterns that writhed endlessly on the gaslit walls of Victorian front parlors. Within the past ten years, a renascence has taken place in the field of interior decoration that is restoring to the design of wallpaper some of the contemporary charm and significance that it possessed as a graphic art in the 18th Century. The 18th Century was the "golden age" of wallpaper. It was then that the process of printing from woodblocks was perfected in France and England, and many beautiful papers were printed from designs by leading artists of the time. The 19th Century introduced the wallpaper printing machine and standards of wallpaper design and printing suffered. With the exception of Designer William Morris in England and a few of his contemporaries, there was little of importance contributed to wallpaper, and the industry resorted to copying 18th Century patterns, some of which still have a vogue today. Now, many leading artists are once again designing wallpapers. Modern masters, such as Matisse, Miro and Calder have designed wallpapers and printed wall panels which reflect the spirit of the 20th Century in their imaginative handling of line, color and form. Their work has brought new dignity to wallpaper and given it creative stature among the decorative arts. Simultaneously, new and improved printing methods, such as silk-screen, offset lithography and photo-chemical processes, are permitting the reproduction of various techniques of drawing and painting which could not be approximated a few years ago. The wallpapers shown here are from Katzenbach and Warren Inc., a contemporary-minded firm which has consistently pioneered modern design in the wallpaper industry.

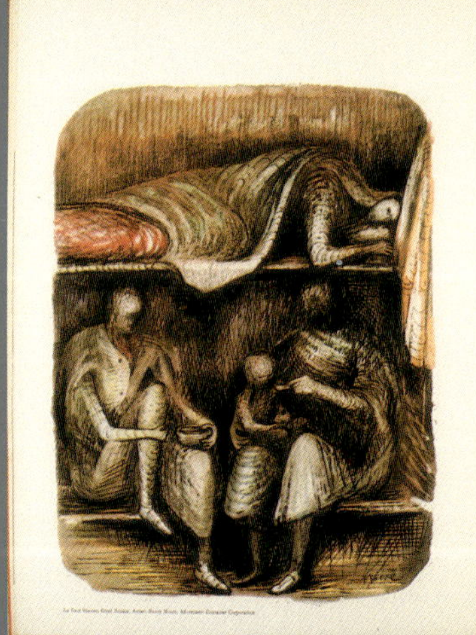

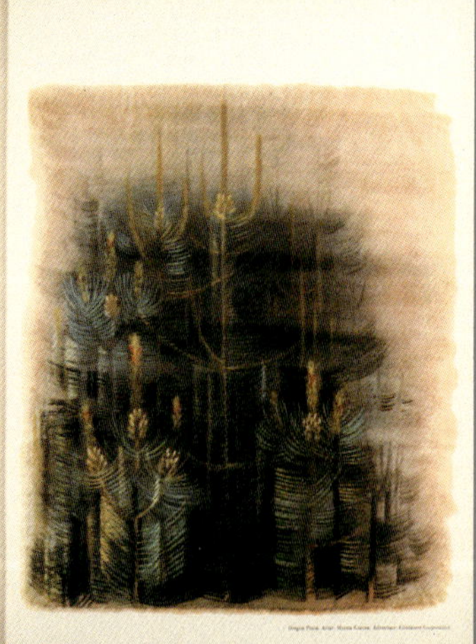

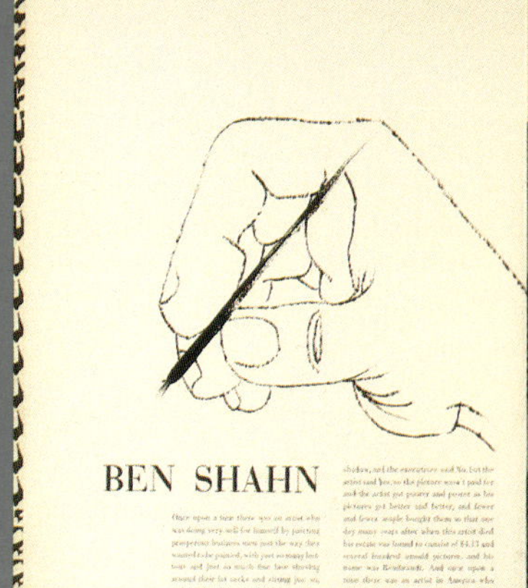

BEN SHAHN

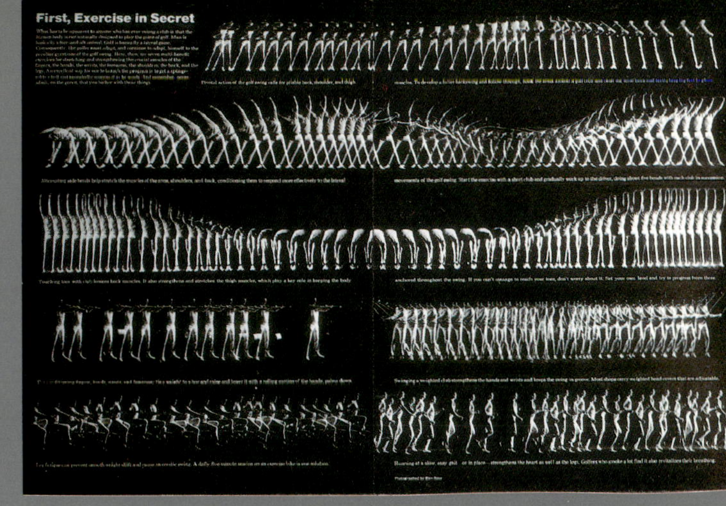

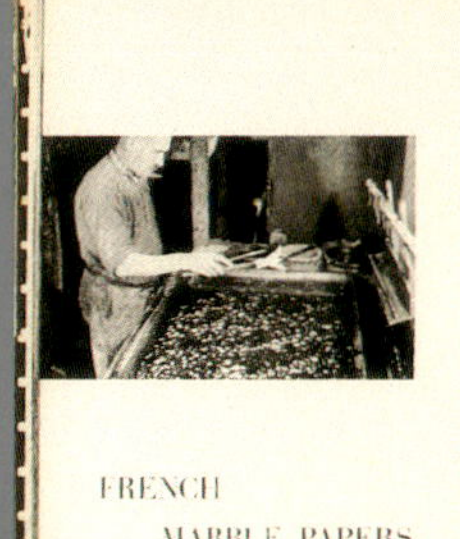

FRENCH MARBLE PAPERS

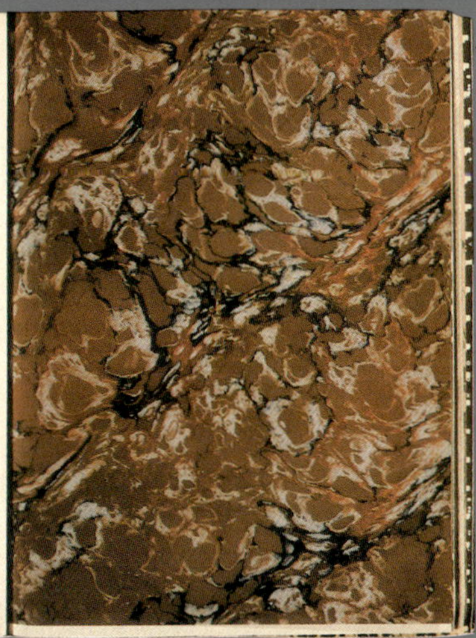

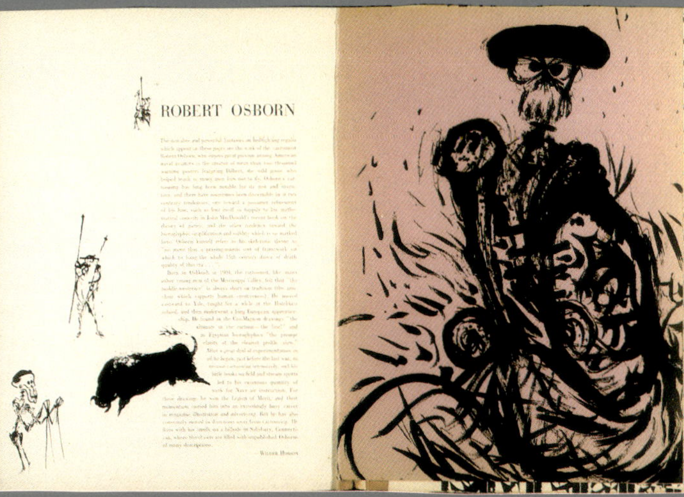

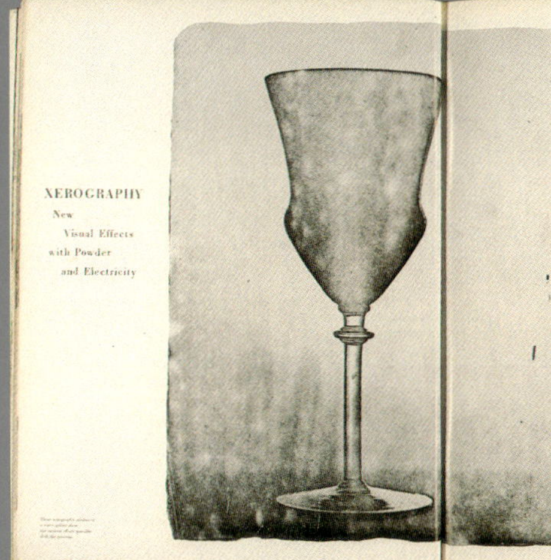

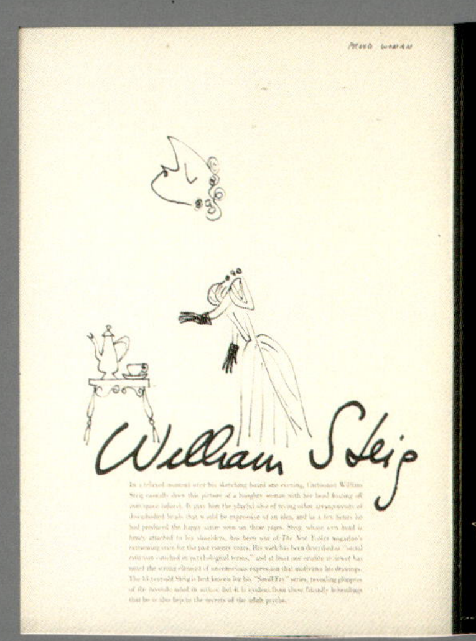

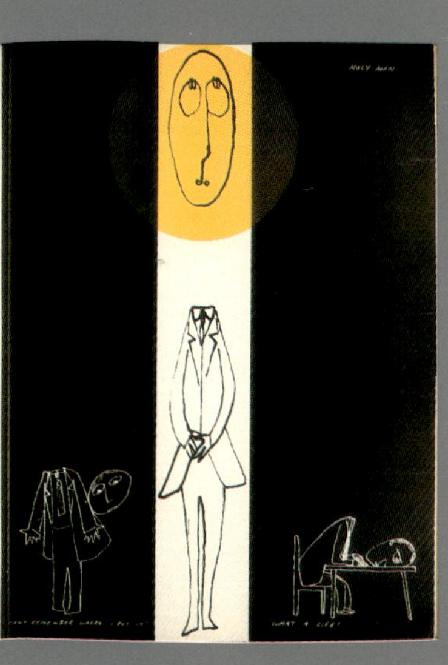

SKIRA'S BOOKS

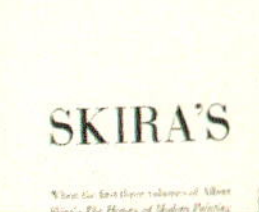

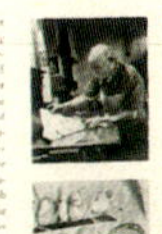

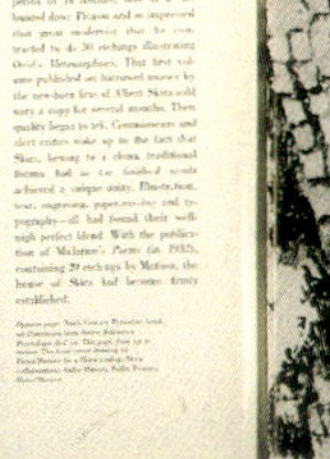

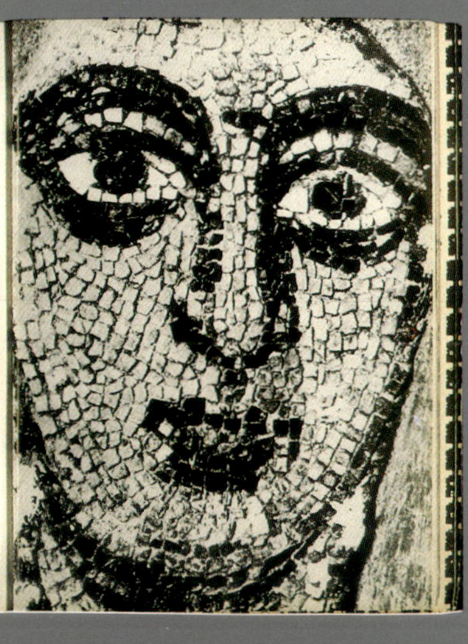

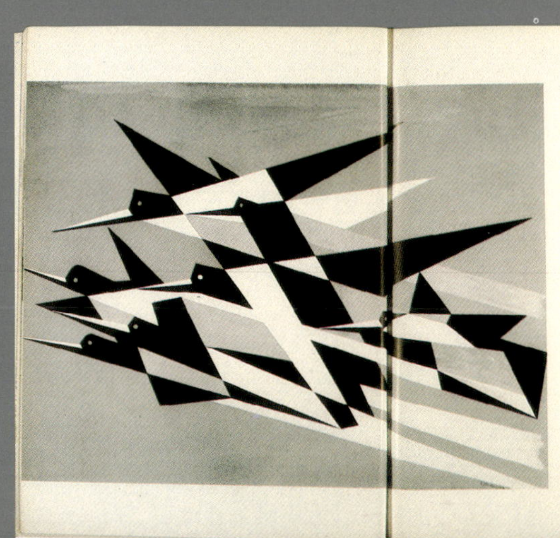

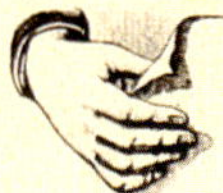

ADVERTISING ART IN 1900

The half-way point of the twentieth century is a logical time to glance back at advertising in its adolescent period—that awkward age when the voice had more volume than control; the manner, more exuberance than poise; and the behavior, more vigor than taste. The year 1900 was an era of childlike naivete in merchandising. Customers were far less sophisticated and there was no fishy-eyed Federal Trade Commission to demand that an attempt be made to separate dreams from facts. Claims for a product were limited only by the number of superlatives in the copy-writer's vocabulary. The artist needed only a slight drawing ability and a totally uninhibited hand with primary colors. In the salad days of advertising before 1900, most sellers promoted their wares with big, splashy lithographed posters that decorated groceries, drug stores and drygoods shops. The art was primitive (in a non-Rousseau sense) and the copy painful, but the flavor was as pure Americana as Currier and Ives. More important, these early placards sold goods. Ivory Soap, Hershey Chocolate and Quaker Oats are but three of the highly successful businesses that first captured their markets through this humble medium. The development of the half-tone about the turn of the century made much of this sort of advertising obsolete. As soon as photographs and wash drawings could be reproduced, publication advertising emerged, almost overnight, as the main generator of mass sales for American industry. The following seven pages were reproduced from original material in the files of New York's Warshaw Collection of Business Americana.

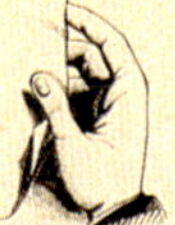

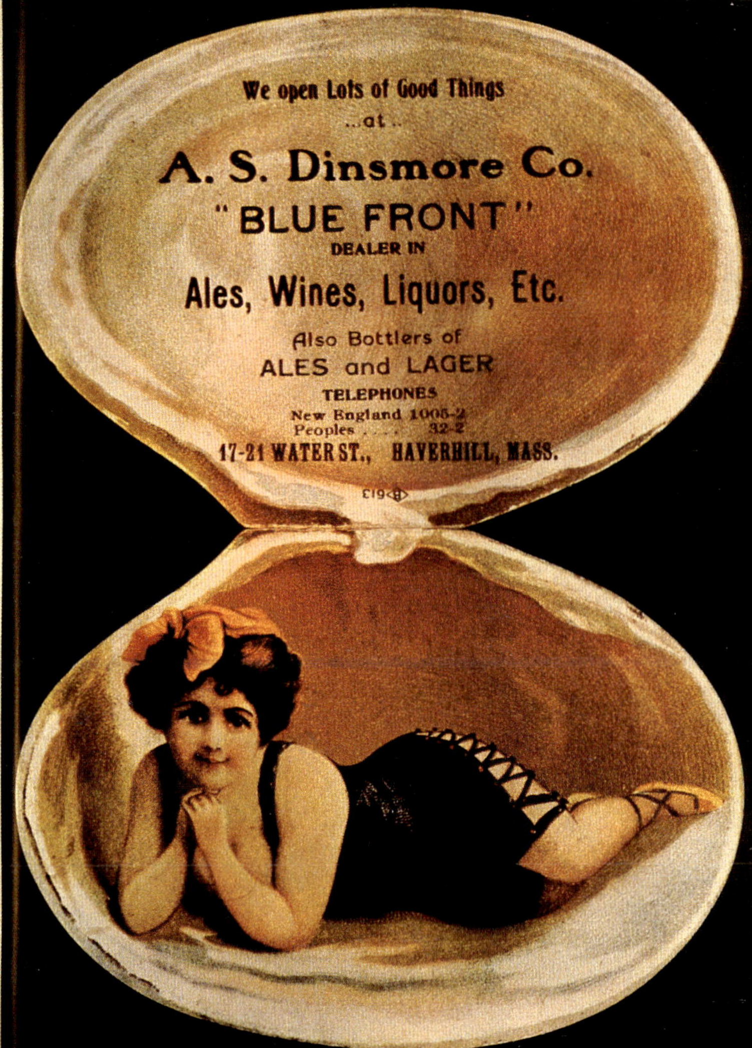

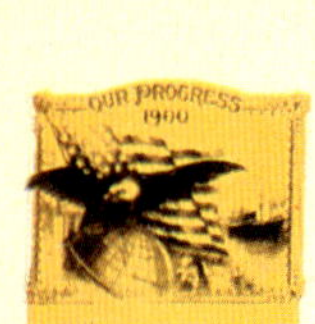

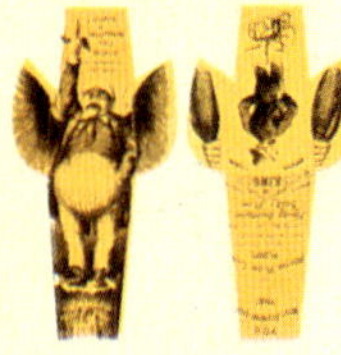

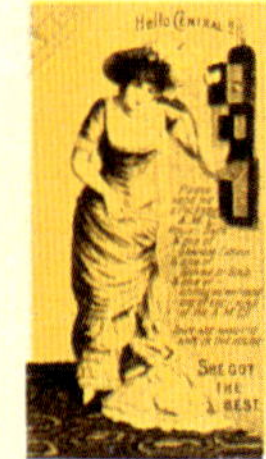

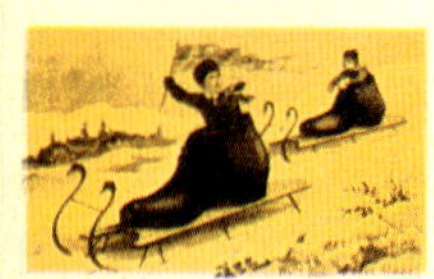

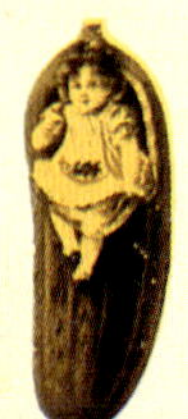

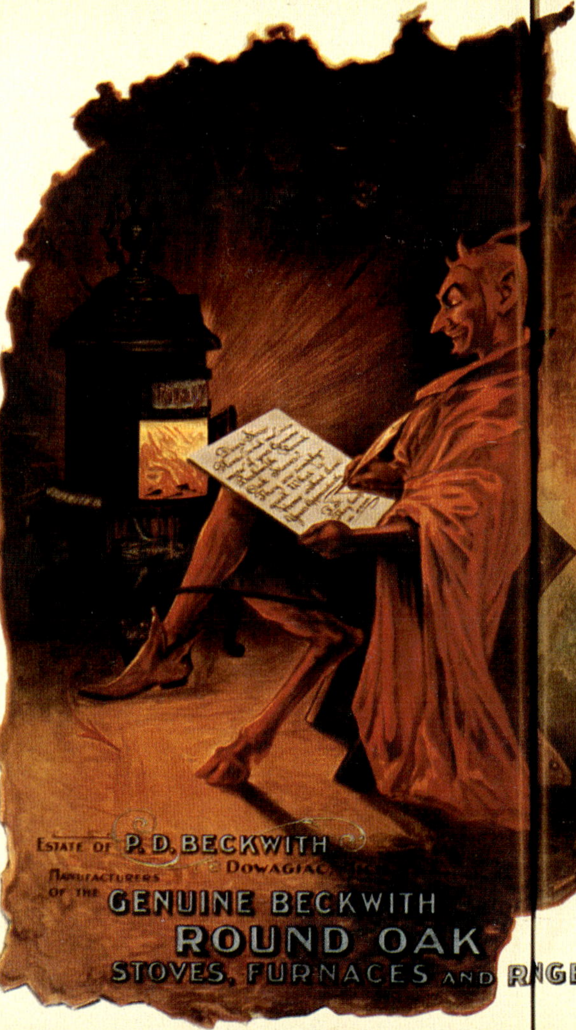

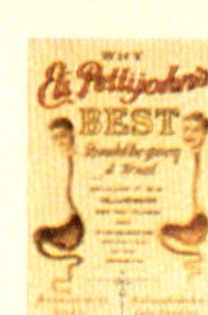

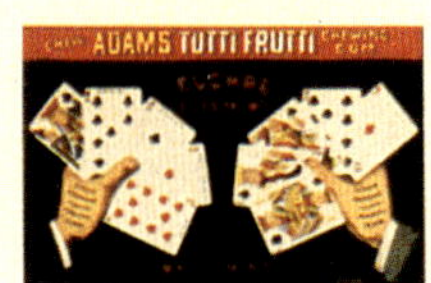

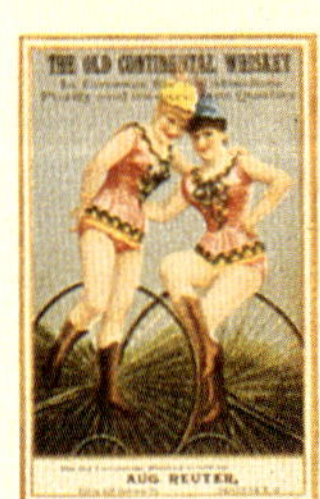

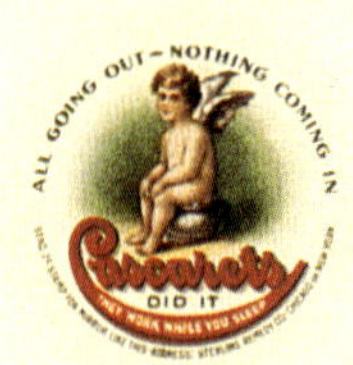

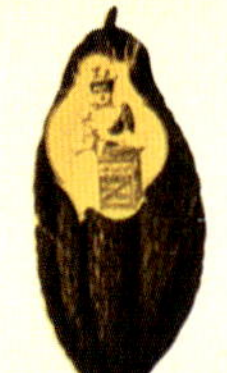

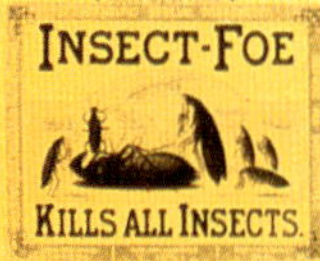

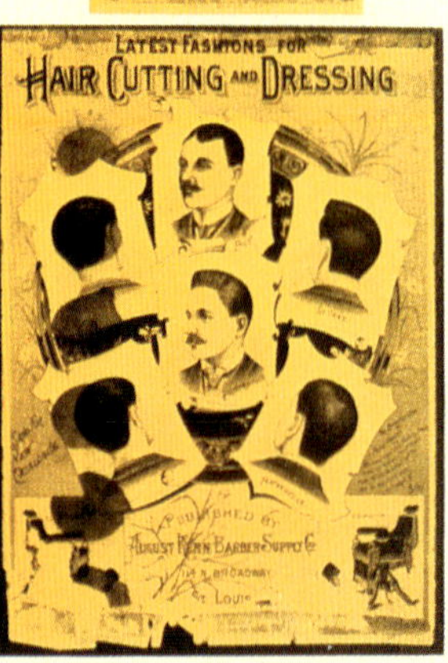

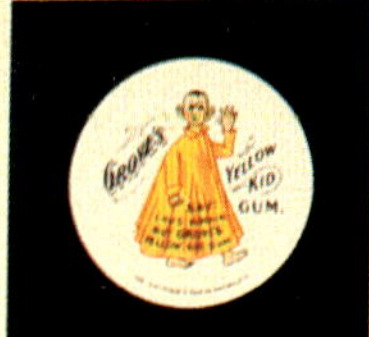

Here is the grandfather of Li'l Abner—the daily comic strip that goes commercial. A half century ago, advertisers discovered the selling power of a popular cartoon character and the idea has been in use ever since. The Yellow Kid, first U. S. comic strip, was an early enthusiasm of American newspaper readers and Adams Chewing Gum put him to work plugging their product. He appeared on the wrappers and on a long series of cards that were avidly collected by youngsters all over the country.

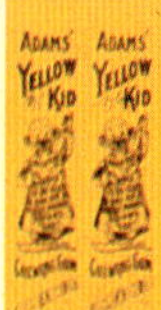

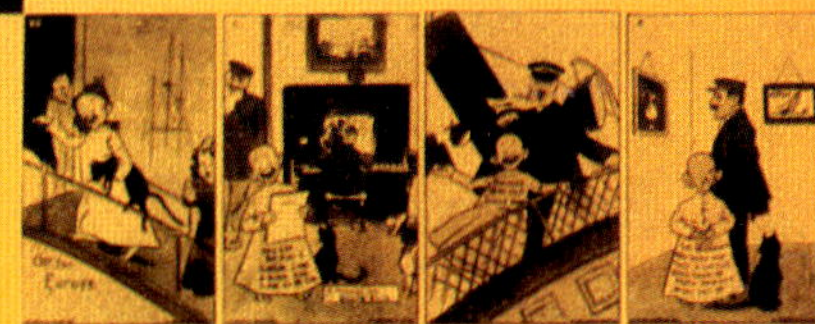

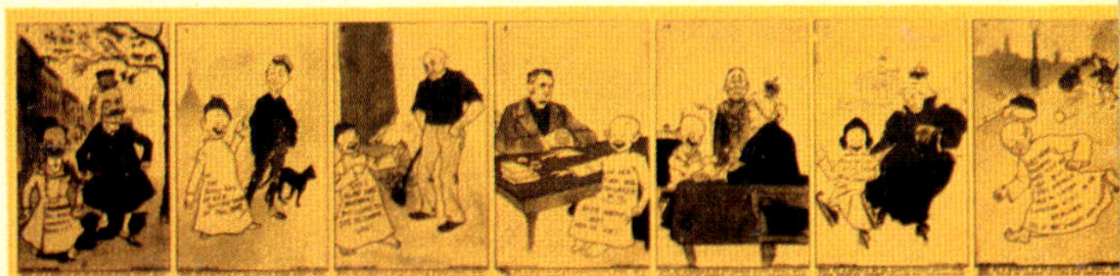

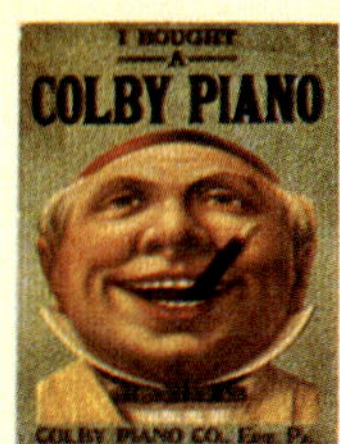

Opposite Page: "A Barnyard Tragedy" or "What the Hell, It's Only Blood." The nonchalant horse, gushing gore like the last act of "Hamlet," calmly awaits its master and the flagon of Silver Pine Healing Oil. This miraculous remedy gave rise to the ancient bromide about a severed artery, "It's no worse than a bad cold."

The Colby Piano Company went in for the stark simplicity school of copy and the backward-child cult of art. They—any of the above points will serve as antecedent—are no longer in business.

Photographic trademarks were a kind of advertising novelty in 1900 but they took on increased importance with the introduction of the half tone engraving. Some of the original trademarks, such as the Uneeda Biscuit boy and the Victor dog, remain in use today.

Two versions of the same broken leg. Father enjoys a prolonged vacation at home with the accident and health company playing the rich and generous uncle, or risk tempting the lady of the house to shoot you for your life insurance.

Hershey Chocolate is the only nationally marketed product which has never advertised in magazines or newspapers. The company did, however, use posters and business cards in the last century to keep its name before the public.

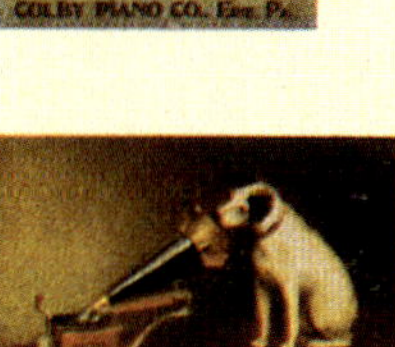

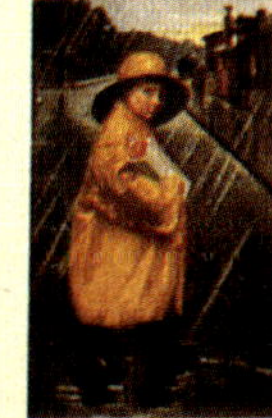

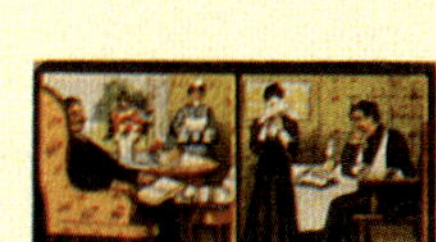

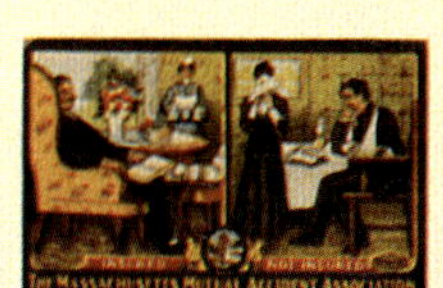

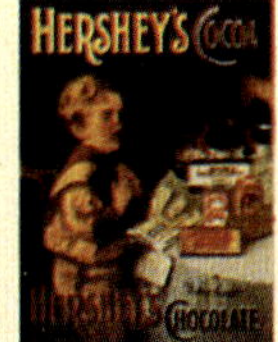

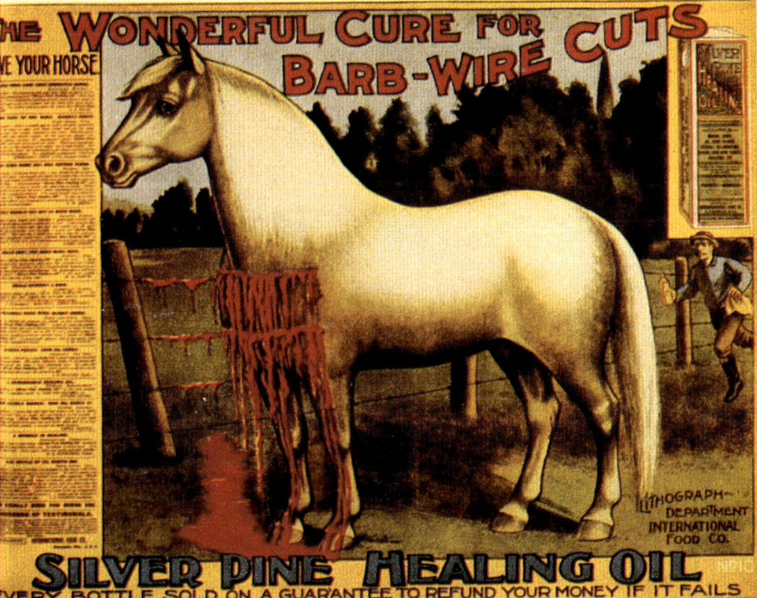

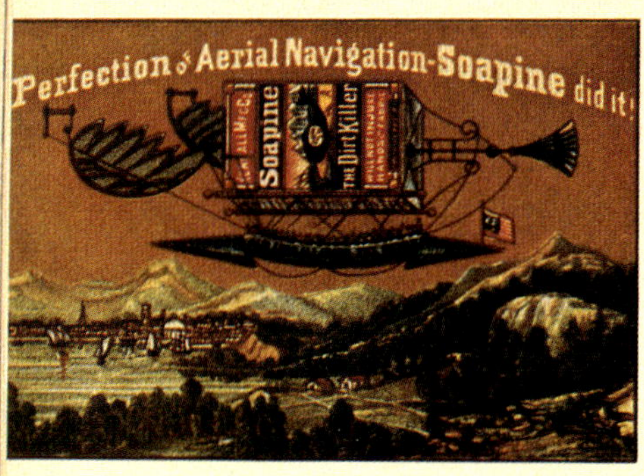

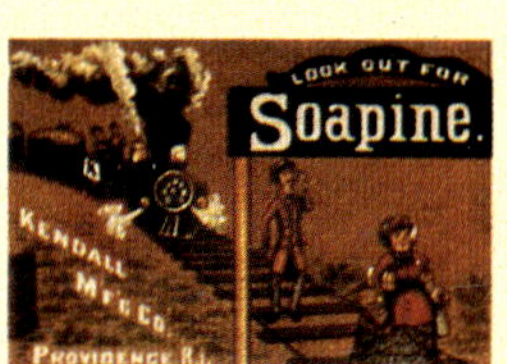

The man who conceived the Soapine campaign undoubtedly had the soul of a circus promoter. With big, garish posters, millions of highly colored give-away cards, a flashy package and a rousing slogan, "The Biggest Thing Ever Put in Water," Soapine bucked the tough competition of such products as Sapolio and Pearline and became one of the biggest selling soaps in the nation. Soap manufacturers were the first industry to make advertising a basic policy in merchandising and the tone they set carries over. Soap is still sold with all the restraint of a calliope. Soapine, however, is no longer in the field. It disappeared quietly in the 1920's.

Soapine DID IT!

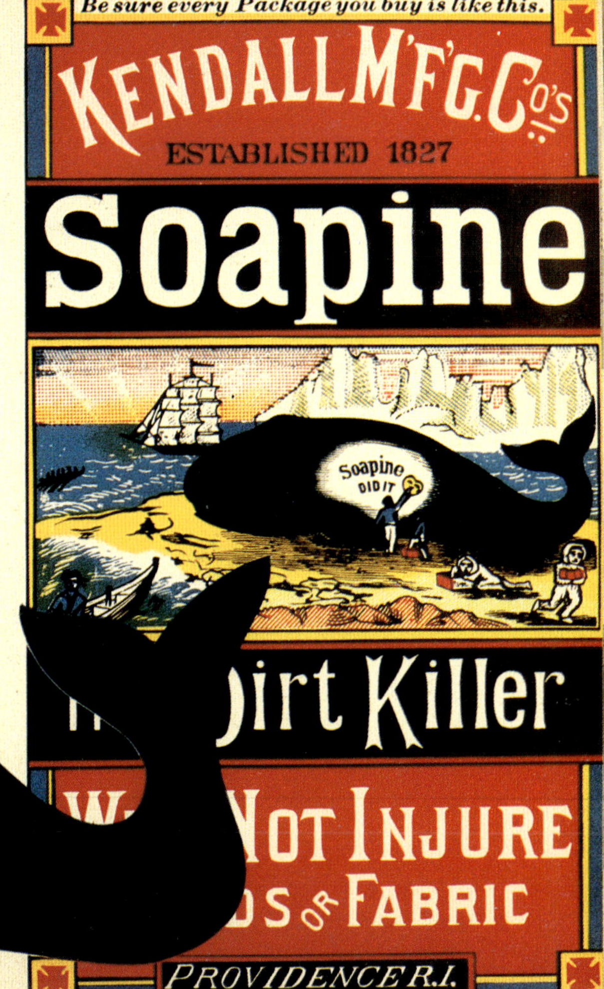

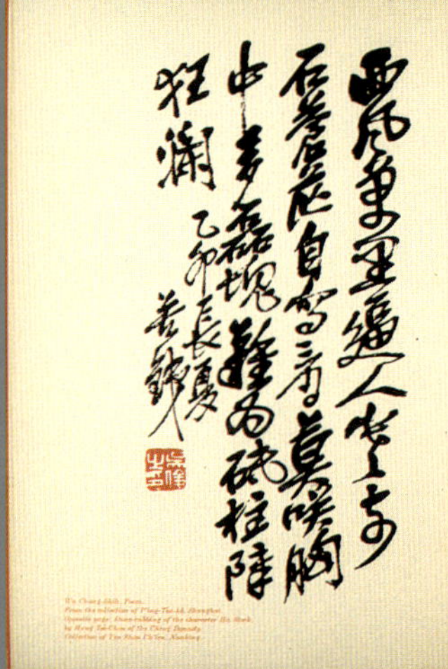

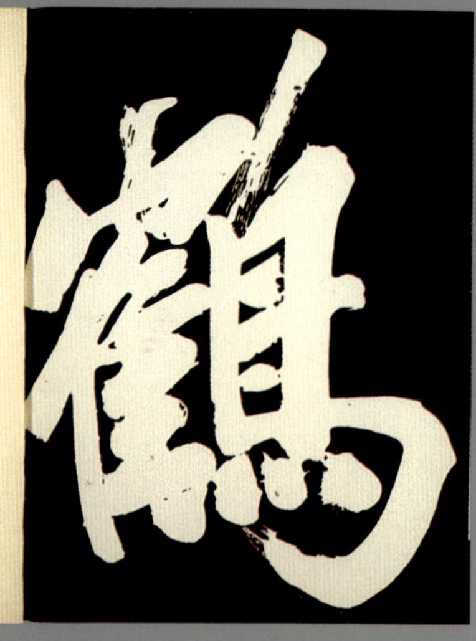

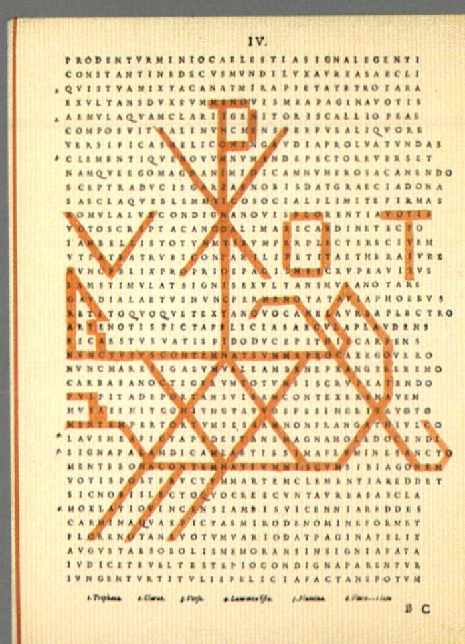

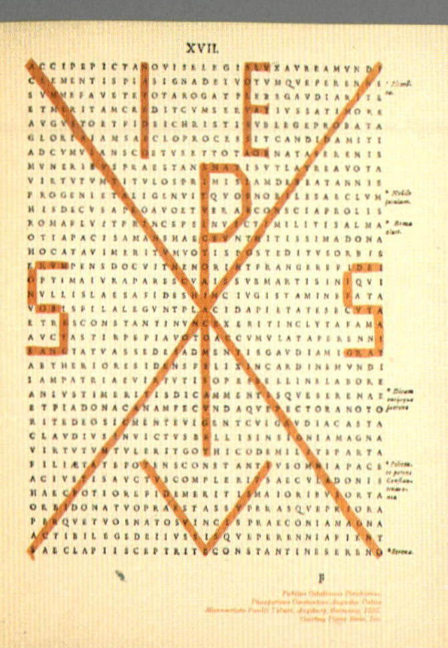

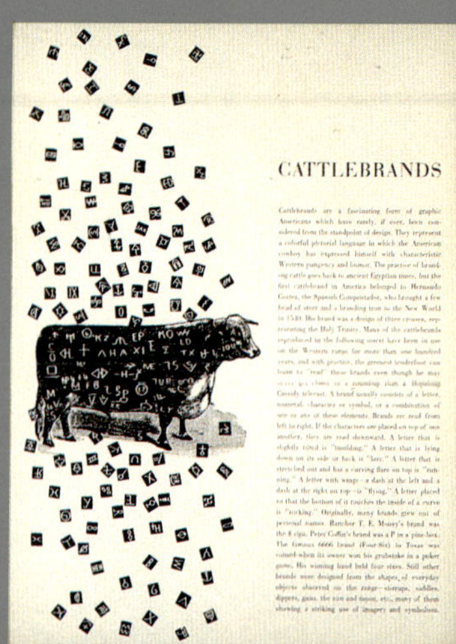

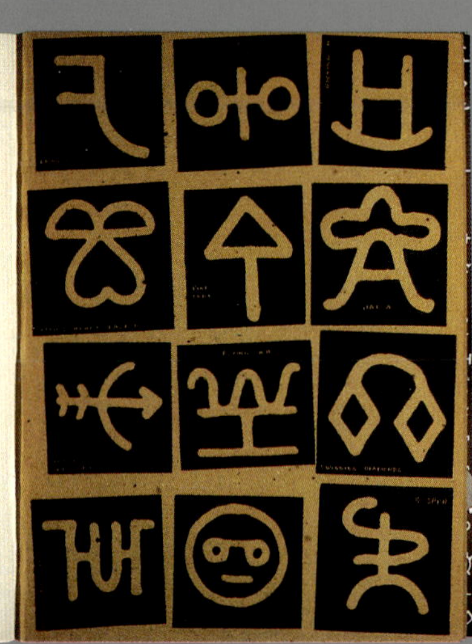

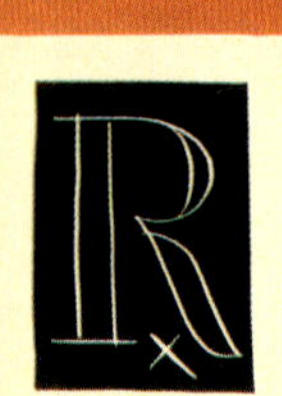

Rarely is the printed page considered a medium of plastic invention. Its design has become standardized, a machine-like element devoid of feeling and esthetic significance. This is cause for regret, for the variety of forms possible when typography and calligraphy are creatively used approaches that of abstract painting. On the following seven pages, Portfolio reproduces in facsimile a number of unusual pages which possess real visual charm and excitement. First is the modern French poet Guillaume Apollinaire's sensitive arrangement of his poem Il Pleut (It Rains), trickling down through the clean white air of the page opposite like a gentle spring shower. It is followed in turn by two curious pages from an early Christian panegyric, printed in 16th Century Germany and stenciled with mysterious religious symbols—a superb example of that now extinct form of literary expression known as "carmen figurato" (figured poem). Next is a contemporary spread from Pierre Reverdy's poem Le Chant des Morts (Song of the Dead Ones), with the text in the poet's script and illustrated with lithographs by Pablo Picasso, who derived the abstract form of his designs from the skull, the bone and the straight line. Last is a poem by Wu Chang-Shih, one of the greatest of modern Chinese calligraphers, written in the calligraphic style known as Ts'ao-Shu, or "grass" style, because of the impromptu nature of the strokes with which the characters are formed. For designers chafing under the conventional discipline of the printed page and seeking new directions, these pages should bring both pleasure and inspiration.

IL PLEUT

Il pleut des voix de femmes comme si elles étaient mortes même dans le souvenir
c'est vous aussi qu'il pleut merveilleuses rencontres de ma vie ô gouttelettes
et ces nuages cabrés se prennent à hennir tout un univers de villes auriculaires
écoute s'il pleut tandis que le regret et le dédain pleurent une ancienne musique
écoute tomber les liens qui te retiennent en haut et en bas

Guillaume Apollinaire, Il Pleut, from Arts et Metier Graphiques. Paris, France, 1930.

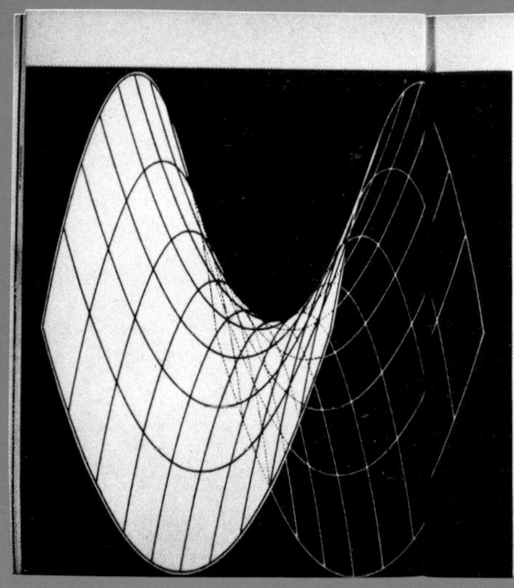

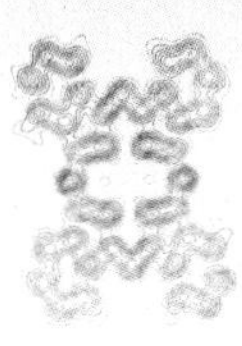

DESIGN FROM THE MATHEMATICIANS

Mathematics, a philosopher once said, possesses not only truth but great beauty. Recently, a group of professional mathematicians have made their science the basis of a fascinating new kind of art. They are demonstrating that beautiful graphic designs can grow from a geometrical theorem. Their exhibit gallery is the Scripta Mathematica, an internationally famed quarterly published by Yeshiva University in New York, under the editorship of Dr. Jekuthiel Ginsburg. The magazine's erudite contributors regularly decorate its pages with the curious forms and dynamic patterns which result when complicated algebraic equations are graphically projected into two dimensions. They offer exciting possibilities to the designer looking for fresh visual ideas.

1 2 3 4

specimen books of them only to advertise his press. Since his death the Bodoni types, punches, and matrices have passed into the hands of the Italian government, which guards them as national treasures. (A number of them are on loan to Dr. Hans Mardersteig, head of the Officina Bodoni in Verona, Italy, who uses them in hand-setting and hand-printing limited editions of fine books.) Modern Bodoni such as the American Type Founders, Lanston, Monotype, Ludlow, Intertype, and Linotype, is a composite impression rather than a strict copy. Some of the versions are excellent adaptations, but others are sufficiently far removed from the original typeface in spirit and form as to cause Bodoni to squirm in his grave, as surely he must have on the day in 1872 when the citizens of Saluzzo, Italy, his birthplace, erected a statue in his honor and carved his name on it in old-style roman letters.

5 6 7 8

BODONI PAGES: This insert reproduces four specimen pages from books designed by Giambattista Bodoni in 18th Century Parma. They are printed by offset on hand-made paper from Cartieri Miliani, the 675-year-old mill in Fabriano, Italy, which supplied Bodoni with similar paper. They appear in the following order: 1. Title page, Q. Horatii Flacci Opera 1791. An example of Bodoni's pure, unornamented style. 2. Opening page, Poems by Mr. Gray 1793. One of Bodoni's few books in English, it is noteworthy for its narrow type page, wide margins. 3. Text page, Anacreon 1785. A tour de force, this book is set entirely in capital letters, including footnotes. 4. Text page, Manuale Tipografica 1818. A box of Scotch rules encloses the type matter on each page of Bodoni's famous specimen book, published posthumously by his widow. To see how modern designers are using Bodoni's typeface, turn to the News Portfolio in the back of the magazine.

9 0

This page: **Arabic Numerals from Bodoni's *Manuale Tipografico***
Opposite page: **Portrait of Giambattista Bodoni**

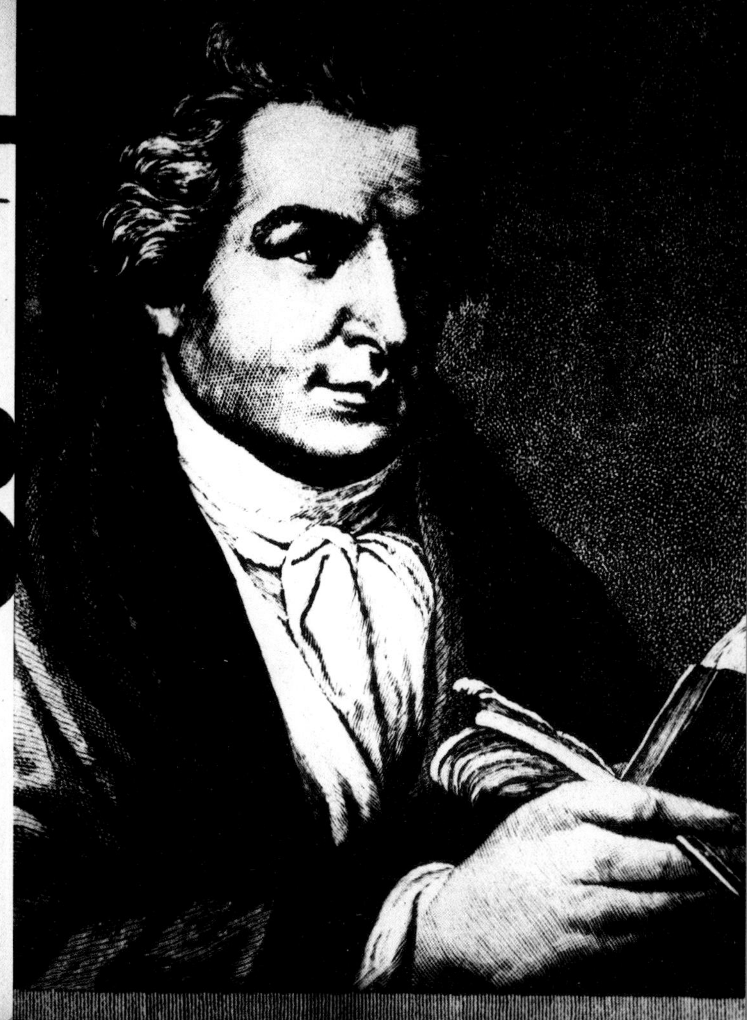

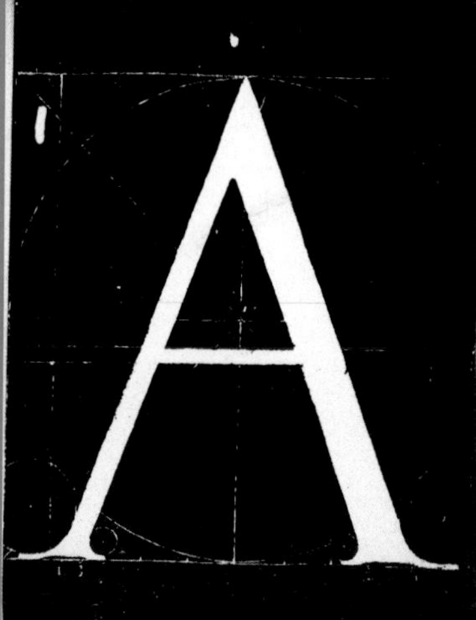

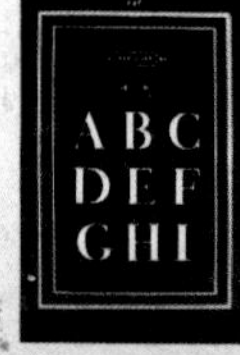

THE CINEMATIC EYE

4

"A sequence of pages is a cinematic book."
—EL LISSITZKY

Despite the suggestion in some biographical accounts that he had known Le Corbusier in Paris, and may have assisted him in designing an automobile,[26] Brodovitch was always an intuitive designer. True, he lined up headlines and captions with the edges of photographs, or with significant horizontal elements within them, but his layouts never seem mechanical, or mathematically derived, or "modular." His assistants recall him shuffling dozens of photostats of various sizes until he "saw" the right one for the page.[27] Much as it might serve other designers, the grid was too mechanical for Brodovitch's taste.[28]

If there is any way to understand Brodovitch's design technique, it is to be found in an analogy with film. He believed that magazines and books, like films, are experienced sequentially and over time. Thus he was especially attuned to the flow of the layouts as they were to appear in the magazine. He always designed his layouts by spreads; except for the columns in the front and back of every issue, the only single-page layouts to be found in *Harper's Bazaar* are the right-hand introductory pages that open the editorial section. And he often revised these layouts as the issue was being made up, when it became clear which spread would follow another.

Frances MacFadden, the *Bazaar*'s managing editor for much of Brodovitch's tenure, explained his working method in 1972:

It was a pleasure to watch him work. He was so swift and sure. In emergencies, like the time the Clipper bearing the report of the Paris Collections was held up in Bermuda, his speed was dazzling. A quick splash or two on the cutting board, a minute's juggling of the photostats, a slather of art gum, and the sixteen pages were complete. His layouts, of course, were the despair of copywriters whose cherished tone poems on girdles or minks had to be sacrificed to his sacred white space. Just before we went to press, all the layouts were laid out in sequence on Carmel Snow's floor, and there, under his eye, re-arranged until the rhythm of the magazine suited him.[29]

It was not up to Brodovitch alone to decide how to assemble the pages of *Bazaar* every month, however. It was also the province of the editor, who had her own strong opinions about what should be in the magazine. As Brodovitch and his assistants finished their layouts of facing pages, with photo-

MARC KACZMAREK, *ALEXEY BRODOVITCH, NEW YORK, 1966*

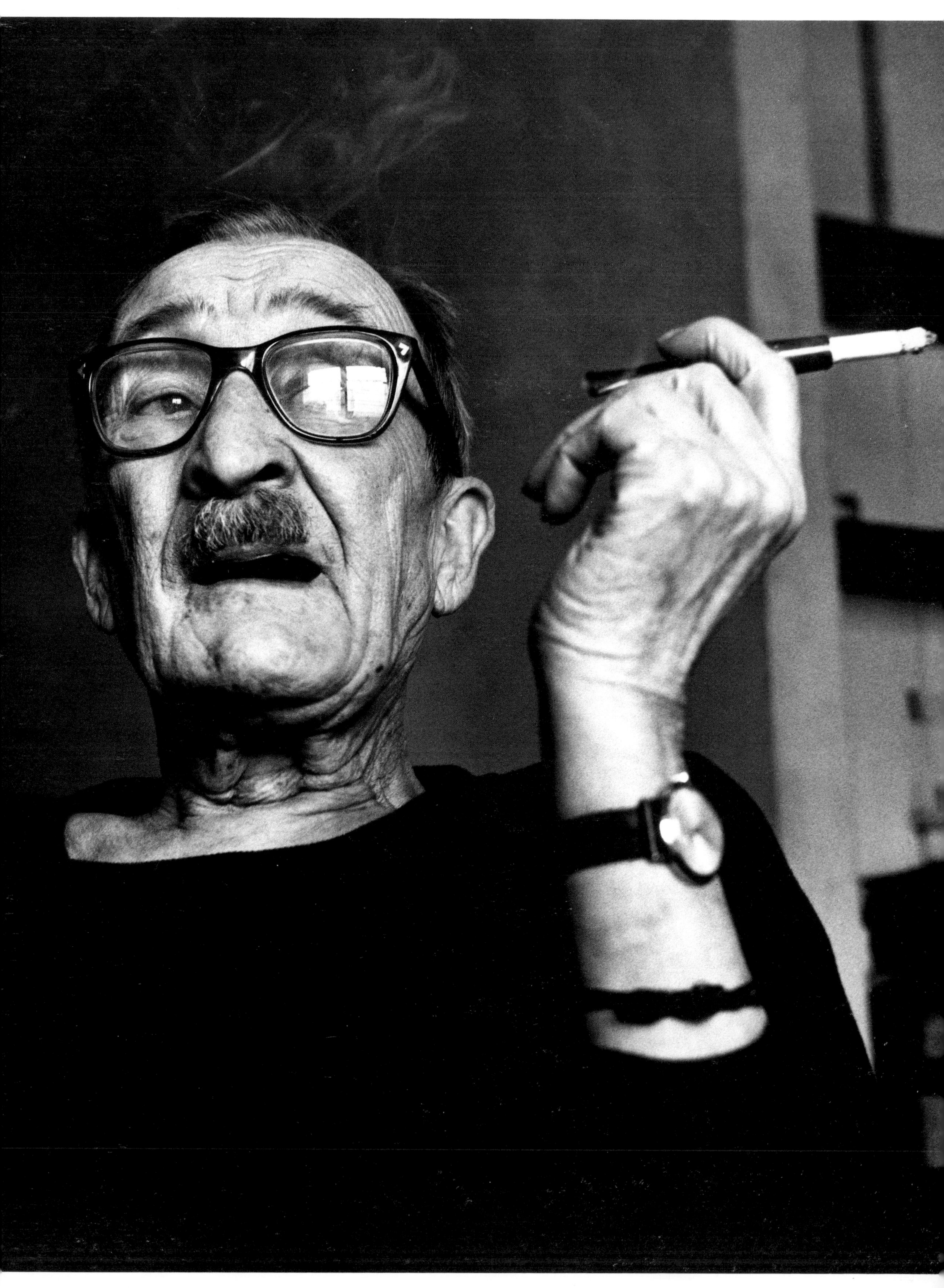

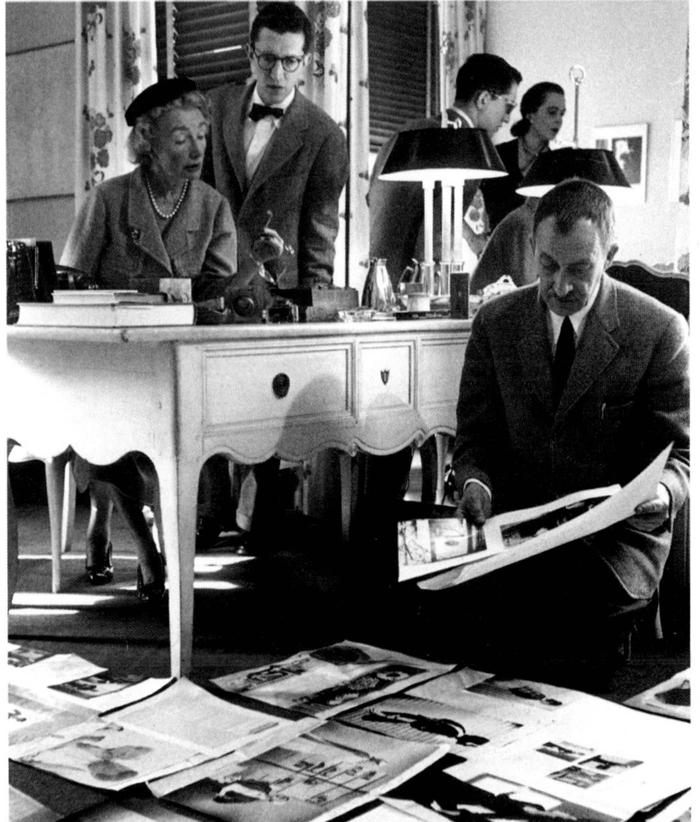

CARMEL SNOW, SEATED LEFT, AND BRODOVITCH, KNEELING RIGHT, IN SNOW'S OFFICE AT *HARPER'S BAZAAR*, 1953

Flow in action: When preparing an issue of *Harper's Bazaar*, Brodovitch started with individual spreads, which would be assembled on the floor of Carmel Snow's office. The final sequence of the pages was determined by Brodovitch under Snow's eye, as shown here.

stats trimmed to size and type positioned using "dummy" copy, they were approved first by the article editor and then by Snow, and ultimately, as MacFadden describes, arrayed on the floor of Snow's large office, in front of her desk. When it was time to send the entire issue to the printer, Snow, Brodovitch, and other senior staff members gathered in front of the layouts. By shifting a spread from the beginning of the issue to the end, for example, the sense of pace of the entire issue could be altered. Occasionally Snow and Brodovitch would decide that a particular layout was not working in its allotted place, and he would go off to his office to prepare a variant that would suit. Finally, when all were satisfied, the imposition—the exact order of all the pages, as they would be printed—would be sent to the printer.

While Snow and the others might worry over how the clothes looked, or whether the dresses of certain fashion designers appeared too prominently, and the production people might police where pages with color could fall, Brodovitch's goal was to ensure a lively sense of pace throughout the issue. Flow was the word he used to describe this essentially narrative quality. For Brodovitch, flow did not mean a seamless, uniform consistency, but a temporal, visual experience with peaks and valleys. This meant that some of his most dynamic layouts had to be sandwiched between quiet, unobtrusive ones. It is obvious in looking at issues of *Bazaar* during his tenure that this alternation between layouts of high visual drama and those that almost whisper was both consciously created and necessary.

Another consequence of this method of magazine makeup is that articles tended to be confined to two pages. When they were longer—as the Paris fashion sections always were—each spread had to have a certain independence, since there was no guarantee where it would be placed in the issue.

Overleaf:
Besides visualizing the entire editorial "well" of the *Bazaar* as a film, and treating art direction as if it were equivalent to film direction, Brodovitch occasionally adopted the narrative conventions of film for individual stories. Here, in "Idyll of the Parkway," an editorial fantasy told entirely with photographs of reflected surfaces (see page 102-103), the joining of the prints into a series makes them read as frames in a sequence; in fact, the order in which they appear is merely arbitrary, the designer's conceit. Elsewhere, Brodovitch added film-sprocket borders to groups of pictures to make them even more "filmic" (see page 106).

Overleaf:
HARPER'S BAZAAR,
MARCH 1937.
PHOTOGRAPHER:
MARTIN MUNKACSI

But Brodovitch sometimes tried to work around this restraint, with limited success. In certain issues of the magazine, spreads that obviously were intended to be seen in sequence are widely scattered. Nonetheless, this method of "editing" the visual appearance of a publication became so much a part of his working method that he used it even when working independently of the *Bazaar*.[30]

There are, needless to say, strong similarities between Brodovitch's practice of magazine design and Sergei Eisenstein's ideas about film. Eisenstein, whose practice exemplified his own theory, emphasized what he called conflicts, both within the frame—direction, scale, volume, mass, and depth—and between adjacent frames, which create new meanings by their juxtaposition and sequencing. As Michael S. Konetzka has written in his study of Brodovitch's design roots,

These concepts of image relationship and conflicts of formal considerations were explored by Brodovitch in his editorial designs. The phrase "conflicts within the frame" could easily be "conflicts within the page," for both frame and page serve similar functions.[31]

To Konetzka, Eisenstein's theory of film is central to any understanding of Brodovitch's graphic design.

If Brodovitch never read Eisenstein's writings on film or saw his films, he could have acquired similar notions from Léger, whose strong ideas about the role of art in the mechanical age Brodovitch often cited to his students. (Léger's pioneering abstract film, *Le Ballet Mécanique*, premiered in Paris in 1924; it is likely that Brodovitch would have seen it.) He also might have been influenced by the theories of El Lissitzky, who in spelling out the Constructivist principles of typography in 1923 wrote the startling sentence, "A sequence of pages is a cinematic book." Indeed, Brodovitch's entire design practice seems modeled to a remarkable extent on Lissitzky's article "The Typography of Typography." Lissitzky wrote:

1. Printed words are seen and not heard.

2. Thoughts are communicated by the appropriate words and formed by letters of the alphabet.

3. Thoughts should be expressed with maximum economy, optically not phonetically.

4. The composition of text on a page is governed by the laws of typographical mechanics—it should reflect the flow and rhythm of the contents.

5. Illustrative material should be used to organize a page in accordance with the new visual theory.

6. A sequence of pages is a cinematic book.

7. A new book requires new means of writing—the inkwell and quill are a thing of the past.

8. A printed book has conquered time and space. Printed pages and the infinity of books must be conquered. Electro-library.

But whether influenced by any one individual or theory, or (as is more likely) by the general climate of Europe in the 1920s, Brodovitch's graphic design—more than any other contemporaneous designer's—shows the stamp of cinematic structure.

Sometimes this cinematic quality is explicit, as in a March 1937 *Bazaar* spread titled "Idyll of the Parkway" (pages 102–103). Across two pages, photographs by Martin Munkacsi —"all taken in the reflection of mirrors or the shining parts of a car," the caption notes—describe a young couple's encounter with a traffic cop. The layout emphasizes the narrative quality of the pictures by butting them together and running the resulting strips in rows; the effect is filmic both in concept and in appearance. The layout is also an example of Brodovitch's fondness for reflections and similar disturbances of reality, which serve Surrealist ends. The mirrored images in the photographs and the cinematic presentation conspire to convey a single message: that the fashionable "good life" depicted takes place at one remove from reality, in a world not of substance but of dreams.

Elsewhere the designer's indebtedness to film is made clear by the joining of images with film-sprocket motifs. At other times it is less obvious but no less present, carried simply by the narrative sequencing of pictures on the page. But his understanding and use of cinematic technique extended beyond the design of single spreads. It can be seen, if not precisely explicated, in terms of the entire content of an issue of the magazine—an experience to which practically anyone who has leafed through a vintage copy of *Bazaar* can attest. And it extended even to his own functioning as a designer.

As a magazine art director, Brodovitch adopted the role of the film director in all its aspects. Like his

IDYLL OF THE PARKWAY

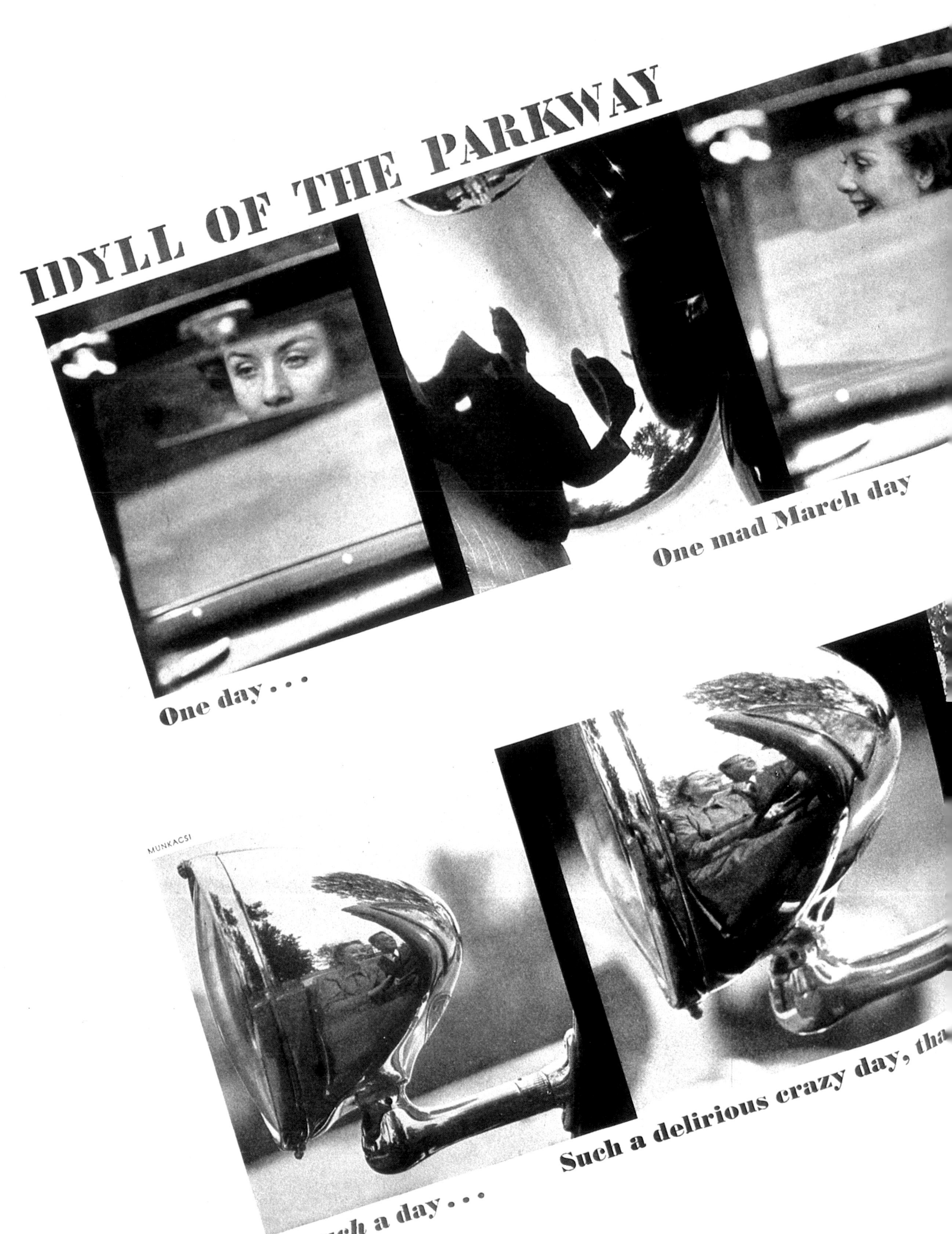

One day . . .

One mad March day

MUNKACSI

It was *such* a day . . .

Such a delirious crazy day, tha

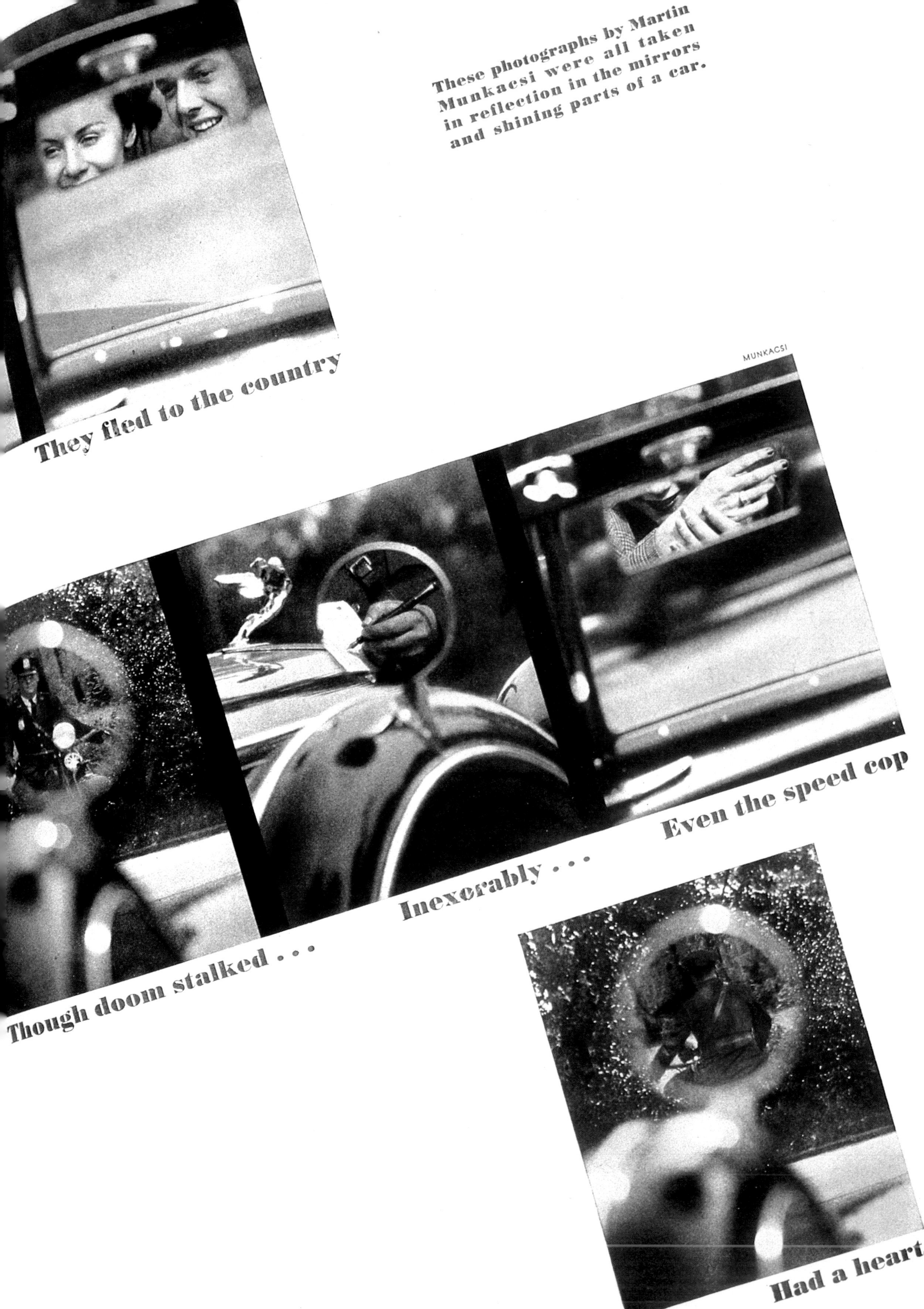

These photographs by Martin Munkacsi were all taken in reflection in the mirrors and shining parts of a car.

MUNKACSI

They fled to the country

Though doom stalked . . .

Inexorably . . .

Even the speed cop

Had a heart.

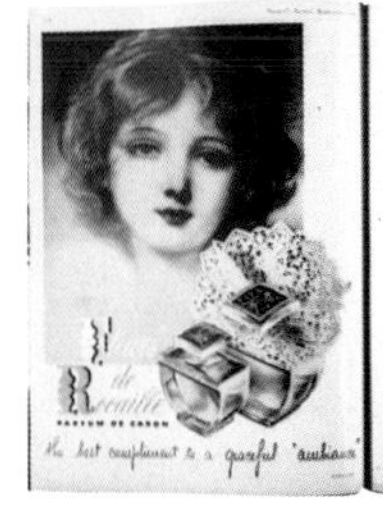
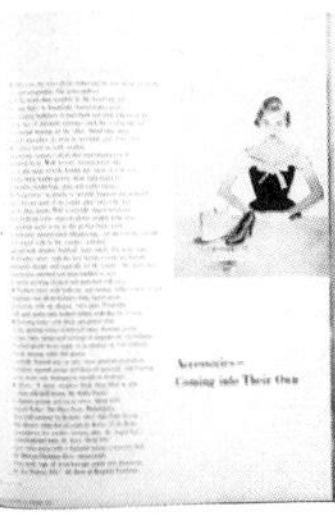
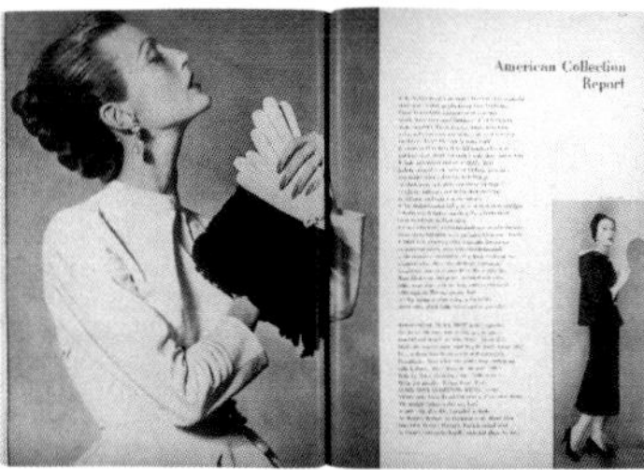
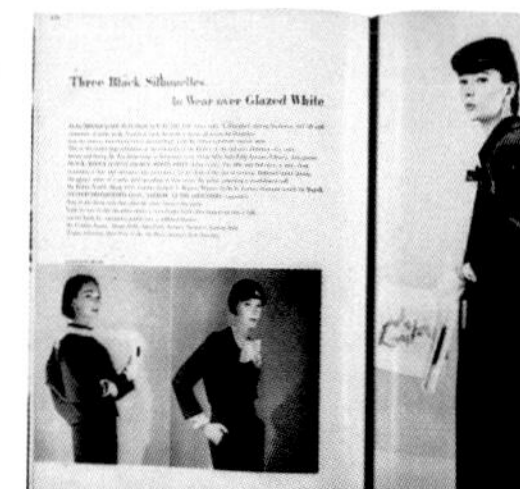
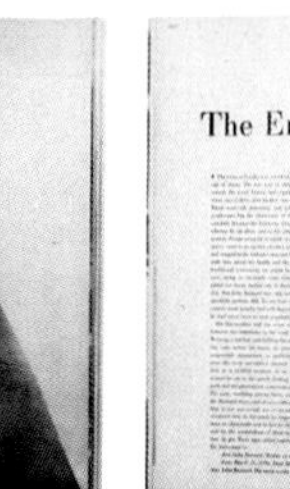
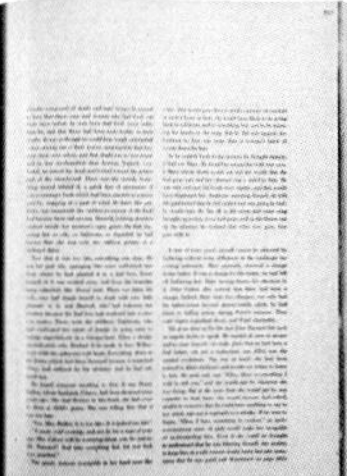
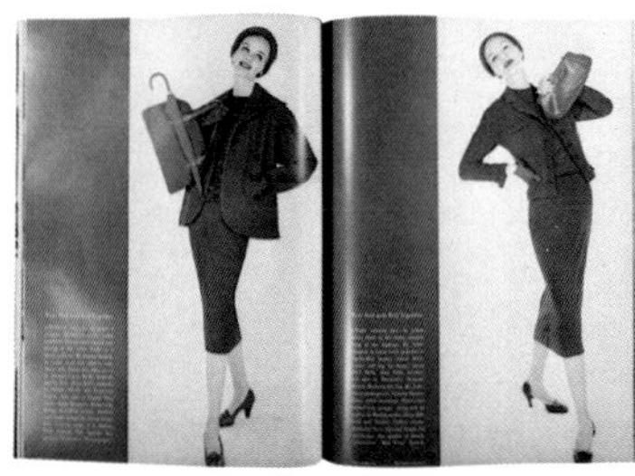
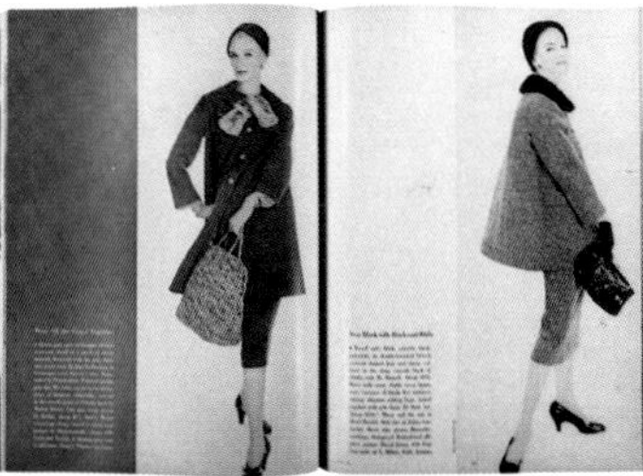
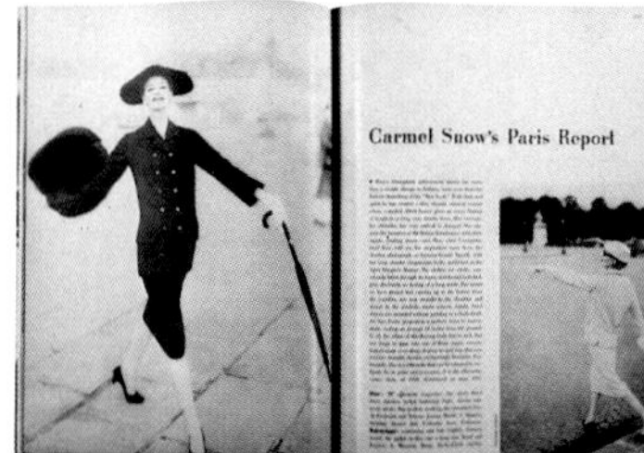
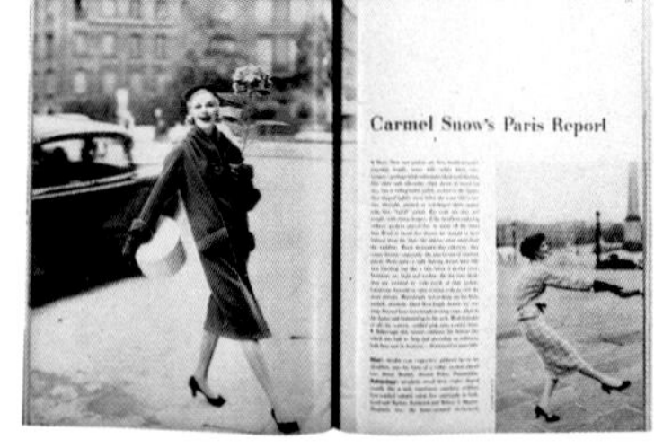
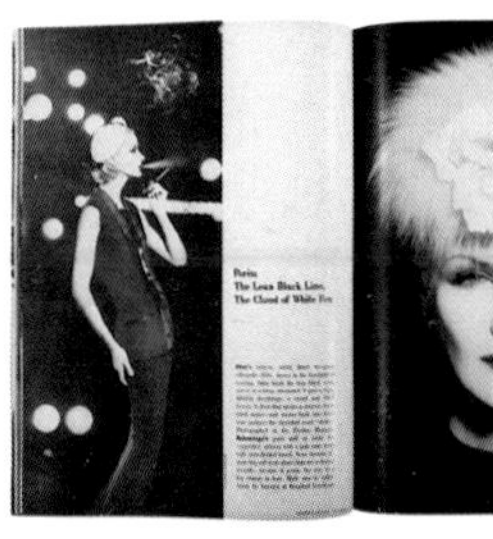
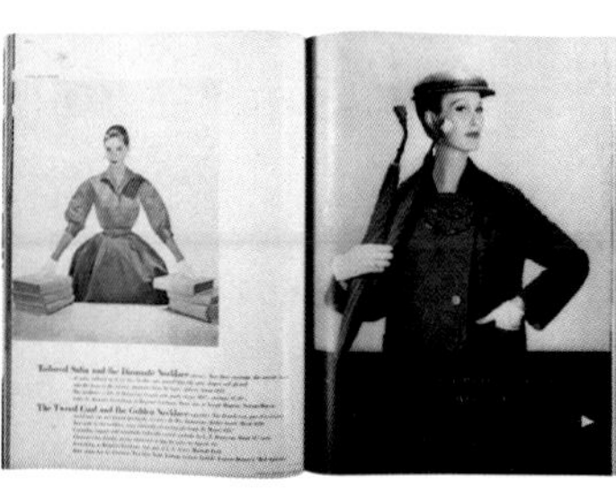
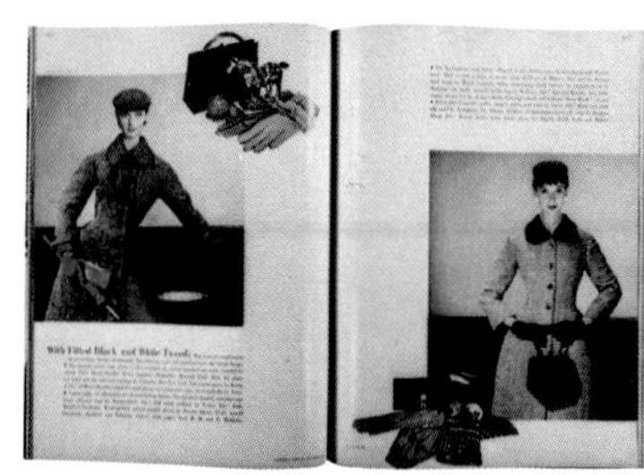
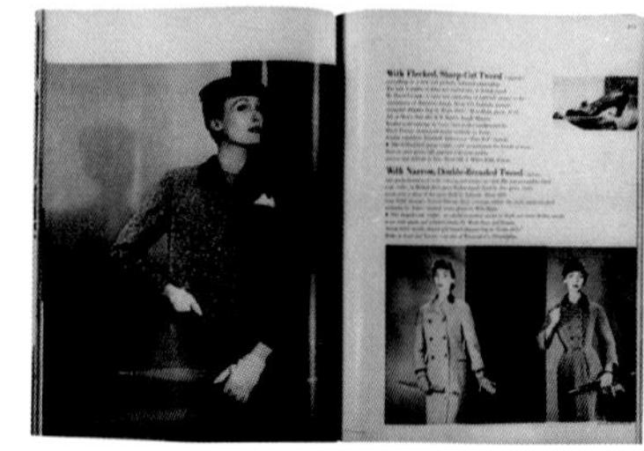
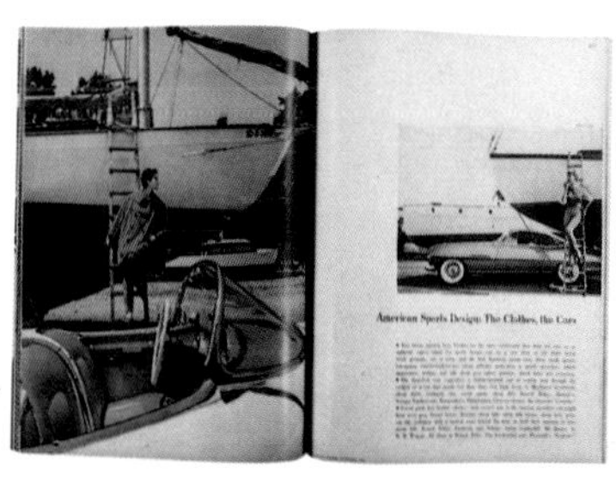
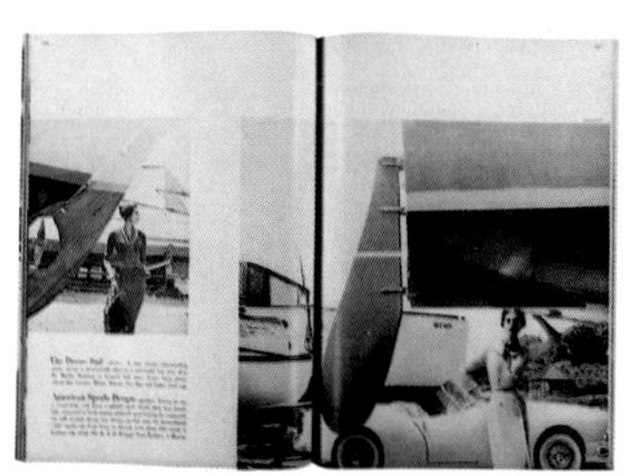
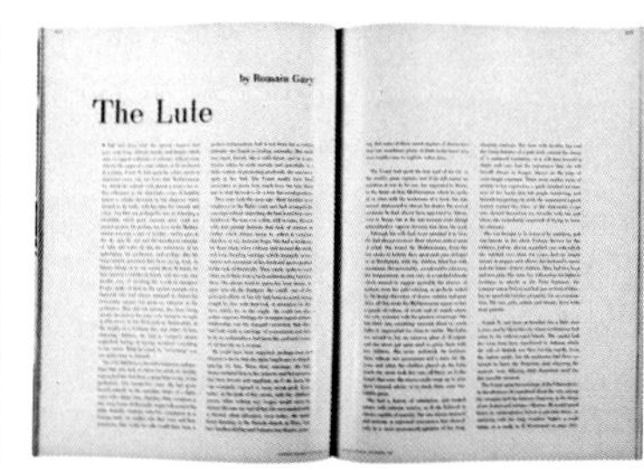
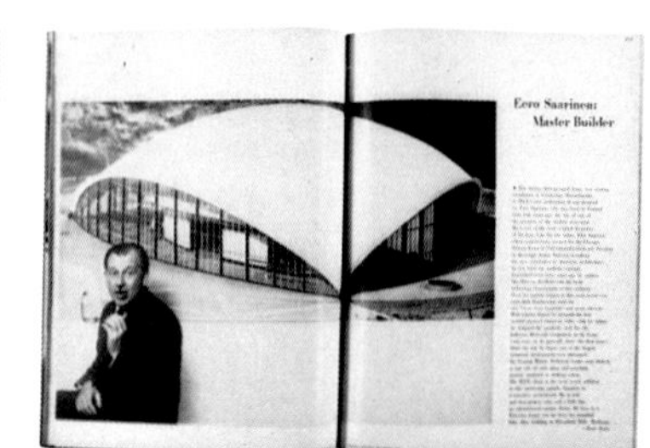
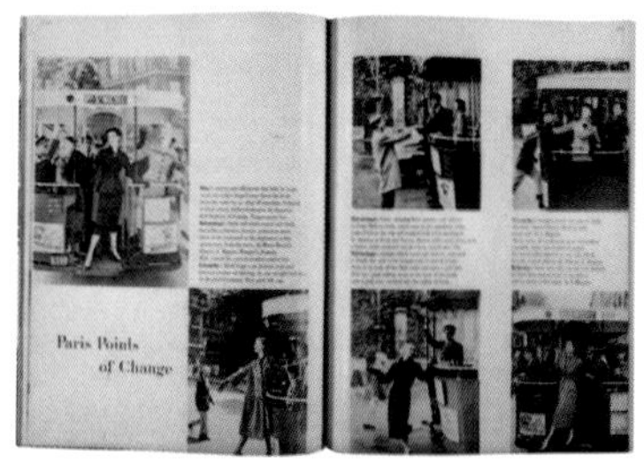
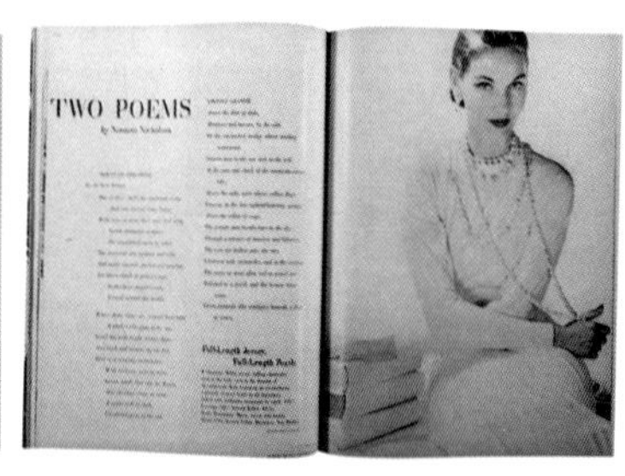
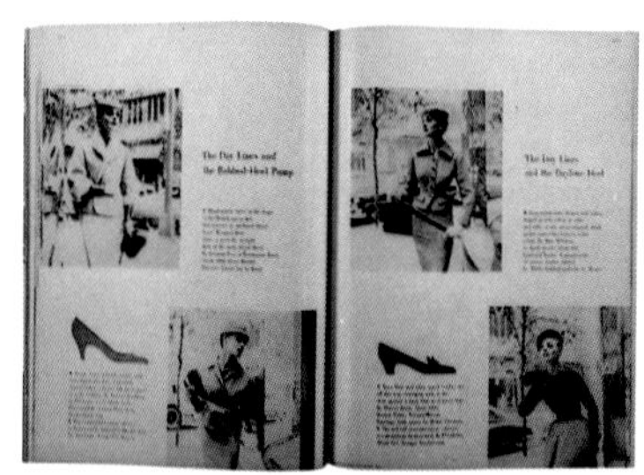
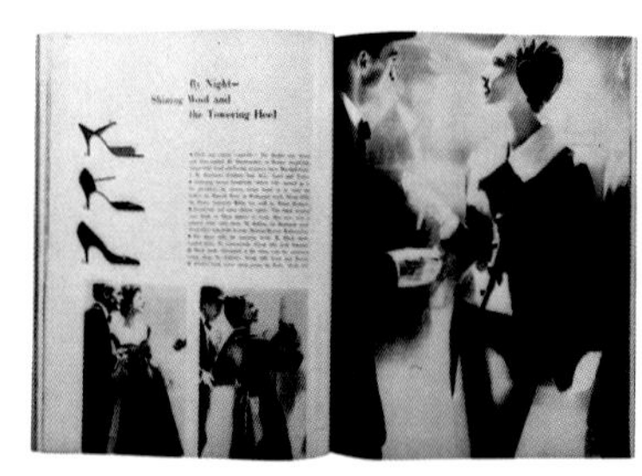
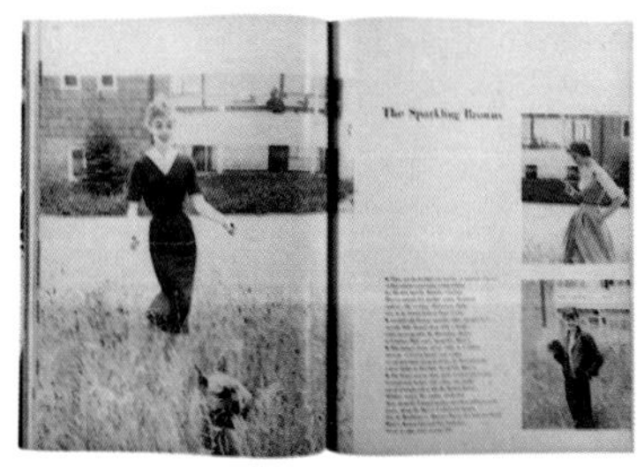
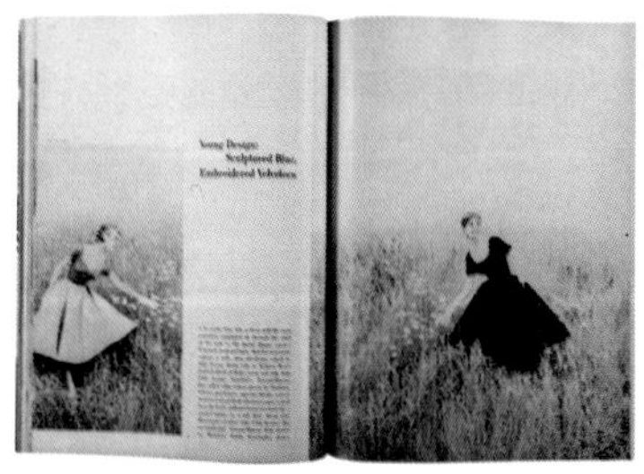
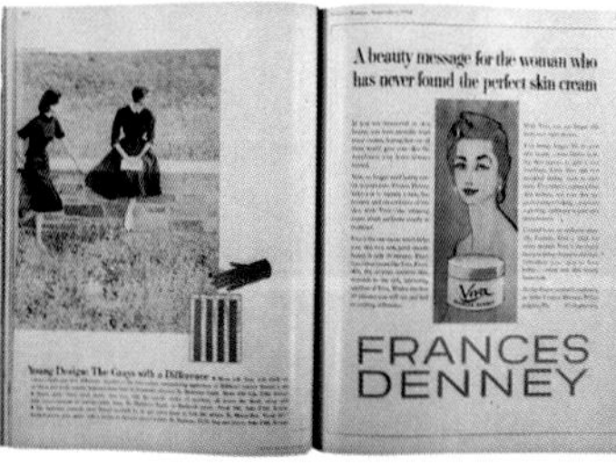

HARPER'S BAZAAR, SEPTEMBER 1954. SHOWN IS THE COMPLETE EDITORIAL SECTION OF THE ISSUE, IN ITS ORIGINAL SEQUENCE

Brodovitch's use of film as a model for the graphic appearance of *Harper's Bazaar* extended to the entire editorial "well," or center section of the magazine. With Carmel Snow's collaboration, he sequenced each issue's pages to provide the most dramatic visual progression possible. While he almost always balanced his experimental pages with quiet, relatively conventional spreads, he made the act of perusing an issue visually compelling. No previous publication designer had understood so thoroughly the linkage of graphic display and temporal experience.

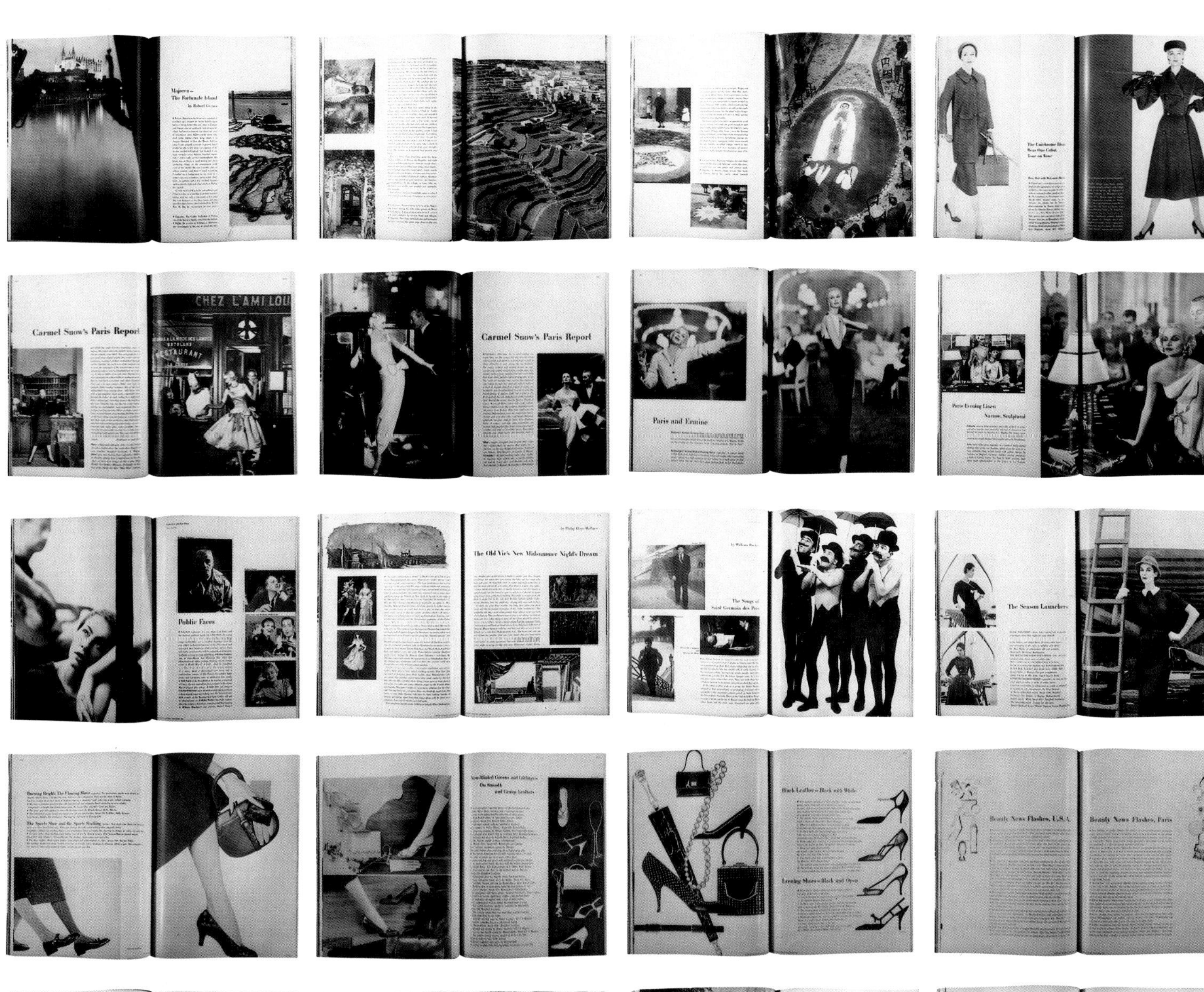

counterparts in film, he was the person responsible for creating a coherent visual whole, and he necessarily had to rely on others to help achieve it. In the case of film directors, these others include cinematographers, set designers, lighting crews, and film editors. In Brodovitch's case, he relied on the contributions of his design assistants, free-lance photographers and illustrators, and the magazine's editors. His function was like that of an impresario, pressing people into the service of his vision, cajoling and flattering them into doing the tasks he assigned them, incorporating their talents and contributions into his larger design scheme. He was patriarchal and sometimes autocratic in the process, but paradoxically also democratic. If a student produced something of value, he adopted it (or appropriated it) as readily as he would a contribution from an experienced illustrator with whom he had worked for years. Because of this, he became known for recognizing young and untested talent.[32]

Designing the Page

Typically, Brodovitch started designing with the illustrations in hand. Although Mary Fullerton, the Philadelphia student who became his first assistant and later an illustrator for the *Bazaar*, received sketches of possible page layouts from Brodovitch, photographers were usually left to fend for themselves. According to Louise Dahl-Wolfe, who was on the *Bazaar*'s payroll as a staff photographer from 1936 to 1958,[33] she usually would be told only what the subject was, how many pages there were and, sometimes, which pages would face one another. Freelancers on fashion assignments were told to come up with something new and unusual, and sometimes given a prod in the right direction. Brodovitch once sent Lisette Model, who was known for her attraction to life's

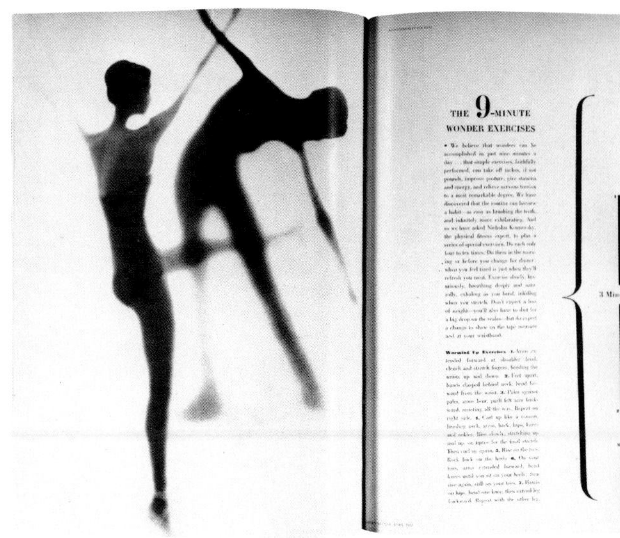

seamier side, to Times Square to photograph fashion models; the pictures were never used, and Model did not try shooting fashion again. In short, Brodovitch's favorite exhortation, "Astonish me," was put into practice literally.

When the pictures arrived he would select those he found most interesting—usually those that seemed most visually active—and have photostats made in a wide variety of sizes. From these he, or his assistants, fashioned layouts, a spread at a time. According to one former assistant, Adrian Taylor, a typical Brodovitch day started with the art director marking up photographs to send out for photostats, usually in an astounding variety of sizes. He would then break for lunch, downing at least two martinis and very little food, returning to the offices somewhat wobbly and with a bead of sweat hanging from the end of his nose. He repaired immediately to the paper cutter, where he proceeded to trim the completed photostats into the proportions he envisioned.[34]

While undoubtedly enhanced in the retelling, this account reveals how intuitively Brodovitch functioned. For while his intellect could not have been at its sharpest point at mid-afternoon, his ability to fashion precisely balanced layouts seems to have been unimpaired. Indeed, the assistant was impressed that so casual a process could result in such rigorous design; somehow, he never expected order to emerge from the pile of photostats that had been sized so nonchalantly.

It is tempting to argue that the Russian's taste for liquor spoiled his taste in magazine design, resulting in issues of *Harper's Bazaar* that are wildly uneven to today's eyes. But there are several more likely reasons for the quite ordinary, boilerplate pages that seem always to accompany Brodovitch's most inspired layouts. One is the notion of cinematic flow itself, which calls for sections of calm and conventionality alongside sections of drama and innovation. Another can be attributed to the compromises inherent in the designer's working situation at *Harper's Bazaar*—compromises that are a fact of life for most all editorial art directors. Snow and the editors were beholden to the fashion world, not the design world, and their concerns about certain dresses being seen and certain designers highlighted often overrode Brodovitch's desires as an art director. He took to preparing alternate layouts for most spreads, giving Snow the benefit of a choice.

Fortunately, the relationship between the editor and art director of the *Bazaar* remained respectful and reciprocal, and Snow usually deferred to Brodovitch when it came to judging visual material. She was not above vetoing his decisions, however, or even signaling her displeasure at entire layouts. By Snow's own account, she once sent back to Brodovitch a layout of Avedon's photographs of Balenciaga dresses (Balenciaga happened to be her favorite designer) with the word "No" scribbled repeatedly across the photostats.[35] As for Brodovitch, who could seem imperious to his assistants and students, he apparently was intimidated by his editor. Robert Frank remembers the art director's extreme deference to her when he was introducing Frank as his latest discovery; the photographer found it at odds with Brodovitch's otherwise confident European

While most of the Surrealist devices used by Brodovitch in the 1930s had disappeared by the issues of the fifties, his attraction to film and cinematic devices persisted. Here, as is true of all the *Harper's Bazaar* issues he designed, the film-strip motif represents action and movement.

Above:
HARPER'S BAZAAR, APRIL 1950. PHOTOGRAPHER: BEN ROSE

Opposite:
HARPER'S BAZAAR, MARCH 1952

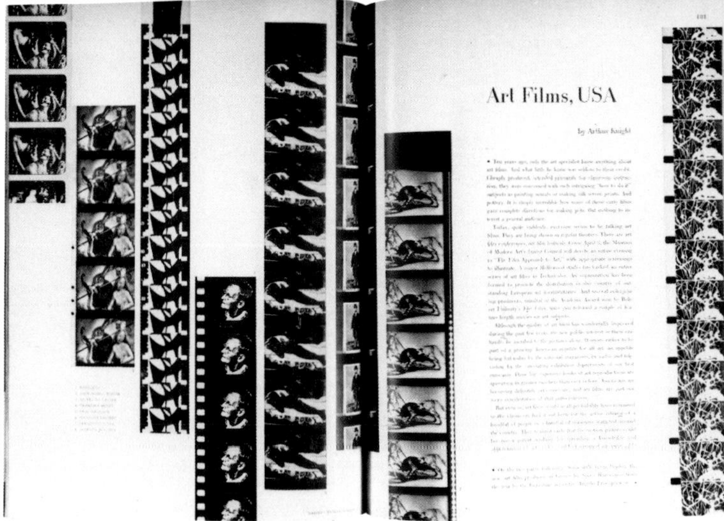

manner.[36] Others recall that the designer never would argue with her if her mind clearly was made up.

Nevertheless, Snow trusted Brodovitch in all matters of visual taste, and usually agreed with his enthusiasms about artists and photographers. She even allowed him to continue working as a designer on a free-lance basis, for clients that included as least one advertiser, Saks Fifth Avenue—something he could manage because for much of his tenure at the *Bazaar* he spent only part of the day in the office. (Snow apparently countenanced the arrangement, although his assistants felt the need to cover up his absences, which often were ascribed to sickness.) And it was away from *Harper's Bazaar*, freed of the constraints of fashion and editorial oversight, that Brodovitch produced some of his best work.

Portfolio and *Observations*

In 1949 George S. Rosenthal, the son of an Ohio magazine publisher, and Frank Zachary, a young and ambitious editor, asked Brodovitch to design a new magazine of the graphic arts they were planning, called *Portfolio*. Conceived as a quarterly, and lasting only three issues, the magazine shows Brodovitch at his most inventive and imaginative (pages 86–97). He was the publication's art director and art editor, meaning that he both conceived of articles and nurtured them onto the page.

Among the artists, photographers, and designers featured in the issues of 1950 and 1951 were Richard Avedon, Alexander Calder, Charles Eames, Irving Penn, Paul Rand, Ben Shahn, and Saul Steinberg. In addition, there were articles devoted to anonymous and commercial design in its least noticeable forms, such as cattle brands and shopping bags. But besides its innovative and sophisticated approach to content, *Portfolio* was most remarkable for its design. Pages folded out, paper stock changed from thick to thin and from glossy to matte, 3-D stereo viewers and swatches of shopping bags were bound in. And the pages themselves showed off Brodovitch's immense versatility, ranging from photomontage, in a layout of his students' photographs of Philadelphia's mummers parade (pages 126–127), to an eight-page article on sculptor Alexander Calder in which each spread has a distinctive appearance.

As he did at *Harper's Bazaar*, Brodovitch worked on *Portfolio* by laying out spreads, assembling them on the floor as he went along. But the freedom to have the articles run whatever length they required, and his own involvement with their subject matter, gave his work a sense of expansiveness similar to that of his Paris years and glimpsed only intermittently at *Harper's Bazaar*. Scale, proportion, and contrast are all used to dislodge the viewer's eye from its impartial gaze; the same elements serve to create a three-dimensional effect that made the page itself not so much a background curtain as a theater proscenium.

Because it reflects both his youthful enthusiasm and his mature self-confidence as a designer, *Portfolio* is the best and most consistent example of Brodovitch's talent as a magazine designer. The foremost example of Brodovitch's work as a book designer is the 1959 volume *Observations*, featuring Richard Avedon's photographs and commentary by Truman Capote, another regular contributor to *Bazaar*. In *Observations*, each spread functions like a movie screen (pages 108–113). Making the most of Avedon's washed-out backgrounds, the designer shifted between pages of silhouetted images and pages of rectangular blocks of images and text, all surrounded by ample quantities of white space. For all the clarity and simplicity of the presentation, there is an enormous visual variety in the book. Like Avedon's photographs, the design shocks the eye to attention, but its elegance never breaks the implicit contract between the page and the viewer.

Portfolio and *Observations* mark the height of Brodovitch's signature style, one characterized by a liberal use of white space, restraint in terms of type and headlines, and a reliance on the power of photography to convey emotion without recourse to artifice. Indeed, it was a growing appreciation of, and fascination with, the photograph that inspired Brodovitch's most original work. As he grew older, he forsook the sometimes gimmicky illusionism of Surrealism for daring, attention-getting expanses of white, on which photographs became the major—and in some cases the only—characters. Like actors on a bare stage, they become the center of attention and, more importantly, centers of emotional energy. ■

A GATHERING OF SWANS

From the journal of a Mr. Patrick Conway, aged 17, during the course of a visit to Bruges in the year 1800: "Sat on the stone wall and observed a gathering of swans, an aloof armada, coast around the curves of the canal and merge with the twilight, their feathers floating away over the water like the trailing hems of snowy ball-gowns. I was reminded of beautiful women; I thought of Mlle. de V., and experienced a cold exquisite spasm, a chill, as though I had heard a poem spoken, fine music rendered. A beautiful woman, beautifully elegant, impresses us as art does, changes the weather of our spirit; and that, is that a frivolous matter? I think not."

The intercontinental covey of swans drifting across our pages boasts a pair of cygnets, fledglings of the prettiest promise who may one day lead the flock. However, as is generally conceded, a beautiful girl of twelve or twenty, while she may merit attention, does not deserve admiration. Reserve that laurel for decades hence when, if she has

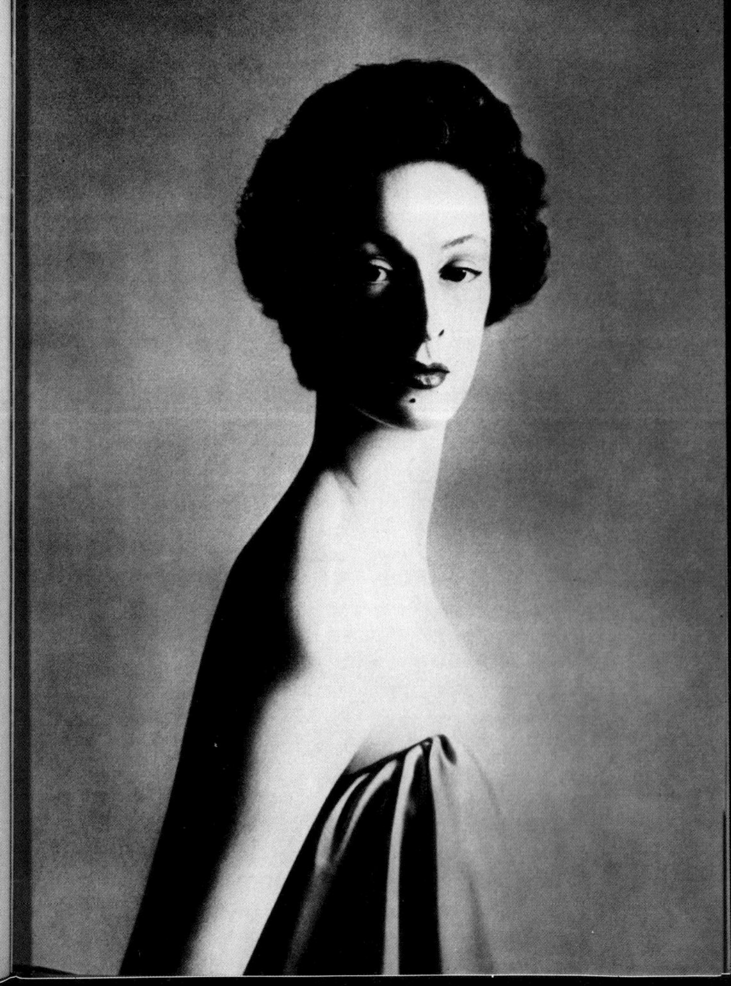

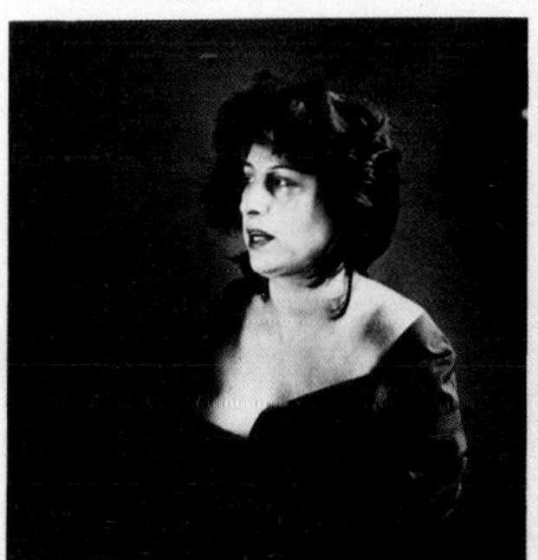

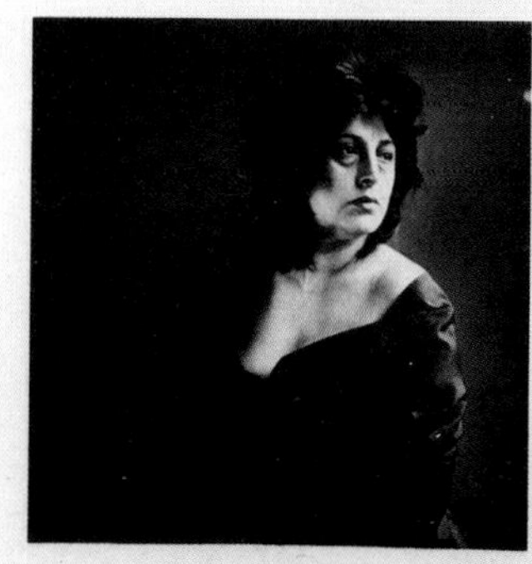

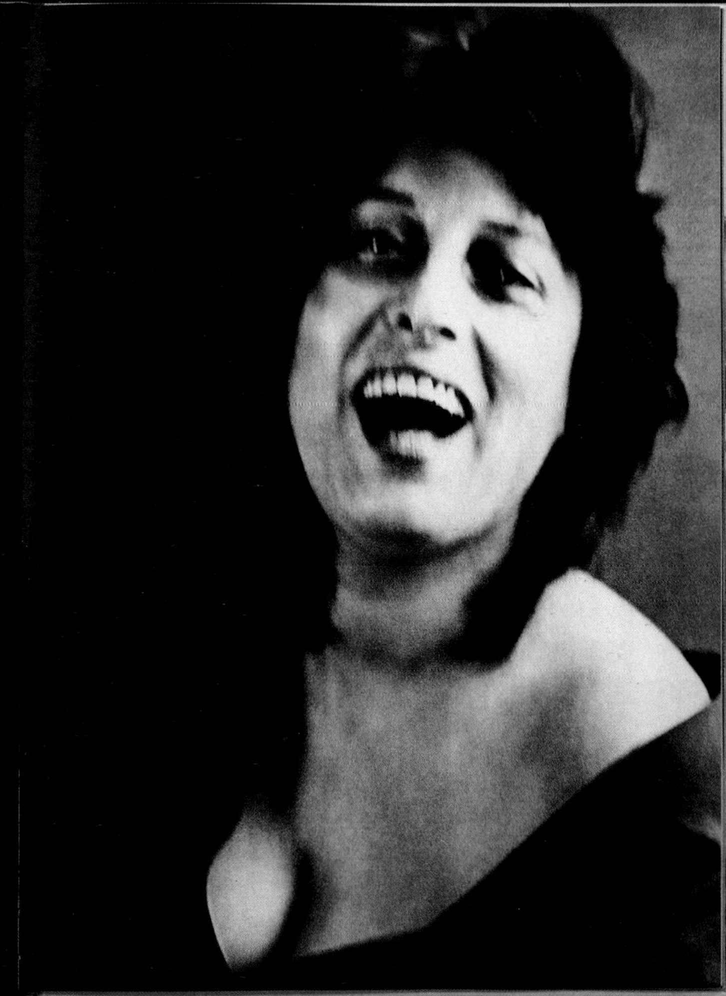

kept buoyant the weight of her gifts, been faithful to the vows a swan must, she will have earned an audience all-kneeling; for her achievement represents discipline, has required the patience of a hippopotamus, the objectivity of a physician combined with the involvement of an artist, one whose sole creation is her perishable self. Moreover, the area of accomplishment must extend much beyond the external. Of first importance is voice, its timbre, how and what it pronounces; if stupid, a swan must seek to conceal it, not necessarily from men (a dash of dumbness seldom diminishes masculine respect, though it rarely, regardless of myth, enhances it); rather from clever women, those witch-eyed brilliants who are simultaneously the swan's mortal enemy and most convinced adorer. Of course the perfect Giselle, she of calmest purity, is herself a clever woman. The cleverest are easily told; and not by any discourse on politics or Proust, any smartly placed banderillas of wit; not, indeed, by the presence of **any** positive factor, but the absence of one: self-appreciation. The very nature of her attainment presupposes a certain personal absorption; nonetheless, if one can remark on her face or in her attitude an awareness of the impression she makes, it is as though, attending a banquet, one had the misfortune to glimpse the kitchen.

To pedal a realistic chord—and it must be sounded, if only out of justice to their cousins of coarser plumage—authentic swans are almost never women nature and the world has at all deprived. God gave them good bones; some lesser personage, a father, a husband, blessed them with that best of beauty emollients, a splendid bank account. Being a great beauty, and **remaining** one, is, at the altitude flown here, expensive: a fairly accurate estimate on the annual upkeep could be made—but really, why spark a

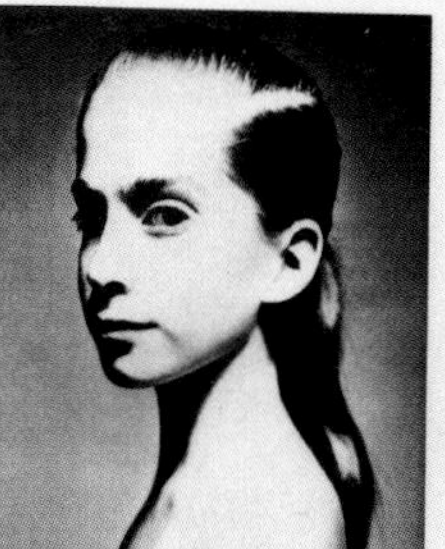

revolution? And if expenditure were all, a sizable population of sparrows would swiftly be swans.

It may be that the enduring swan glides upon waters of liquefied lucre; but that cannot account for the creature herself—her talent, like all talent, is composed of unpurchasable substances. For a swan is invariably the result of adherence to some aesthetic system of thought, a code transposed into a self-portrait; what we see is the imaginary portrait precisely projected. This is why certain women, while not truly beautiful but triumphs over plainness, can occasionally provide the swan-illusion: their inner vision of themselves is so fixed, decorated with such clever outer artifice, that we surrender to their claim, even stand convinced of its genuineness: and it **is** genuine; in a way the **manqué** swan (our portfolio contains two excellent examples) is more beguiling than the natural (of which, among present company, the classic specimens are Mme. Agnelli, the European swan **numero uno**, and America's superb, unsurpassable Mrs. William S. Paley): after all, a creation wrought by human nature is of subtler human interest, of finer fascination, than one nature alone has evolved.

A final word: the advent of a swan into a room starts stirring in some persons a decided sense of discomfort. If one is to believe these swan allergics, their hostility does not derive from envy, but, so they suggest, from a shadow of "coldness" and "unreality" the swan casts. Yet isn't it true that an impression of coldness, usually false, accompanies perfection? And might it not be that what the critics actually feel is fear? In the presence of the very beautiful, as in the presence of the immensely intelligent, terror contributes to our over-all reaction, and it is as much fright as appreciation which causes the stabbed-by-an-icicle chill that for a moment murders us when a swan swims into view.

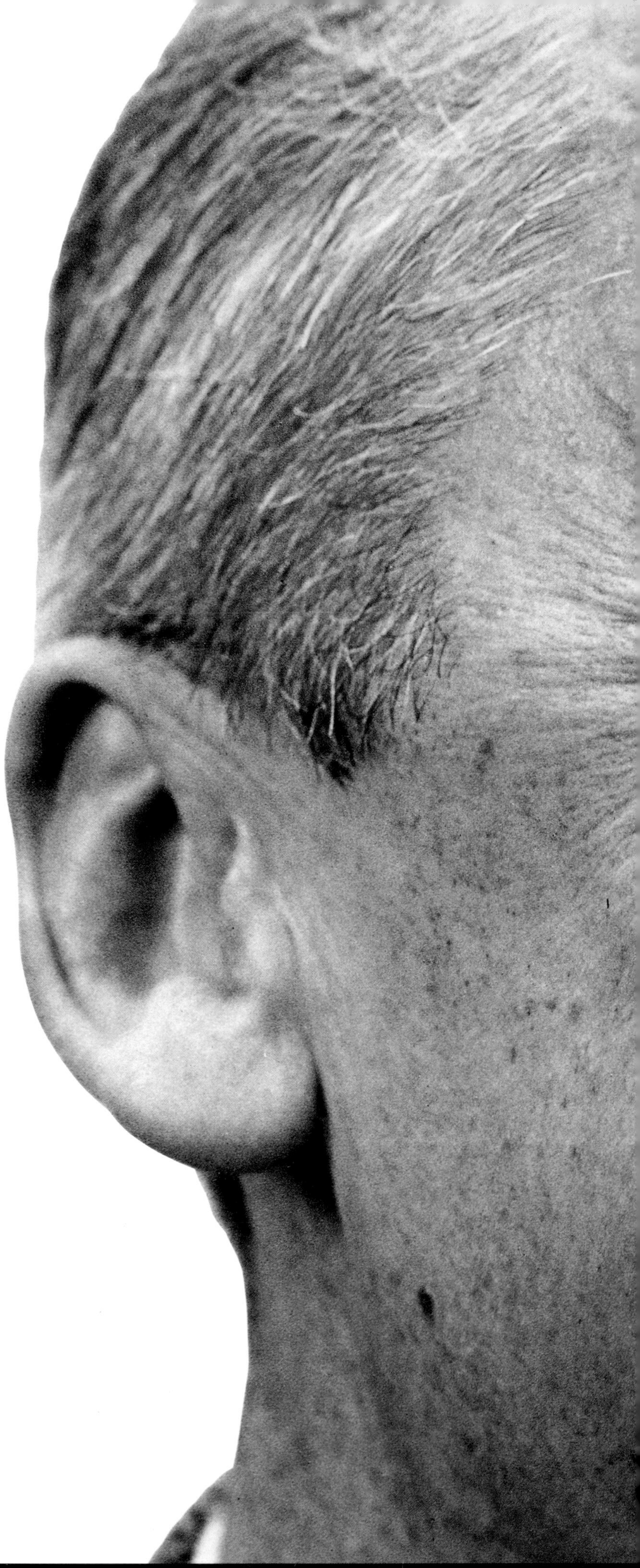

This portrait of undersea explorer Jacques Cousteau was taken for *Observations*. Three of the uncropped portraits from the sitting are shown here, superimposed on the one that was finally selected as cropped by Brodovitch for the book.

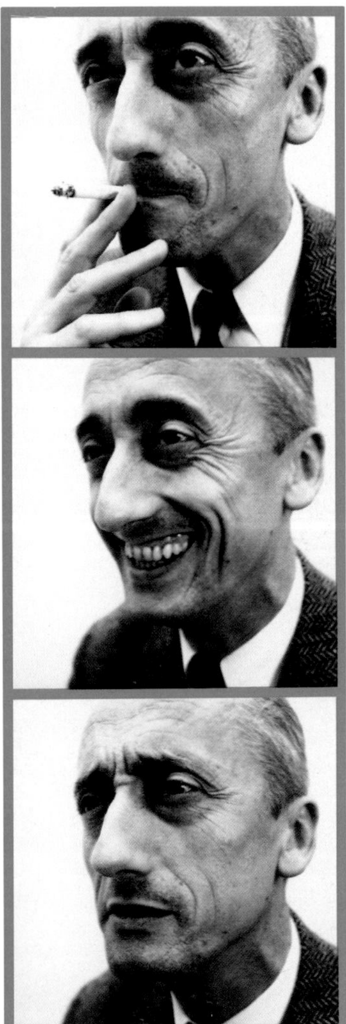

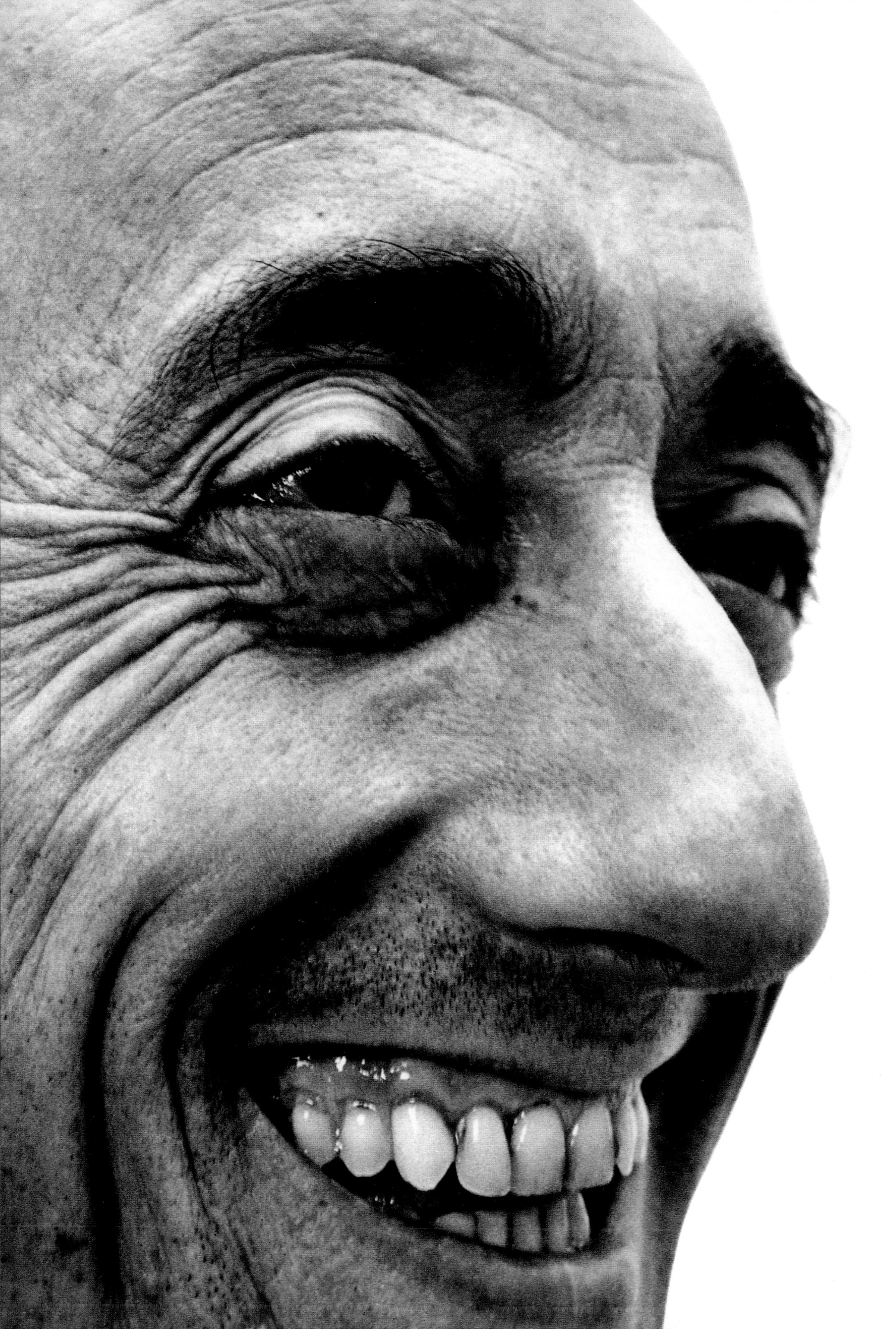

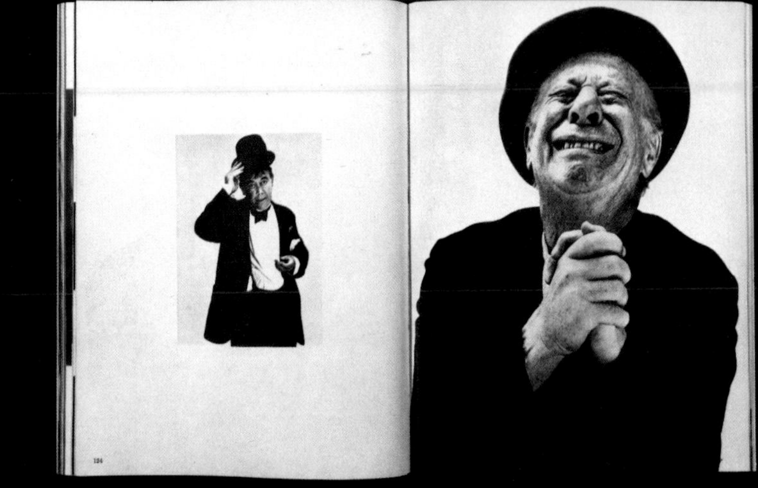
124

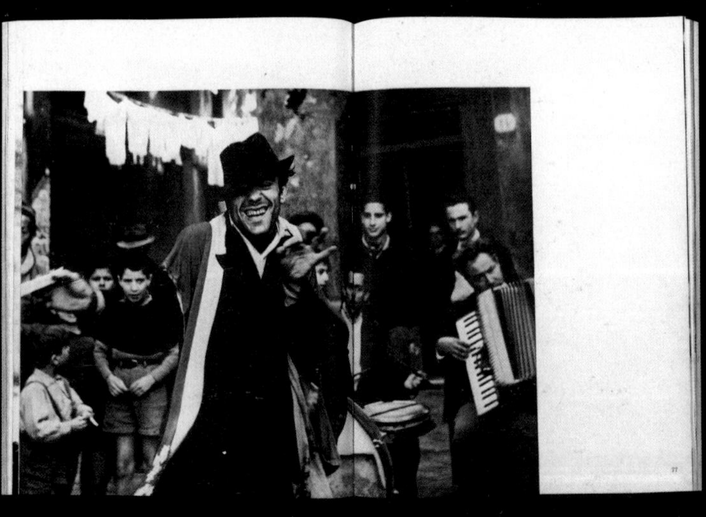
77

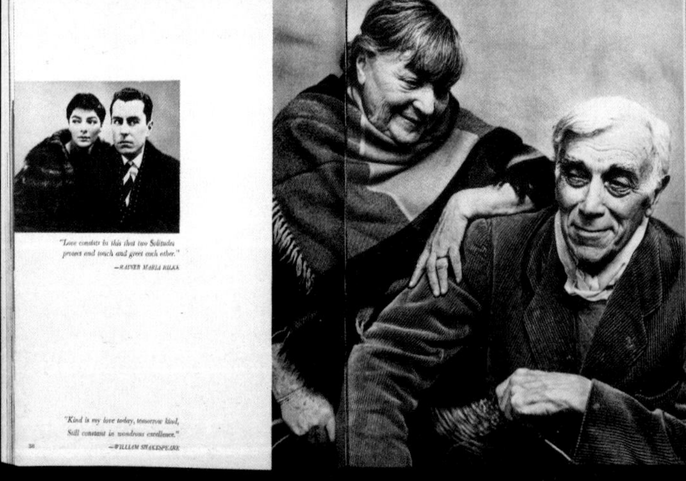
"Love consists in this that two Solitudes protect and touch and greet each other."

—RAINER MARIA RILKE

"Kind is my love today, tomorrow kind,
Still constant in wondrous excellence."

—WILLIAM SHAKESPEARE

38

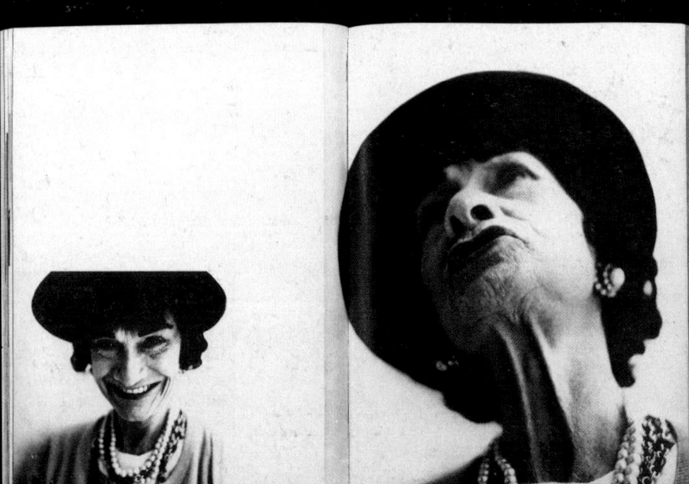

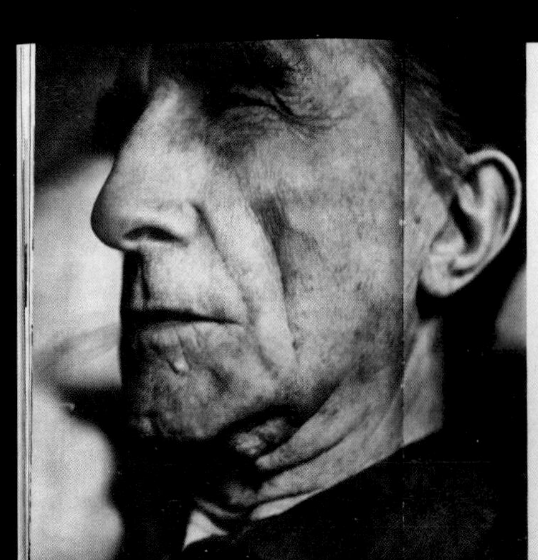

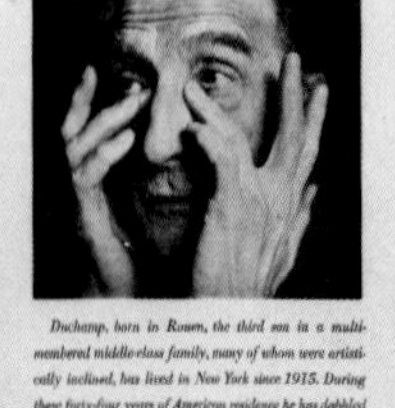

Duchamp, born in Rouen, the third son in a multi-membered middle-class family, many of whom were artistically inclined, has lived in New York since 1915. During these forty-four years of American residence he has dabbled away at only one painting (Bride Stripped Bare by Her Bachelors, Even—an oil, on transparent glass, the size of a church window), and finished none; for all prac-

53

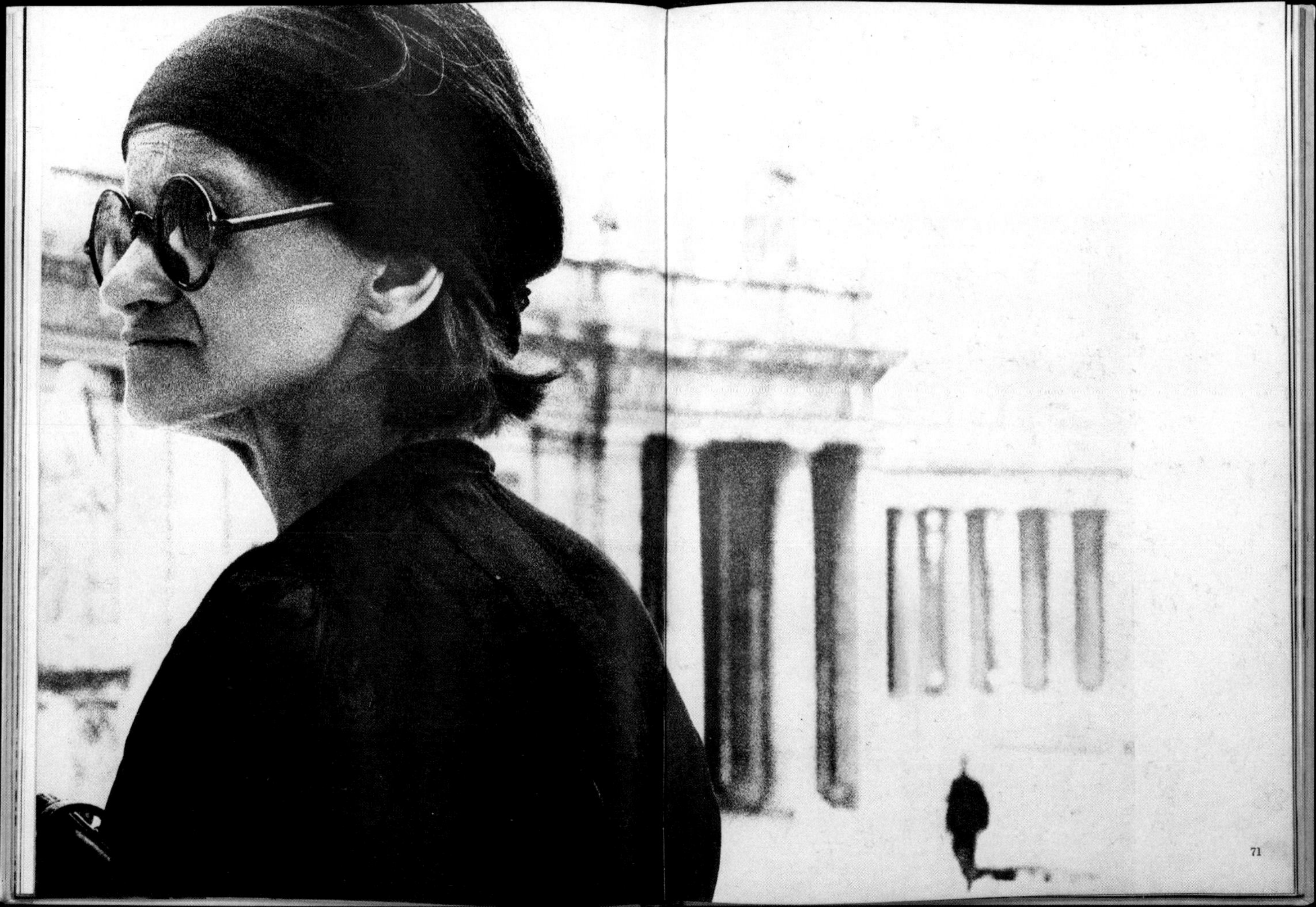

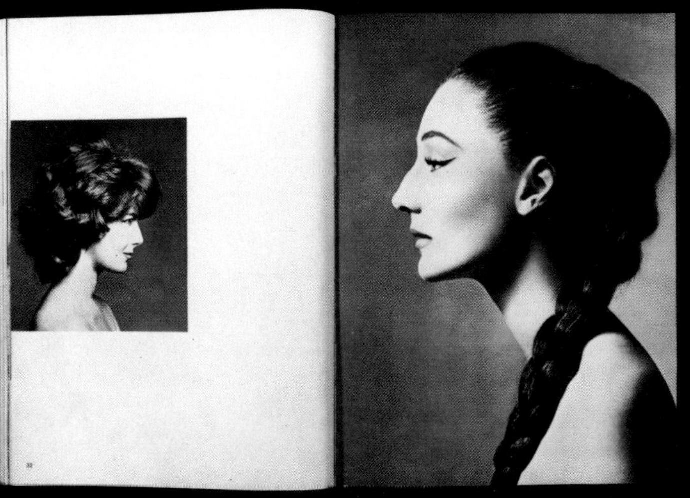

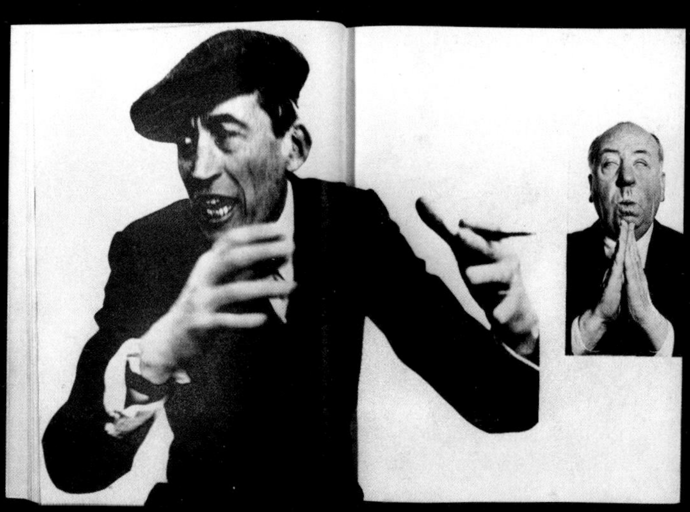

City's foremost philosophers (The Mind and Heart of Love) and emissaries into atmospheres of wealth and/or intellect, year after year bustles, a rusty-black miser-like figure, always pinched and poor-looking, between continents, beseeching the rich in support of Catholic good-works, lecturing the already Enlightened and, as a sort of Monsignor Sheen to the intelligentsia, converting to the Faith many of the century's cleverest minds (it was Darcy who first convinced, then instructed, Evelyn Waugh and Graham Greene). A mentally modernized Savonarola, Darcy is swift in pursuit of man's soul, the undyable self is his concern; Mr. Oppenheimer is, on the other hand, troubled by the all too perishable aspects of humanity: definitely he doesn't want to see us evaporate inside a mushroom-contoured cloud—a possibility which, in theory so to say, holds no horrors for Catholic Darcy, who has the not-to-be-mocked-at comfort of a true after-life vision. Meanwhile, we may as well (why not?) allow ourselves to hope that the separately directed prayers of this man who hopes he is heard by God, and this man who hopes he is heard by men, will somewhere gain audience. Amen.

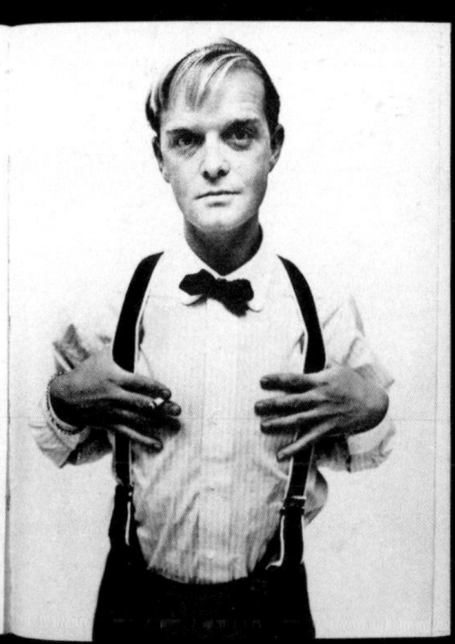

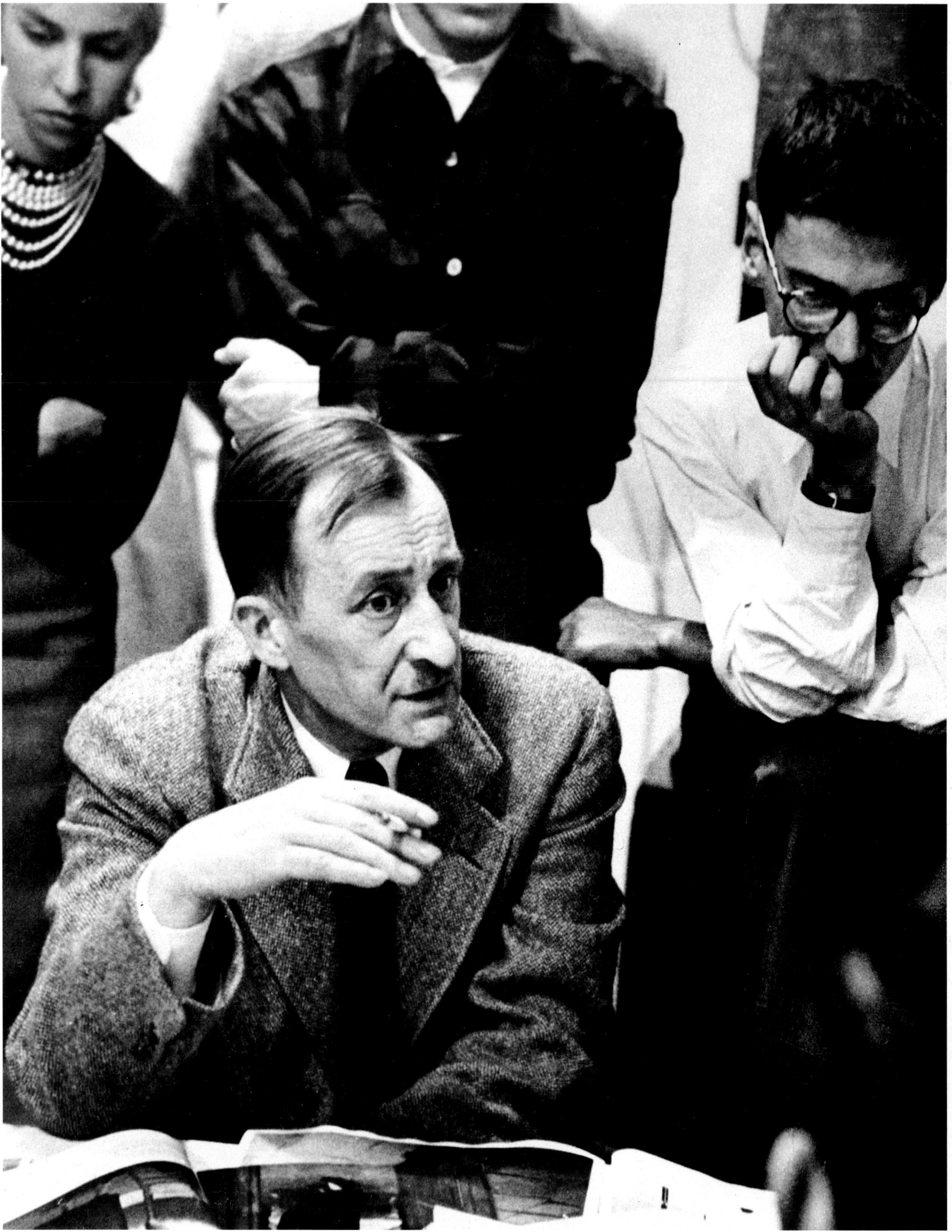

MEDIUM OF THE IMAGINATION

5

"Industry today gives the publicity artist not only a new vision but also a variety of new materials and instruments as a means for realizing ideas."
—ALEXEY BRODOVITCH[37]

As the art director of one of the leading picture-oriented magazines of the day, as a teacher, and as a photographer himself, Brodovitch came to have an enormous impact on the practice of photography. His career coincided with the widespread adoption of photography as a medium of mass communication and as an instrument in the creation of consumer desire. And it extended into a period of fundamental change in how photographs were viewed as works of art.

During Brodovitch's first years in the United States, American publishing and advertising underwent a fundamental transition, in which photographs replaced hand-drawn illustrations as the predominant medium of visual communication on the printed page. While *The National Geographic* had been using camera images as its main staple for years, and while photographs were already significant features of *Vogue* and *Vanity Fair*, it was only in the 1930s that photography finally usurped the place of illustration in large-circulation American magazines. This was true both on the editorial pages and in the advertisements that accompanied them. The birth of *Life* in 1936 signaled the beginning of an era in which photographs would be the major source of news, information, and cultural iconography to the nation—an era that would last until photography was in turn supplanted by television in the 1960s.

Technological, financial, and cultural factors played a role in this transition. As half-tone reproduction advanced from its infancy in the late nineteenth century, it became economically feasible and even advantageous to use photographs in place of hand-drawn illustrations. Photographs were preferable for journalistic purposes because they could be produced more rapidly. And because photographs were widely believed to represent reality directly and without inflection, they conveyed events, personalities, products, and symbols with an unmatched authority. To a world suffering both economically and spiritually from the Depression, photographs seemed more real, more believable, and more compelling than the imaginative creations of illustrators—never mind that they were often manipulated to convey specific messages, or that they, like the Hollywood films of the time, might deal largely in fantasy.

In Europe the shift had begun soon after World War I. As a novice designer and

ALEXEY BRODOVITCH TEACHING THE DESIGN LABORATORY, WITH EVELYN AVEDON, LEFT, AND RICHARD AVEDON, RIGHT. C. 1930

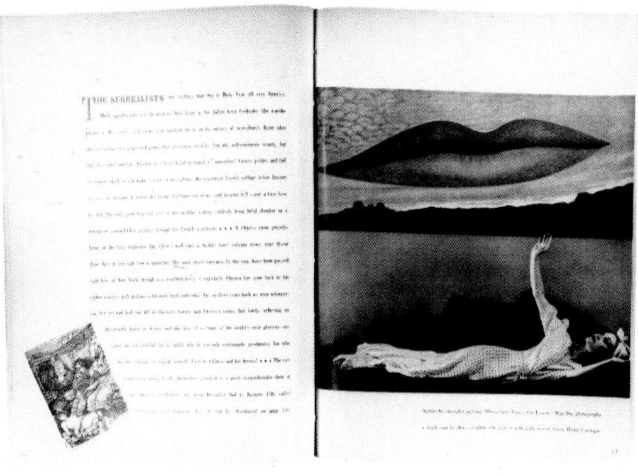

From the very first issue of *Harper's Bazaar* that he designed, Brodovitch sought out new and arresting kinds of photographic imagery. Besides using Martin Munkacsi, a pioneer of active outdoor fashion photography who had been recruited by Carmel Snow, he regularly published pictures by Man Ray, who was among the most experimental of the photographers of the 1930s. The American expatriate artist's Surrealist-inspired fashion pictures, solarized portraits, photograms, X–ray images, and this "photographic impression of a new fashion 'coming over' the short waves" appeared on the pages of the magazine throughout the thirties.

illustrator in Paris in the twenties, Brodovitch would have been acutely aware of the surging interest in photography and its graphic potentials. An aesthetic of visual dynamism, created out of a widespread urge to find a new visual order appropriate to a new age, was charging the medium with a sense of possibility, and it was being widely disseminated throughout Europe in news and picture magazines. Photography was not only a means of conveying information but also an image-making system that could reveal new vistas and truths about the world. Not surprisingly, the new stylistic approaches and formal experimentation in European photography led to new ideas about design.

The Futurists in Italy, Constructivists in Russia, and Surrealists in France all saw the camera as an integral part of their avant-garde activities. The efforts of Futurist photographer Anton Giulio Bragaglia to represent kinetic forces in visual terms, begun in 1911, prefigured a wide range of photography in the 1920s devoted to capturing instants of time in a single image. For László Moholy-Nagy, Alexander Rodchenko, and other Constructivist and Constructivist-inspired photographers, the discovery of new points of view was paramount, as was the disruption of conventional single-point perspective. For Surrealists such as Man Ray, photography's fascination lay in its seemingly magical revelation of unexpected realities.

The development of portable hand cameras of high quality helped nourish the seeds of a new European Modernist style of photography. The concept of the "candid" image, so important to contemporary photojournalism, was put into practice on a large scale following the introduction of the Leica camera in 1924. In the hands of such photographers as Brassaï, Cartier-Bresson, and Kertész, candid imagery became recognized as a new kind of art, one based on contingency and lyricism. Meanwhile other photographers, including Man Ray and Moholy-Nagy, were practicing a cameraless, studio-based photography, in which the photographic paper was treated like a blank canvas, to be drawn on with light.

All these currents flourished during Brodovitch's years in Paris, since many of the leading photographers of the day were then living there. Man Ray arrived there a year after Brodovitch; Berenice Abbott was already in residence. Brassaï came in 1924, André Kertész a year later. Maurice Tabard and Bill Brandt both appeared on the scene by the decade's end. At the same time that these artists pursued aesthetic innovations, a more commercial practice—fashion and portrait photography—helped sustain them. Man Ray, for example, did both portraiture and fashion assignments to earn money; others, such as George Hoyningen-Huené and James Abbe, were in Paris specifically to serve the growing market for fashion and portrait photographs.

Brodovitch came under the spell of more than individual photographers, however. In France and Germany, the rise of photographically illustrated magazines helped prompt a new consideration of the relationship of type and photography on the printed page. In magazines such as the *Municher Illustrierte Presse*, where Stefan Lorant was editor, and *Vu*, published in Paris and edited by Lucien Vogel, a reliance on photographs to carry the magazines' "content" presaged a radical shift in the traditional relationship of type and

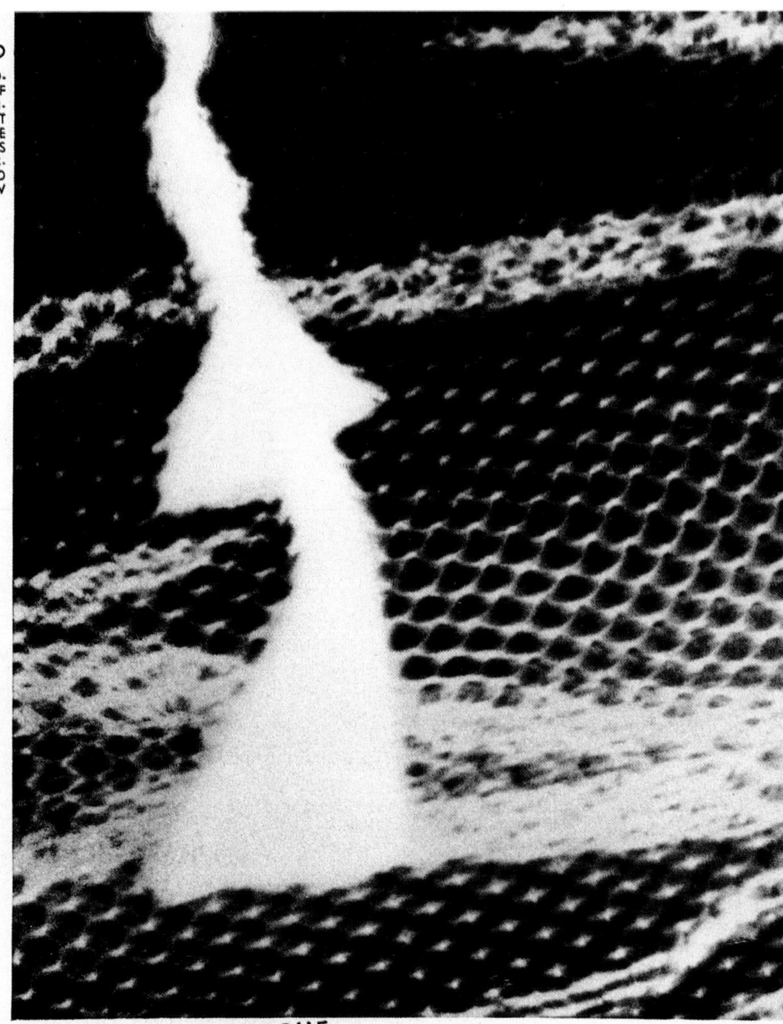

FASHIONS BY RADIO

MAN RAY'S PHOTOGRAPHIC IMPRESSION OF A NEW FASHION "COMING OVER" THE SHORT WAVES. IN THIS ISSUE FIVE PAGES OF FASHIONS FROM THE NEW COLLECTIONS WERE RADIOED FROM PARIS TO NEW YORK.

ALL COLLECTIONS VIOLENTLY PICTURESQUE
LOOK 1880 ONE MINUTE, 1950 THE NEXT
THE MOST FANTASTIC MODERN MATERIALS
STIFF AS INFANTAS IN THE EVENING
EVERYONE IS CUTTING WHOOPSY BANGS
DO NOT BELIEVE THAT DERRIERES ARE FLAT
CROWNS ZOOM HIGH AS HUSSARS
WONDERFUL NEW SHADE OF VIOLET BLUE

45

Right:
HARPER'S BAZAAR,
NOVEMBER 1936.
PHOTOGRAPHER: MAN RAY

Opposite:
HARPER'S BAZAAR,
NOVEMBER 1936.
PHOTOGRAPHER: MAN RAY

image on the page. Henry Luce reportedly once said that without the example of *Vu*, *Life* would never have existed.

This intense interest in photographs and their appearance on the printed page was part of a wider revolution in visual consciousness. The increasing ease, economy, and sophistication of printing, and the development of better halftone reproduction technology, fueled the demand for images of all sorts. What was then called "publicity" and is now called advertising was in the process of becoming a field of its own, with its own styles, conventions, and masters. Large industrial corporations hired designers to shape everyday objects ranging from pencil sharpeners to locomotives. These new fields of activity became hothouses for what we now call modern design, and design itself became a distinct profession with its own division of labor. Thus, for Brodovitch, photography functioned both as a symbol of modernity and, less obviously, as an analogue of his own career.

Photomontage

For graphic designers like Brodovitch, one of the most important artistic innovations of the twenties was photomontage—the practice of combining separate images into one "seamless," but artificial, whole. As pioneered in the late 1910s by the Berlin Dadaists—George Grosz, Raoul Hausmann, Hannah Hoch—photomontage was a way of dismantling photography's insistent realism, replacing it with disruptive juxtapositions as unusual

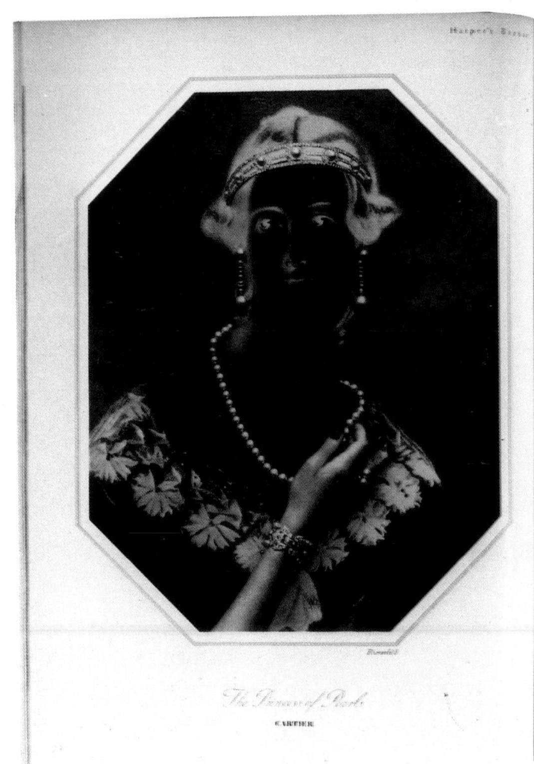

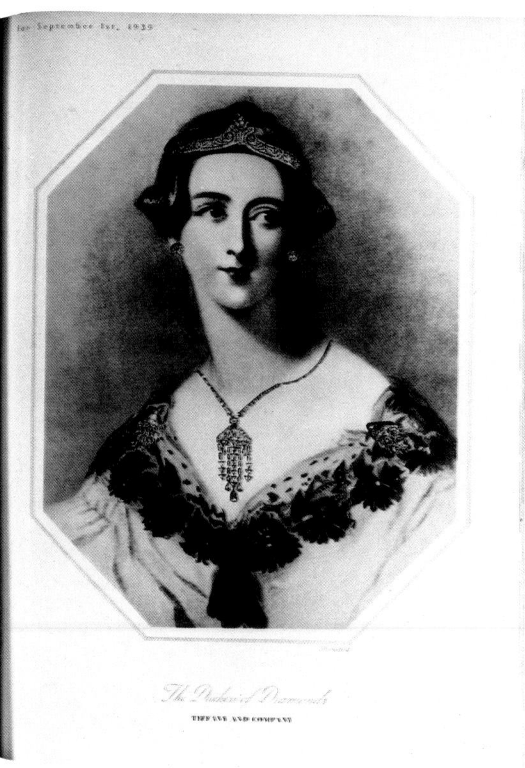

Among the influences that formed Brodovitch's style, none seems more central than photomontage, the practice of combining several photographs into one image. In the thirties and forties, the photographer Erwin Blumenfeld took many photographs for the *Bazaar* that utilized montage techniques within the photographic frame.

and challenging as the radical spaces of Cubist painting. Almost simultaneously, the Russian Constructivists conceived of photomontage as a political instrument in a wider sense, for communicating directly with the Soviet masses—one that was inexpensive to reproduce, repeatable, and easy to understand. Their propaganda posters, film advertisements, and exhibition installations were intended to provide the Soviet state with a revolutionary graphic style. On the other hand, the Paris Dadaists, and later the Surrealists, saw photomontage as a kind of visual automatic writing, producing the chance, subconscious juxtapositions they treasured.

Both strains of photomontage had an important impact on graphic design as a whole and Brodovitch in particular. As Dawn Ades has written in her book *Photomontage:*

From about 1923 until well into the thirties, the uses of photomontage were rapidly extended in the fields of commercial publicity and political propaganda, for posters, book covers, postcards, magazine and book illustrations, and exhibition installations.[38]

Although he retained an allegiance to illustration in his own work even in the thirties (for example, in his ads for Climax Molybdenum, page 56), Brodovitch had already demonstrated a sophisticated working knowledge of the visual lessons of photomontage in his advertisements for the Aux Trois Quartiers department store in the late twenties.

From the Berlin Dadaists and the Constructivists, Brodovitch gleaned a sense of the photograph as malleable instrument of mass communication. From Parisian Dada and Surrealism, he acquired a taste for the visually disruptive, for combinations of images that challenged the public's conventional understanding of visual order. As a designer, Brodovitch intuitively understood that such disruptions need not rely solely on subject matter—as does, for example, Max Ernst's photomontage that blends a woman's legs with an airplane fuselage.[39] They also could function in purely graphic ways: in terms of disparities of scale, tonality, and composition.

At *Harper's Bazaar*, his ability to pair photographs and type so that they become part of a single, organic composition, and to use photographs together so that their combined effect is greater than their effect individually, made his graphic design unique and, to the American mind of the time, "European" and "modern." To a public used to seeing photographs treated in magazines as boxy, unwieldy rectangles, the effects were astonishing. Even in the fifties, when he

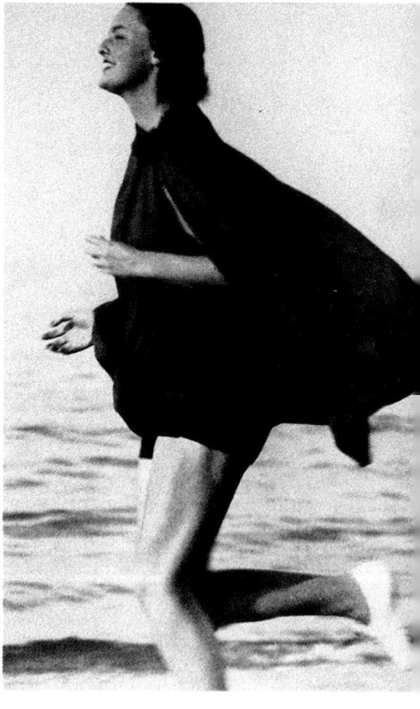

Brodovitch's love of spontaneity and activity in graphic design led him to use photographs that had the same qualities. In the 1930s Martin Munkacsi regularly supplied the *Bazaar* with quasi-candid images; Herman Landshoff and Richard Avedon helped carry Munkacsi's precedent into the forties and fifties. As fashion photography's goal came to be more about fashioning image than portraying substance, Brodovitch increasingly encouraged blur and other nontraditional uses of the medium

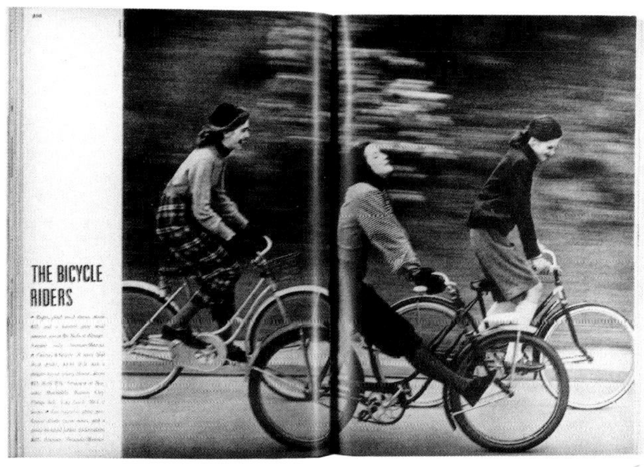

Both pages, left to right:
HARPER'S BAZAAR, SEPTEMBER 1, 1939. PHOTOGRAPHER: ERWIN BLUMENFELD

HARPER'S BAZAAR, DECEMBER 1933. PHOTOGRAPHER: MARTIN MUNKACSI

HARPER'S BAZAAR, AUGUST 1946. PHOTOGRAPHER: HERMAN LANDSHOFF

had abandoned the most obvious uses of photomontage, Brodovitch continued to create combinations of photographs and text that worked together in ways that recall Constructivist poster designs.

A New Impressionism

Some accounts suggest that the designer was predisposed to photography from the start, that as a child in Russia he had used a camera, although no pictures from this period are known to exist. However, there is evidence that he carried a camera during field trips in Philadelphia, and testimony that he encouraged students to do the same. His pictures of performances by the Ballets Russes, taken from the wings of the stage with long shutter speeds, date from the mid-thirties (pages 48–53). While the blurred forms of the dancers are formally innovative, the dreamlike atmosphere in which they move also captures a sense of Brodovitch's nostalgia for his Paris years and yearning for his native Russia.

Spurred perhaps by these slow-shutter pictures, which suggest the influence of Munkacsi, he began to encourage other photographers to experiment with stop-action, blurred motion, and out-of-focus optical effects, and to explore unusual, unexpected points of view. Since he relied heavily on photographs to keep the pages of the *Bazaar* full of vitality, it was to his advantage to nurture a generation of innovative photographers. In the last decade of his career at *Harper's Bazaar*, and from then until the end of his life, he devoted himself to the development of fresh ways of seeing with the camera. In the process, he became a leading exponent of a new style of photography.

While expressive abstraction was as widespread an interest among photographers as it was among painters, the style Brodovitch fostered was radical and controversial. It abjured any pretense to reportage, stressing emotional immediacy through such devices as imprecise focus, large foreground forms, and blurs to suggest movement—precisely the qualities to be found in his own ballet photographs. Technically, it was one hundred and eighty degrees from the precise control and "previsualization" admired by the school of Stieglitz, Strand, and Weston. Instead, imperfections of craft were cherished as indicators of that most prized of artistic virtues, honesty.

At the time photographers spoke in terms of the "available light" aesthetic (disdaining flash, they only recorded with the light that existed). They took pains to emphasize the putative honesty of their pictures through the grainy, chalky, smudged half-light of their prints. The evocation of raw emotion and the direct transcription of feeling was the aim, not technical perfection or finesse. In reality, of course, producing such pictures often required a great deal of technical skill and craftsmanship.

Not everyone was delighted with the kind of photography Brodovitch encouraged and propagated through *Harper's Bazaar*. As John Szarkowski, director of photography at the Museum of Modern Art, has recently written, "The new photographers were referred to by unsympathetic observers as the *quality-be-damned* school." Szarkowski goes on to suggest the possible virtues of such photography:

The goal of the new work was not clarity but authenticity. It did not so much describe its subject as allude to it . . . . If [these photographers'] pictures seemed gratuitously casual even by the relatively

• Last September we ran a want ad in this very spot. "Wanted," we said, "a new word for accessories, a new generic term for all those precious small possessions which bring a dress to life." Apparently, we had found a weak spot in Webster, for though we offered no cash, no cars, no television sets as prizes, the suggestions streamed in. Among them: *accelerators, accentories, dramadditions, animators, completements, extracessories, enhanceries, vitalizers, catalysts, finessories.* To show what an essential role they thought accessories played in fashion, two readers christened them *necessories.* Three others came up with the term *successories.*

• Right: a *successory* if ever there was one— a tight little ski helmet of printed chiffon, to wear with your gray flannel suits. You pull your face through the porthole, then wrap the ends around to the front to make an ascot tie. By John Frederics, in Brooke Cadwallader chiffon (rose, brown and black figures on a white ground). $25.

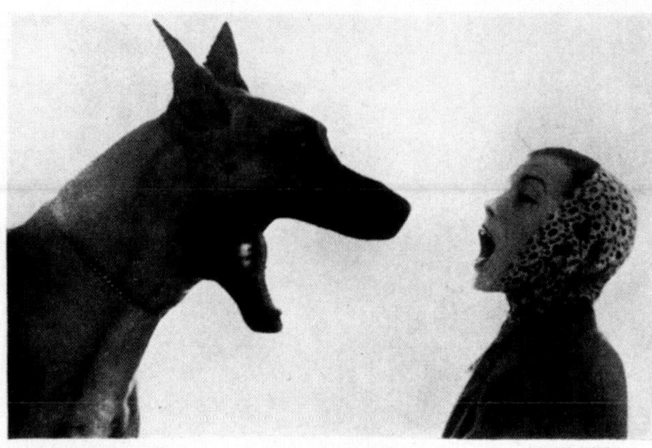

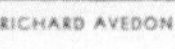

RICHARD AVEDON

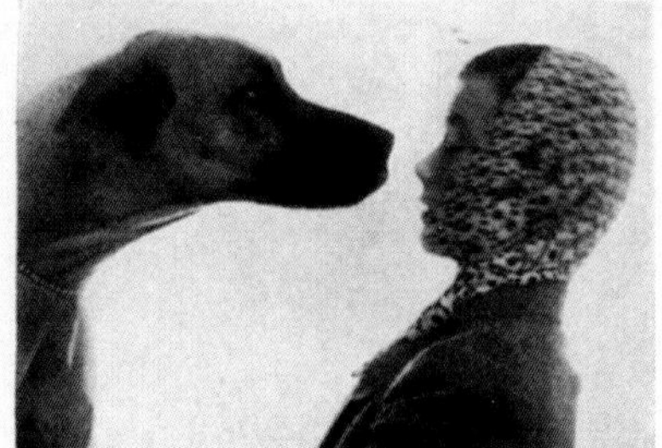

JOHN FREDERICS HELMET

Found: new ways to say "Accessory"

AZAAR, MARCH 1st 1950

permissive standards of photojournalism, they also seemed to be lifted directly and spontaneously from the flow of real life; they seemed formed not by rules and calculation, but by intuition and strong feeling.[40]

Intuition and feeling were precisely what Brodovitch treasured in photographs, and what he tried to teach photographers to treasure as well.

But it may be oversimplifying to limit Brodovitch's influence to a particular style. While it would seem clear that he favored impressionism over precision, preferring the suggestive qualities of a fuzzy, nearly indecipherable image to one that limned the world in front of the lens in great detail, he also was able to appreciate photographs that rendered the most miniscule object in microscopic detail. What mattered to him ultimately was not the technique used to achieve the picture, or even its style, but its effect. It had to be bold, shocking, and close to the photographer's skin.

By encouraging these values in his teaching and through the pictures he chose to reproduce in *Harper's Bazaar*, Brodovitch helped create a climate in which the expressive potentials of photography were felt to be sympathetic, if not synonymous, with the honest depiction of social realities. Unlike the followers of Stieglitz, for whom the photograph served as personal metaphor, and unlike the adherents of the Photo League, for whom straightforward documentation was the only permissible means of political advocacy, the photographers under Brodovitch's spell could have it both ways. Their pictures could be personally expressive *and* documentary. But the subject of the photograph in some ways mattered less than the audience for it. The photographer always had to find a way to grab the viewer's attention, to shock him out of a state of boredom and satiation.

The Example of Avedon

Brodovitch's most important protégé is Richard Avedon. More than any other photographer, Avedon exemplifies the notion that the reaction of the viewer is what matters most in making a picture, and more than anyone else his career has been shaped by Brodovitch's direct influence. He was not yet twenty-one and fresh out of the Merchant

Of the dozens of photographers whose careers Brodovitch nurtured in their formative stages, none has had as much impact on fashion and art as Richard Avedon. Delighted by the camera's ability to dissemble as well as describe, Avedon produced both candid, slice-of-life fashion pictures and calculated studio portraits for *Harper's Bazaar* from the mid-forties through the fifties.

Besides giving Brodovitch the white space he craved, Avedon also sought the surprising juxtapositions favored by Brodovitch's Surrealist aesthetic of the thirties.

Opposite:
HARPER'S BAZAAR,
MARCH 1, 1950.
PHOTOGRAPHER:
RICHARD AVEDON

Left:
HARPER'S BAZAAR,
DECEMBER 1957.
PHOTOGRAPHER:
RICHARD AVEDON

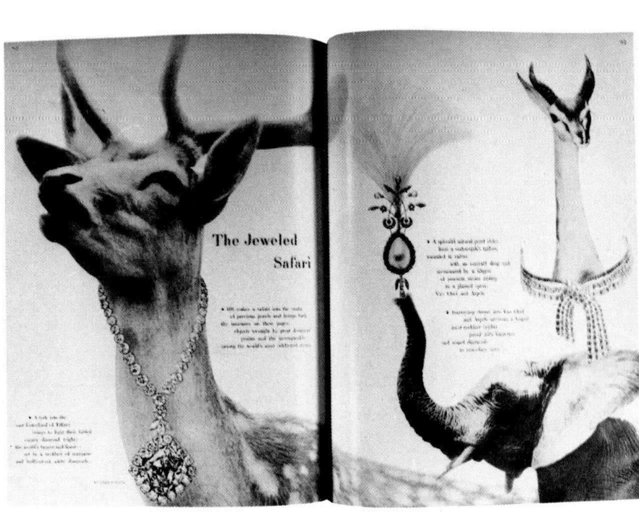

Marine when he encountered Brodovitch, and he quickly became the long-sought successor to Martin Munkacsi, *Harper's Bazaar*'s photographer of dynamic movement. Under the designer's wing, Avedon developed a repertory of stylistic effects that included blurred motion, activity frozen in mid-stride, out-of-focus faces, incongruous subject matter, and a cinema vérité look that resembled the "available light" school of photojournalism. Having grown up an admirer of the *Bazaar* and Munkacsi's pictures in particular, Avedon was primed to follow in the latter's footsteps even before he received his first assignment.

While working for Brodovitch as a free-lance photographer, both for *Harper's Bazaar* and its short-lived spin-off, *Junior Bazaar*, Avedon attended the Design Laboratory at the New School in the mid-forties, doing weekly design assignments based on layout, packaging, and other graphic-design problems. One that has since become legend was to design a neon sign. Avedon protested to Brodovitch that he was unable to complete the assignment because he could not draw. Brodovitch's droll reply, "Why not to use spaghetti?," became the talisman of inventiveness that the photographer would keep with him for the rest of his career.[41]

Brodovitch encouraged Avedon to imbue his pictures with a feeling of movement. As a consequence, many of the fashions and personalities they depict are blurred and indistinct. But Brodovitch did not seem to mind these technical "flaws"; his response was to use the pictures as large as the page size would permit. Neither, apparently, did the photographs' lack of descriptive definition upset the fashion arbiters on the *Bazaar's* staff, including Diana Vreeland and Carmel Snow; their acceptance of Avedon's fuzzy-edged style stands as a clear indication that by the late forties fashion magazines were moving toward a reified, abstract idea of fashion itself. Instead of simply picturing clothes—which, in the years just after World War II, were in short supply—photographs were called on to depict a fashionable image. And no one captured the essence of that image as well as Avedon.

Avedon's unpolished and immediate imagery also signaled a new frankness in postwar fashion photography, an apparent willingness to deal with real lives in everyday, outdoor settings. In part it was inspired by Carmel Snow's belief in utilitarian fashion, itself partly inspired by the naturalism of American clothing designers such as Claire McCardell. But it also coincided with a movement in photography that found its home on city streets, where "real life" was believed to reside. The apparent new candor in fashion photography—which remained, like fashion itself, rooted in illusion—is evident in Avedon's 1948 pictures of the new Paris fashions. Taken on the streets of Paris itself, they show slender models dressed in couturier clothes in the company of street acrobats and other picturesque representatives of life outside of fashion. Like Edward Steichen, Baron de Meyer, and George Hoyningen-Huené before him, Avedon took portraits of authors, artists, and other cultural figures besides doing fashion assignments.

Before the war, Brodovitch had relied on descriptive, full-toned images by the likes of Hoyningen-Huené, George Platt Lynes, Jean Morel, and Leslie Gill. Even Man Ray's fashion images toed the line in terms of showing fine detail with elaborate lighting and a sharp lens. Only Martin Munkacsi's work pointed the way toward a new style. During and after the war, using photographers such as Herman Landshoff, Lillian Bassman, Paul Himmel, Karen and Paul Radkai, Hiro, and Avedon, Brodovitch featured pictures using movement, silhouettes, double exposures, and other techniques that limited the amount of descriptive information being

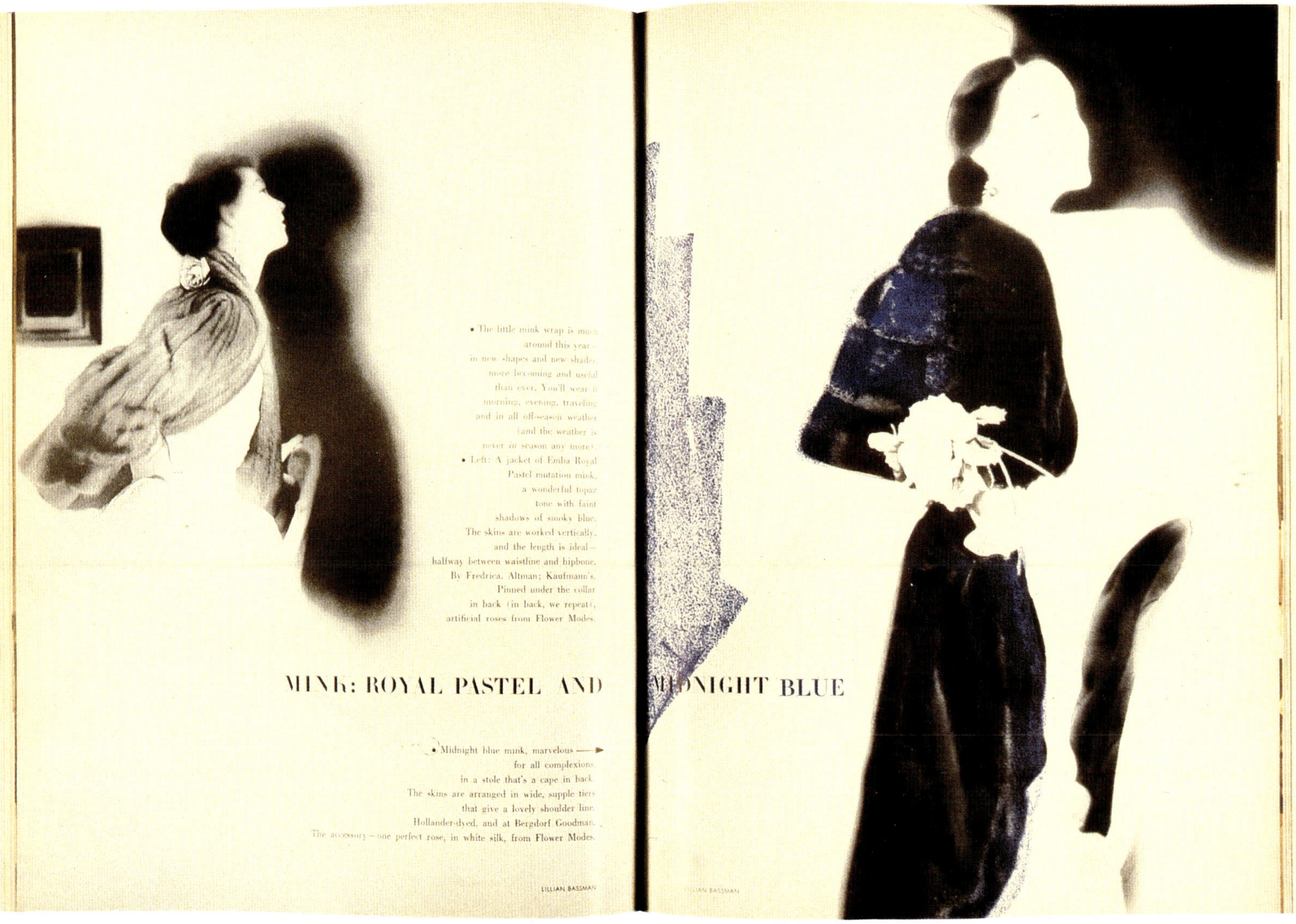

• The little mink wrap is much around this year—in new shapes and new shades, more becoming and useful than ever. You'll wear it morning, evening, traveling and in all off-season weather (and the weather is never *in* season any more).

• Left: A jacket of Emba Royal Pastel mutation mink, a wonderful topaz tone with faint shadows of smoky blue. The skins are worked vertically, and the length is ideal—halfway between waistline and hipbone. By Fredrica. Altman; Kaufmann's. Pinned under the collar in back (in back, we repeat), artificial roses from Flower Modes.

MINK: ROYAL PASTEL AND MIDNIGHT BLUE

• Midnight blue mink, marvelous → for all complexions in a stole that's a cape in back. The skins are arranged in wide, supple tiers that give a lovely shoulder line. Hollander-dyed, and at Bergdorf Goodman. The accessory—one perfect rose, in white silk, from Flower Modes.

LILLIAN BASSMAN

LILLIAN BASSMAN

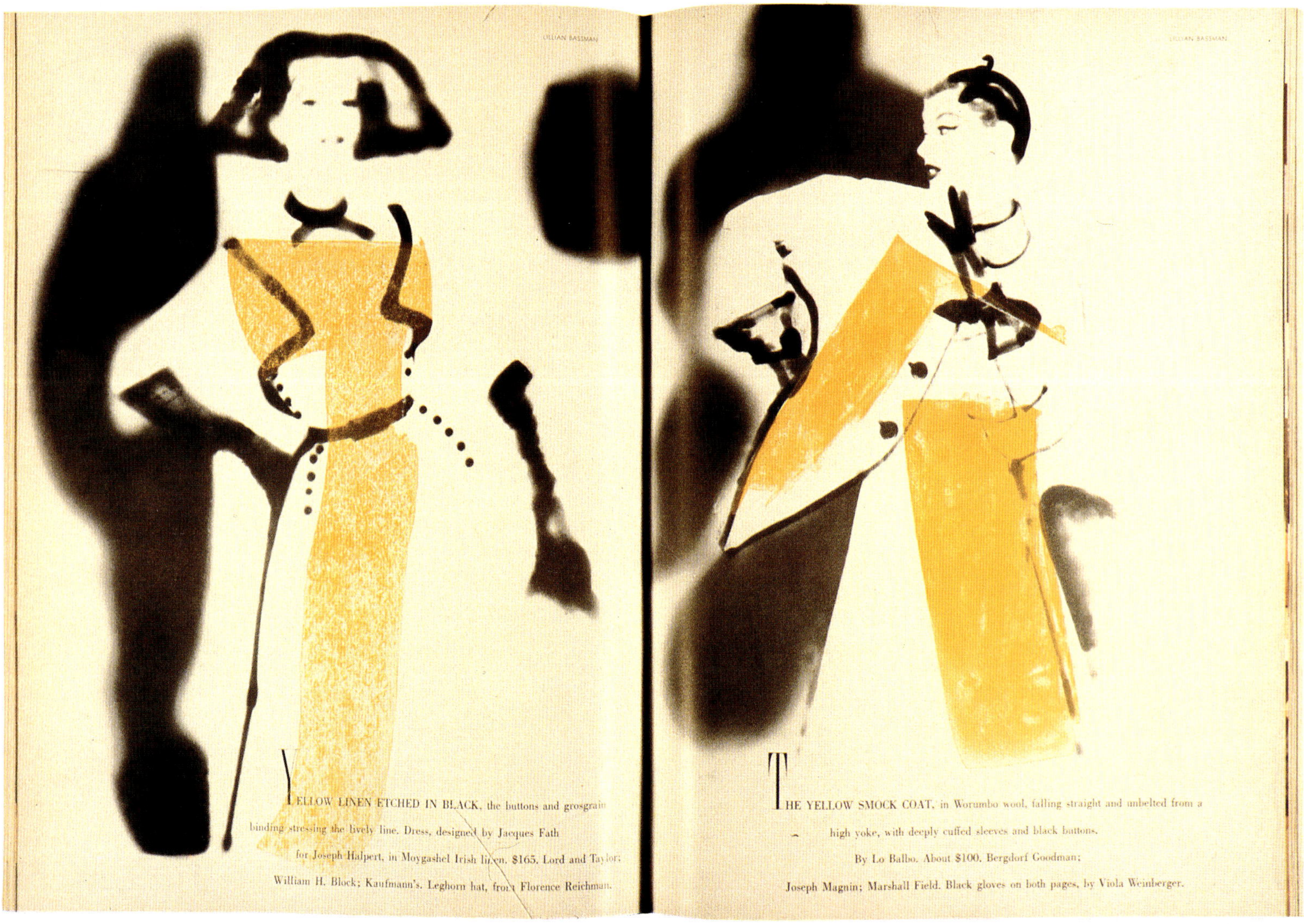

LILLIAN BASSMAN

LILLIAN BASSMAN

YELLOW LINEN ETCHED IN BLACK, the buttons and grosgrain binding stressing the lively line. Dress, designed by Jacques Fath for Joseph Halpert, in Moygashel Irish linen. $165. Lord and Taylor; William H. Block; Kaufmann's. Leghorn hat, from Florence Reichman.

THE YELLOW SMOCK COAT, in Worumbo wool, falling straight and unbelted from a high yoke, with deeply cuffed sleeves and black buttons. By Lo Balbo. About $100. Bergdorf Goodman; Joseph Magnin; Marshall Field. Black gloves on both pages, by Viola Weinberger.

By the 1950s, Brodovitch's taste for impressionistic stylization had reached such an extreme that the clothes themselves almost vanished from the page. The art director encouraged photographers like Lillian Bassman, Paul Himmel, and Karen and Paul Radkai to convey the feeling of fashions without necessarily describing their details. The resulting pictures were often provocatively experimental and, in terms of traditional fashion-magazine photography, radically new. Pictures like these, by Bassman, coincided with a new journalistic style of photography that valued immediacy and expressiveness above precision and craft.

HARPER'S BAZAAR, MARCH 1950. PHOTOGRAPHER: LILLIAN BASSMAN

conveyed. Even Avedon's mercilessly sharp portraits were printed in "high key," so that the highlights disappeared into the white of the page. Only one photographer—Louise Dahl-Wolfe, whom Carmel Snow had invited onto the staff—managed to weather the transition.

Outside the fashion pages, however, Brodovitch remained attached to a more familiar notion of documentary photography. In the forties and fifties he regularly assigned Bill Brandt, Brassaï, and Henri Cartier-Bresson to take pictures for the magazine, and he often used their independently produced images for their own sakes, as picturesque glimpses of far-off places, or as examples of photography's artistic potential. For the most part, though, they worked for Brodovitch as cultural reporters, producing single pictures and small essays that were essentially travelogues of European customs and off-the-beaten-track byways. Since all three worked in predominantly reportorial, slice-of-life styles, they helped bring "the real world" into the realm of the fashion magazine.

Other photographers of whom Brodovitch was fond included the émigrés Robert Frank and Lisette Model. Frank was put to work on fashion assignments, but quickly tired of the idea. Model, who was to succeed Brodovitch as a teacher and mentor to young photographers, brought the art director her candid street photographs, which Brodovitch managed to get published in the *Bazaar*. Both photographers were essentially realists, but with a strong emotional resonance in their work. In terms of fashion photography, however, and in terms of the work he encouraged in his workshops for photographers, Brodovitch increasingly favored impressionistic photography over its descriptive counterpart, and expressionist photography over reportage.

Brodovitch's involvement with photography in the last twenty years of his life, and especially after he was dismissed as art director of the *Bazaar*, undoubtedly helped him to keep functioning in the world despite his failing health, alcoholism, and emotional decline. Part mentor, part guru, and part father figure to scores of young men and women, he taught them to believe in their own instincts and to find the source of their creative lives inside themselves. He was the medium of their imagination. Thanks to them, his memory has been kept alive. But the kind of photography he advocated is no longer in the forefront of current practice. A calculated, intellectual approach that he could have neither foreseen nor condoned now dominates the discussion of photography as an art form. While many of his students became successful as photographers during his lifetime—David Attie, Ed Feingersh, Hiro, Art Kane, and Bert Stern among them—only a few—including Avedon, Bruce Davidson, Irving Penn, and Garry Winogrand—have established significant reputations in contemporary creative photography. ■

DESIGN LABORATORY

From 1930, when he first set foot in the United States, until 1966, when he returned to France, Brodovitch promoted the tenets of modern graphic design by teaching. Despite his protestations that he was only a "can opener," not a teacher, he trained and inspired a generation of postwar designers, illustrators, and photographers. Central to his method was the peripatetic Design Laboratory, an always-evolving seminar course over which Brodovitch presided with imperious authority.

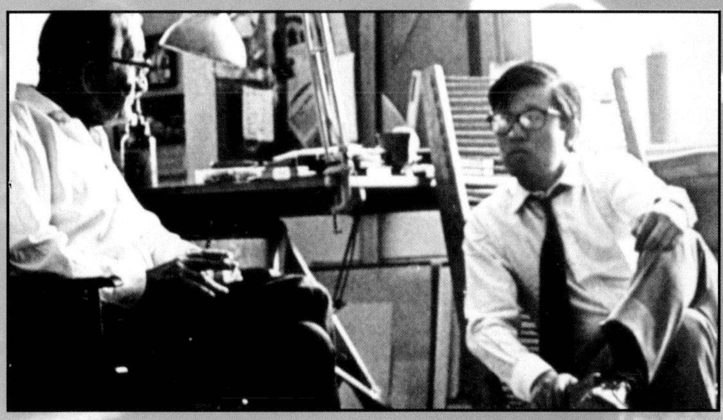

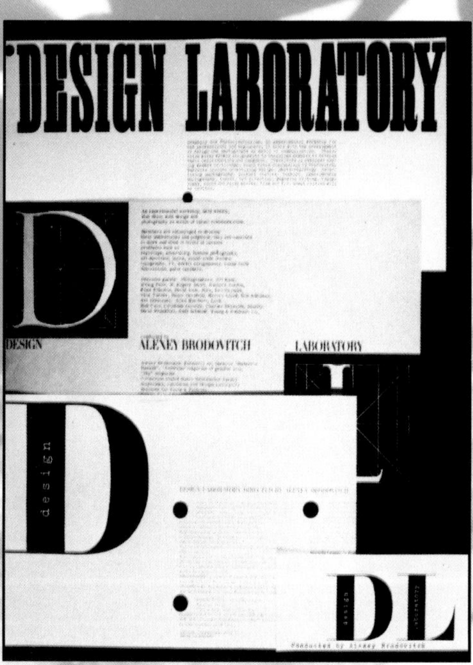

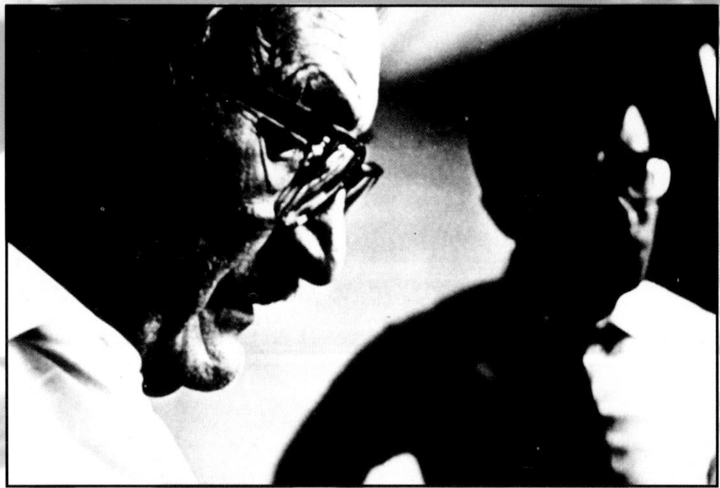

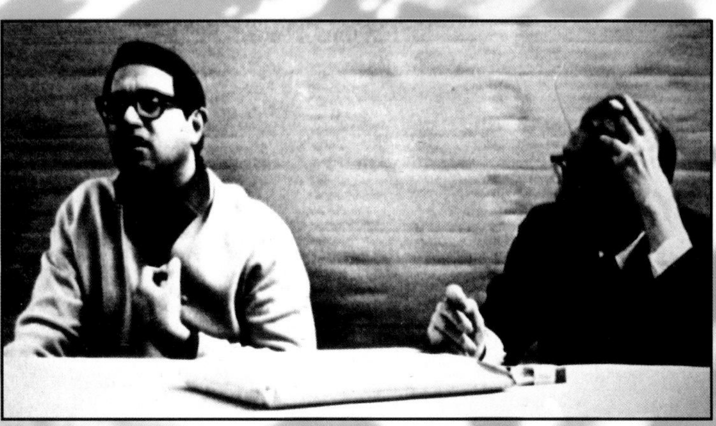

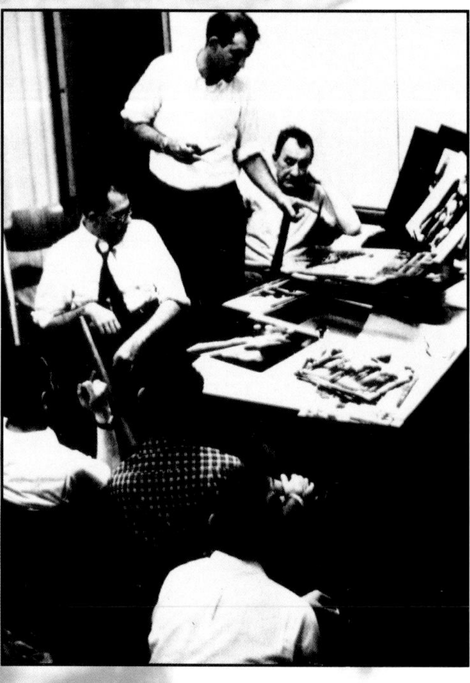

THE MUMMERS' PARADE

Brodovitch used the classroom as a source of fresh material—some of which later found its way into print. A dramatic example is the *Portfolio* article on the Philadelphia Mummers Parade (below and overleaf), which students at the Philadelphia Museum School of Art where Brodovitch first taught were assigned to document. The text does not make clear whether the assignment came from the designer himself, but it is typical of the kinds of assignments he would give in Design Laboratory sessions devoted to photography. The spectacular fold-out presentation is characteristic of the no-expense-spared design of *Portfolio*.

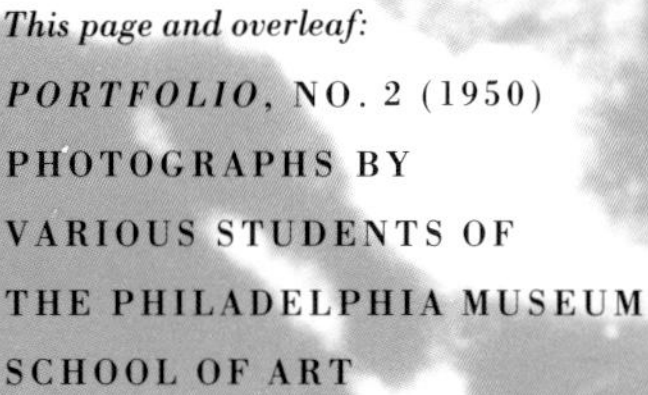

This page and overleaf:
PORTFOLIO, NO. 2 (1950)
PHOTOGRAPHS BY VARIOUS STUDENTS OF THE PHILADELPHIA MUSEUM SCHOOL OF ART

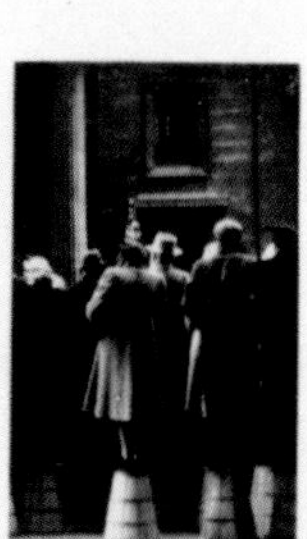

THE MUMMERS PARADE

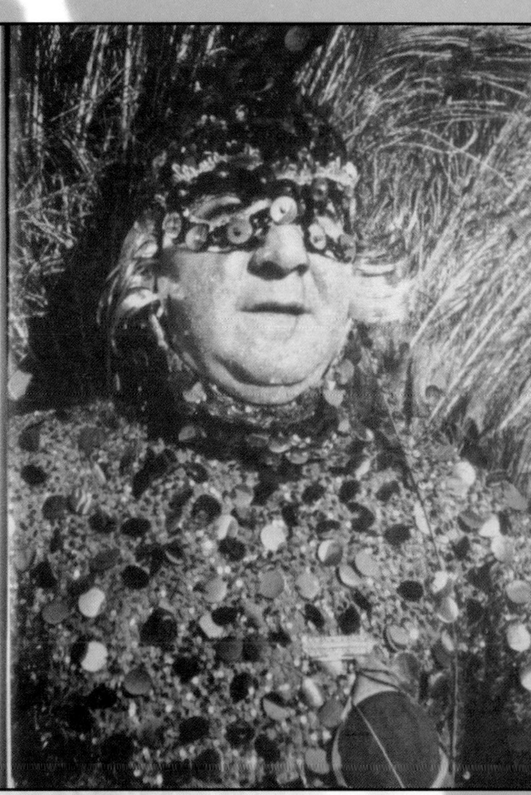

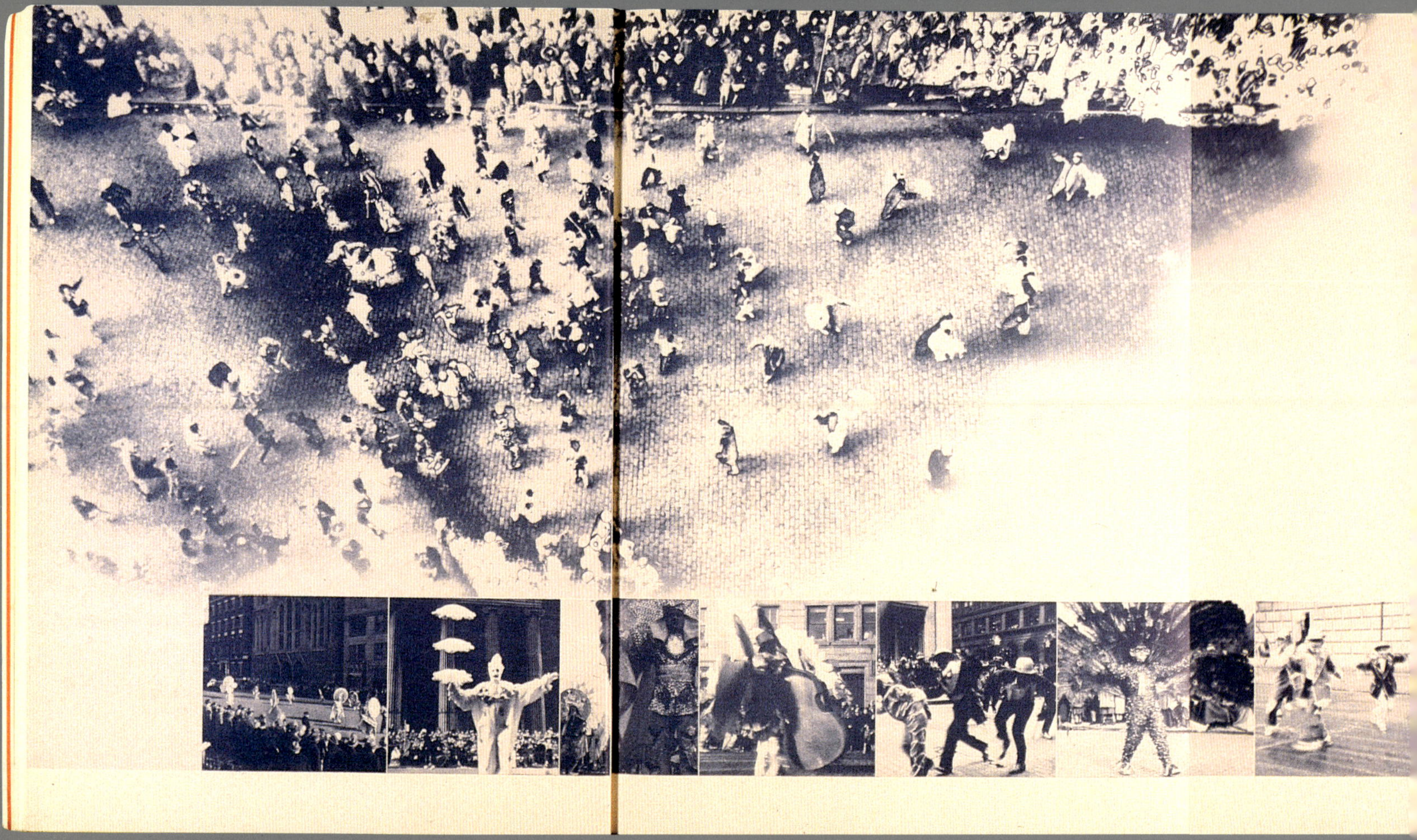

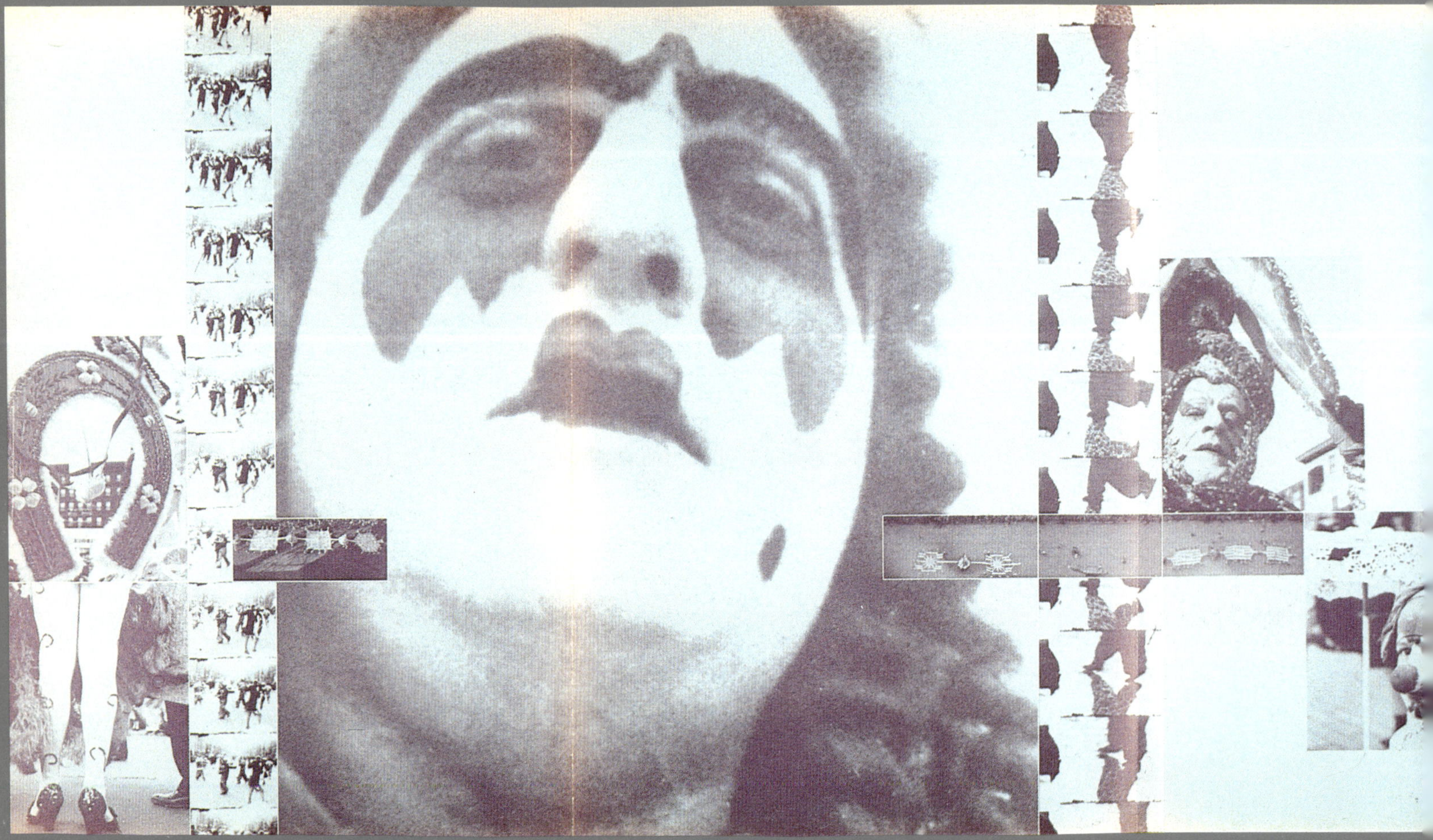

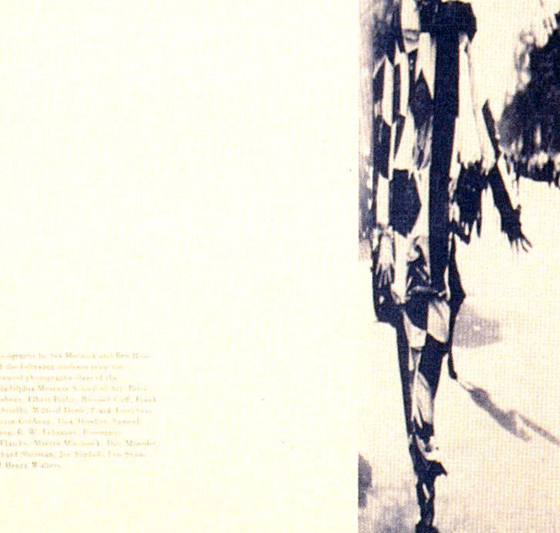

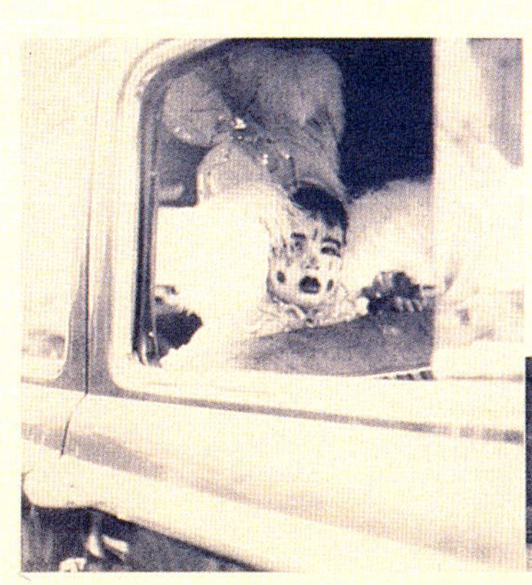
SOUTH PHILA
PHONEYS
WITH THE
BE-BOP-LOOK

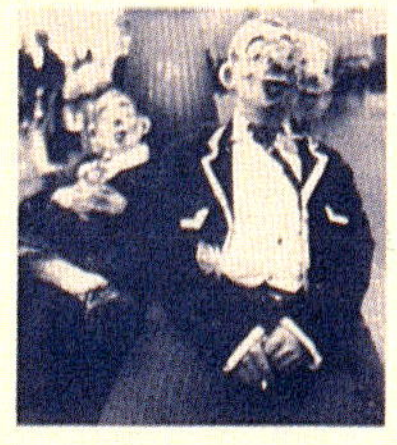

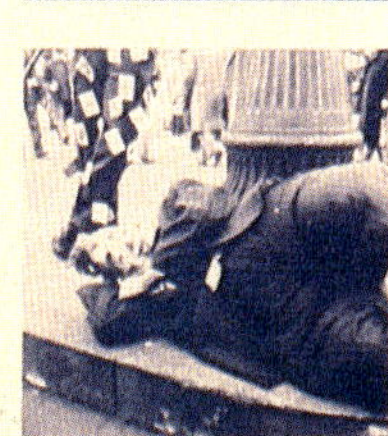

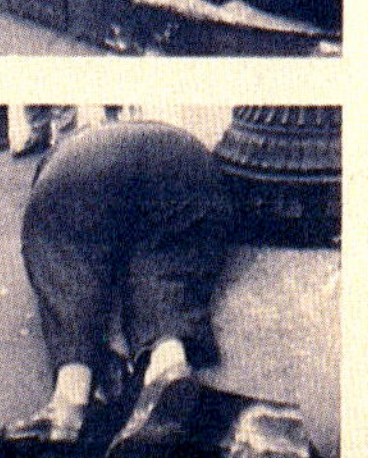

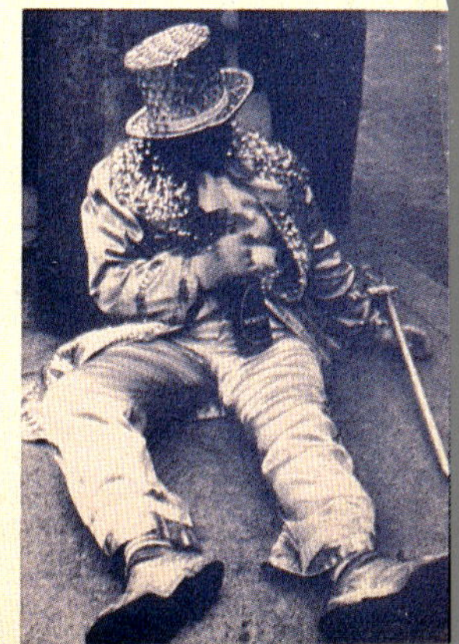

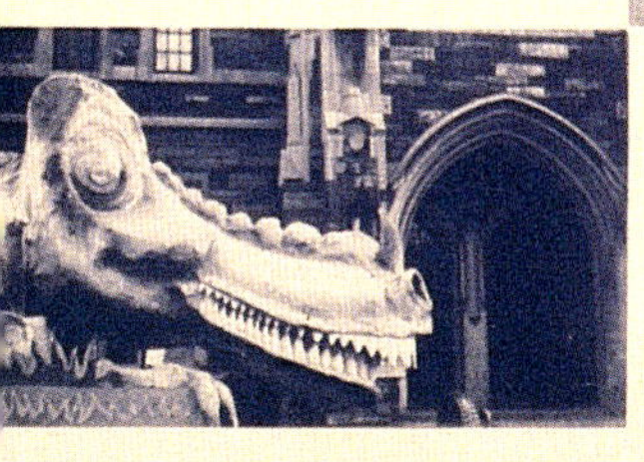

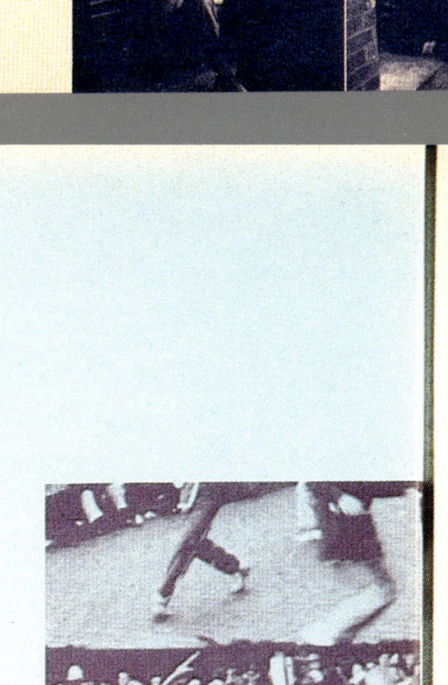

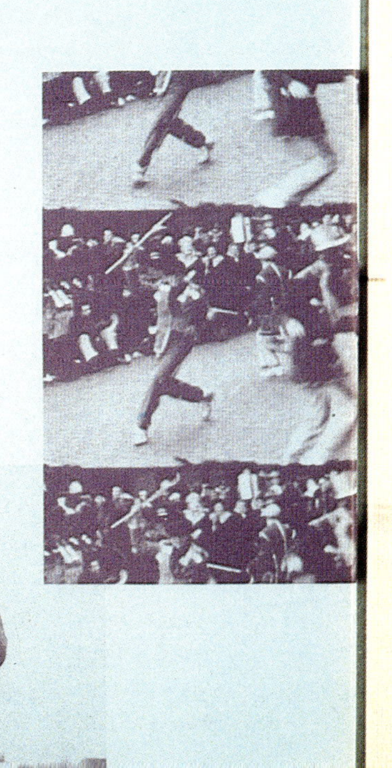

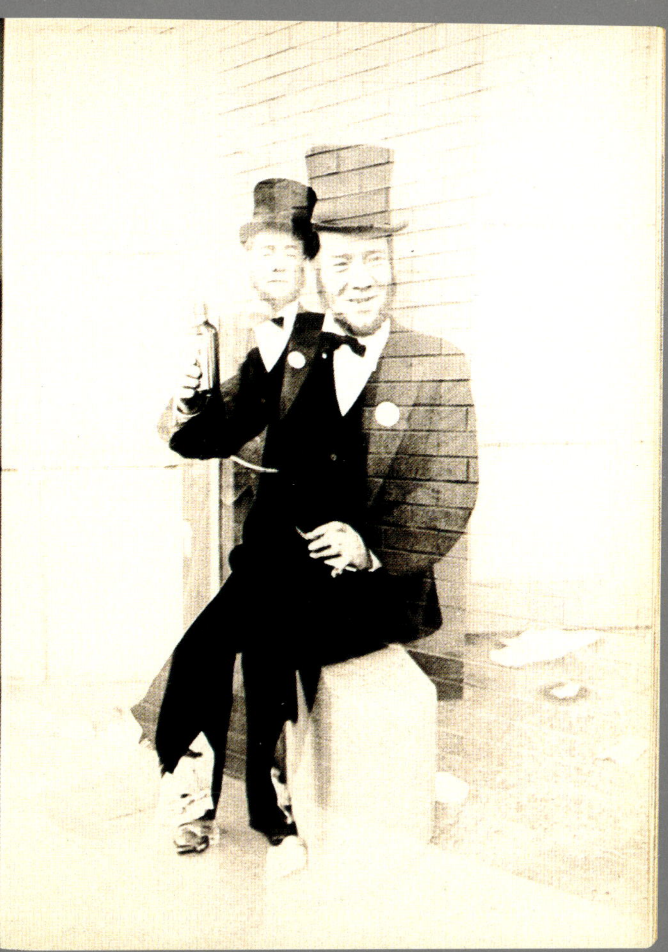

A LABORATORY OF INVENTION

6

Brodovitch's growing involvement with photography cannot be understood only in terms of the growth of interest in the medium itself, or its increasing visibility in the form of reproductions. It is also a symptom of the post–World War I reconstruction of the Western world, which was fueled by an almost religious faith in industrial technology. The most obvious manifestation of this faith was the fascination with machinery, speed, and transportation. In the eyes of the interbellum faithful, the disorder and chaos that resulted in the war might be replaced by a rational and well-organized social system that functioned like a machine. This belief in the machine, as a social model and as the symbol of a new age, is readily apparent in the subject matter of the art of the period. It also manifested itself as an urge to use new industrial materials and technology to make new kinds of art.

Brodovitch was not immune to this urge. A great deal of his European reputation rested with his use of innovative tools and materials. In addition to using the airbrush for illustration, he made drawings using photographic film as the base material and a dentist's drill, surgical knives, and steel needles as the engraving implements. In place of traditional oil paints, he substituted industrial lacquers. He also reportedly invented a method of engraving glass using sandblasting equipment. Brodovitch was excited by the visual impact of industrial technology, and he sung its praises in a 1930 article that appeared in the British graphic-design magazine *Commercial Art*:

Blinking lights of a city. The surface of the revolving phonograph record, the fantastic reflection of the red tail light and the tread of an automobile tyre on the wet pavement, the heroism and daring in the silhouette of an aeroplane. The rhythm of the biographical or statistical diagram.

In the same article, titled "What Pleases the Modern Man," Brodovitch declared, "In the monotony and drudgery of a work-a-day world, there is to be found new beauty and aesthetics." He added:

Industrial lacquers, airbrush, a thin ray of light, perfected hard, flexible steel needles, surgical knives and even dental implements may also adequately take the place of watercolor, undurable and clumsy brushes, and charcoal pens and crayons. Handmade engraving and printing are things of the past, and while they have not yet become anachronisms, their proper place should be on the dusty shelves of snobbish collectors.[42]

The Design Laboratory

When Brodovitch arrived in Philadelphia in 1930, he brought his Machine Age zeal with him. In an early draft of his prospectus for the Design Laboratory—an advanced seminar that was an adjunct of his advertising design program—he described the workshop as "an organization for studying new formulas, new materials, new ideas, devices of the past in order to establish new devices for the future, Rationalism, Logic and practicability—and their artistic interpretation to the needs of industry."[43] As a believer in the possibilities of the Machine Age, he also believed that America was the ideal environment for promulgating his vision of harmony between art and technology. Listed on the prospectus was this agenda: "Excursions to factories, industrial laboratories, plants, shopping centers, building developments, etc. An intimate contact with all developments in art in general: museums, exhibitions, lectures, theatres, concerts, etc." Idealistically, but not uniquely, he envisioned a unification of the arts and industrial society—a process in which design would play a central role.

In his belief in the reconciliation of the artistic avant-garde with the needs of modern industrial society, Brodovitch is aligned with the visionary Bauhaus artist László Moholy-Nagy. One of the primary theorists of Bauhaus pedagogy, Moholy-Nagy also was among the first to proclaim the primacy of photography among the arts in the modern age. He argued that photography could teach mankind to see the world in a new, "objective" way. Thus armed with a "new vision," Moholy-Nagy believed, the peoples of the world would be able to perceive solutions not just to design problems but to social and political problems as well. His interest in photography as an objective, machine-based means of depiction—and in film as an extension of photography into the realm of motion—was carried to the United States when Moholy-Nagy came to Chicago in 1937 to start a school of design that initially was called the New Bauhaus.

In his draft prospectus for the Design Laboratory, Brodovitch managed to sound a clarion call to the new age that strikingly resembles the language later used by Moholy-Nagy in a brochure for the New Bauhaus. He wrote that, "The class is conducted in the way of laboratory research to prepare students as industrial designers, art directors, and free-lance artists," adding:

It is a class for study and experimenting in new ideas, new formulas, and new materials. Devices of the past are studied in order to adapt their principles to the present and future. Rationalism, logic and practicality are also considered as part of the artistic interpretation of the needs of Industry.[44]

Moholy-Nagy's "objectives" for the Institute of Design in Chicago were not that different:

To develop a new type of designer for today's new needs. To train a man so that he will be able to face every requirement, scientific and technical, social, aesthetic and economic . . . not because he is necessarily a genius but because he has the right method of approach to new problems and an advanced knowledge of new and old materials.[45]

Moholy-Nagy's insistence on "fundamental principles and facts" echoes Brodovitch's belief in "rationalism, logic and practicality," and both perceived a vocational need for designers trained in the "new ideas" and "new problems."

Although their ideas about design's social functions are similar—they both appear to have been derived from Constructivism's agenda—Brodovitch and Moholy-Nagy had quite distinct temperaments. Moholy-Nagy was an active and enthusiastic writer, developing his theoretical position in books and articles. Brodovitch, on the other hand, wrote little more than letters and, despite a career as a teacher that lasted more than thirty years, never formulated his enthusiasms into a coherent and consistent body of thought. Whereas we can turn today to Moholy-Nagy's writings to reconstruct his ideas about design and design pedagogy, all that remains of Brodovitch's thoughts are a few articles and some meager aphorisms.

Just as Moholy-Nagy gave photography a privileged position within the foundation course he designed at the Institute of Design in Chicago, Brodovitch stressed camera literacy in

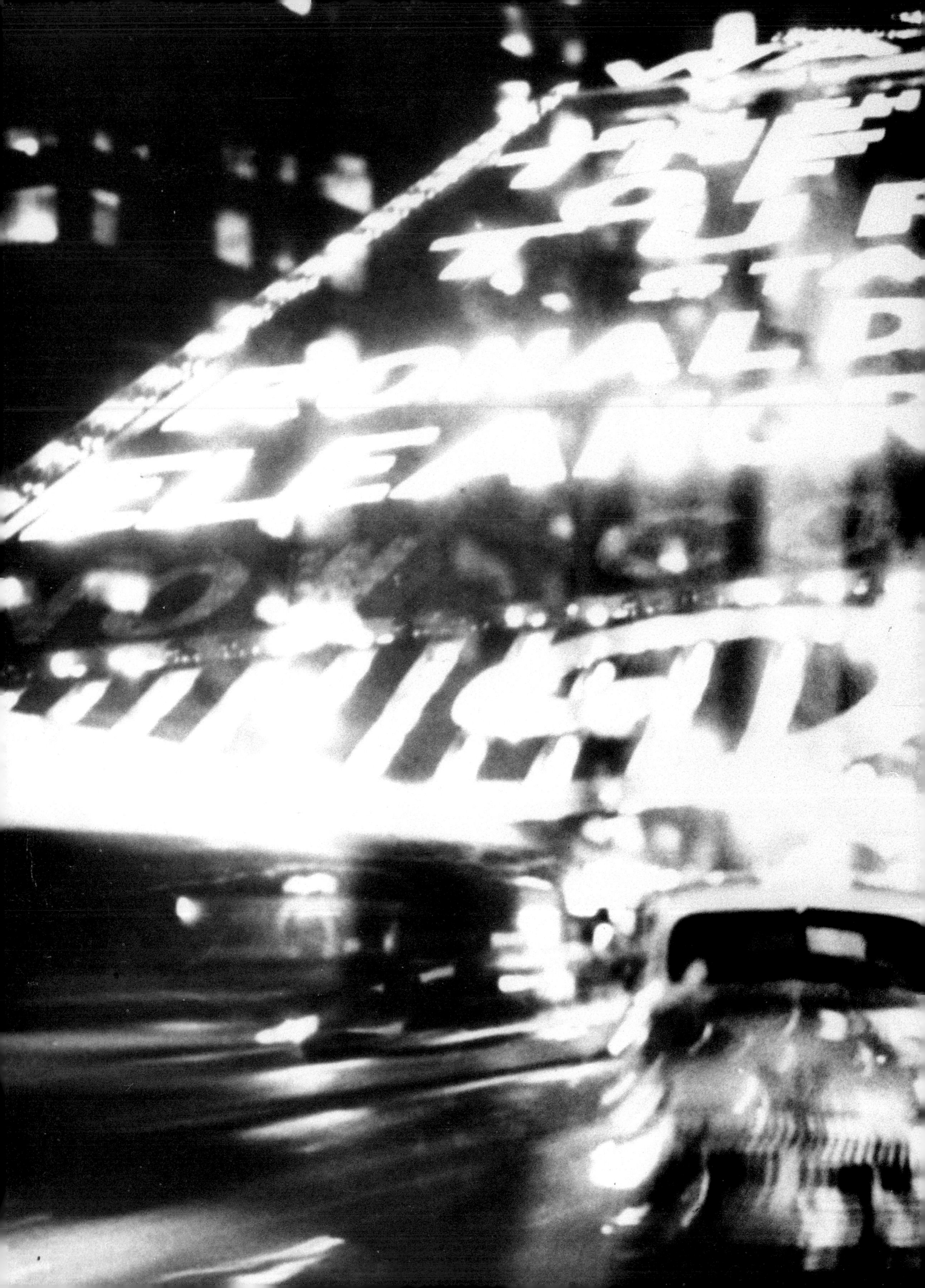

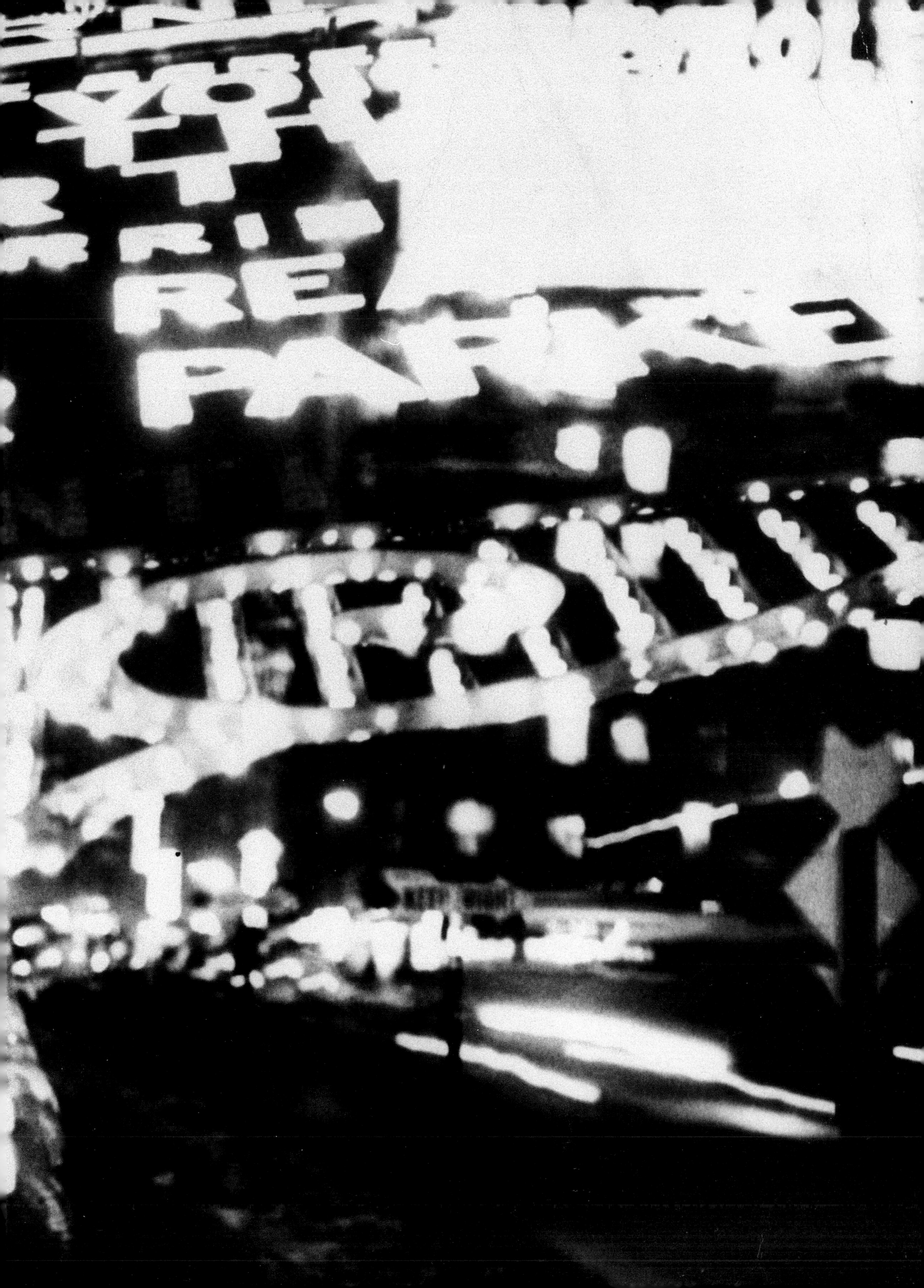

his early design courses. On the class's field trips to factory sites, teacher and students alike carried cameras along. A "Surrealist Ball" at the Philadelphia school was extensively photographed. But while Moholy-Nagy's assignments were exercises in pure form, Brodovitch developed no program for instilling in students a sense of photography's transformative potential, and the students' "problems" in his Design Laboratory were oriented toward the actual needs of the workplace. As a result, they stressed illustration, layout, and other professional skills.

Brodovitch's "Yearly Report" on the Design Laboratory, dated 1937–38, is especially revealing about his early teaching aims and methods. Citing a need to prepare "free-lance artists, stylists, art directors," for jobs in a technological society, he lists the "problems" assigned, the field trips taken, and the free-lance assignments accomplished by the students. They prepared dummy ads for department stores, public service posters, designs for packages, and editorial illustrations. None of the classroom assignments specifically required the taking of photographs or the use of them in layouts. But the field trips included a journey to New York to see Beaumont Newhall's pioneering history of photography exhibition at the Museum of Modern Art. Students also visited the Julien Levy Gallery, which specialized in vanguard European art and photography, and, closer to the Machine Age spirit, a printing plant and a steel mill.

The course description in a New School catalogue, written to appeal more to designers than to photographers, neatly summarizes Brodovitch's approach to teaching (the ellipsis is Brodovitch's):

The aim of the course is to help the student to discover his individuality, crystallize his taste, and develop his feeling for the contemporary trend by stimulating his sense of invention and perfecting his technical ability. The course is conducted as an experimental laboratory, inspired by the everchanging tempo of life, discovery of new techniques, new fields of operation . . . in close contact with current problems of leading magazines, department stores, advertising agencies and manufacturers. Subjects include design, layout, type, poster, reportage, illustration, magazine make-up, package and product design, display, styling, art directing. Analysis and discussion of ideas and problems. Guest critics.

The passage couples Brodovitch's rhetorical appeal to the new, carried over from his Paris years, with the inherently American (and postwar) concept of education as a field in which one could "discover his individuality." In later years Brodovitch would deny being a teacher at all, insisting instead that he was merely "a can opener" for his students' imaginations.

Confrontation and Inspiration

In practice, Brodovitch's teaching method had little to do with theories about the new vision and the new order of things. Instead, he emphasized the discovery of one's inner, creative resources through a paradoxical process of submission and rebellion. First, he would challenge students, making their defenses bristle and forcing them to respond emotionally. Only later would he grudgingly acknowledge their efforts to impress him with unique solutions to the design problems he had assigned them. This kind of encounter-group pedagogy may account to a large degree for the intense loyalty and

IRVING PENN. *OPTICIAN'S SHOP WINDOW*, NEW YORK, C.1939

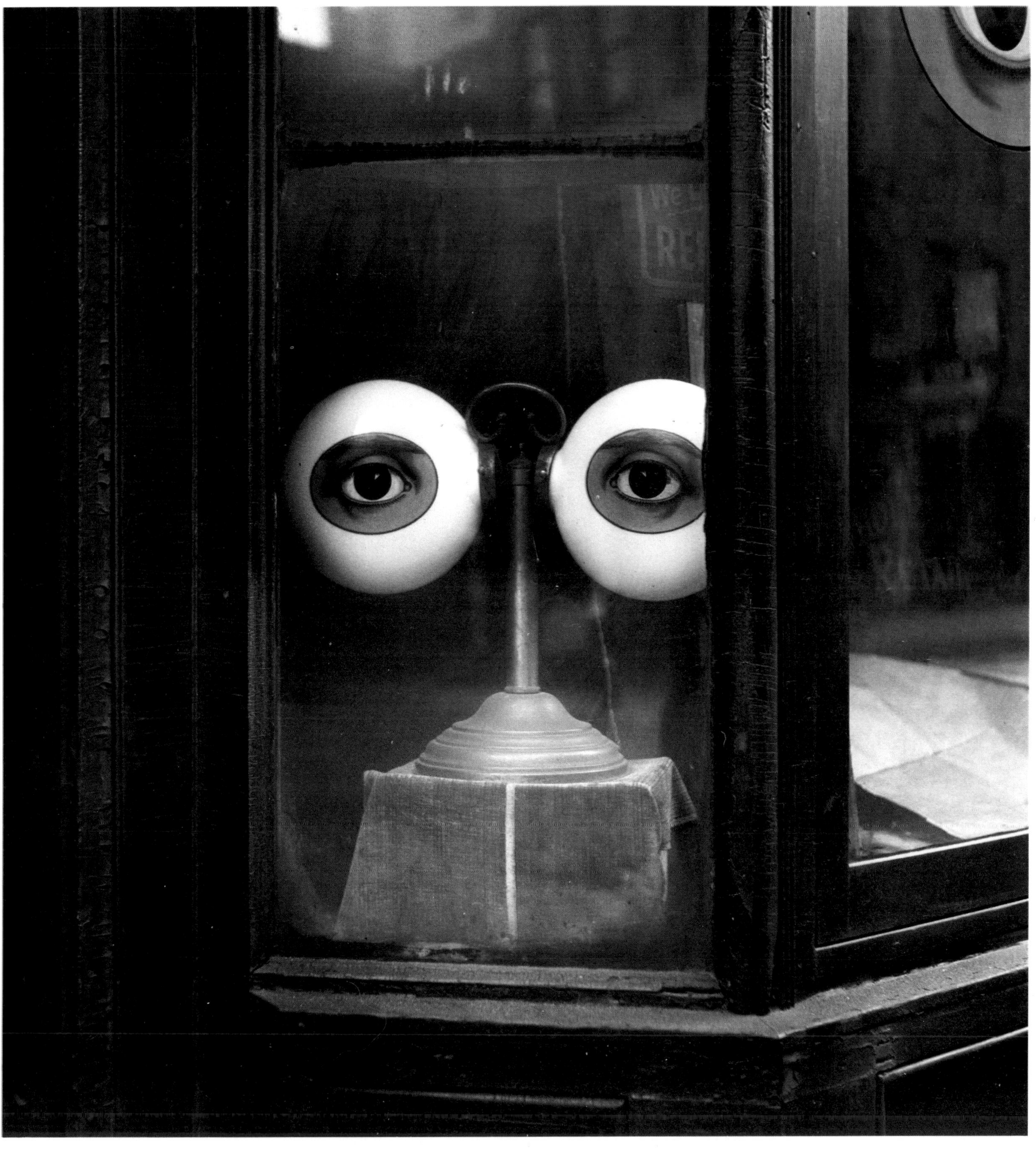

admiration toward Brodovitch expressed by those who studied with him.

Among Brodovitch's students in Philadelphia in the thirties was Irving Penn. Now known for his photography, Penn at the time was interested in painting and drawing. Penn recalls showing his "cartoonlike" student drawings to Brodovitch on the first day of class, and Brodovitch's cold reaction. "I have nothing to teach you and I'd like you to leave my class," Penn remembers his teacher saying with some finality. But rather than disappear, the young art student persevered. He destroyed all his prior work and gave himself over to Brodovitch's way of doing things. A year later, according to Penn, Brodovitch made him his summer assistant at *Harper's Bazaar.* Although Penn did not become a photographer until he began working at *Vogue* under Alexander Liberman, he feels that Brodovitch's influence was crucial to his artistic development.[46]

Brodovitch's demeanor could be intimidating, especially to young people just out of high school. With his aristocratic bearing and curt way of expressing himself, he commanded students' attention much as he must have commanded the troops that served under him during World War I. Penn remembers that when Brodovitch walked into the classroom, all the students stood up, European fashion. Such formality served to establish a psychological distance between the master and his pupils.

After starting work at *Harper's Bazaar*'s offices in midtown Manhattan, Brodovitch could no longer teach full-time in Philadelphia, but he continued to hold classes there. He enlisted former students—Mary Fullerton, for one—to teach the design sessions, while he would preside over the critiques, which were held on Fridays once or twice a month. He coined the name "Design Laboratory" to describe these seminar-style classes.

In the spring of 1941, having resigned from teaching at the Philadelphia Museum School, he transferred the concept of the Design Laboratory to the New School for Social Research in New York City. There, in two sessions a week, he taught a course listed as "Art applied to Graphic Journalism, Advertising, Design, and Fashion."[47] As before, he ran the classroom like a workshop, giving students assignments and then critiquing the results. Often

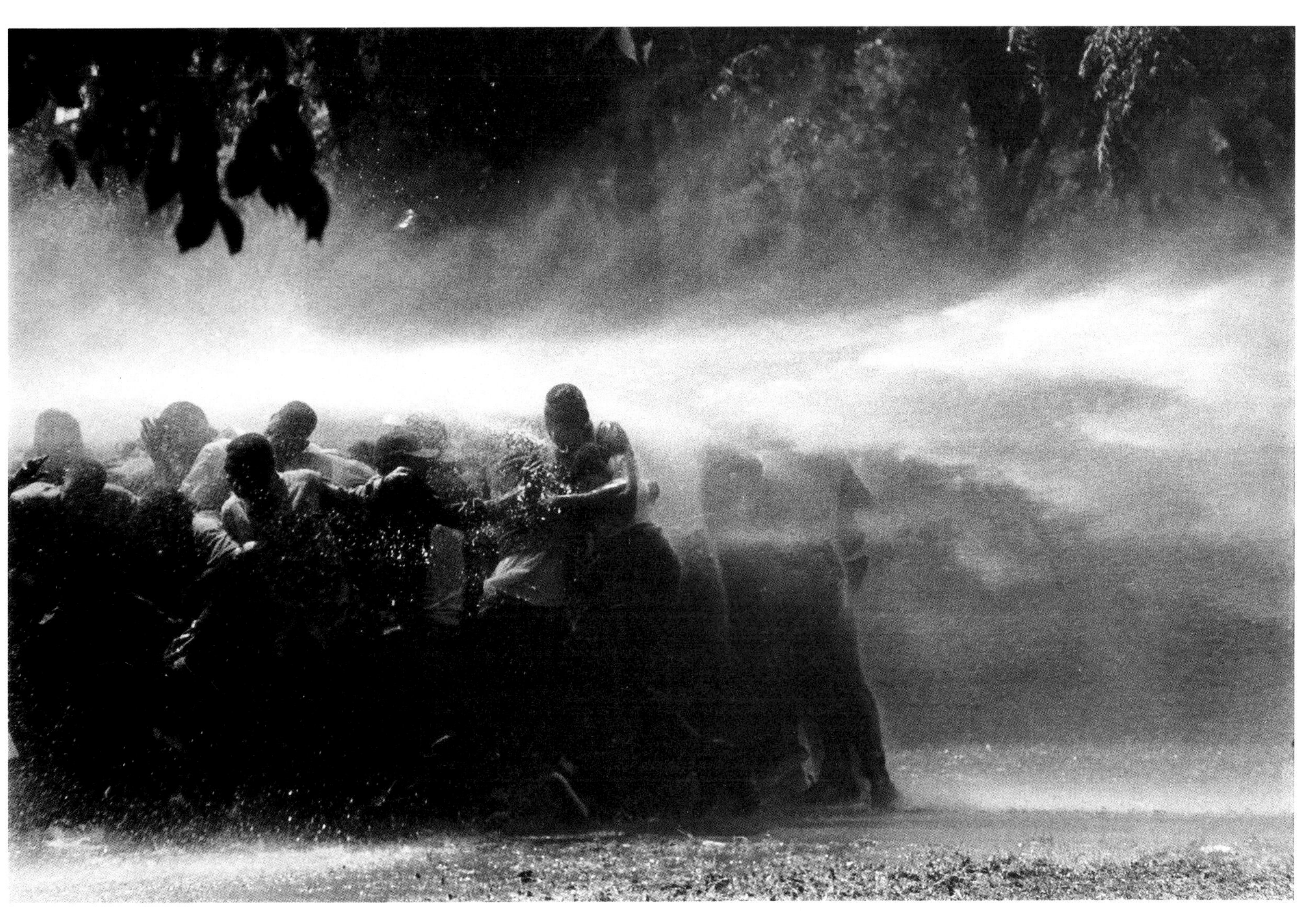

BOB ADELMAN.
DOWN HOME, 1963

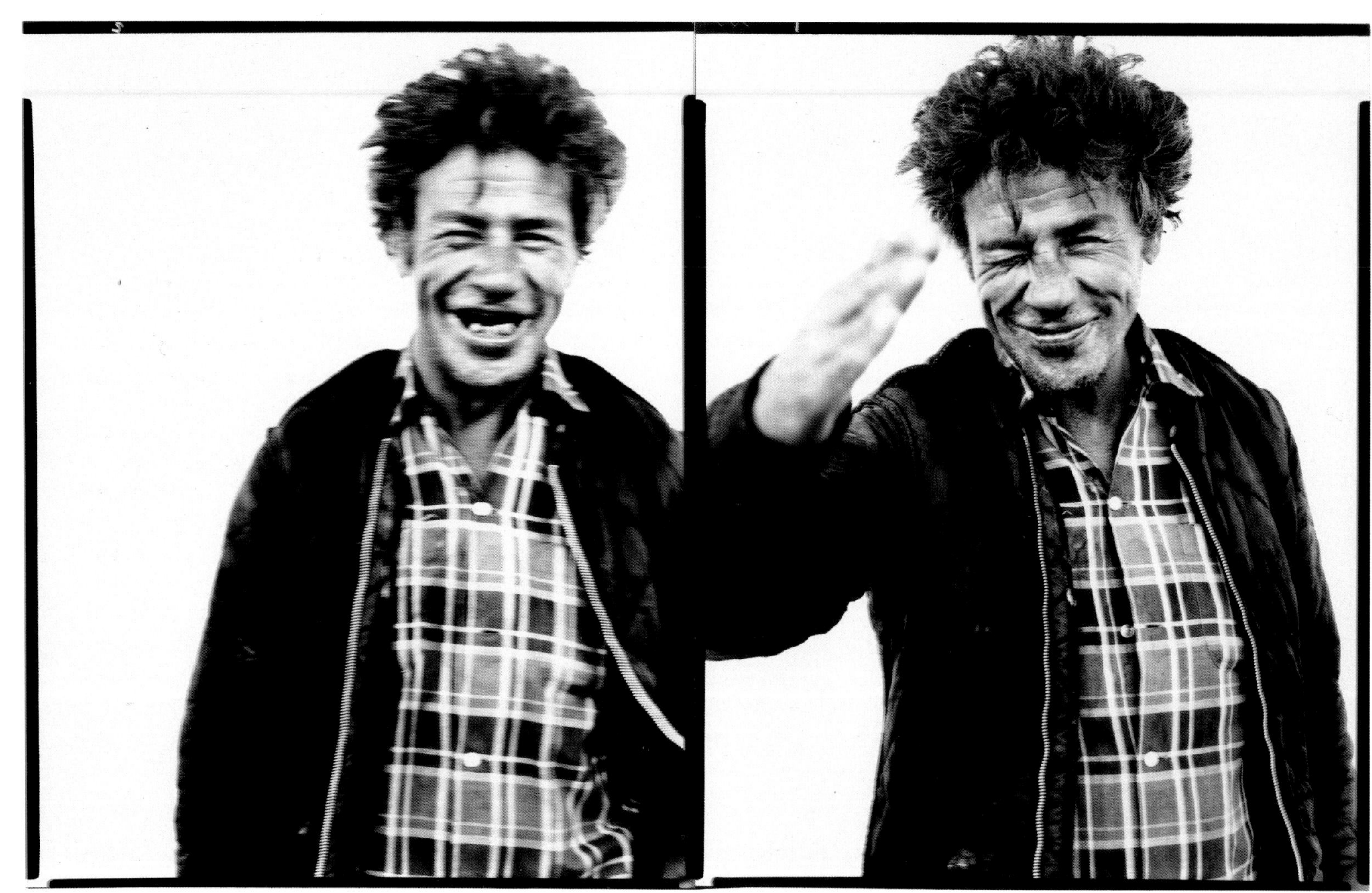

RICHARD AVEDON.
GORDON STEVENSON, DRIFTER.
INTERSTATE 90,
BUTTE, MONTANA, 8/25/79.

these assignments paralleled, or were the same as, projects he was working on at *Harper's Bazaar;* if the magazine's needs were met in the classroom, the art director considered it a bonus.

Lillian Bassman, a Brodovitch student at the New School in the early forties, remembers that he presided over two simultaneous but distinct sessions, one devoted to illustration and the other to page design. She entered with hopes of being a fashion illustrator, but after being told by Brodovitch that she knew nothing about fashion, she switched into the design section. Brodovitch, apparently recognizing a nascent talent, arranged a scholarship for her; at the end of the term, he asked her to be his apprentice at the *Bazaar*—a position that, while unpaid, was "the plum" for students every year. Later, during the war, Lillian Bassman became Brodovitch's first full-time, paid assistant at the magazine.

"He never allowed you to be satisfied with what you were doing," Bassman recalls. "He was always trying to goad you into doing better than you had done, so there never really was a point at which he would say that what you did was marvelous. It was always 'It's okay. You can do better.' "[48] Not everyone could adjust to his demanding style, she notes: "He was always needling everybody. If you didn't have a powerful ego you just fell by the wayside." Richard Avedon, who attended the Design Laboratory even while seeing his pictures published in *Harper's Bazaar,* puts it even more bluntly: "He never complimented me, to his death."[49]

But the art director's inability to praise his students did not dampen their desire to please him, even if his ingenuity usually outpaced theirs. Hiro, one of the last "discoveries" introduced on the pages of the *Bazaar* during Brodovitch's tenure there, once spent months photographing shoes at Brodovitch's urging. Each time he showed his best efforts, Brodovitch sent him off to try again. Finally, Hiro succeeded in photographing a pair of shoes in a way that Brodovitch had never seen before; his reward, naturally, was having his pictures published in the *Bazaar.*

While officially under the aegis of the New School, the workshops were often held off the school's premises. At times Brodovitch used the photography studios of Richard Avedon, Steve Colhoun, and Paul and Karen Radkai. By the fifties, the title of his course had changed from "Art Applied to Graphic Journalism" to "Visual Communications," and a section devoted specifically to photography had been added. From 1951 to 1959, what Brodovitch continued to call his Design Laboratory was dedicated to design and photography, and photographers especially flocked to study with the man who by that time had become one of their medium's most influential arbiters.

Brodovitch taught his classes using what Avedon calls "the Socratic method." That is to say, students would put their work down on a large table for his inspection, and he would ask questions about whatever interested him. But as much as anything he said, what he left unsaid was a vital part of the instruction. "Not interesting" was about the best he could manage to say about some solutions to his assignments; more likely, he simply would ignore work that seemed to him derivative, hackneyed, or precious. "It was like the sixties, very confrontational," photographer Bob Adelman remembers of the sessions he attended in the sixties.

"Two thirds of the students felt rejected and became defensive and withdrawn. One third took up the challenge."[50]

In the photography classes, Brodovitch encouraged the "available light" style of candid shooting, seeking a reconciliation of reportage's look of truth and fashion photography's graphic immediacy. Bob Cato, who served as the art director's "man Friday" in the late forties, during the period when Brodovitch was recovering from injuries resulting from being struck by a truck, says that he favored "an active camera." "Brodovitch encouraged involved street photography, not observation," Cato recalls of the New School class he assisted, in which most students—Ted Croner was one—used available light in a journalistic manner.[51]

Brodovitch used essentially the same teaching techniques for his design classes as he did for his photography classes. Students received weekly assignments, which were submitted and critiqued the following week. By the fifties his reputation as a teacher and graphic designer had grown to the point that he was invited to be a "guest critic" at Yale University's School of Design. Commuting there on Friday nights, as he had in Philadelphia more than a decade earlier, he analyzed students' design projects before a rapt audience. Among the students there were Marvin Israel, who would become art director of *Harper's Bazaar* in the sixties, and Bruce Davidson, soon to be recognized as a gifted young photographer.

Brodovitch continued to teach even after his professional and personal life declined precipitously at the end of the fifties. In 1958 he lost his job at the *Bazaar*, in a shift that was due partly to management changes (Carmel Snow was forced out shortly thereafter) and partly to his increasing inability to control his drinking. In 1959 his wife died and he suffered a second major house fire. Ill and depressed, he checked into the state mental hospital on Ward's Island while he tried to regain a hold on his life. Meanwhile, his former students rallied around him, trying to establish his Design Laboratory independently, since he was no longer associated with the New School.

A Sample Session

One fruit of these labors was a series of sessions attended by the creative staff of the New York office of the Young & Rubicam advertising agency. Organized by Steve Frankfurt, one of the agency's art directors and a former Brodovitch student, this was one of the last Design Laboratories held, and as far as can be ascertained the only one to be recorded. The transcripts of the sessions reveal better than any description how Brodovitch conducted his class, and himself, towards the end of his years in the United States.[52]

The first class took place on September 23, 1964. After being introduced by Frankfurt, Brodovitch had this to say:

We must communicate. We must expose ourselves. You know me, but I don't know anything about you. I would like to see samples of your work. How you think, or the way you think. Only then can we communicate much better with each other.

I hate imitation and clichés. I hope we can discover a new way of communication. How can we invent?

Don't believe that I am a teacher. I am a student—a beginner like you are. I don't think we can preach or teach. My way of guiding people is by irritation. I will try to irritate you, to explore you. Dust off

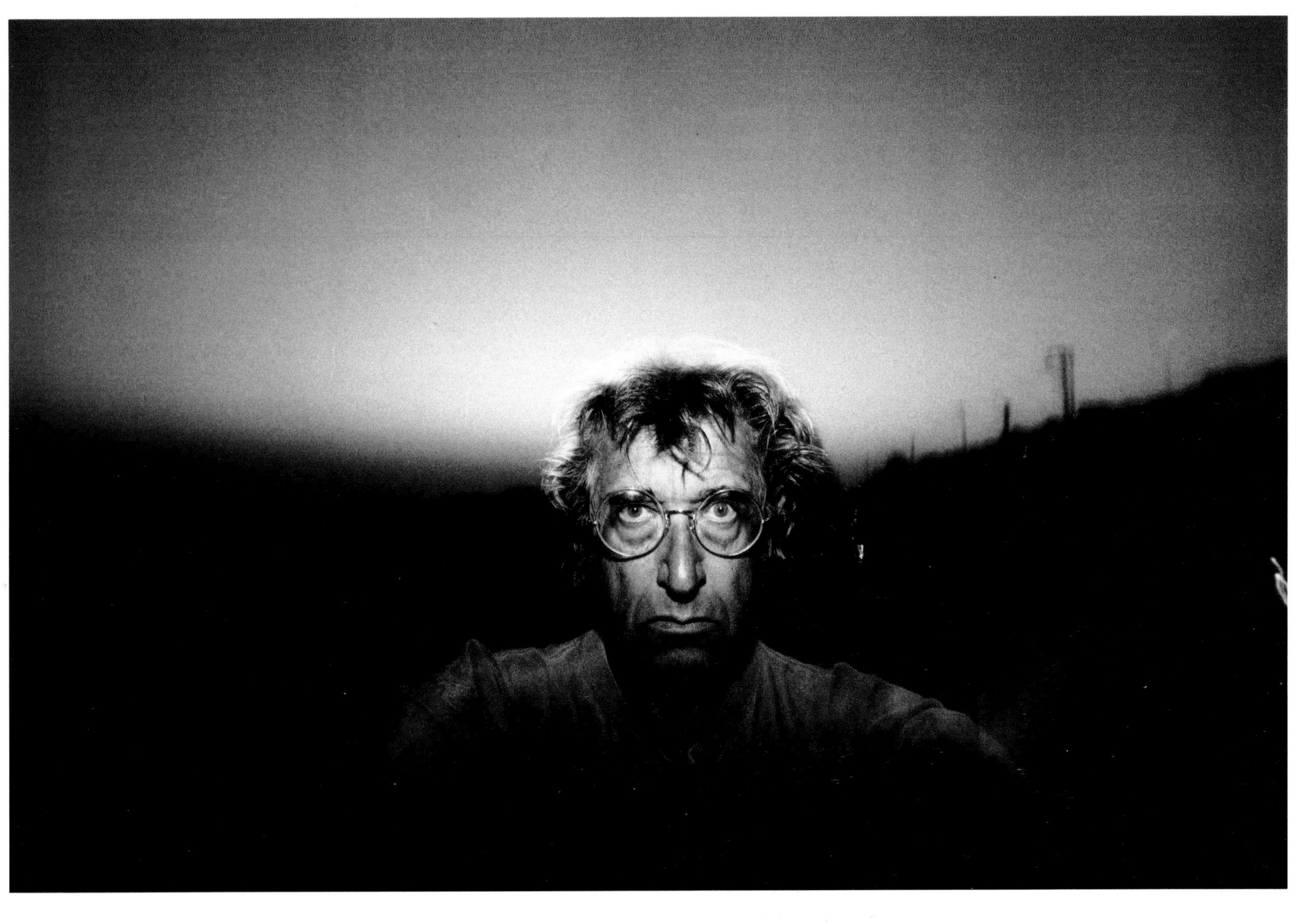

ART KANE.
SELF-PORTRAIT, 1988.
MYKONOS, GREECE

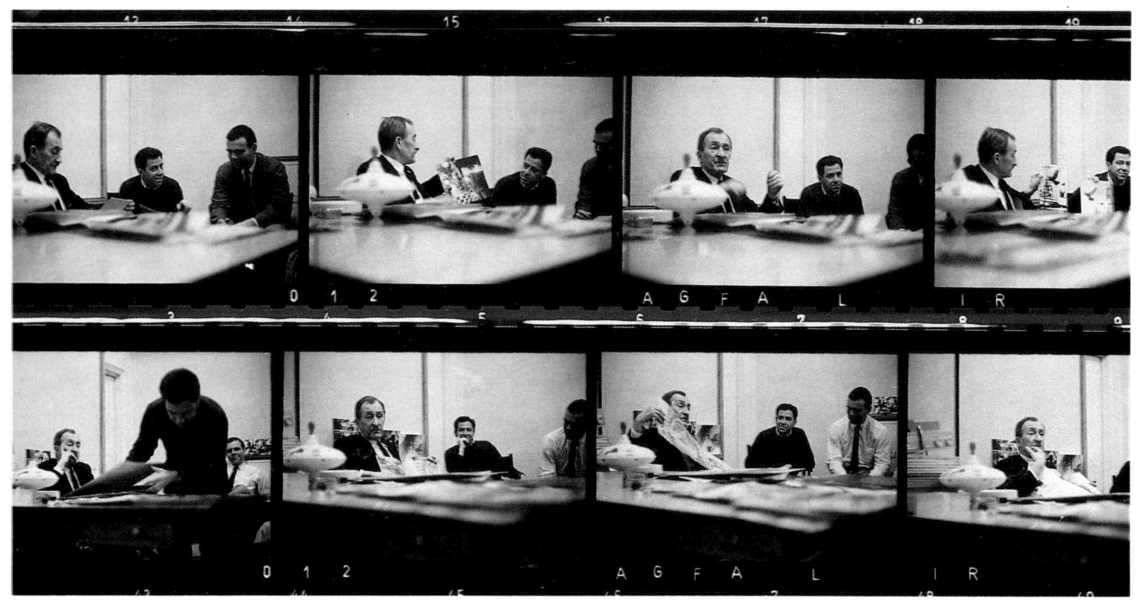

Brodovitch, seated at center, enjoyed the rapt attention of his Design Laboratory students, perhaps because he so seldom spoke at length that they hung on every word. The workshop sessions were often held in the studios of photographers and designers who had studied with him earlier.

tradition. Dust off old habits. We are here to brush off our shoulders the dust of tradition, and this will be the first step of our evolution. I hope you will help me by participation in discussion of the subjects at hand. We are here to achieve a goal. What is the goal? We must discover new ways of communication.

Everybody has stage fright, and I am always camera shy in the first few sessions.

We are to irritate each other. You should provoke me, and only then can I provoke you back. I believe in this backfire technique. I have here a list of your backgrounds and achievements. I must get to know you. Only then can I help you. Maybe not.

You see, I never believe in miracles, but I would like to see your handwriting and samples of your work. I think you should be exposed to me. And you should expose to me so much of your ideas, your thoughts, or your voice, or what not.

I will have guest speakers, and you should provoke him, or I will irritate you. Sometimes our sessions will be successful. It depends. Sometimes they are dull as anything. I'm not a miracle man. Our sessions will only be successful by your participation.

After proposing that "we should start with doodles, abstract doodles," Brodovitch responded to Frankfurt's criticisms of the advertising of the day:

See, we are dealing with the audience. Psychoanalysis of the audience. I must awaken his interest. We must provoke the interest of the audience. Everybody is not creative in the way of thinking.

We should be irritated, and should resist imitation. The most important thing in communication is how to provoke this. How to present. How to shock. Whether it be visual, or by sound, or by any other means. Maybe, in a few years, TV will produce an aroma. A total communication with the eye, the ear and the nose, by smell.

BRUCE DAVIDSON.
CAFETERIA, 1976

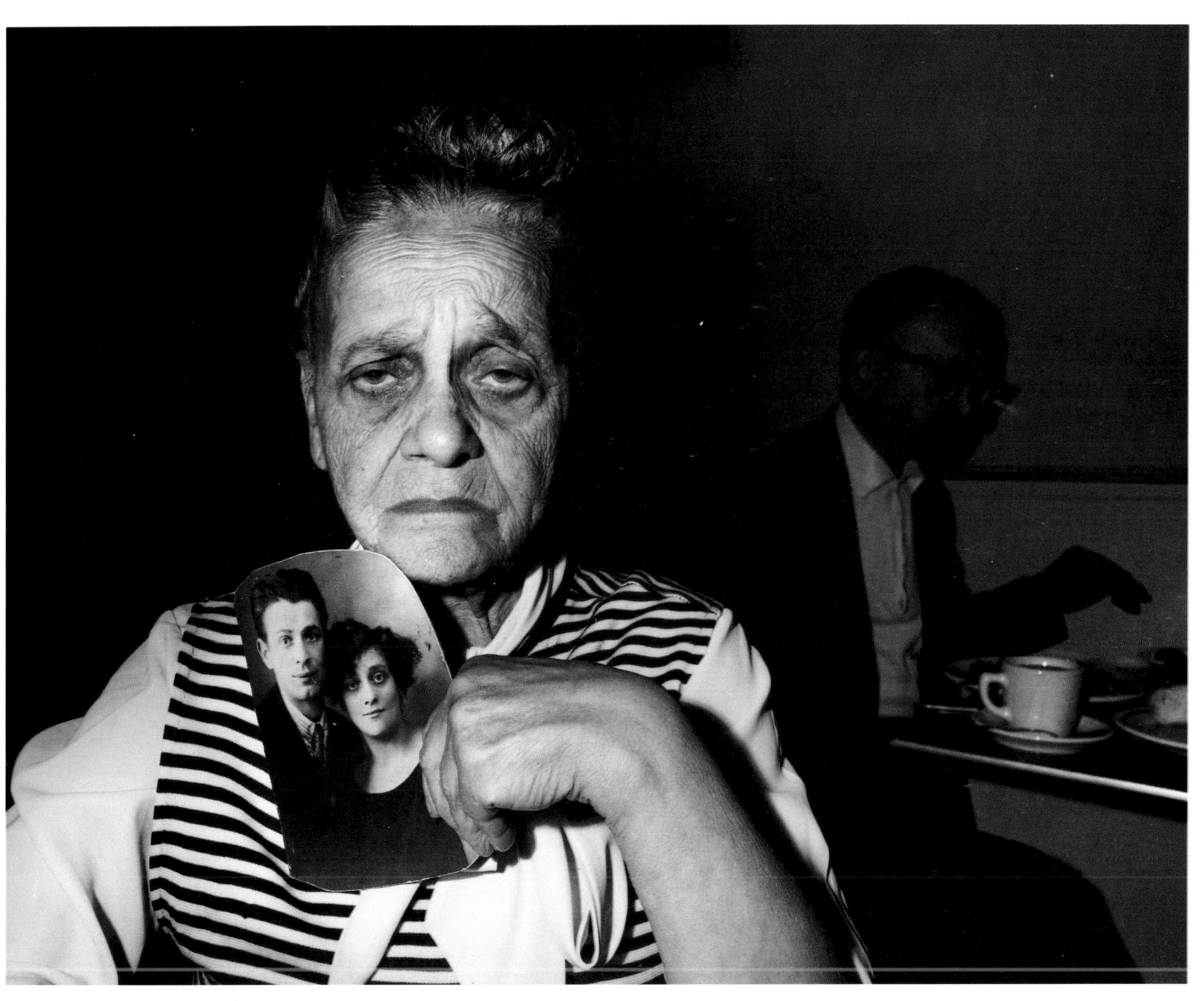

We should be prepared for anything. I am a firm believer in progress. This is my motto.

He proceeded to crumple a piece of paper and throw it onto the center of the table, challenging those around it to "give me a report on this object here." It was the first week's "problem," or assignment. "We are here to doodle and relax," Brodovitch concluded, not a little ironically.

In later sessions, both teacher and students loosened up considerably, trading quips about the work done for class. Just how direct Brodovitch could be in his critique sessions can be seen in this exchange with an unidentified student regarding a student's two-page color picture, of what apparently is a heavily made-up transvestite, done in response to an assignment focusing on cosmetics:

Brodovitch: What is your message? What do you like to sell—lipstick, eyes, nose or what not?

Student: It's a statement on the camouflage of make-up.

Brodovitch: I frankly think it's very dull.

Another student: What about the other page? (He shows a picture of a man's hairy chest.)

Brodovitch: I think it's much worse.

Another student: It's pretty shocking.

Brodovitch: I beg your pardon. You don't communicate to me any idea, and you really don't tell me any story. You don't amuse me. You disgust me.

Student: But, by disgusting you, it communicates a message and tells you a story, disgusting as it may be.

Brodovitch: What is the story? What is the message? Can you tell me? . . .

Finally, Brodovitch tells the student:

Brodovitch: You see, in our business we must capture the eye of the audience. I don't know. I personally would never be excited about this. I would never really be interested in it. What does this mean? To me, it deserves the garbage can. I beg your pardon. I hope you won't take my words personally.

Student: Can I explain it?

Brodovitch: Yes, please.

Student: It shows a picture of a platinum blonde and says, "Do blondes have more fun?," and when you open it up on the inside, it says, "Be a Clairol blonde and see," and there are pictures of men putting on cosmetics. What I tried to show was the "Guys of Cosmetics." I don't feel it came across as strong as the one we saw previously.

Brodovitch: Well, everybody

HIRO.
DONNA MITCHELL, FASHION MODEL. CRATERS OF THE MOON, IDAHO, 9/21/68

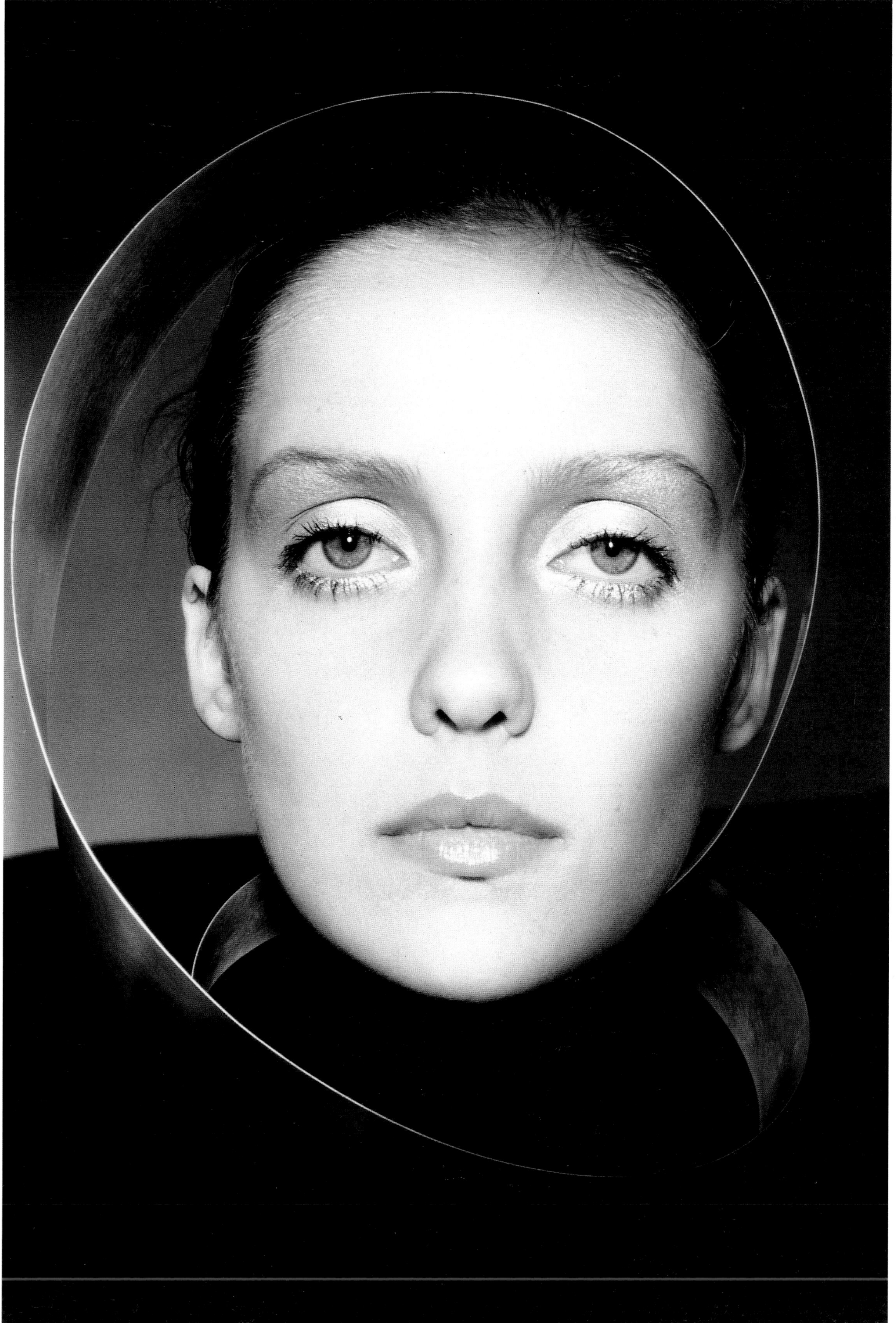

makes mistakes. (Laughter.) And it's the best way to learn. How about the rest of you? Come on, let's fight.

Throughout his teaching, Brodovitch maintained an honesty and integrity that could be brutal or helpful, depending on the student's resilience in the face of criticism. He turned his inability to dissemble about his emotional responses to creative work into an advantage: If he ever said he liked something, one could take it as high praise indeed. When he sent photographers off to document the presidential elections, or asked designers to devise fresh approaches to political ads, what mattered was not so much the assignment as the freshness of the response. As with all aspects of his life, boredom and habit were his archenemies.

During the sixties, besides the Young & Rubicam sessions, Brodovitch taught Design Laboratory courses under the sponsorship of the American Institute of Graphic Arts in New York and at the Corcoran School of Art in Washington, D.C. But his health continued to decline; in 1965 he was readmitted to Ward's Island, and in 1966 he broke his hip. A fragile and failing man at age sixty-eight, he left New York for France, where he spent the last five years of his life.

Today, some ninety years after his birth and more than fifteen years after his death, Brodovitch's legacy is kept alive by the hundreds of photographers, designers, and other "graphic journalists" who first sensed their own creative potential under his insistent guidance. There are perhaps as many stories about him as there are surviving students. But his style of graphic design is dramatically in eclipse.

No magazine published today has the combination of elegance, flair, and sense of surprise that *Harper's Bazaar* had when it was designed by Brodovitch. In large part this is due to the economics of publishing: Faced with tighter budgets and greater competition for editorial space, magazines can no longer afford the vast expanses of white that are the closest thing to a Brodovitch design trademark. Also, just as fashions in clothing change, so do fashions in magazine design. The shift to busy, chockablock layouts, so much a part of the mass-market magazines of the eighties, can be considered the apogee of a pendulumlike reaction to Brodovitch's style. The same could be said of the shift in photography to calculated, often stilted setups taken in the studio, which represent the opposite of the direct, documentary naturalism espoused by Brodovitch throughout the fifties.

Nevertheless, Brodovitch's pivotal influence on American visual experience remains a fact that transcends fashion—even though fashion was the arena in which his influence first made itself felt. By bringing the practice and ethos of modern design to the United States, by spreading its message through the pages of one of the most innovative magazines of the mid-century, and by keeping its spirit of constant renewal and experimentation alive through some of history's most inauspicious times, Alexey Brodovitch established a model that many art directors have emulated, but few have equalled. ■

MARVIN ISRAEL AND YOLANDA CUOMO. POSTER FOR THE ALEXEY BRODOVITCH EXHIBITION AT THE GRAND PALAIS, PARIS. 1982

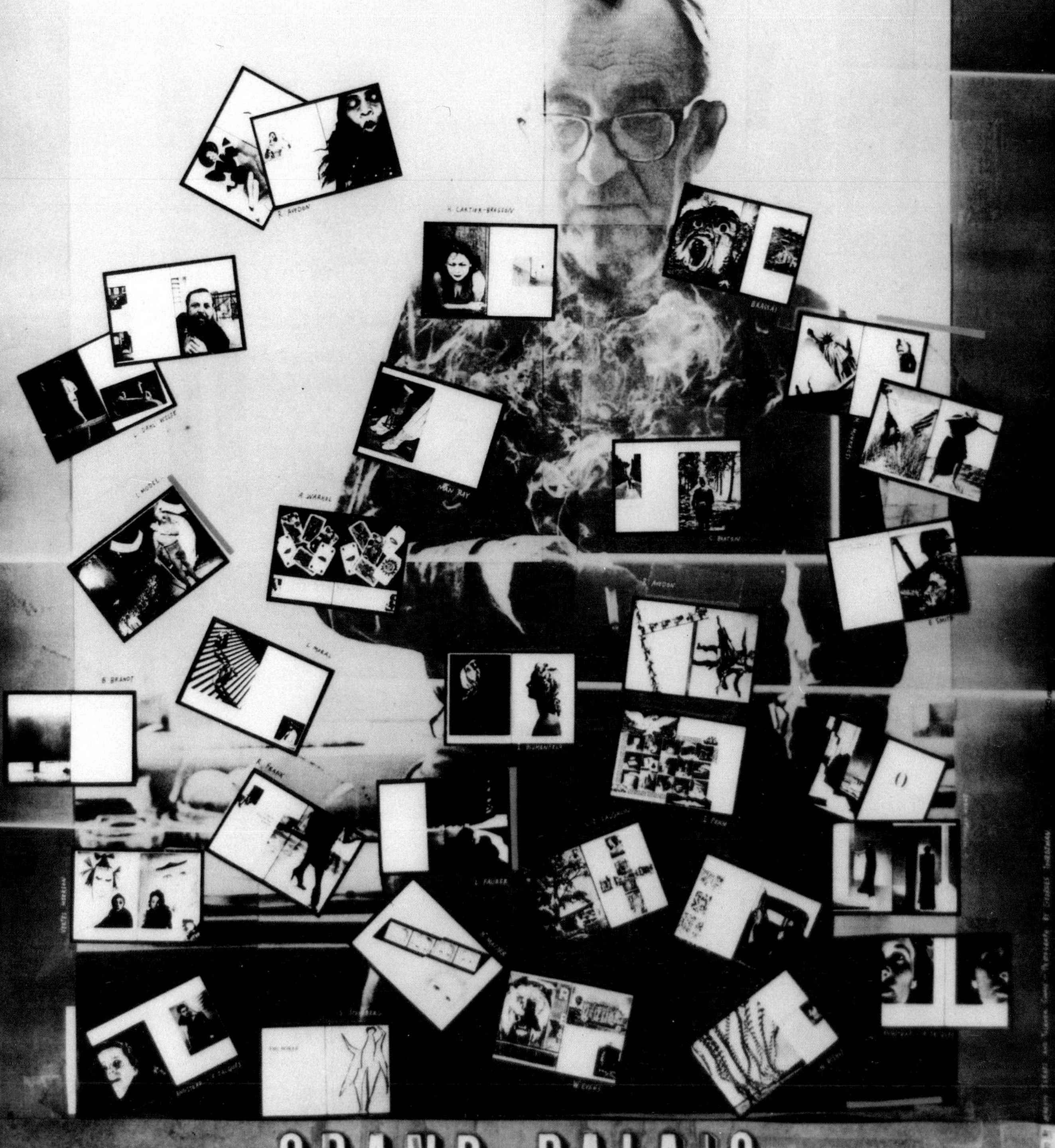

MINISTÉRE DE LA CULTURE RIP MAIRIE DE PARIS
DANS LE CADRE DU MOIS DE LA PHOTOGRAPHIE ORGANISÉ PAR PARIS AUDIO-VISUEL
HOMMAGE A
ALEXEY BRODOVITCH
GRAND PALAIS
ENTRÉE PLACE CLEMENCEAU DU 28 OCTOBRE AU 29 NOVEMBRE 1982

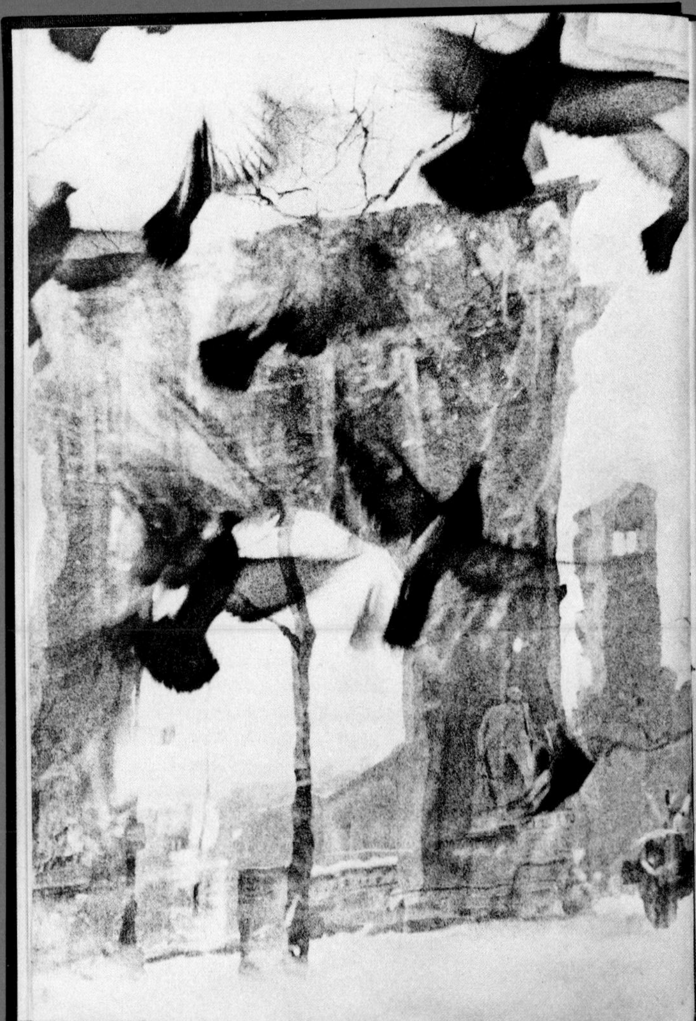

My first clue that my friends knew I was back in town was the champagne and sherbet in my orange juice the Saturday morning I got back. "I brought along some crazy rum for later, too," my old friend A. E. Kugelman yelled, pouring more champagne over the orange ice. "Some of that 168-proof Puerto Rico go-to-the-moon rum. Cigars, too. Smoke, smoke, *smoke!*"

He ran to the phone. "Hello, Kitty, it's me—Kugel. Yes, yes, he's back. Listen, Kitty, you bring that thing over here now, we're turning on. Don't tell me about early in the morning, we'll pull the shades. We'll wear dark glasses. Yeah, yeah, bring her, too. But tell her she brings that stupid with her, I'll cook him. I can't stand him. *I'll bake him!* Yeah, yeah, O.K., O.K., so take an aspirin and start on beer."

He called twenty or thirty other people. "The champagne is going to run out you don't bring that thing over here in a hurry," he screamed at them. "Listen, it's only Saturday morning—we got time to have a hell of a party!"

7

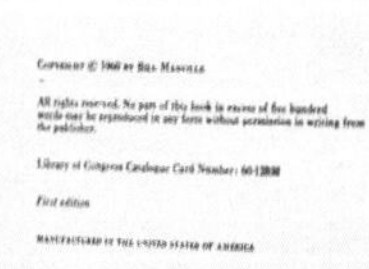

Library of Congress Catalogue Card Number: 60-[illegible]

First edition

MANUFACTURED IN THE UNITED STATES OF AMERICA

Grateful acknowledgment is made to *The Village Voice*, in which the sections of this book first appeared in different form.

"There was a fountain in the center of the room of a bar I used to make when I first came to the Village. I remember a brass merman perpetually sounded a sea trumpet there, forever calling surrounding mermaids to a wilder dance. No cold water flowed from that fountain—something better: the great basin offered all the bottled wines of the world. It all seemed an image of the way I wanted to live—generous, naked, overabundant, and noisy."

A. E. Kugelman

It was A. E. Kugelman; I yelled at him for a few minutes and then agreed to meet him at the Riviera.

He wasn't there himself, of course, when I arrived. I met Danny East, though, who bought me a drink. "What was that?" Danny suddenly said: a woman was shrieking. Then somebody yelled and heads began to turn. A long, beautifully shaped woman's leg was up on the bar, her black pumps nestling among the shot glasses. From the angle, she had to have her head on the floor, her skirt tangled in her necklace. When I got there, I saw it was Kugel, and the leg was his: "I bought it from a guy went bankrupt selling cheap rayon stockings on Eighth Avenue. It's a new number," he said.

I told him he looked tired. He ignored me. "How about some action," he said to the bartender. "Bill, too."

Harry was still laughing about the leg as he poured the stuff for us.

Kugeloo held his glass in his hand, looking around. "Listen to them, the jukebox, the laughing—you listen to the noise, you'd think they were happy." He knocked back his drink in one take, and turned to say something to a tall blonde his leg act had brought over.

A loser whose name I can't remember came in with his ex-wife. They'd busted up when she'd run off with a Jersey City cop. Kugel gave me a fast sideways look when he spotted them together. The guy stopped beside us, but his wife walked on to the can. Kugel watched her disappear and then said to the stud: "Listen, don't wait. Before she comes back, run quick to your psychoanalyst and get all your money back."

We had another drink, and Kugel bought one for the blonde. "My advice to

20

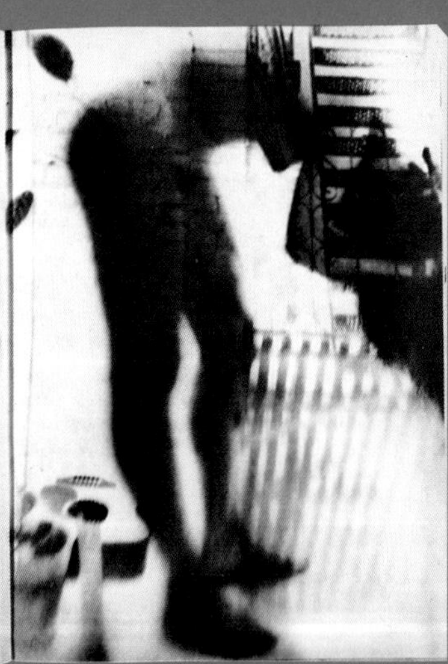

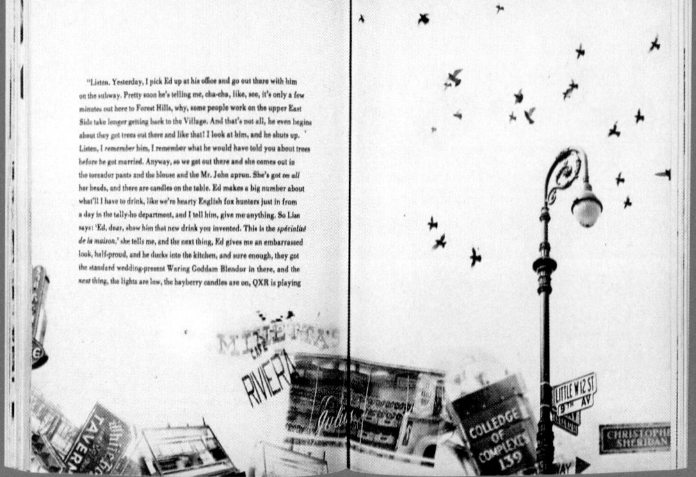

"Listen. Yesterday, I pick Ed up at his office and go out there with him on the subway. Pretty soon he's telling me, cha-cha, like, see, it's only a *few* minutes out here to Forest Hills, why, some people work on the upper East Side take longer getting back to the Village. And that's not all, he even begins about they got trees out there and like that! I look at him, and he shuts up. Listen, I *remember* him, I remember what he would have told you about trees before he got married. Anyway, so we get out there and she comes out in the toreador pants and the blouse and the Mr. John apron. She's got *on all* her beads, and there are candles on the table. Ed makes a big number about what'll I have to drink, like we're hearty English fox hunters just in from a day in the tally-ho department, and I tell him, give me anything. So Lise says: 'Ed, dear, show him that new drink you invented. This is the *spécialité de la maison,*' she tells me, and the next thing, Ed gives me an embarrassed look, half-proud, and he ducks into the kitchen, and sure enough, they got the standard wedding-present Waring Goddam Blendor in there, and the *next* thing, the lights are low, the bayberry candles are on, QXR is playing

In Focus:

SALOON SOCIETY

One of Brodovitch's last design projects was the book *Saloon Society* (1960), a combination of Bill Manville's tale of inebriation and David Attie's swirling, exuberant photographs. While good use is made of white space, and the overall look is typically elegant, the page-to-page impact of *Saloon Society* falls short of Brodovitch's best publication designs, like those for *Observations* and the magazine *Portfolio*.

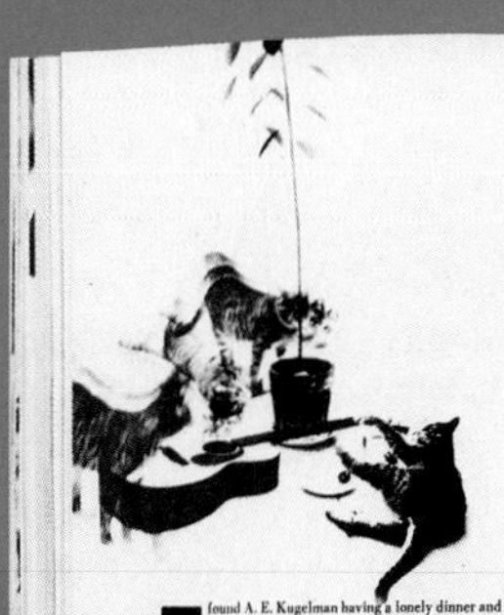

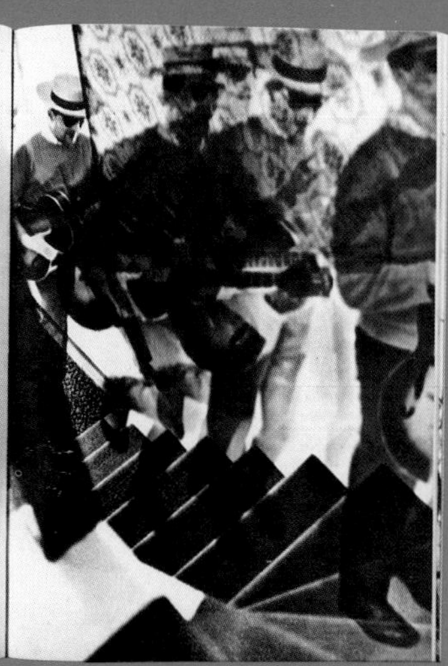

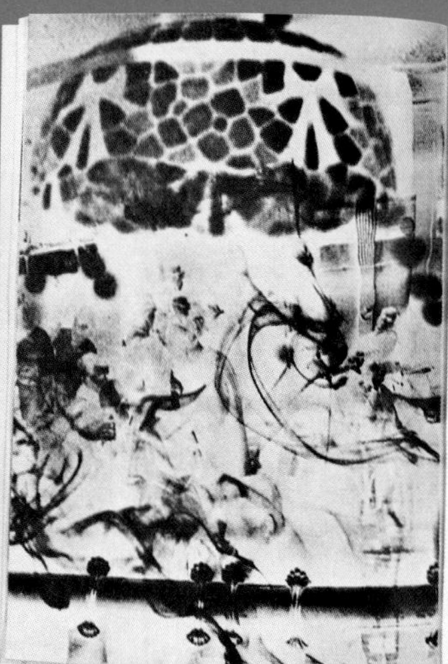

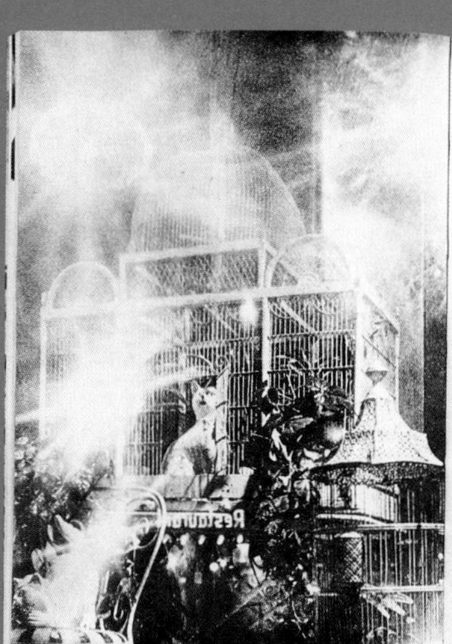

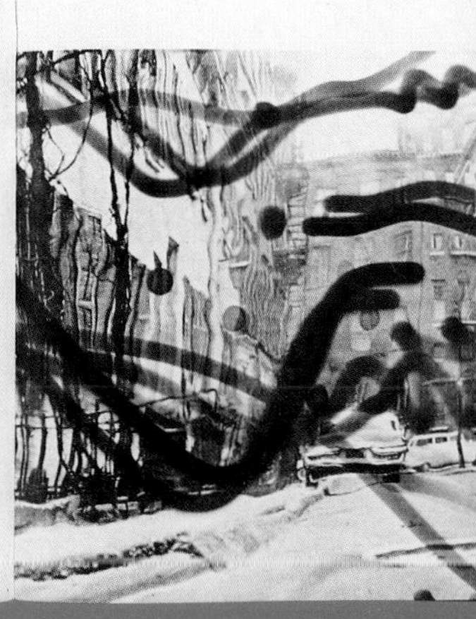

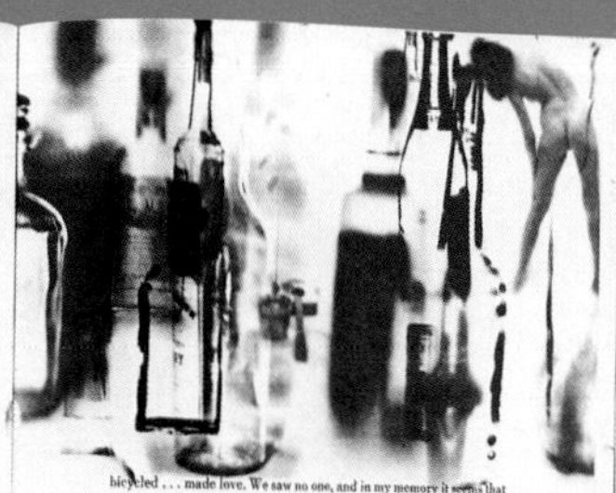

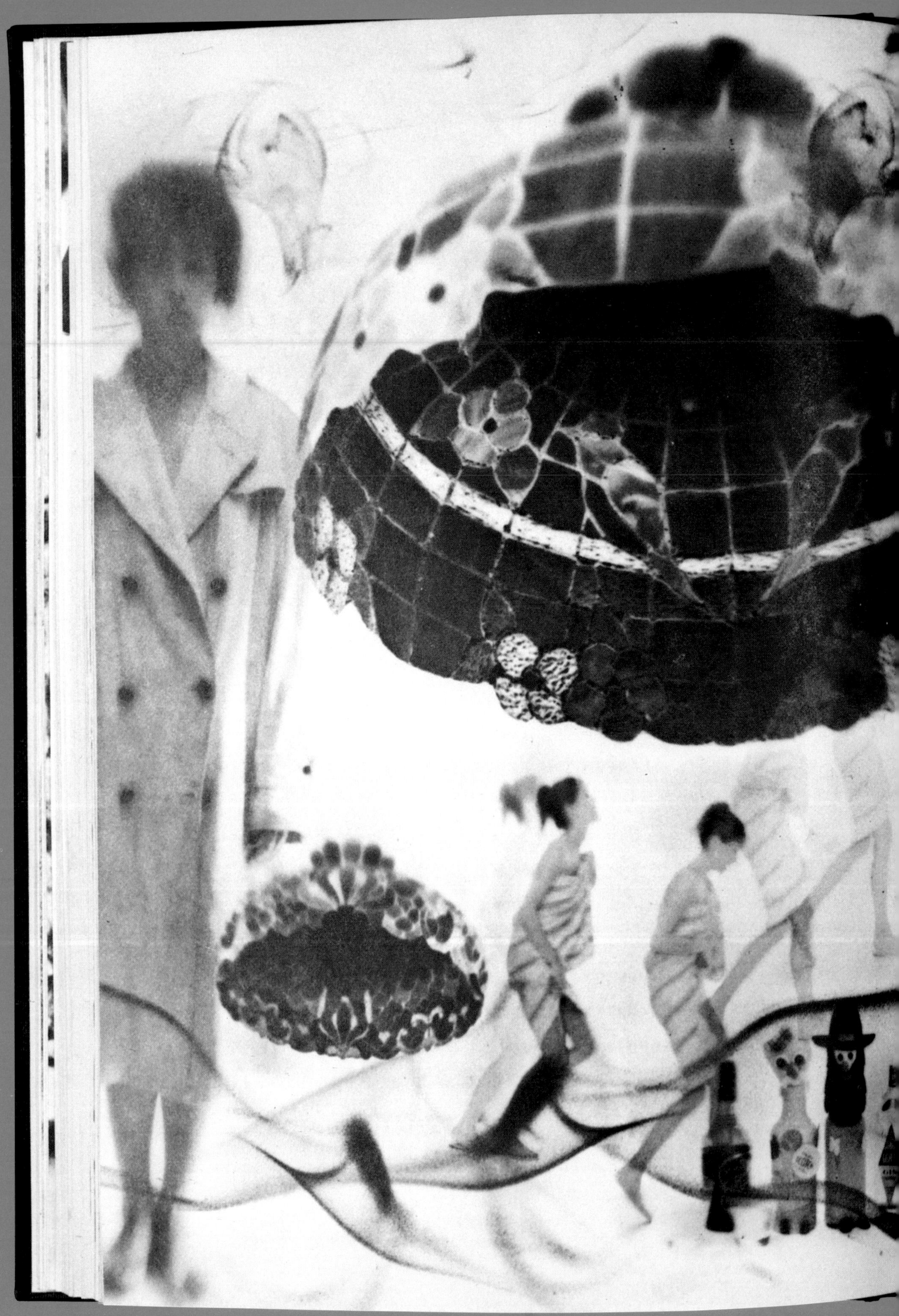

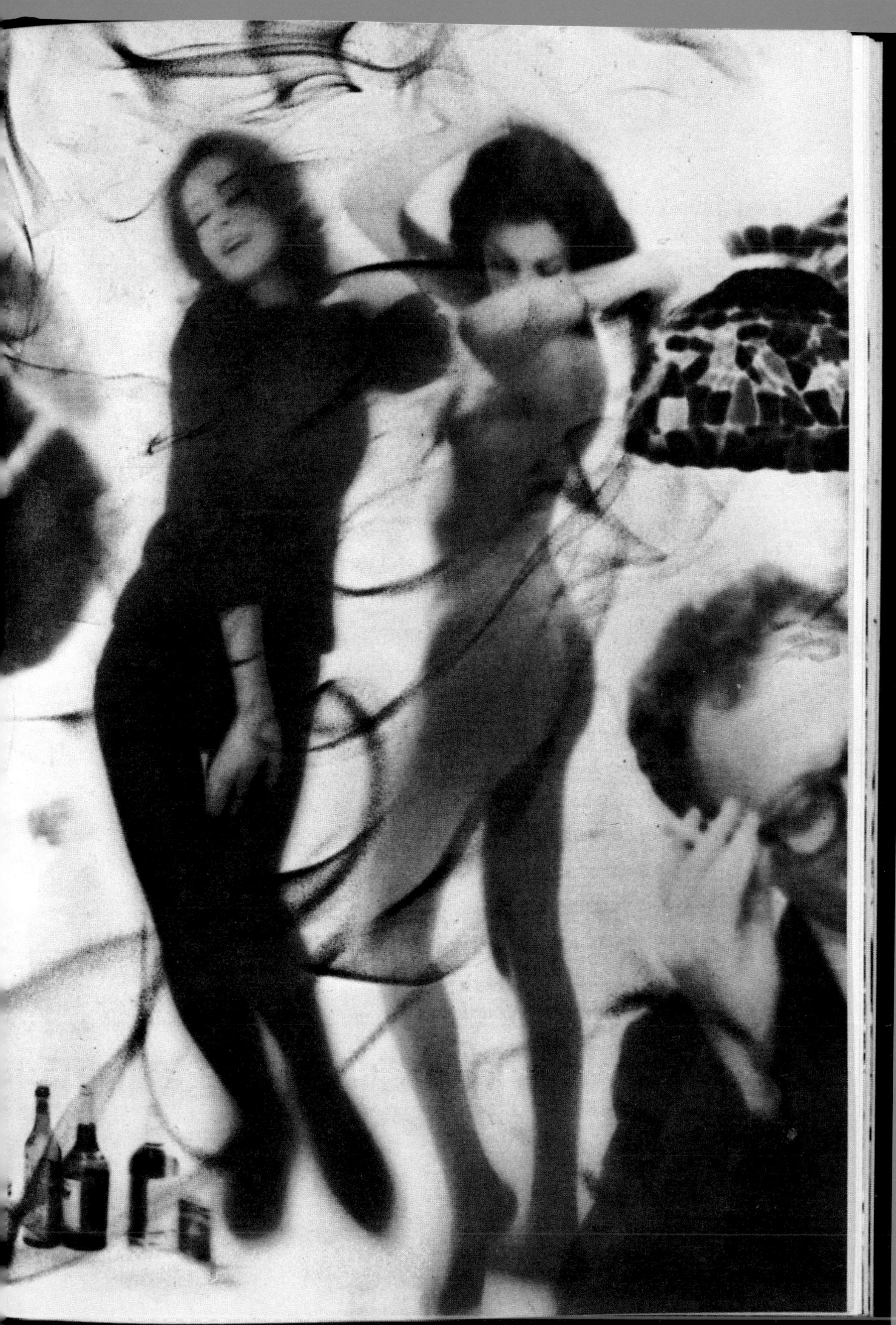

WARD'S ISLAND

While confined to Ward's Island in 1960, Brodovitch photographed his fellow patients. The pictures form a kind of coda to Brodovitch's earlier photographs, published in the book *Ballet*, since they have a similar sense of freedom and spontaneity. As poignant as they are, however, they were never published during Brodovitch's lifetime, and knowledge of their existence has been confined largely to a close circle of his former students.

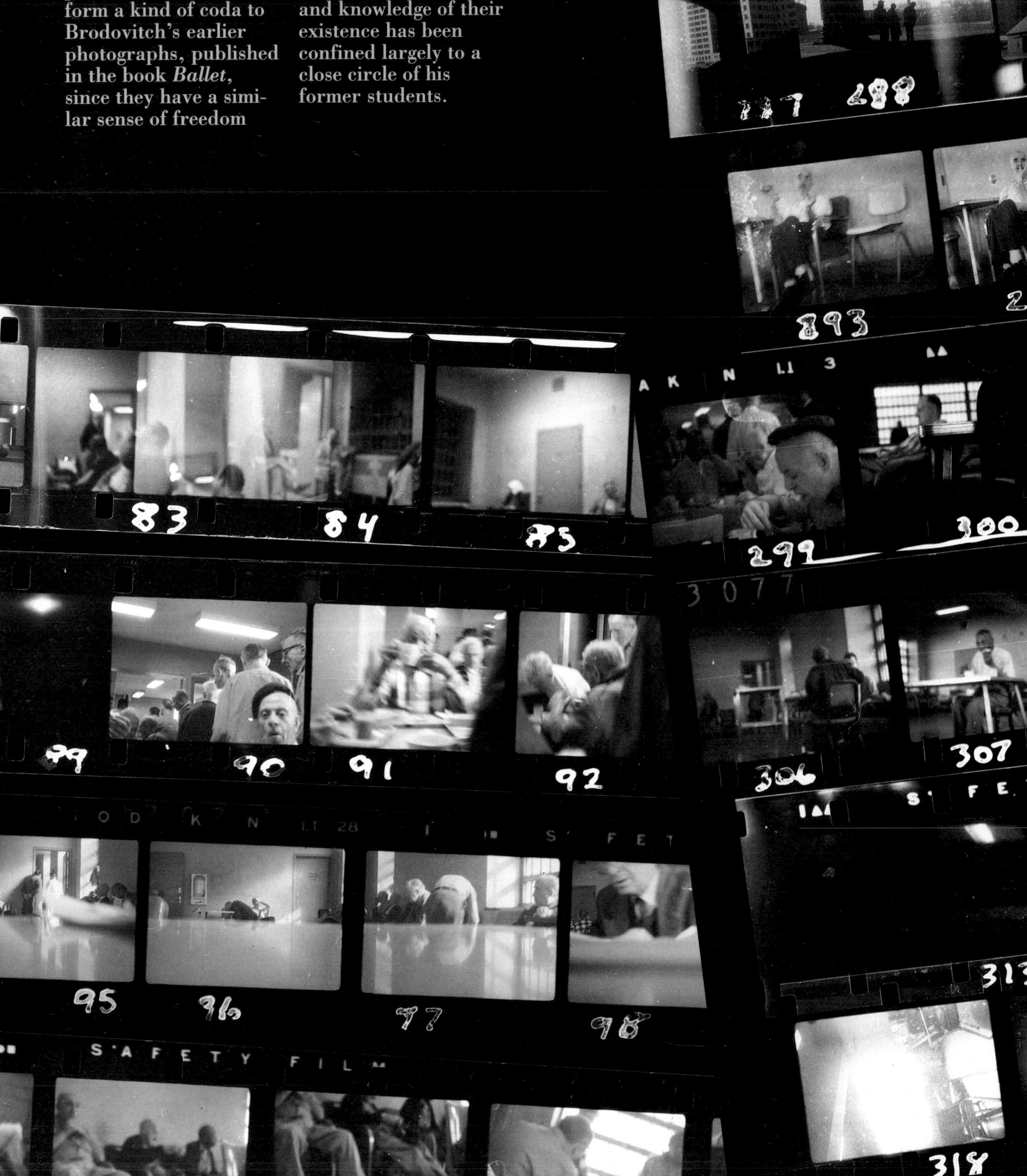

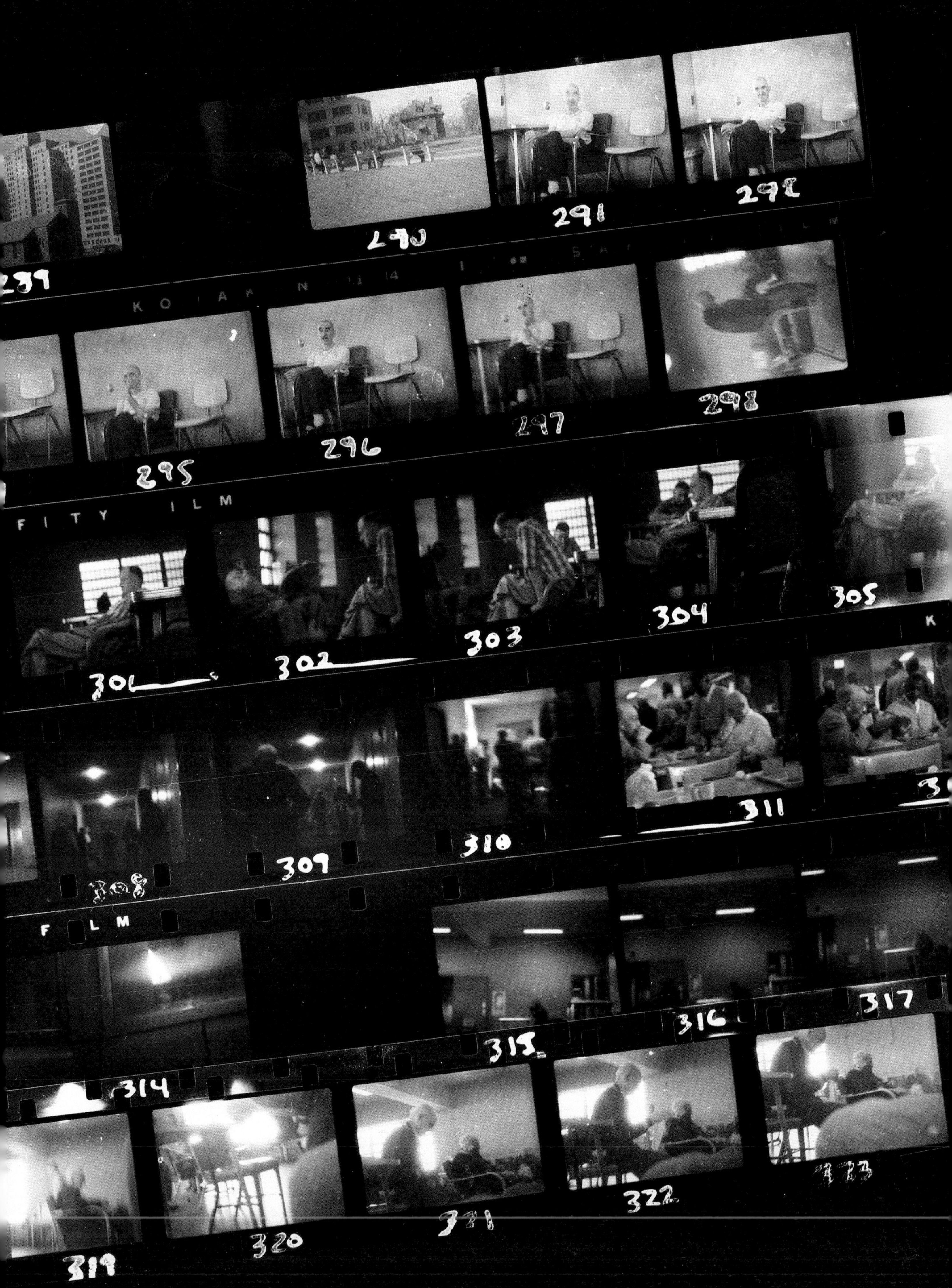
289
290
291
292
295
296
297
298
301
302
303
304
305
308
309
310
311
314
315
316
317
319
320
321
322
323

CHRONOLOGY

What is known about Alexey Brodovitch's life before 1930 is, with few exceptions, based on his own accounts and reminiscences; certain details may have been embroidered over time, and others expurgated. Information about his years in the United States is generally more reliable and comes from published sources and the memories of former assistants, students, and friends.

1898–1920 Russia

1898 Born in a hunting lodge in northwestern Russia near the Finnish border, of well-to-do Russian parents. His father is a physician/psychiatrist, his mother an amateur painter.

1905 Moves to Moscow with family. Reportedly photographs Japanese prisoners of war at hospital his father headed. Later attends school in St. Petersburg, now Leningrad.

1914 At start of World War I, abandons goal of entering the Academy of Arts, runs away from home, and joins the Russian army. Soon thereafter he is brought home by his father.

1915 Enrolled in military school, reportedly meets the czar, graduates as a lieutenant (later promoted to captain). Joins cavalry, fights in Romania.

1918 Wounded while fighting with White army against Bolsheviks in Odessa. During mass retreat from Kislovodsk, in the Caucasus, first meets Nina, a nurse, his future wife. After retreat southward, reunited with Nina and his family in Istanbul.

1920–1930 Paris

1920 Moves to Paris. Paints houses for a few months, then begins to paint sets for Sergei Diaghilev's Ballets Russes. Supplements income with illustrations for books and designs for porcelain, china, and glassware. (Examples do not survive.) Does layouts for *Arts et Métiers Graphiques*, a design magazine published by the type house Deberny-Peignot, and *Cahiers d'Art*. Marries Nina.

1924 Designs poster for Bal Banal, receives first prize and first public recognition as a designer. Son, Nikita (Nicky), is born.

1925 Receives five medals for design work at the Exposition des Arts Décoratifs et Industriels Modernes, in Paris (gold medals for kiosk and jewelry design, silver medals for fabric designs, top award for best pavilion). Numerous design commissions and illustration assignments follow, from Martini, Bon Marché, Le Printemps. Paints, draws on glass and celluloid, uses photographic (cliché verre) processes.

1927 Commissioned to decorate Prunier restaurant and design menu.

1928 *Monsieur de Bougrelon*, by Jean Lorrain (Jonquieres) is published, with scratchboard-style illustrations by Brodovitch.

1928–30 Works for Athelia, design studio of Aux Trois Quartiers department store, under Robert Block. Designs temporary facade of store, advertisements for Madelios, the store's luxury shop, and interiors for the store's clients.

1930 Publishes "What Pleases the Modern Man," a manifesto of his ideas about the function of the "publicity artist," or graphic designer.

1930–1934 Philadelphia

1930 Moves to Philadelphia, organizes Department of Advertising Design at the Pennsylvania Museum School of Industrial Art (now the Philadelphia College of Art) at instigation of John Story Jenks, the museum's vice-president.

1931 Receives advertising design assignments from N.W. Ayers agency. Works on Steinway and Climax Molybdenum campaigns.

1933 Holds first Design Laboratory, for his advanced advertising design students, at the museum school. One-man exhibit of his paintings at Crillon Gallery, Philadelphia.

1934 Designs installation of Art Directors' Club of New York 13th Annual Exhibition of Advertising Art, with his Philadelphia students. Receives honorable mention for illustration of Climax Molybdenum ad.

1934–1966 New York

1934 Named art director of *Harper's Bazaar* and moves to New York. Continues to teach in Philadelphia, commuting by train. Continues free-lance art direction, book design, and illustration.

1936 Receives medal from Art Directors' Club in the

category "Posters–Irrespective of Classification," for poster based on February 1936 *Harper's Bazaar* cover.

1937 Organizes "New Poster" show at Franklin Institute, Philadelphia. Also designs the catalogue and installation.

1938 Wins third prize in Museum of Modern Art, New York, knock-down furniture design competition. Entry illustrated in "Prize Designs for Modern Furniture," MOMA catalogue. Buys farmhouse in Phoenixville, Pa., his weekend retreat for next eighteen years.

1939 Designs mural for educational pavilion of New York World's Fair. Designs women's fashion pages of Sears, Roebuck catalogue.

1939–41 Two-year contract as art director of Saks Fifth Avenue; executes and commissions store's ads with Irving Penn as his assistant. Also, free-lance art direction for I. Miller & Son.

1941 Begins holding Design Laboratory in New York at the New School for Social Research, under the title "Art Applied to Graphic Journalism, Advertising Design and Fashion." Also works as a consultant for the American National Red Cross and various government agencies as part of war effort; designs posters.

1945 *Ballet*, a book of 104 photographs taken by Brodovitch at performances of the Ballets Russes during the thirties, published by J. J. Augustin. Text by dance critic and poet Edwin Denby. *Day of Paris*, a book of photographs by André Kertész that is designed by Brodovitch, published by J. J. Augustin.

1947–49 Design Laboratory, under New School aegis, held at the studio of Richard Avedon.

1949 Struck by Hearst delivery truck on 57th Street, injures hip.

1949–51 Designs three issues of *Portfolio*, a journal of the graphic arts. Serves as art director and art editor, with Frank Zachary as editor.

1951 Three photographs from his ballet series are included in the exhibition "Abstraction in Photography," at the Museum of Modern Art. New School workshops listed as "Visual Communication: Art Applied to Graphic Journalism/Design/Photography."

1953–55 Teaches at the Yale School of Design, where he is guest critic.

1956 Fire destroys Brodovitch's country house in Phoenixville, Pa. Buys a new home in East Hampton, Long Island.

1958 Resigns from *Harper's Bazaar.*

1959 *Observations*, with photographs by Richard Avdeon, text by Truman Capote, design by Brodovitch, published. Fire destroys home in East Hampton. His wife, Nina, dies.

1960 *Saloon Society*, with text by Bill Manville, photographs by David Attie, and design by Brodovitch, published. Hospitalized for depression, presumably the consequence of alcoholism, at Manhattan State Hospital on Ward's Island. Takes pictures of fellow patients with concealed camera.

1964 Revives Design Laboratory at Avedon Studio under auspices of the American Institute of Graphic Arts. In the fall, teaches Design Laboratory workshop at the School of Visual Arts, sponsored by Young & Rubicam advertising agency and attended by its creative staff. Designs dummy issues of *Sky* magazine, which fails before publication.

1965 Teaches Design Laboratory for two semesters at the Corcoran Gallery of Art, Washington, D.C. Readmitted to Manhattan State Hospital.

1966–1971 France

1966 Gives up teaching activities. Breaks hip. Moves with his son Nikita to Oppède-le-Vieux, France, to a remote house brought in 1938.

1968 Moves to Le Thor, France, near Avignon, where his brother Georges is an architect.

1971 Dies at Le Thor, April 15. In June, Doctor of Fine Arts degree conferred posthumously by the Philadelphia College of Art.

1972 "Alexey Brodovitch and His Influence" exhibition at the Philadelphia College of Art. Inducted into the Art Directors Club Hall of Fame, New York.

1982 "Hommage à Alexey Brodovitch" exhibition at Grand-Palais, Paris.

NOTES

1. Personal interview with Ben Fernandez, March 30, 1988.
2. Personal interview with Lillian Bassman, October 24, 1986.
3. Philadelphia College of Art, *Alexey Brodovitch and His Influence*, pp. 32–33.
4. Brodovitch's use of the term, "I am a can opener," is widely quoted by his former students, and is mentioned in his obituary in *The New York Times* of April 24, 1971.
5. His description of the aims of his Design Workshop, for example, is quite similar to the contemporaneous brochure for the New Bauhaus in Chicago, written by Laszlo Moholy-Nagy. See page 129 for a more detailed discussion of these similarities.
6. For a time in the 1930s Rand and Brodovitch shared a studio in Manhattan. However, according to Steve Heller, the two men never worked together. Still, the younger Rand looked up to Brodovitch as an exemplar of modern design.
7. For a more general discussion of the expanded role of the art director, see Lorraine Wild, "Trends in American Graphic Design, 1930–1955."
8. Personal interview with Lillian Bassman, October 24, 1986.
9. It is possible, though undocumented, that Brodovitch painted sets of their design, thus coming to know their work firsthand.
10. Richard Avedon, for one, believes that Le Corbusier's modular principles provided the foundations for Brodovitch's design style. Personal interview, October 1, 1986.
11. See, for example, *Arts et Métiers Graphiques*, November 29, 1930, which reproduces a Brodovitch-designed ad for Athelia, the design studio. The same issue contained Robert Block's "L'Expression graphique des Trois Quartiers," which was reprinted from the English magazine *Commercial Arts* (July & December, 1929). *Gebrauchsgraphik*, a German graphic-arts magazine supplemented with English texts, published an article on Brodovitch by R. L. Dupuy in January, 1930.
12. For this and many other examples, see Richard Martin, *Fashion and Surrealism*. The hat, designed in 1937, is illustrated on page 111.
13. Wild, "Trends in American Graphic Design,"p.1.
14. "Resumé." Collection Mary Faulconer.
15. "Ideas on Advertising." Mary Faulconer.
16. Personal interview with Irving Penn, July 18, 1986.
17. Carmel Snow, *The World of Carmel Snow*, p. 90.
18. Ibid., p. 91.
19. "What he does for *Harper's Bazaar* would not necessarily be suitable to another publication, Brodovitch points out. *Harper's* deals with fashion and fashion is a butterfly...here today and gone tomorrow. Fashion, he explains, is only good because within three months or less it will be old-fashioned. This is the key to *Harper's* pages." George Herrick, "Alexey Brodovitch," *Arts and Industry*, pp. 166–67.
20. Snow, *The World of Carmel Snow*, p. 50.
21. Polly Devlin, *The Vogue Book of Fashion Photography*, p. 120.
22. Ibid., p. 120.
23. Personal interview with Richard Avedon, October 1, 1986.
24. Quoted in Charles Reynolds, "Focus on Alexey Brodovitch," *Popular Photography*, December, 1961, p. 81.
25. *Harper's Bazaar*, January 1943.
26. See Michael S. Konetzka, "An Essay on the Graphic Design of Alexey Brodovitch."
27. Personal interview with Lillian Bassman, October 24, 1986.
28. "Like Brodovitch in *Harper's Bazaar*, [Will] Burtin uses no discernible grid." Wild, "Trends in American Graphic Design," p. 41; "[Brodovitch] completely abandoned use of any framework to be followed in layout." Herrick, "Alexey Brodovitch," pp. 168–69.
29. Philadelphia College of Art, *Alexey Brodovitch and His Influence*, pp. 33–35.

30. Frank Zachary, for example, recalls how Brodovitch and he spread out the layouts of *Portfolio* in the hallways of the New York hotel they used as an office. Personal interview, November 19, 1986.
31. Konetzka, "An Essay on the Graphic Design of Alexey Brodovitch," p. 9.
32. Brodovitch also was a jazz fancier, and one could argue that his magazine design is as much informed by musical phrasing as by cinematic devices. But music is more a metaphoric way of understanding what Brodovitch did on the pages of the *Bazaar:* There are few explicit references in the design to music or jazz, the way there are references to cinema.
33. See Louise Dahl-Wolfe, *A Photographer's Scrapbook*. Dahl-Wolfe apparently was hired by Carmel Snow, or at least protected by her, since Brodovitch was never her greatest fan. She is said to have complained to Snow that the art director was using too many pictures by Richard Avedon, at her expense.
34. Personal interview with Adrien Taylor, November 19, 1986.
35. Snow, *The World of Carmel Snow*, p. 203.
36. Personal interview with Robert Frank, May 17, 1986.
37. Alexey Brodovitch, "What Pleases the Modern Man," *Commercial Art*, p. 60.
38. Dawn Ades, *Photomontage*, p. 84.
39. Variously referred to as *Untitled* or *The Murderous Airplane*. See Ibid., p.115.
40. John Szarkowski, *Winogrand: Figments from the Real World*, p. 12.
41. Personal interview with Richard Avedon, October 1, 1986.
42. Brodovitch, "What Pleases the Modern Man," p. 60.
43. "Yearly Report, 1936–1937. Design Laboratory." Collection Mary Faulconer.
44. Ibid.
45. "Institute of Design, 1944." Collection the author.
46. Personal interview with Irving Penn, July 18, 1986.
47. Noelle Hoeppe, "Faculty Photo Dept., New School," unpublished listing of faculty, 1931–1973.
48. Personal interview with Lillian Bassman, October 24, 1986.
49. Personal interview with Richard Avedon, October 1, 1986.
50. Personal interview with Bob Adelman, September 5, 1986.
51. Personal interview with Bob Cato, December 30, 1986.
52. The following excerpts come from "Alexey Brodovitch Workshop Sessions." Collection Harvey Lloyd.

BIBLIOGRAPHY

Books and Articles by Alexey Brodovitch

Ballet. Text by Edwin Denby. New York: J.J. Augustin, 1945.

"Brodovitch on Brodovitch." *Camera* (Lucerne), February 1968, pp. 6–19.

"Brodovitch on Photography." *Popular Photography,* December 1961, pp.107–109.

"What Pleases the Modern Man." *Commercial Art,* August 1930, pp. 60–70.

Selected Books Designed by Brodovitch

Avedon, Richard. *Observations.* Text by Truman Capote. New York: Simon & Schuster, 1959.

Kertész, André. *Paris by Day.* Text by George Davis. New York: J.J. Augustin, 1945.

Manville, Bill. *Saloon Society.* Photographs by David Attie. New York: Duell, Sloane and Pierce, 1960.

Snow, Carmel and Mary Louise Aswell. *The World of Carmel Snow.* New York: McGraw-Hill, 1962.

On Brodovitch

CATALOGUES

Grand-Palais, Paris. *Alexey Brodovitch.* Introduction by GeorgesTourdjman. October 27–November 29, 1982.

Philadelphia College of Art, with the Smithsonian Institution. *Alexey Brodovitch and His Influence.* By George R. Bunker et al. April 1972.

ARTICLES

Block, Robert. "The Publicity of a French Store." *Commercial Art,* July/December 1929, pp. 195–200.

________. "L'Expression graphique des Trois Quartiers." *Arts et Métiers Graphiques* 14, 1930, pp. 851–856.

Bondi, Inge. "The Photographer's 'Two Masters,' " *Print,* March 1959, pp. 22–29.

Carroll, Mark. "Brodovitch and Portfolio." *Typographic,* October 1986, pp. 2–7.

Depuy, R. L. "A. Brodovitch, a Graphic Alchemist." *Gebrauschgraphik,* January 1930, pp. 44–49.

Downes, Bruce. "Brodovitch and Ballet." *Popular Photography,* September 1945, pp. 31–34.

Edwards, Owen. "Zen and the Art of Alexey Brodovitch." *American Photographer,* June 1979, pp. 50–61.

Esten, John. "Alexey Brodovitch." *Contemporary Photographers.* New York: St. Martin's Press, 1982, p. 104.

Ettenberg, Eugene. "The Remarkable Alexey Brodovitch." *American Artist,* December 1961, pp. 25–31.

Finke, J. A. "Profile: Alexey Brodovitch." *Upper and Lower Case,* March 1977.

Herrick, George. "Alexey Brodovitch." *Art and Industry* 29 (November 1940) , pp. 164–169.

Hurlburt, Allen F. "Alexey Brodovitch: The Revolution in Magazine Design." *Print,* January/February 1969, pp. 55–59 ff.

Kraus, H. Felix. "Modern Photography." *Tricolor,* June 1945, p. 64.

Larson, Peter. "Life as a Brodovitch Student." *Photography* (London), February 1964, pp. 20–21.

Lloyd, Harvey. "Alexey Brodovitch." *Photography* (London), February 1964, pp. 14–19.

Maingois, Michel. "Hommage a Alexey Brodovitch." *Zoom* 9, November/December 1971, pp. 25–35. (Reprinted in Grand-Palais, Paris, *Alexey Brodovitch.*)

Phillips, Christopher. "Brodovitch on Ballet." *American Photographer,* December 1981, pp. 74–82.

Reynolds, Charles. "Focus on Alexey Brodovitch." *Popular Photography,* December 1961, pp. 80–87. (Reprinted in Grand-Palais, Paris, *Alexey Brodovitch.)*

________."Alexey Brodovitch: 1900–1971." *Popular Photography,* September 1971, p. 60.

Rose, Ben. "Alexey Brodovitch." *Infinity,* June 1971, pp. 12–17.

Soupault, Philippe. "Alexey Brodovitch." *The Bulletin,* August 1930, pp. 908–910. (Reprinted in Grand-Palais, Paris, *Alexey Brodovitch.*)

Steinberg, Claire. "Alexey Brodovitch: 1900–1971." *Photography Annual*, 1972, pp. 156–168.

THESES

Konetzka, Michael S. "Brodovitch: An Essay on the Graphic Design of Alexey Brodovitch." Yale University, 1985.

Sednaoui, Karim H. "Alexey Brodovitch, His Work, His Influence." Trent Polytechnic and Derby College of Art and Technology, 1974.

Wild, Lorraine. "Trends in American Graphic Design, 1930–1955." Yale University, 1982.

Related Reading

BOOKS

Baldwin, Neil. *Man Ray, American Artist*. New York: Clarkson N. Potter, 1988.

Blumenfeld, Erwin. *My One Hundred Best Photos*. Text by Hendel Teicher, translated by Philippe Garner. New York: Rizzoli, 1981.

Bojko, Szymon. *New Graphic Design in Revolutionary Russia*. New York: Praeger Publishers, 1972.

Dahl-Wolfe, Louise. *A Photographer's Scrapbook*. Preface by Frances McFadden. New York: St. Martin's/Marek, 1984.

Devlin, Polly. *Vogue Book of Fashion Photography: The First Sixty Years*. Introduction by Alexander Liberman. New York: Quill/William Morrow, 1979.

Friedman, Mildred, ed. *De Stijl: 1917–1931, Visions of Utopia*. New York: Abbeville Press/Walker Art Center, 1982.

Hall-Duncan, Nancy. *The History of Fashion Photography*. New York: International Museum of Photography/Alpine Book Company, 1979.

Honour, Hugh and John Fleming. *The Visual Arts: A History*. Englewood Cliffs, N.J.: Prentice-Hall, 1982.

Martin, Richard. *Fashion and Surrealism*. New York: Rizzoli, 1987.

Phillips, Sandra S., David Travis, and Weston J. Naef. *Andre Kertész: Of Paris and New York*. New York: Thames and Hudson, 1985.

Rand, Paul. *Thoughts on Design*. Introduction by E. McKnight Kauffer. New York: Wittenborn, Schultz, 1947.

Read, Herbert, ed. *Surrealism*. New York: Praeger Publishers, 1971.

Szarkowski, John. *Winogrand: Figments from the Real World*. New York: The Museum of Modern Art, 1988.

Trahey, Jane, ed. *Harper's Bazaar: 100 Years of the American Female*. New York: Random House, 1967.

White, Nancy and John Esten. *Style in Motion: Munkacsi Photographs of the Twenties, Thirties, and Forties*. New York: Clarkson N. Potter, Inc., no date.

CATALOGUES

Arco Center for Visual Art, Los Angeles. *Herbert Bayer: Photographic Works*. Introduction by Leland Rice, essay by Beaumont Newhall. April 19–May 28, 1977.

New Orleans Museum of Art. *Leslie Gill: A Classical Approach to Photography, 1935–1958*. Foreword by Tina Freeman, essay by Owen Edwards. November 20, 1983–January 15, 1984.

Photofind Gallery, Woodstock, New York. *Martin Munkacsi*. May 4–June 9, 1985.

Zabriskie Gallery, New York. *French Photography: Selections from the Zabriskie Gallery Collection*. December 16, 1986–January 17, 1987.

Unpublished Material

"Alexey Brodovitch Workshop Sessions," typed transcripts of tapes recorded during Young and Rubicam Design Laboratory, September–November 1964, unattributed.

Hoeppe, Noelle. "Faculty, Photo Dept, New School," typed manuscript, 1983.

"Hospital Interview/Biography of Alexey Brodovitch," typed manuscript, undated and unattributed.

Newhall, Beaumont. "A Chronology for the Years 1900–1940 of certain publications, collections, museums and exhibitions pertaining to the history of photography," typed manuscript, 1978.

ACKNOWLEDGMENTS

The literary critic Denis Donaghue recently observed that biographies serve not merely to satisfy our curiosity about other human beings, but to make large-scale events and historical shifts comprehensible. "A biography of one man may give a more intimate sense of [an] institution than any other form of description," he said—which perhaps explains why the members of Documents of American Design, in seeking to create a critical literature for their profession, commissioned this publication.

Because I believe that historical and social forces play at least as strong a role as personality in the development of graphic design, my text generally approaches Brodovitch's work apart from his individual temperament. Yet I could not have even begun this task without the reminiscences and memories of many individuals who were his students, colleagues, and friends.

Mary Faulconer Saalburg, one of the designer's first students and his first assistant, was especially helpful in providing information about Brodovitch's earliest years in the United States, and she gave me free access to her considerable collection of original typescripts, tearsheets, and photographs.

Another former assistant, Lillian Bassman, who was art director of the short-lived *Junior Bazaar* and later became a photographer, provided lucid memories of working at *Harper's Bazaar* in the 1940s. I am indebted to her for many of the details of how the magazine was put together. Other former assistants whose insights proved valuable include Bob Cato and Adrian Taylor.

Frank Zachary, former editor of *Portfolio*, shared his memories of working alongside Brodovitch while creating that remarkable publication. Dorothy Wheelock Edson, an editor at the *Bazaar* after the war, helped bring alive the cultural flavor and excitement of those times.

Richard Avedon, Louise Dahl-Wolfe, and Irving Penn spoke with me at length about their years with Brodovitch and *Harper's Bazaar*. (Penn, it should be noted, became a photographer only after leaving Brodovitch's employ.) Bob Adelman, Ben Fernandez, and Robert Frank were among the other photographers who shared their accounts of the designer's impact on their photography and their careers.

Without photographer Harvey Lloyd's archive of Brodovitch material, collected since his days as a Design Lab student, this book would still be an idea. Since original material is almost nonexistent, his collection of slides, publications, and copies of *Harper's Bazaar* and *Portfolio* was crucial. Ben Fernandez's collection also was helpful.

Valuable guidance in my research was provided by Nicholas Callaway, Diana Edkins, Alvin Eisenman, Steve Heller, Katie Homans, and Bethany Johns. To them, and to all others who helped blaze a path for me, my deepest appreciation.

Finally, I would like to thank Sarah Bodine, the project editor for Documents of American Design, who supplied needed direction and support in equal measure; Will Hopkins, the project advisor; Ray Komai, whose striking design surely would have caused Brodovitch pleasure; and, at Harry N. Abrams, Eric Himmel, who took a personal interest in the book.

Any errors of fact, of course, are on my own account. Since so little verifiable evidence of Brodovitch's career exists, I can only hope that this enterprise spurs the discovery of much that is now unknown or uncertain.

Photograph Credits

Pages 2–3, Collection Eric Himmel, New York; Page 34 left, The Museum of Modern Art, New York. Lillie P. Bliss Bequest; Page 34 center, The Solomon R. Guggenheim Museum, New York; Page 34 right, Private Collection; Page 35 left, Kunstmuseum Basel; Page 35 second from left, Philadelphia Museum of Art. Louise and Walter Arensberg Collection; Page 35 third from left, The Solomon R. Guggenheim Museum; Page 36 left, Culver Pictures; Page 36 second from left, The Museum of Modern Art, New York. Van Gogh Purchase Fund; Page 36 third from left, National Gallery of Art, Washington, D.C.; Page 40 left, The Museum of Modern Art, New York; Page 40 right, The Museum of Modern Art, New York; Page 41 left, Philadelphia Museum of Art. Louise and Walter Arensberg Collection; Page 42 top left, Altoona Area Public Library; Page 42 top right, © 1969 Bauhaus-Archiv, Darmstadt; Page 42 bottom right, Bauhaus-Archiv, Darmstadt; Page 43 left, The Museum of Modern Art, New York; Page 43 second from left, Bauhaus Archiv, Darmstadt; Page 43 right, Niedersachsische Landesgalerie, Hannover; Page 54–55, © Arnold Newman; Page 100, Walter Sanders, Life Magazine © Time Inc.; Page 133, © 1948 (renewed 1976) by The Condé Nast Publications Inc.; Page 143, © HIRO.

"I am not a teacher.
I can irritate
and intrigue you
but you must
teach yourself."

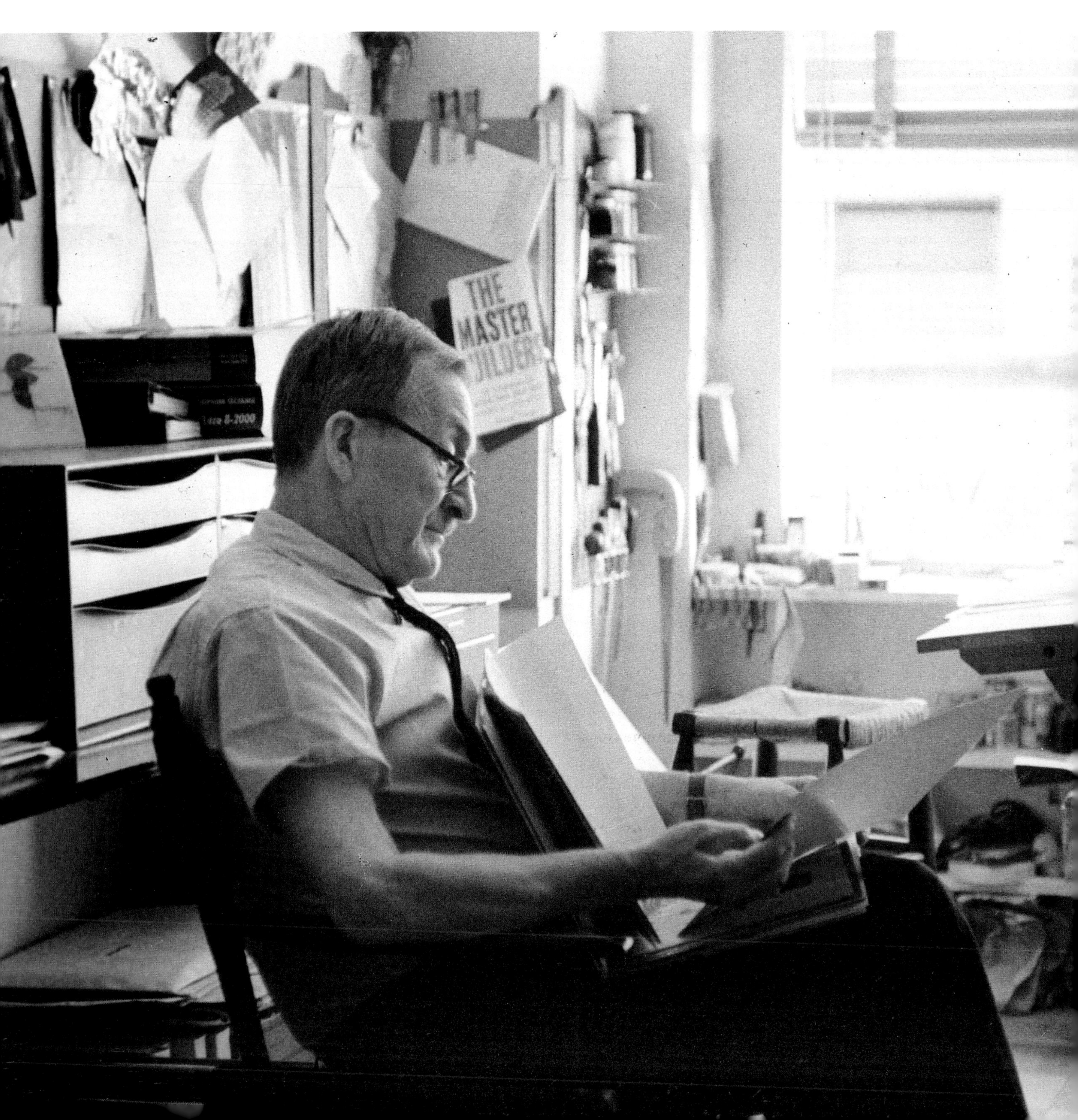

DOCUMENTS OF AMERICAN DESIGN

Documents of American Design is a nonprofit corporation established in 1984 by a group of graphic designers, art directors, and educators to assess and preserve the record of America graphic design. Its projects include exhibitions, seminars, and books, of which *Brodovitch* is the first book in the *Masters of American Design* series.

These undertakings are intended to inform professional and general audiences and to further the knowledge of the history and role of graphic design in our culture. Future projects will include Frederic Goudy, Saul Bass, and Will Burtin.

Documents of American Design is deeply indebted to many individuals and organizations for their help and support. This book and the books that follow could not happen without their advice and contributions. We are very grateful to them.

Our benefactors include Aaron Burns and the International Typeface Corporation, The Cooper Union for the Advancement of Science and Art, Cowles Charitable Trust, Jean Coyne and Richard Coyne of *Communication Arts* Magazine, Carl Fischer, Alvin Grossman, Kit Hinrichs, Neil Shakery, and Linda Hinrichs of Pentagram, Ken Lieberman of Ken Lieberman Labs, The National Endowment for the Arts, and James Stockton of James Stockton & Associates.

Contributors to the development of **Documents of American Design** and this book include Jennifer Antupit, Mary K. Baumann, Barbara Berger, Kathy Corrigan, Dan Erkkila, Annie Fink, Patricia Galteri of Meyer, Souzzi, English, and Klein, Alan Green, David L. Green, Amy K. Hughes, Bill N. Lacy, Joseph Lee, David Matava, Susan B. Moore, Peg Patterson and Tom Wood of Patterson and Wood, Judith Rew, Michael Saridis, Debora K. Schuler, Arthur Tarlow, and Phyllis Wender of Rosenstone-Wender.

While every attempt has been made to include proper and accurate credits for our sponsors and for all work appearing in this book, we apologise for any oversights. Errors will be corrected in future editions.

ALEXEY BRODOVITCH: 1898-1971

1880

1890

1898 Alexey Brodovitch is born in a hunting lodge in northwestern Russia near the Finnish border to well-to-do Russian parents. His father is a physician/psychiatrist, and his mother is an amateur painter.

1900

1905 He moves to Moscow with his family. He reportedly photographs Japanese prisoners of war at a hospital his father heads. He later attends school in St. Petersburg, now Leningrad.

1880 New York City streets are first lit by electricity.

Stephan Horgan invents the halftone process; it is perfected by Max and Louis Levy in 1888.

1881 First photomechanical color illustrations appear in *L'Illustration* in Paris.

1882 Oscar Wilde lectures in America, influencing the "aesthetic movement."

1883 Brooklyn Bridge opens to traffic.

The Home Insurance Building, one of the first skyscrapers, is completed in Chicago.

Cyrus Curtis founds *Ladies Home Journal.*

1884 Linn Boyd Benton invents the punch-cutting machine, which mechanically produces the molds needed for casting metal type.

Oxford English Dictionary is published.

1885 George Eastman begins manufacturing coated photographic paper.

Clark Bryan founds *Good Housekeeping*.

1886 Ottmar Mergenthaler invents the Linotype machine, a keyboard-driven device that casts complete lines of lead type; it reverses the centuries-old method of assembling and then redistributing prefabricated lead characters.

Tolbert Lanston invents the Monotype machine, which casts single characters rather than full lines.

The U.S. adopts the standard "point" system for measurements in the graphic arts.

1887 Celluloid film is invented.

1888 George Eastman perfects the portable box camera and introduces rolls of paper film, whose price includes processing and finishing.

The English designer and social critic William Morris begins designing the neogothic typeface Golden.

The electric motor is invented.

1890 First mechanical computer, using punch cards, is employed for the U.S. Census; it is designed by Herman Hollerith, who will later found IBM.

1892 George Eastman founds the Eastman Kodak Company.

Edna Chase founds *Vogue*.

1893 Sears, Roebuck, and Co. is founded in Chicago.

John Joly in Dublin produces the first color photograph that can be viewed without any external apparatus.

1894 Frederic Goudy starts the Camelot Press, inspired by William Morris and the fine-press movement in America.

Thomas Alva Edison's Kinetoscope machines, viewed like a peep show, are installed in a Kinetoscope Parlor in New York.

1895 The brothers Louis and Auguste Lumiere introduce the first motion-picture projector, which casts a moving image on a screen.

1896 The avant-garde art periodicals *Die Jugend* and *Simplicissimus* are published in Munich, featuring "Jugenstil" graphics.

The magazine *Poster Lore* notes that there are over 6,000 poster collectors in America.

To aid his photographic studies of motion, Eadweard Muybridge invents the first camera shutter, which exposes a photographic plate for a fraction of a second.

1897 A group of artists and designers, led by Gustav Klimt, form the Vienna Secession, abandoning the official academic artists' organization.

1898 The Spanish-American War ends, affirming U.S. dominance in the Americas.

The German firm Berthold designs a sans serif typeface that is called Standard in the U.S. and Akzidenz Grotesque in Germany.

1902 Alfred Stieglitz forms the Photo-Secession in New York; the following year he publishes the first issue of *Camera Work*, promoting photography as a legitimate form of fine art.

Animal Crackers box is designed.

1903 Russian Social Democratic Workers' Party splits into Mensheviks and Bolsheviks.

The Great Train Robbery is produced; 12 minutes in length, it is the world's longest motion-picture film.

The Wright Brothers fly a powered airplane.

1905 Ernest Elmo Calkins declares that advertising is becoming a "profession" equivalent to "law, medicine, and divinity."

Between 1905 and 1914, nearly 10.5 million immigrants enter the U.S.

1906 The first Yellow Pages telephone directory is published.

200,000 postcards pass through the New York City post office in one week.

1907 The first exhibition of cubist painting is held in Paris.

The German electrical utility AEG hires architect Peter Behrens to direct the design of factories, products, and graphics.

Alfred Stieglitz opens the Little Galleries of the Photo-Secession at 291 Fifth Avenue, New York, popularly known as "291".

Leo H. Baekeland develops Bakelite, the first completely synthetic plastic.

1908 A group of painters in New York committed to the realistic depiction of urban life forms the Ashcan School.

Ford builds the first Model T.

1909 F.T. Marinetti invents a new avant-garde movement when he publishes the "Futurist Manifesto" in a Paris newspaper.

1 Three of Brodovitch's Ballets Russes ographs appear in the Museum of ern Art exhibition "Abstraction in ography."

'-1955 He is guest critic at the design am of the Yale School of Art.

1958 Resigns from *Harper's Bazaar.*

1959 The book *Observations*, with photographs by Richard Avedon, text by Truman Capote, and design by Brodovitch, is published.

Wife Nina dies.

1960 The book *Saloon Society*, with photographs by David Attie, text by Bill Manville, and design by Brodovitch, is published.

He is hospitalized for depression, presumably the consequence of alcoholism.

He takes pictures of his fellow patients with a concealed camera.

1964 Revives the Design Laboratory at Avedon's studio, under the auspices of the AIGA. In the fall, he holds the Design Laboratory at the School of Visual Arts, sponsored by Young & Rubicam ad agency and attended by its staff.

Designs a dummy for *Sky* magazine, which fails before publication.

0 North Korea invades South Korea President Truman sends U.S. troops to rvene; war ends in 1953.

tainer Corporation of America begins eat Ideas of Western Man," using fine and design as institutional advertising.

seum of Modern Art holds biannual od Design" exhibitions between 1950 1955, promoting such modernist values bstraction, truth to materials, and ability to function.

1 William Golden designs the CBS eye, odel for corporate identity in the 1950s gn program of the Yale School of Art.

ter Paepcke and Egbert Jacobson d the International Design Conference spen; its goal is to promote design as a tion of management.

2 McDonald's Golden Arches signage is gned by architect Stanley Meston.

3 Henry Wolf becomes art director of *uire*, contributing to the trend towards eptual photography in magazine gn.

4 Senator Joseph McCarthy's anti-nunist trials are televised in the U.S.

an Frutiger designs the type family ers in Switzerland.

n Glaser, Edward Sorel, Seymour ast, and Reynolds Ruffins found Push Studio in New York.

5 Industrial designer Henry Dreyfuss shes *Designing for People*, populariz-rgonomics" in the U.S.

Bass designs the title sequence for Otto inger's film *The Man with the Golden* considered one of the first applica- of modernist graphic design to a ire film.

ew York, Edward Steichen's exhibition e Family of Man" opens at Museum of lern Art.

1956 Paul Rand designs corporate identity for IBM, in collaboration with architect Elliot Noyes.

Southdale Shopping Center, one of the first indoor, climate-controlled shopping malls, opens in Minneapolis.

Allen Ginsberg publishes *Howl.*

1957 Dr. Seuss publishes *Cat in the Hat.*

Max Meidinger and Edouard Hofmann design the typeface Helvetica.

Vance Packard publishes his popular critique *The Hidden Persuaders*, attacking advertising as psychological warfare: it tries "to invade the privacy of our minds."

Roland Barthes publishes *Mythologies*, a linguistic analysis of design, advertising, cooking, etc.: "cars today are almost the exact equivalent of the great Gothic cathedrals...."

1958 European Economic Community is established.

Communication Arts magazine begins publication.

Beatnik movement spreads across Europe and the U.S.

Mies van der Rohe and Philip Johnson design Seagram Building in New York, setting a standard for the urban corporate architecture of the 60s.

1959 Emil Ruder publishes "The Typography of Order" in multilingual journal *Graphis.*

Harley Earl designs the Cadillac Eldorado, marking the climax of his interest in low, long, ornate automobiles.

1960 U.S. spends more than $11 billion on advertising.

Chermayeff & Geismar Associates, New York, designs corporate identity for Chase Manhattan Bank, utilizing a non-figurative, non-typographic mark.

1961 Berlin Wall is constructed.

Soviet Union sends humans into space.

1962 U.S. Military Council is established in Vietnam.

Cuban Missile Crisis leads to confrontation between U.S. and U.S.S.R.

Andy Warhol begins painting *Campbell's Soup Cans.*

Eero Saarinen designs TWA Terminal, New York, a monument of late modern-expressionism.

Marshall McLuhan publishes *The Gutenberg Galaxy*, proclaiming the end of print culture and the beginning of the electronic age.

1963 John F. Kennedy is assassinated.

Martin Luther King delivers his speech "I Have a Dream."

Stanley Kubrick directs the Cold War film fantasy *Dr. Strangelove.*

Pop Art exhibition at the Guggenheim features work by Warhol, Johns, Rauschenberg, and others.

1964 U.S. invades North Vietnam.

Beatles invades the U.S.

Maurice Sendak publishes *Where the Wild Things Are.*

1930

1940

1930 Publishes "What Pleases the Modern Man," a manifesto on the role of the "publicity artist" or graphic designer.

He and his family move to Philadelphia, where he is asked to organize the Department of Advertising Design at the Pennsylvania Museum School of Industrial Design (later the Philadelphia College of Art).

1931 Receives advertising design commissions from the agency N.Y. Ayer.

1933 Holds first Design Laboratory, for his advanced students at the museum school.

Crillon Gallery, Philadelphia, holds a one-man show of his paintings.

1934 He becomes art director of *Harper's Bazaar*.

1936 Receives a medal from the Art Directors Club for a poster based on a *Harper's Bazaar* cover.

1937 Organizes and designs "New Poster" show at Franklin Institute, Philadelphia.

1938 Wins third prize in Museum of Modern Art's knockdown-furniture competition.

1939 Designs mural for educational pavilion at the New York World's Fair. He designs women's-fashion pages for Sears, Roebuck catalogue.

Receives a two-year contract as art director of Saks Fifth Avenue, with Irving Penn as his assistant.

1941 Begins conducting the Design Laboratory in New York at the New School for Social Research.

1945 J. J. Augustin publishes *Ballet*, a book of photographs taken by Brodovitch of the Ballets Russes during the 1930s, and *Paris*, a book of Andre Kertesz photographs, designed by Brodovitch.

1947-1949 Supported by the New School, the Design Laboratory is held at the studio of Richard Avedon.

1949 Is hit by a Hearst delivery truck on 57th Street, injuring his hip.

1949-1951 Is art director and art editor of three issues of *Portfolio*, a journal of the graphic arts. Frank Zachary is editor.

1930 The flashbulb becomes available to photographers.

A working phototypesetter is installed by Waterlow & Sons in the U.K.

Henry Luce founds *Fortune*, a design-conscious coffee-table magazine for the business community.

1931 The Empire State Building is completed and Rockefeller Center is begun.

Stanley Morison designs Times New Roman, a typeface for the London *Times*.

Over two thirds of the men working in ad agencies are college educated, compared to only half in 1916. They are nearly all white, male, and of Anglo-Saxon descent.

1932 Henry-Russell Hitchcock and Philip Johnson promote the term "International Style" in architecture with their Museum of Modern Art exhibition.

Aldous Huxley publishes *Brave New World*.

1933 Hitler is appointed chancellor of Germany and Nazis erect first concentration camp.

Approximately 60,000 artists emigrate from Germany between 1933 and 1939.

The Bauhaus closes in Berlin.

Black Mountain College opens in North Carolina; its faculty includes former Bauhaus master Joseph Albers.

1934 The graphic design magazine *P.M.*, *(later called A.D.)*, is founded by Dr. Robert Leslie.

1935 WPA Federal Art Projects begin under Roosevelt's "New Deal."

1936 Mussolini and Hitler proclaim Rome-Berlin Axis.

Allen Lane founds Penguin Books.

Dale Carnegie publishes *How to Win Friends and Influence People*.

Henry Luce founds *Life* magazine; the following year, Gardner Cowles and John Cowles found *Look*.

The Museum of Modern Art organizes "Fantastic Art, Dada, Surrealism," complementing the museum's tendency towards cubism, abstraction, and functionalism.

1937 *Hindenburg* disaster is reported over first transcontinental radio.

Picasso paints *Guernica* in response to the bombing of a Basque town during the Spanish Civil War.

The New Bauhaus opens in Chicago, with Moholy-Nagy as director; Gropius and Breuer are teaching at Harvard.

Merganthaler Linotype introduces Bell Gothic, for use in American phone books.

E. McKnight Kauffer exhibits poster designs at the Museum of Modern Art.

1938 William Addison Dwiggins designs the typeface Caledonia.

Mies van der Rohe becomes director of the Armour Institute (later Illinois Institute of Technology) in Chicago.

1939 World War II begins.

U.S. economy is revitalized by wartime production.

Innovative U.S. products include nylon stockings and IBM Mark I, the first digital computer.

Joseph Binder, Donald Deskey, Norman Bel Geddes, Paul Rand, and other prominent designers contribute to the New York World's Fair.

Exhibition "Bauhaus: 1918-1928" is held at the Museum of Modern Art.

1940 Museum of Modern Art holds the exhibition "Organic Design in Home Furnishings," featuring a molded-plywood chair designed by Charles Eames and Eero Saarinen.

1941 Japan bombs Pearl Harbor; U.S. enters World War II and begins Manhattan Project to develop nuclear weapons.

Regularly scheduled television broadcasts begin in the U.S.

1943 Italy surrenders and declares war on Germany.

Mondrian paints *Broadway Boogie Woogie*.

1945 World War II ends.

Will Burtin becomes art director of *Fortune* magazine.

1946 Xerography process is invented.

Paul Rand publishes *Thoughts on Design*, promoting stylistic interchange between modern art and advertising.

Florence and Hans Knoll found the modernist furniture manufacturer Knoll Associates.

1947 Herbert Land invents the Polaroid-Land process.

The former avant-gardist Jan Tschichold works for Penguin Books typography.

Armin Hofmann and Emil Ruder begin teaching at the School of Design in Basel.

1948 State of Israel is founded.

1949 North Atlantic Treaty Organization (NATO) is established.

Apartheid becomes the official policy in South Africa.

George Orwell publishes *1984*.

The advertising firm Doyle Dane Bernbach is founded; it appeals to a sophisticated audience with conceptual photography and witty copywriting, becoming crucial to the "New Advertising" of the 1950s and 60s.

1910

1920

1914 At the start of World War I, he abandons his goal of entering the Academy of Arts and runs away from home to join the Russian army. Soon thereafter he is brought home by his father.

1915 Enrolled in a military school, Brodovitch reportedly meets the czar. He graduates as a lieutenant and is later promoted to captain; he joins cavalry and fights in Romania.

1918 Wounded while fighting in the counter revolutionary White Army against the Bolsheviks in Odessa. During mass retreat from Kislovodsk in the Caucasus, he meets Nina, a nurse, whom he will later marry. After retreat southward, he is reunited with Nina and his family in Istanbul.

1920 Moves to Paris, where he paints houses and later stage sets for Sergei Diaghilev's Ballets Russes. He pursues illustration and decorative arts commissions, and does layouts for *Arts et Metiers Graphiques*, a design magazine, and for *Cahiers d'Art*. He and Nina marry.

1924 Designs poster for Bal Banal competition; he wins first prize and receives his first public recognition as a designer. His son Nikita (Nicky) is born.

1925 Receives five medals for design work at the Paris Exposition des Arts Decoratifs et Industriels Modernes. Numerous commissions for design and illustration follow. His techniques include painting, drawing on glass and celluloid, and photographic (cliche verre) processes.

1927 Commissioned to decorate Prunier restaurant and design its menu.

1928 *Monsieur de Bougrelon* by Jean Lorrain (Jonquieres) is published, with scratchboard-style illustrations by Brodovitch.

1928-1930 Works for Atelia, the design studio of Aux Trois Quartiers department store, under the direction of Robert Block. He designs ads, interiors, and architectural decorations.

1910 Eastman invents the Photostat photocopying machine.

1911 Publisher Cyrus Curtis invents modern "market research" by commissioning studies of his readers' buying habits.

Frederick Winslow Taylor invents "Taylorization" by analyzing human factory labor into a series of simple repeatable motions.

1912 Pablo Picasso produces *Still-Life with Caning*, one of his first works of "collage."

1913 Cass Gilbert designs the Woolworth Building, a New York skyscraper in the Gothic style, then the tallest building in the world.

The Armory Show shocks the U.S. with European avant-garde art.

Premier of Futurist opera "*Victory Over the Sun*" in St. Petersburg. Malevich does first black square on white backdrop as stage set.

1914 World War I begins in Europe.

The American Institute of Graphic Arts is founded in New York.

1916 Tristan Tzara reads the first *Dada Manifesto*, in Zurich.

1917 U.S. enters World War I.

In Russia the October Revolution is followed by a civil war, which ends in 1920 with the triumph of the Red Army.

In neutral Holland Theo van Doesburg founds the De Stijl movement.

1918 World War I ends.

The first manifesto of the Berlin Dadaists proclaims the need for an art "which has been visibly shattered by the explosions of last week...."

1919 The Art Directors Club is established in New York.

The Bauhaus is established in Weimar.

1920 The Vkhutemas (Higher Technical Art Studios) established in Petrograd.

1921 The New York Dadaist Man Ray moves to Paris, where he engages in both commercial and experimental photography.

1922 The Union of Soviet Socialist Republics (U.S.S.R.) is formed.

Aleksei Gan publishes the *Constructivist Manifesto*, announcing the active role of art in Soviet culture.

The tomb of Tutankhamen is discovered, inspiring an international fashion for Egyptoid motifs.

Reader's Digest is founded.

1923 The Bauhaus mounts its first major exhibition in Weimar, receiving international publicity.

Henry Luce and Britton Haddon found *Time* magazine.

1924 In Paris Andre Breton publishes the first *Surrealist Manifesto*, demanding the liberation of art from the constraints of reason, aesthetics, and morality.

In Germany the Leica 35mm camera is manufactured, liberating the photographer from the constraints of bulky, immobile equipment and conventional perspective views.

In New York the French illustrator Erte is hired to design covers for *Harper's Bazaar*.

1925 In Paris the Exposition des Arts Decoratifs et Industriels Modernes generates international enthusiasm for what is later called the "Art Deco" style.

In Detroit General Motors hires Harley Earl, believing that visual styling will sell cars.

In the Soviet Union Sergei Eisenstein directs *Battleship Potemkin*; sequences such as the battle on the Odessa steps demonstrate his theory of cinematic montage.

The New Yorker is founded.

1926 El Lissitzky, referring to the vast audiences created by modern mass media, writes, "The book is becoming the most monumental work of art."

1927 Society of Typographic Arts (STA) is founded in Chicago.

1928 Inspired by modern art and machinery, Jan Tschichold writes *The New Typography*, and Paul Renner designs the typeface Futura.

Inspired by modern art and machinery, the American typographer Morris Benton designs the typeface Broadway.

Conde Nast invites the European designer Dr. M. F. Agha to art direct American *Vogue*.

Mickey Mouse makes his first appearance in the silent film *Plain Crazy*; he is later identified by Sergei Eisenstein as "America's most original contribution to culture."

1929 Wall Street stock market crashes and the Great Depression begins.

The Museum of Modern Art opens in New York.

Marshall Fields department store in Chicago uses a futuristic dwelling designed by Buckminster Fuller as a display for home furnishings. The store calls it the "Dymaxion House."

1970

1980

1965 He teaches the Design Laboratory for two semesters at the Corcoran Gallery of Art, Washington, D.C.

He is readmitted to the hospital.

1966 Gives up his teaching activities.

Breaks his hip and moves in with his son Nikita to Oppede-le-Vieux, France, to a remote house bought in 1938.

1968 Moves to Le Thor, France, near Avignon, where his brother Georges works as an architect.

1971 Alexey Brodovitch dies at Le Thor on April 15.

In June, he is posthumously awarded a Doctor of Fine Arts degree by the Philadelphia College of Art.

1972 The exhibition "Alexey Brodovitch and His Influence" is held at the Philadelphia College of Art, April.

Brodovitch is inducted into the Art Directors Club Hall of Fame, New York.

1982 The Exhibition "Homage a Alexey Brodovitch" is held at the Grand-Palais, Paris.

1965 The black American leader Malcolm X is assassinated.

Beatles' *Rubber Soul* album features distorted "psychedelic" type.

Claes Oldenburg produces *Soft Toilet*.

Massimo Vignelli cofounds Unimark International in Chicago.

Bernard Rudofsky curates the exhibition "Architecture without Architects" in New York, fanning the enthusiasm for "vernacular" design.

1966 International Days of Protest are held against U.S. policy in Vietnam.

Dot Zero, a theoretical design magazine, is founded in New York.

1967 U.S. bombs Hanoi.

Milton Glaser designs Bob Dylan poster; nearly 6 million copies are printed.

British model Twiggy becomes emblem of the U.S. fashion scene.

Victor Papanek publishes *Design for the Real World*, proposing commonsense, low-tech, low-waste, and anti-aesthetic design.

1968 Martin Luther King, Jr. and Robert F. Kennedy are assassinated.

Warsaw Pact allies invade Czechoslovakia and install pro-Soviet government.

Students revolt across Europe and the U.S.

The Basel School of Design institutes its Advanced Course in graphic design.

Tom Wolfe publishes *The Electric Kool-Aid Acid Test*.

British troops enter Belfast to quell Protestant-Catholic fighting.

Neil Armstrong walks on the moon.

Sesame Street begins broadcasting.

1969 Gatti, Paolini, and Teodora design the "Sacco" chair, a shapeless bag filled with polystyrene; it is also known as the "bean-bag" chair.

1970 Ohio National Guard kills four students at Kent State University.

International Typeface Corporation (ITC) is founded by Aaron Burns, Herb Lubalin, and Edward Rondthaler.

1971 Vietnam War spreads to Laos and Cambodia.

Cigarette ads are banned from U.S. television.

The microprocessor, basic component of the microcomputer, is invented.

1972 Richard Nixon visits China and the Soviet Union.

Robert Venturi, Denise Scott Brown, and Steven Izenour publish *Learning from Las Vegas*, proclaiming the virtues of commercial vernacular design over the elitism and abstraction of modernism.

Wolfgang Weingart lectures in Europe and the U.S. on "How Can One Make Swiss Typography?"

1973 Vietnam cease-fire is signed, but fighting continues.

Roe vs. Wade gives U.S. women the right to choose abortion.

1975 Cambodia and South Vietnam fall to the Communists, and U.S. evacuates.

1976 Socialist Republic of Vietnam is proclaimed.

Blacks battle police in Soweto, Johannesburg, and Cape Town, South Africa.

1977 Steven Jobs founds Apple Computers.

1978 Matthew Carter designs Bell Centennial for "CRT" typesetting.

1979 Communist Sandinistas overthrow Nicaraguan government.

Ayatollah Khomeini establishes Islamic Republic in Iran.

Soviet forces invade Afghanistan.

1980 The labor union Solidarity is formed in Poland; martial law is declared the following year, and Solidarity leaders are arrested.

Border war between Iran and Iraq begins.

Keith Haring begins drawing in the subways of New York.

Milton Glaser designs complete corporate identity for the Grand Union supermarket chain.

1981 Richard Serra installs *Tilted Arc* in a New York office plaza, causing controversy over the relationship between public art and the public.

Tom Wolfe attacks modernism in *From Bauhaus to Our House*.

1982 Vietnam Veterans Memorial is installed in Washington, D.C., causing more controversy over the relationship between public art and the public.

Michael Graves completes Public Services Building in Portland, Oregon, launching his career as a post-modernist.

1983 U.S. invades Grenada.

Niels Diffrient designs the Jefferson Chair, a reclining leisure/labor unit with a built-in telephone and computer workstation.

1984 Philip Johnson's AT&T Building, begun in 1978, is completed in New York.

1985 President Botha declares state of emergency in South Africa.

U.S. military industry begins work on Star Wars.

1987 Under the leadership of Mikhail Gorbachev Soviet Union announces new policy of openness, *glasnost*.

U.S. and U.S.S.R. sign arms-reduction pact.

1988 U.S. shoots down Iranian civilian plane in Persian Gulf.